News Writing
Student Study Guide
Second Edition

Peter F. Berkow

The Annenberg/CPB Telecourse

Part of a college-level telecourse that includes
Writing and Reporting News: A Coaching Method, Second Edition
written by Carole Rich
and published by
Wadsworth Publishing Company

Produced by Peter F. Berkow

Wadsworth Publishing Company

I(T)P® An International Thomson Publishing Company

Belmont, CA • Albany, NY • Bonn • Boston • Cincinnati • Detroit • Johannesburg • London • Madrid
Melbourne • Mexico City • New York • Paris • San Francisco • Singapore • Tokyo • Toronto • Washington

For more information, contact Wadsworth Publishing Company, 10 Davis Drive, Belmont, CA 94002
or electronically at http://www.thomson.com/wadsworth.html.

International Thomson Publishing Europe
Berkshire House 168-173
High Holborn
London, WC1V 7AA, England

International Thomson Editores
Campos Eliseos 385, Piso 7
Col. Polanco
11560 México D.F. México

Thomas Nelson Australia
102 Dodds Street
South Melbourne 3205
Victoria, Australia

International Thomson Publishing Asia
221 Henderson Road
#05-10 Henderson Building
Singapore 0315

Nelson Canada
1120 Birchmount Road
Scarborough, Ontario
Canada M1K 5G4

International Thomson Publishing Japan
Hirakawacho Kyowa Building, 3F
2-2-1 Hirakawacho
Chiyoda-ku, Tokyo 102, Japan

International Thomson Publishing GmbH
Königswinterer Strasse 418
53227 Bonn, Germany

International Thomson Publishing Southern Africa
Building 18, Constantia Park
240 Old Pretoria Road
Halfway House, 1685 South Africa

ISBN 0-534-52254-8

This book was developed for use by students enrolled in *News Writing*, an Annenberg/CPB Project telecourse.
This telecourse consists of fifteen half-hour video programs broadcast on PBS, this Student Study Guide,
the Wadsworth textbook *Writing and Reporting News: A Coaching Method*, *Second Edition* written by Carole
Rich, and a Faculty Guide.

News Writing is produced by Peter Berkow, in association with the Golden Empire Television Corporation.

Major funding was provided by the Annenberg/CPB Project.

ARRANGEMENTS FOR USE

Colleges, universities, and other educational institutions may:

• License the use of *News Writing* as a complete telecourse or acquire an off-air or off-satellite taping
  license through the PBS Adult Learning Service. For information, phone 1-800-257-2578; in Virginia,
  phone 703-739-5360.
• Acquire copies of the programs on video to use in the classroom or media center. (1/2" videocassettes,
  $39.95 each or $299 for the entire 15-part series on eight cassettes.) To order, phone 1-800-LEARNER.
• For information on purchasing a duplication license, please phone 1-800-LEARNER.

The Annenberg/CPB Project

Funding for *News Writing* is provided by The Annenberg/CPB Project. The Project was created in 1981
with the goal of increasing opportunities for Americans to acquire a high-quality college education using
telecommunications and information technologies. The Project leads a national movement to make innovative
technology-based educational materials widely available for educational institutions, libraries and individuals.

This book is dedicated to Anita Berkow, who is more than just my best friend (and, coincidentally, my wife). More accurately, Anita should be listed as the co-author of the student study guide and the co-producer of the Annenberg/CPB telecourse *News Writing*. She ran the camera on all of the interviews and many of the live shots, lugged equipment from hotel rooms to cabs to elevators to stairwells to cabs to hotel rooms—often in the rain or snow. She transcribed more than a hundred interviews, arm wrestled with me about editorial style, debated instructional content and ate from the same plate in the restaurant when funds got scarce. She researched, faxed, filed and phoned. She collaborated in raising my child and in feeling every conceivable human emotion listed in the thesaurus during the five-year process it took to complete this project—together.

She even argued with me about the grammar in this dedication.

Thanks, Anita.

Peter Berkow

TELECOURSE PERSONNEL

HOST/PRODUCER FOR NEWS WRITING

Peter Berkow is an educator and working journalist. Currently the school newspaper adviser for Shasta College in Redding, California, he also teaches courses in news writing, mass communications, editing, computers and English composition. He has worked for several newspapers, currently writes a weekly column for a syndicated news service and has been published as a freelance writer in many national magazines.

NEWS WRITING ADVISORY BOARD

Field Experts

Peter Bhatia
Managing editor, *The Oregonian*
(Portland, OR)

Lorraine Dechter
Reporter/Producer, KCHO-Radio and
KIXE-TV, Redding, CA

Dr. Richard Ek
Professor emeritus, California State
University, Chico

Mark Hall
Telecommunications instructor,
Butte College, Oroville, CA

Gerald Larson
Palo Alto Bureau Chief, *San Jose
Mercury News*

Sigrun Kristamie
Journalism program administrator,
University of California, Santa Cruz

Carole Rich
Journalism professor, University of Kansas

Tom Rolniki
Executive Director, Associated Collegiate
Press and the National Scholastic Press
Association

Harry Smith
Anchor, "CBS This Morning," CBS News

Mitchell Stephens
Journalism Department Chair,
New York University

Curriculum Evaluation Team

Dr. Robert Main,
Head Professor of Mass Communication,
California State University, Chico

Dianne Conrad
The Evergreen State College,
Olympia (WA)

Scott Hanson
Yuba College (Yuba City, CA) and
Butte College (Oroville, CA)

Roberta Mantooth
Peninsula College (Port Angeles, WA)

Bart Potter
South Puget Sound Community College
(Olympia, WA)

INTERVIEWEES

(A partial list)   * Pulitzer Prize winner   ** Emmy Award winner

Joel Achenbach
Columnist/feature writer, *Washington Post*

JoNel Aleccia
Reporter, Medford, *Mail-Tribune*

Susan Antilla
Financial reporter, *The New York Times*

Richard Aregood*
Editorial writer, *Philadelphia Daily News*

Terry Armour
Columnist, *Chicago Tribune*

Elizabeth Arnold
Congressional reporter, National Public Radio

Dave Barry*
Syndicated columnist, *The Miami Herald*

Peter Bhatia
Managing editor, *The Oregonian* (Portland, OR)

Michael Brown
Managing editor, *Chicago Defender*

Bobby Calvan
Political reporter, *Record Searchlight* (Redding, CA)

Jack Cappon
National news editor, Associated Press, New York

Roy Peter Clark
Associate Director, The Poynter Institute

Joyce Davis
Foreign editor, National Public Radio

Monica Davey
Reporter, *St. Petersburg Times*

Anthony DeCurtis
Music editor, *Rolling Stone*

John DeNatale
Senior producer of national affairs, "MacNeil/Lehrer News Hour," PBS

Sam Donaldson**
Anchor, "Prime Time Live," ABC

Brian Donlon
TV reporter, *USA Today*

Roger Ebert* **
Film critic, *Chicago Sun Times*

Linda Ellerbee
Anchor, "Nick News"

Carri Geer
Crime Reporter, *Las Vegas Review-Journal*

Bernard Goldberg
Correspondent, CBS

Mark Goodman
Attorney, Student Press Law Center

David Hatfield
Public relations, Golden State Warriors

Thomas Hylton*
Editorial writer, *The Mercury* (Pottstown, PA)

Charles Jackson
Editor, *The Tribune* (Oakland, CA)

Rick Kaplan**
Executive producer, "ABC World News Tonight"

Larry King**
Talk show host, CNN and Mutual Radio Network/*USA Today*

Jane Kirtley
Attorney, Reporter's Committee for Freedom of the Press

John Katsilometes
Sports reporter/columnist, *Record Searchlight* (Redding, CA)

Ron Kotulak*
Science reporter, *Chicago Tribune*

Steve Kroft**
Correspondent, "60 Minutes," CBS

Tom Knudson*
Environmental writer, *Sacramento Bee*

Charles Kuralt**
Anchor, "Sunday Morning," CBS

Bruce Lang
Anchor/news director, KHSL-TV, Chico, CA

Dominique Leompora
Public Relations, Capitol Records

Kurt Loder
News announcer, MTV

Andrew Loschilin
Correspondent, ITAR-TASS News Agency

Bill Mitchell
Editor, Merc Center, San Jose (CA)

Russ Mitchell
Correspondent, CBS

Scott Ostler
Columnist/sports writer, *San Francisco Chronicle*

Gene Policinski
Sports page editor, *USA Today*

Neil Postman
Author/media critic, New York University

Sam Quinones
Crime reporter, *The News Tribune* (Tacoma, WA)

Dorothy Rabinowitz
Editorial writer/media critic, *Wall Street Journal*

Andy Rooney**
Correspondent, CBS News

Claudio Sanchez
Education reporter, National Public Radio

Barrett Seamann
Editor, *Time* magazine

Gene Siskel**
Film critic, *Chicago Tribune*

Harry Smith**
Anchor, "CBS This Morning," CBS

Mitchell Stephens
Chair, Department of Journalism and Mass Communications, New York University

Steve Tetreault
News service editor, Donrey Media Group

Helen Thomas
White House correspondent, UPI

George Thurlow
Editor, *Chico News and Review*

Michael Tomasky
Political reporter, *Village Voice*

Miki Turner
Sports reporter, *Orange County Register*

Michael Waldholz
Science/medicine writer, *Wall Street Journal*

Andy Webster
Copy editor, *Rolling Stone*

Randall Weissman
Associate managing editor, *Chicago Tribune*

Kathy Wilson
News producer, KHSL-TV, Chico, CA

Deborah Wilgoren
Police reporter, *Washington Post*

Jack Winning
Managing editor, *Chico Enterprise Record*

Bob Woodward
Investigative reporter, *Washington Post*

John D. Zelezny
Attorney/instructor/author, Fresno State University

(Affiliations shown are at the time of interviewing.)

CONTENTS

Course Overview   vii

Unit One   What Is News?   1

Unit Two   The Summary Lead   25

Unit Three   News Language and Style   41

Unit Four   News Writing Story Development   55

Unit Five   Interviewing, Quotes and Sources   77

Unit Six   Writing Versus Reporting   103

Unit Seven   Beat Reporting   127

Unit Eight   Broadcast News Writing   149

Unit Nine   Public Relations Writing   175

Unit Ten   Writing Beyond the Summary Lead   197

Unit Eleven   Feature News Writing   217

Unit Twelve   Editorial, Opinion and Column Writing   239

Unit Thirteen   Covering Disasters   261

Unit Fourteen   Journalism Ethics   283

Unit Fifteen   Media Law   311

News Writing is a 15-part PBS telecourse providing the most comprehensive series on journalism ever produced. The programs are the equivalent of video field trips into the best news rooms in the country. Featuring interviews with more than 150 journalists, the television segments and student study guide offer opportunities to learn from celebrity journalists in major markets (including many Pulitzer Prize, Emmy, Peabody and ASNE award winners) as well as from recently graduated reporters just a few years beyond the campus newsroom. Students see how news writing skills are applied at newspapers, television stations and radio stations. The use of journalism skills in public relations and on-line computer services is also discussed.

Since our modern society is absorbing information from many rival sources, journalists must develop competitive reporting techniques and writing styles. Through this telecourse, viewers will learn journalistic traditions, discover innovative techniques, explore contemporary issues, learn about the future of journalism and gain an understanding of the ethical and legal considerations that confront journalists. This inside-view of present-day media practices is designed to make students more critical consumers of news today—and better writing professionals tomorrow.

News Writing can be used as a college credit course fulfilling a one-term requirement for a beginning writing or reporting course. In addition, the entire series or individual programs can be used in a variety of ways:

COURSE OBJECTIVES

News Writing is designed as an introductory journalism course. Several strands or themes have been "woven" throughout the curriculum, including:

- an awareness of media ethics issues,

- mastery of journalism language and style,

- a respect for the traditions of good reporting, and

- a foreshadowing of evolutionary changes in news writing.

The course is designed to help you:

- develop a news sense,

- learn the summary lead,

- master AP style,

- design story architectures,

- deal with sources,

- blend the best techniques of writing and reporting,

- find a vocational niche,

- see the difference between broadcast and print news writing,

- understand the interrelationship between PR and news,

- create new lead styles,

• discover the relationship between feature news and hard news,

• explore opinion writing styles,

• prepare for reporting of disasters,

• create your own code of ethics, and

• introduce you to the basics of media law.

COMPONENTS OF THE TELEVISION COURSE

15 half-hour television programs, also available on videocassettes, help students learn how to start, develop and polish hard news and feature news stories. In addition, related styles—such as editorial and column writing—are explored along with isues of language use, media ethics and media law. The series covers both traditional and emerging journalism styles in broadcast and public relations as well as print journalism.

The textbook, *Writing and Reporting News: A Coaching Method, Second Edition* by Carole Rich, professor of journalism at University of Kansas, focuses on the process of writing as it sequentially addresses conceiving the story, gathering information, constructing the story and polishing it to "make the reader see, make the reader care." Based on the coaching method, widely used by newspapers today to improve writing and reporting abilities of their staffers, the book features a wealth of activity exercises based on actual newspaper stories.

Wadsworth Publishing Company. © 1997. ISBN: 0-534-50879-0.

The *Workbook for Writing and Reporting News: A Coaching Method Second Edition* also by Carole Rich, expands the text, with exercises suitable for homework assignments or use in the journalism lab. In addition, the workbook contains style quizzes, information on how to seek internships and jobs in journalism and an optional resume form. This perforated, three-hole punched workbook is available for sale to students at instructor's option.

Wadsworth Publishing Company. © 1997. ISBN: 0-534-50880-4.

An Instructor's manual, designed for use with the textbook and workbook, contains chapter-by-chapter teaching tips, followed by suggestions for using the textbook activities and workbook exercises (discussion of exercises contains the original stories on which the exercises are based). The manual includes a full explanation of the coaching method and how it can be used with students, a sample evaluation form and teaching plan. Complimentary to adopters of the text.

Wadsworth Publishing Company. © 1997. ISBN: 0-534-50881-2.

A telecourse study guide, by Peter Berkow. Please read the description on the following page.

Wadsworth Publishing Company. © 1997. ISBN: 0-534-52254-8.

A faculty guide, also by Peter Berkow, directly coordinates the television programs and the telecourse study guide with the Carole Rich textbook. It presents guidelines for organizing and teaching the telecourse and includes test banks, reading assignments and activities for each unit. The guide also offers information on licensing agreements, suggestions for promoting and scheduling the telecourse, guidelines for arranging for course credit and suggestions for school newspaper advisers. One copy of the faculty guide is provided at no charge to institutions licensing the telecourse.

Wadsworth Publishing Company. © 1997. ISBN: 0-534-52255-6.

ABOUT THIS STUDY GUIDE: Each of the 15 units of the *News Writing* telecourse contains a half-hour television program and a corresponding chapter in the student study guide. The study guide is designed to prepare you to view each television program critically and to help you evaluate your understanding of what you have seen. It also integrates the program material with the textbook and reinforces strands of instruction woven throughout the entire telecourse. Many of the journalists featured in the television programs offer additional insights in the student study guide. They have also contributed excellent example news stories for your consideration. Each unit shows reporters working on actual news stories, and many of those stories are featured in the student study guide.

It is natural for good writing techniques to grow from a lot of reading. The television programs are not intended to replace reading assignments. And, the reading assignments should be supplemented with as much reading of daily newspapers, news magazines and other sources of news reporting as possible. You can absorb the textures of good news writing through a lot of reading; you can also learn what to avoid by reading poor reporting, and learning to judge with a critical eye.

The units of the student study guide include the following sections:

An Introduction—designed to orient you toward the unit's topic.

Objectives—designed to help you set learning goals for the unit.

Program Guide—designed to help you organize and think critically before, during and after you watch the television program for the unit.

The Lesson—designed to coordinate the student study guide directly with the television program and to reinforce or elaborate upon major points.

You Should Read . . .—designed to guide you to specific sections in the first edition of Carole Rich's book *Writing and Reporting News: A Coaching Method* that expand on the unit's focus.

Did You Know . . . ?—designed to bring up additional fine points to supplement the main points of the unit.

Example Stories—designed to show you completed news stories that illustrate the lessons learned in the unit.

Alternative Views—designed to show you other opinions that might differ creatively from the conventional, subjective judgments made in the unit.

Glossary—designed to clarify terms and concepts used in the television program or student study guide.

Suggested Writing Exercises—designed to stimulate your writing abilities and evaluate (or expand) your understanding of the key concepts for each unit.

Quiz—designed to help you evaluate your understanding of the key concepts for each unit.

Self-test—designed to stimulate your writing abilities and evaluate (or expand) your understanding of the key concepts for each unit.

TAKING THE NEWS WRITING TELECOURSE

Find out the following information as soon after registration as possible.

• What books are required for the course

• If and when an orientation session has been scheduled

• When *News Writing* will be broadcast in your area

• When course examinations are scheduled (mark these on your calendar)

• If any additional on-campus meetings have been scheduled (plan to attend as many review sessions, seminars, and other meetings as possible)

To learn the most from each unit:

1. Before you view the television program, read the student study guide and pay particular attention to the Objectives, Program Guide and Glossary.

2. Read the textbook assignment given by your instructor or listed in the student study guide.

3. View the program, keeping the Objectives and Program Guide in mind. Be an active viewer. Some students find that taking notes while viewing the programs is helpful. There may be several opportunities for you to watch and review the program. If you have access to library tapes or personal copies, many students find multiple viewings reveal several additional levels of understanding.

4. Read the "After You Watch" section of the student study guide, and review "The Lesson" to reinforce important concepts and expand on what you have seen.

5. Attend class discussions, or complete journal assignments.

6. Complete the multiple-choice quiz and self-test and turn them in to your instructor for evaluation. Much of the learning can be accomplished by finding out what concepts you missed on the tests, so pay careful attention to corrections.

7. Complete writing assignments in the student study guide or those given by your instructor-of-record and seek out as much feedback as possible from teachers, peers or professional journalists.

8. Keep up with the course on a weekly basis. Each unit of the telecourse builds upon knowledge gained in previous units. Stay current with the programs and readings. Make a daily checklist and keep a calendar, noting scheduled activities such as meetings, discussion groups, instructor conferences and examinations. Be sure to block out time for viewing, reading and completing assignments.

9. Stay in touch with your instructor. If possible, get to know him or her. You should have your instructor's mailing address, E-mail address, phone number, office hours and telecommuting (or call-in) hours. Your instructor would like to hear from you and know how you are doing. He or she will be eager to clarify any questions you have about the course. Students interested in communicating with producer Peter Berkow about the course may contact him through the following E-mail address: PBerkow@aol.com.

10. Keep a portfolio of your work. Published clippings, especially, are very valuable when applying for a journalism job or internship. Portfolios of work may also be used for end-of-term evaluation.

WHAT
IS
NEWS?

This is the introductory unit and program to the telecourse. In this first program, the Poynter Institute's Roy Peter Clark—one of the most respected journalism researchers in the world—speaks of a skill developed by the best news writers: an ability to recognize news where the average person can't even see a story. This first lesson will help you start developing that skill.

By taking a behind-the-scenes glimpse into several real newsroom environments, you should also get a feel for the practical, artistic and ethical decisions that news professionals must make daily when they decide what to report as news.

In the process, you will be prepared to write your first news stories (in the next few weeks of the course) by learning the process of focusing on a news event and distilling it to the essence.

A wide variety of journalists are featured in this program. They work for the mainstream press (major metropolitan newspapers such as the *Washington Post* and the *Chicago Tribune* and smaller community newspapers such as the *Chico Enterprise-Record* in northern

California), and they work for broadcast news organizations ranging from National Public Radio, ABC and CNN to rural CBS affiliate KHSL in the Chico-Redding market. They also work for publications ranging from a widely respected African-American daily newspaper, the *Chicago Defender*, to a gossip tabloid, the *National Enquirer*.

All of these journalists acknowledged certain similar concepts when they were asked to define news. Many of them, however, voiced radically different views.

OBJECTIVES

This first lesson will help you start understanding the difference between news writing and other types of writing you may have studied, by introducing the concept of news value. By hearing these journalists define news and watching them make news value judgments in several different newsrooms, you will be able to start the process of creating your own definition of news.

PROGRAM
GUIDE

BEFORE YOU WATCH

This program is designed to introduce beginning journalism students to the ways professional news writers view the world. By listening to several journalists talk about their definitions of news and watching others actually make news decisions, you will begin to develop your own news sense.

•**Pay close attention to the ways journalists and teachers use the following terms:**

News value	What the reader wants to know
Proximity	What the reader needs to know
Time lines	News mix
Local news	Good news
National news	Bad news
	Breaking news

WHILE YOU WATCH

1. Imagine yourself in the place of the various journalists as they make decisions about what news will be published in the newspaper or aired on the television news.

2. Compare and contrast the various definitions of news given by the reporters, editors and television personnel interviewed; look for similarities and differences in their attitudes.

3. Think about the difference between discussing the definition of news from a hypothetical perspective in a classroom and developing an on-the-job news sense.

4. Look for the connection between having a good personal definition of what makes news and becoming a good news writer.

AFTER YOU WATCH

Address the following questions in your journal, or, if there's time, discuss them in class:

1. If you were an editor of the local newspaper or program director for the television station, would you use the story about the high school "spur posse" sex scandal? Why?

2. If you were in charge of the front page for the *Chicago Tribune*, would you feature the story about the child being shot on the freeway? Would you cover the tragedy but put the story on a different page? Why?

3. How does the definition of news change as you move from a small community newspaper to a larger metropolitan area publication?

4. Analyze several issues of your local newspaper. Is there too much "bad" news on the front page? Why?

THE LESSON

Larry King, of CNN, starts off this unit with a rather flippant statement about "good" news. King sounds a bit cynical, but his point is well taken—the only good news that gets published in the newspaper or aired on television is something out of the ordinary. As King suggests, a possible cure for cancer might make the front page. And, sure enough, later in the program we find that it does—as the editors of the *Chicago Tribune* editorial board struggle to balance out an unusually violent day's worth of front-page stories with something positive.

Roy Peter Clark is nationally respected for his research work and teaching at the Poynter Institute for Media Studies—the kind of place a successful editor or reporter would travel to study to become an even better journalist.

Clark suggests that news exists in the world before the journalists package it and convey it to the public. The news, he says, needs to be communicated to the public by a narrator or storyteller—and that's the challenge of being a good news writer.

Michael Brown, managing editor of the *Chicago Defender*, expresses what appears to be a contrasting view. According to Brown, if journalists want to be honest, they will admit that what the public perceives as news is determined, in a large part, by the media. To back his point, Brown says that during the Persian Gulf War many other wars were being waged across the globe, but the American press reported on only one.

Are Clark's and Brown's attitudes mutually exclusive or just views of the same process from different angles?

Both of these journalists' perspectives on the news business are studied in most mass communications courses as part of the **agenda-setting** and **gatekeeping** process.

Mass communications researchers use the term *gatekeeping* as a regular part of their vocabulary. In a survey of mass communications textbooks, you would find gatekeeping usually defined something like this:

Gatekeeping is the process by which reporters, editors, news directors and other journalists decide which events and details get reported as news and which events or details do not get reported.

Agenda setting is slightly more complicated. Many mass communications researchers say that a discrete society (such as a given country) can focus only on a mass group discussion of three to five current event topics at a time—for example, an election, the downfall of a celebrity, a disaster in one region, the state of the economy and the World Series. Most teachers, books and curricula have a definition for the process that is similar to the following:

Agenda setting is the process by which politicians, journalists and others determine which topics and events will be the current focus of societal concern.

In other words, they decide what society should talk and worry about this week. Through the repetitive emphasis of certain types of events (agenda setting), gatekeepers can set the stage for what a society will think *about*—though there is little evidence that the gatekeepers have any influence at all on what the news consumers will actually *think*.

The results of both gatekeeping and agenda setting are that those who are in charge of news decisions tend to emphasize sensational events. Simply put, these events tend to attract more readers, viewers and listeners than mundane occurrences do—even if the results of a (seemingly) mundane event will produce information the news consumers *need* to know.

In Unit One, Brian Williams of the *National Enquirer* characterizes his publication—a grocery counter tabloid—as being "reader friendly." The *National Enquirer* is primarily concerned with printing celebrity gossip and other information that Williams says the public "wants to know." In his paper, Williams says, there shouldn't be a single story that the reader doesn't want to read.

The tabloid papers (and their counterparts—television shows such as "A Current Affair" and "Hard Copy") have been successful participants in the national and worldwide agenda-setting process. Though most of the cover stories in tabloid journalism involve scandals, those same scandals increasingly find their way into more traditional news media, often as the lead stories on network news shows and front-page stories in daily newspapers.

"More and more, I think we're coming closer and closer together," Williams says. "I think the mainstream press is moving to more personality journalism. We've been covering those for a very long time, and I think the rest of the press is catching up with us."

Many journalists would agree that Williams is right, but that doesn't make them feel any better about the phenomenon.

"Too often we say, 'The reader wants to know,'" says Carole Rich, a widely respected journalism teacher and writing coach from the University of Kansas.

"The reader has a right to know what's public record. The reader has a want to know a lot of prurient things, which is why the *National Enquirer* sells more papers than the local newspaper or the *New York Times*. But does the reader really have a need to know?"

Joyce Davis says that even National Public Radio has to be concerned with delivering information that the public wants to know. But, she says, public radio has a "bigger mission" to distribute information the public needs to know.

"I know journalists aren't supposed to have any missions, but we all have something pushing us—or else, we don't stay in this business," Davis says. "We hope it's just a sense of trying to do right, and get a message across and serve the public. We hope it's noble values. The mission of NPR is . . . to try to inform. Not just entertain. And that is a big difference. Entertainment is just feeding what we think your interests are . . . in a way that will keep you there. But I do think NPR has a mission to try to tell you about different parts of the world, parts of the world that will eventually affect you. . . . This is our burden: to make it creative enough and interesting enough that people will listen. And care."

Which is more important? News organizations that only inform, without entertaining, usually flounder financially. News organizations that overemphasize entertainment lack credibility.

Sam Donaldson, of ABC news, says in the program that there are two commodities—information the public wants to know and information the public needs to know—that should be blended and delivered in balance to produce good journalism. Many editors call this **news mix**.

Jerry Lanson, of the *San Jose Mercury News*, offers one example of how that blend might be achieved: "Let's say there's a public hearing about speed bumps . . . about a plan for traffic in which one block is going to get speed bumps to keep the cars out, and the neighbors there are concerned that it's going to have an impact on them because all the traffic will go in their direction. You can go to that meeting and have a lot of talking heads and bureaucrats talking to each other, and write a very boring story. Or you can write a story that has a little bit of a slice-of-life feel to it, where you go out into the community beforehand, talk to the people who are going to be affected, in their homes, and show rather than tell."

In other words, Lanson suggests that the writer learn to package information the public needs to know in such a way as to turn it into information the public wants to know.

Next in the program, we get a look at how the gatekeeping and agenda-setting processes work in smaller markets, as the employees of the *Chico Enterprise-Record* newspaper and KHSL–Channel 12 television examine the identical menu of news stories on the same Thursday and decide which will be showcased to the readers and viewers.

How important is the "scoop" of an arrest in a local murder/arson case that reporter Theresa Dagitz brings into the station from Redding? Channel 12 News Producer Kathy Wilson is willing to plan the whole 6:30 newscast around Dagitz's promise on a two-way radio that it will be a top story, even though she has no details about the story's content. Wilson would rather trust Dagitz's news judgment than take the chance that competitors who might be eavesdropping on the radio frequency will be tipped to the exclusive story.

"If I can say we had that story," Wilson says, "and the other local stations totally missed it, and we had something that was important to our viewers and that was fast breaking and developing and they needed to know, . . . then, yeah, I can say, 'We did a great job. We beat those guys.' Whether you're in insurance, or you're a small business person, there's competition with your brethren in that field. And you're going to be pleased when you say, 'We've got this great product that the others don't have, and we're going to provide a service that no one else has.' That's what keeps everyone on their toes and doing their jobs very well."

The competition for news consumers is intense, even in a remote market like northern California. Four news/talk radio stations in the Chico/Redding listening area vie for listeners 24 hours a day. A half dozen other all-news radio stations come into the market from Sacramento and San Francisco, though they feature little local news of interest for those who live closer to the mountains. On top of that, dozens of local music-format radio stations air reports from scaled-down news departments.

Chico and Redding are an hour's drive apart, and both towns are served by three network affiliate television stations with full-fledged news departments. The 200,000-plus listeners in the same general area are served by three daily newspapers and a half dozen successful weekly and biweekly newspapers, as well as metropolitan newspapers published in Sacramento and San Francisco.

All of those news departments might feature the homicide story that Dagitz and KHSL were able to showcase exclusively 12 to 24 hours before any of their competitors. The local gatekeepers would classify the arrest as information people would both want to know and need to know. The Redding newspaper would display the local homicide story on the front page; Chico's paper, an hour's drive down Highway 5, might give it an inch or two deeper in the paper, next to an ad for used cars.

Proximity is an important element of the news. In fact, proximity is so important, it is the sole reason local news agencies in a market such as this (served by a dozen television news departments from nearby metropolitan areas) can survive. Readers from Chico and Redding might pick up the *Sacramento Bee*, *San Francisco Chronicle* or *USA Today* to read national and international news, but they will find the news they need to know about their own communities only in the hometown newspaper.

There is another reason why the Dagitz story was important as a lead for the 6:30 KHSL Thursday newscast. Simply put: violence fascinates news consumers.

Producer Kathy Wilson is concerned that the news media can tend to present a distorted view of the world as a whole—with too much emphasis on sex, murder and crime—and feels that's not way the world really is.

Wilson's concerns are understandable. Critics of mass media frequently suggest that viewing reality primarily through newspaper and television reports gives an exaggerated impression that things are significantly worse than they are.

However, reporters and editors understand that it is sometimes their duty to expose the ugly side of society. *Washington Post* crime reporter Debbie Wilgoren, who covers the police beat in a city that averages more than one murder per day, explains it this way:

"You see blood on the street. You see people who live in these neighborhoods watching the violence, sitting on their front porches with young children at two in the morning as the medical examiner's van takes away the body of a 20-year-old man who's just been gunned down.

"I come in there and leave as an observer. As a reporter. As someone who documents what happened. The people sitting on their porches live through that every day. And if they can take it, who am I to come in and be so offended, or repulsed, or distraught that I can't even coherently tell the rest of the world about it? If I don't capture it and write it, the people in the neighborhoods where it doesn't happen can pretend it doesn't exist."

Charles Kuralt, of CBS, summarizes the dilemma facing journalists: "I think news is the unexpected event, the event that is out of the ordinary. Frequently, it also is the more depressing things that have occurred.

"My mother used to say, 'Why don't you people ever print any good news?' She even canceled her subscription a couple of times to the newspaper I worked on because she was so upset with the calamities that showed up on page one that sort of ruined her evening. I never did develop a satisfactory answer for my mother. 'Mother, you don't want to read on page one that 89 airplanes took off and landed safely out at the airport today, but that one that came in and had a belly landing and the people were lucky to live through the crash—that's news.' That old answer to my mother is the best answer I can give you. It's the out-of-the-ordinary event."

The alternative is reporting a story that's clearly a ho-hummer.

That same Thursday, both KHSL and the *Chico Enterprise-Record* featured a story about the city council closing a local legalized low-stakes poker game in a downtown bar and putting a moratorium on permits for new bars in the downtown area.

Why did the daily paper play it as the main story? Both KHSL and the paper ran this story, but the television station put a low emphasis on the news value. Clearly, it was not the kind of story that would boost ratings or circulation.

But, as Jack Winning, managing editor of the *Chico Enterprise-Record,* says, it is the job of the local newspaper to package information the public needs to know in a palatable form so readers will want to know about it, also.

Which brings us to the "spur posse" story—a piece about local high school boys who were allegedly playing a game in which they kept score of their sexual conquests.

The television station ran it as the lead story; the newspaper examined the issues and didn't publish a single inch about the event.

Both sides are eloquent in explaining their essentially opposite reasons for running or not running the piece.

Winning says clearly the story is "sexy" and falls into the category of information the public wants to know. But his conservative and traditional journalistic instincts were—for the moment—to shy away from a story in which all of the sources were anonymous and in which there was no hard evidence that a "spur posse" even existed.

Wilson and KHSL reporter Holiday Moore were convinced that the story contained information viewers, especially parents of the teens attending the high school, *needed* to know. Moore was convinced, after peeling away several layers of rumor and getting closer to the original sources, that the spur posse was fact, not fiction, and worthy of reporting.

The challenges facing the *Chicago Tribune* editorial board were completely different. In a large metropolitan area such as Chicago, a simple killing (which might be a daily or near-daily occurrence) would more than likely not make the front page.

Instead, a homicide might merit six inches in the metro section. The front page would showcase international incidents, though even the *Tribune* will look for a local angle.

On this date, reporters were scrambling to find out if the lead story—about a United States military helicopter that was accidentally shot down by American soldiers near Iraq—could be connected to Chicago. If any of the victims were

Chicagoans, the *Tribune* staff would work overtime to **localize** the wire service reports with any kind of angle connecting the home community to the event.

Meanwhile, Randall Weissman, of the *Tribune,* was concerned about the violent and negative tilt the day's front page was taking. A random freeway shooting, in which a child was the victim, was shaping up to be the day's other lead story.

To balance the front page, the *Tribune* emphasized the good news about progress in understanding the causes of breast cancer.

A "lite" story about local teenagers challenging the FCC with pirate radio stations was also displayed on the front page.

But deciding to feature the freeway shooting of the child in suburban Chicago on the front page was not an automatic process.

Several editors pointed out that emphasizing murders in white suburbia while downplaying similar events in the predominantly black South Side of Chicago would reduce the paper's credibility among African-Americans. Weissman and others vigorously defended the decision to play the freeway shooting against any perception of racial motivation by the paper.

The predominant view by members of the editorial board was that this act of random violence on the freeway, regardless of the race of those involved, was something different that had not happened in Chicago before; therefore, it was news.

When defining news—either hypothetically or in real-life decisions—we see that several themes emerge.

News must have impact. It must affect the viewers or readers in the local proximity. News attracts more consumers if it is unusual and, therefore, often negative. But if the news is ordinary and important (many "good news" stories fall into this category), most journalists still feel a duty to find a way to package the information so that it is easy and pleasant to digest.

Other important elements of news might be timeliness, conflict and novelty. Ultimately the decision rests with the consumers of the news. Toward the end of the program, several prominent journalists point out that their definition of news depends specifically on the target audience.

Kurt Loder of MTV news and Linda Ellerbee of Nickelodeon's "Nick News" have completely different audiences but show a common attitude toward defining the news. Loder packages events to communicate to the predominantly teen-age audience viewing his reports between pop music videos. Ellerbee packages some of the same events to communicate to the children who watch the Nickelodeon network.

Tom Knudson, who has won two Pulitzer Prizes for covering environmental issues, packages his news for the readers of the *Sacramento Bee*. His point is that it is too easy for daily newspapers to reduce news coverage to obvious events such as city council meetings, murders and fires when other less obvious occurrences—such as the slow and steady degradation of the environment—are just as newsworthy. Journalists, Knudson maintains, must dig deeper to find the hidden stories to better serve the public.

Will the definition of news change as journalists confront the 21st century? Will the role of daily newspapers and local television stations diminish as the predicted flood of data from the on-line computer "information superhighway" and predicted 500 channels of television invade our homes?

Bill Mitchell, of the San Jose *Mercury News*/Merc-Center on-line computer news service, says that local news organizations will have an even more important role in the future.

"On the issue of gatekeeping or agenda setting, I think newspapers will play, for better or worse, a growing role," Mitchell says. "Because there's going to be so much information out there, I think people will look to us even more than they have in the past. That's not to say that we're not under pressure from alternative forms of publication. I think we are; I think that ain't a bad thing from the readers' point of view, because readers have many more sources of information than they did before, and if we don't measure up, there are ways that people are getting the word out about interesting things that don't necessarily involve the newspaper."

Mitchell's comment provides a natural transition to Unit Two. It is the news writer's duty today—and it will continue to be the journalist's job in the future—to take a mass of information and focus it so that news consumers can understand what's going on.

In her statements in both the program and her textbook, Carole Rich eloquently explains how this is accomplished. Simply put, Rich coaches a writer to explain the story in one sentence. If the writer, student or professional, rambles on for a while, Rich smiles and asks again, "Please focus, and tell me the story in one sentence."

Understanding this process is the essence behind writing a summary lead, the topic of our next lesson. There's a natural link between that unit and this one. If a student is having a hard time reducing a story to one simple sentence, that student probably doesn't yet have a grasp on the news value of the event.

Many of the concepts introduced in this first unit will connect you to other units throughout the telecourse. There is one final reason for having a solid definition for news. This alternate view connects the first program of the telecourse with the final program, which is an introduction to media law.

Mark Goodman, the attorney from the Student Press Law Center, explains that many lawsuits, especially those in the area of invasion of privacy, stem from the fact that the reporter had a murky understanding of the news value of the published information resulting in the lawsuit. In most of those cases, the determining factor in judgment is whether the public's right to know the information outweighs the individual's right to privacy—a balancing act that essentially focuses on the news value of the dispute with a legal definition of "what is news."

We leave you with a final thought from Roy Peter Clark of the Poynter Institute. Clark says good journalists develop a sense that allows them to see news stories where the general public simply sees the mundane and ordinary. "One of the things that I like to do with my students is to take them right outside this building and to walk within essentially a square block and to attempt to identify the stories that are visible to experienced journalists but invisible to others," Clark says.

We recommend that you step outside of the classroom or your home as soon as possible, and start developing that sense.

YOU

SHOULD

READ . . .

The first reading assignment for the telecourse is to read anything you can that will help you to start developing a news sense.

The most important aspect of that assignment is to read as many different types of news reports as possible. If you can, grab two or three daily newspapers a day. Learn to devour news weeklies—either national publications like *Time* or the local weeklies in your home town. Seek out *Sports Illustrated*, *Rolling Stone*, *Omni* or any other magazine that packages specialized news. Through voracious reading, you'll get a feeling of how journalists write. This is the first step toward becoming a good writer yourself.

The Carole Rich textbook *Writing and Reporting News: A Coaching Method* has several great passages that work well with this unit. Students using this textbook should read the first two chapters as soon as possible.

Rich is eloquent in describing the focus method—one of the main points of Unit One. A news-writing student must learn to focus on the news of an event before writing the story. Those who follow Rich's advice in her first chapter—especially her "tell a friend" technique—seldom get a false start in learning their first basic journalism skills.

The discussion of "Changing Concepts of News" in Rich's second chapter is an excellent follow-up to the first program in the telecourse. Pay close attention to Rich's description of how editors are changing their definitions of news at modern newspapers. Notice how Rich's section on "Qualities of News Stories" parallels the decisions made in the newsrooms we visited on the television program.

Chicago Tribune

Friday, April 15, 1994

Chicagoland North

50¢ Newsstand 40¢ Home Delivery

147th Year — No. 112 © Chicago Tribune 8 Sections N

LIVING IN FEAR

Researchers hunting for rogue gene

Scientists on quest to find 'master switch' of cancer

Last in a series examining how far science has come—and how much more remains unknown—in the fight against breast cancer.

By Peter Gorner
Tribune Staff Writer

When she became a cancer patient at 49, Carol Stegall changed forever. Her body had betrayed her. Its security had been breached.

All her life, Stegall had been protected against malignancies by an army of regulatory genes, sentry proteins, repair enzymes and commando white blood cells. As her cells went about their daily business of dividing, that army had functioned smoothly, keeping things in check and ceaselessly patrolling her body, seeking out damaged cells and either repairing or destroying them.

But somehow a mistake in her genetic code had crept in.

"Cancer didn't run in my family," Stegall said, "so I hadn't worried about breast cancer."

However, her mother had died in a fire when Carol was 7, so there was no way to tell if she had been cancer prone. Moreover, surprising new research is showing that Stegall could have inherited a predisposition to breast cancer from her father, even though he would not get the disease.

In any case, whether inherited or due to chance, Stegall's breast cancer—like all cancers—arose from a glitch in her genes.

The glitch could have been as minuscule as a simple point mutation in a single breast cell—the alteration of one critical nucleotide in the DNA sequence of thousands of nucleotides that constitute a normal gene. Sometimes that's all it takes to turn an ordinary, law-abiding gene into a deadly rogue.

The genes that cause cancer are altered versions of normal genes that encode normal proteins with important roles in normal cells. That statement, the outcome of 25 years of hard labor by molecular biologists, marks one of the great milestones in medical history: The demystification of cancer.

No longer is cancer seen as a black box, a mysterious alien plague too complicated ever to be understood. Now it is recognized that we all carry the seeds of our own destruction within us.

Broadly speaking, two types of genes cause cancer when they become mutated or inactivated. Oncogenes (from the Greek

See Cancer, Page 12

Mystery clouds Iraq tragedy

Reuters photo

A grim President Clinton says the 26 people killed over Iraq on Thursday "lost their lives while trying to save the lives of others."

Reuters photo

Defense Secretary William Perry tells a news conference at the Pentagon: "I take full responsibility for today's tragedy."

No explanation why copters fell to 'friendly fire'

By Terry Atlas
Tribune Staff Writer

WASHINGTON—President Clinton promised a full investigation into the "friendly fire" tragedy in which two American F-15C fighter jets mistakenly shot down two U.S. Army helicopters over northern Iraq on Thursday, killing 26 U.S. and allied personnel.

Defense Secretary William Perry and Gen. John Shalikashvili, chairman of the Joint Chiefs of Staff, could not immediately explain the horrible error.

The two American fighters patrolling the "no-fly" zone over northern Iraq mistook Army UH-60 Black Hawk helicopters for Iraqi aircraft and downed them with missiles despite multiple safeguards intended to prevent just this kind of deadly error.

Perry and Shalikashvili cited initial reports indicating that the pilots had visual sightings of the Black Hawks—which differ in major ways from Iraq's Soviet-built Hind helicopters—before firing their missiles during the daylight mission.

In addition, a U.S. Airborne Warning and Control System (AWACS) radar plane, able to sort out friendly and hostile aircraft, was patrolling the disputed airspace.

"Clearly, something went wrong, and an investigation will have to determine exactly what did go wrong," said Shalikashvili, the four-star Army general who commanded the relief effort for the Kurds when it began in 1991.

Within hours of the news, a grim-looking Clinton appeared before television cameras in the White House briefing room to express his sorrow over the incident, the worst U.S. setback in the three-year humanitarian aid effort in northern Iraq known as Operation Provide Comfort.

"Those who died today were part of that mission of mercy" to protect Kurds from Iraqi government repression, Clinton said. "They lost their lives while trying to save the lives of

See Iraq, Page 19

Helicopters shot down over Iraq

Two American fighter jets mistakenly downed two U.S. Army helicopters in northern Iraq Thursday morning, killing all 26 aboard the helicopters. The jets were enforcing the "no-fly" zone protecting Iraq's Kurdish minority from Iraqi government attacks. The helicopters were also part of the allied Provide Comfort task force protecting the Kurds.

Two UN helicopters shot down by two U.S. F-15C jets

Zakho, Aqrah, 36th parallel, 32nd parallel, Baghdad, IRAQ, TURKEY, SYRIA, SAUDI ARABIA, KUWAIT

Key: No-fly zones, established by Persian Gulf war allies to protect the Kurds.

Chicago Tribune. Sources: Jane's All The World's Aircraft, news reports

Mistaken identity

The U.S. fighter jets may have mistaken the Black Hawk helicopters for the Soviet-built Mi-24 Hind which is used by Iraq. A comparison of the two helicopters:

▸ **UH-60A Black Hawk**
Length*: 64 ft. 10 in.
Crew: 3
Passengers: 11

▸ **Mi-24 Hind**
Length*: 70 ft. 6-1/2 in.
Crew: 3
Passengers: 9

*With rotors turning

Safeguards that failed

Procedures for protecting friendly aircraft from attack have come under scrutiny as a major factor in Thursday's tragedy. Some primary identification safeguards are:

▸ **Electronic:** Aircraft electronic recognition signals or beacons that identify aircraft as friendly or hostile.

▸ **AWACS monitoring:** The Airborne Warning and Control System on board these radar aircraft can detect and track all aircraft within a 200-mile radius or more. Targets are normally identified by communication links to intelligence analysis centers. Communications links between radar planes and fighters allow command centers to control the actions of fighters and direct them to their targets.

▸ **Visual:** In situations that allow, pilots can visually confirm friend or foe status of target prior to engaging.

Rules of engagement

▸ The rules under which pilots may engage and fire upon suspected enemy targets are secret and differ from mission to mission. Rules of engagement are generally established by command staff involved directly with the mission. The decision to engage and fire can be relayed to pilots by a command center once positive identification and intent of a suspected target is confirmed or in some cases, that determination can be made by the pilot.

▸ F-15 fighter 70ft. 6-1/2 in.

Boaters get cut off on bridge openings

By Mitchell Locin and John Kass
Tribune Staff Writers

The Coast Guard lowered the boom on Chicago recreational boaters on Thursday, agreeing after a concerted lobbying effort by Mayor Richard Daley to restrict bridge openings that tie up downtown streets.

The only weekday daytime chance for sailors to bring their tall-masted sailboats and big powerboats down the Chicago River during the "spring breakout" to Lake Michigan will be a three-hour block on Wednesdays.

"This action will accommodate the needs of vehicle traffic while providing for the reasonable needs of navigation," says the new rule, signed by Rear Adm. Rudy Peschel, commander of the 9th Coast Guard District, which includes Chicago.

City officials said they had won the battle of the bridges against boaters who sought more flexibility from the Coast Guard, which governs U.S. waterways.

"The mayor is very pleased and he feels this is a reasonable compromise," said Noelle Gaffney, a spokeswoman for Daley. "His intent was to balance the boat owners' needs with the needs of everyone who works or resides or visits downtown, and these new regulations will strike that balance."

The rule, which is scheduled to

See Bridges, Page 15

AP photo

Tobacco chiefs testify: Heads of top American tobacco companies are sworn to testify Thursday before a House subcommittee. They are, from right to left, Philip Morris' William Campbell; R. J. Reynolds' James Johnston; U.S. Tobacco's Joseph Taddeo; Lorillard Tobacco's Andrew Tisch; Liggett Group's Edward Horrigan Jr.; Brown & Williamson Tobacco's Thomas Sandefur Jr.; American Tobacco's Donald Johnston; and Research American Tobacco's Robert Sprinkle III. **Story, Page 3.**

Despite FCC, pirates ride radio waves

By Ted Gregory
Tribune Staff Writer

The end for Power Radio—87.9 FM—came unceremoniously, after 2½ years of broadcasting from the attic bedroom of 15-year-old Peter Sinadinos.

At precisely 8:58 p.m. on March 31, an on-air personality for the unlicensed "pirate" station was cajoling listeners to participate in a phone-in game show when Peter's mother, Denise, burst into the studio and uttered the last words anyone is likely to hear from "The Power":

"FCC's over at the door."

Peter, the station's creator and operator, helped cut off its signal. Static swept over the frequency, and the station, which offered music, game shows and offbeat humor from a suburban Broadview bungalow studio, dissolved into eternity.

The Federal Communications Commission had brought down another casualty in its fight against illegal radio broadcasters.

With a limited band of frequencies available, the FCC is anxious to keep the radio waves clear of interference. The agency is especially afraid that pirate stations might break up police and fire transmissions or air traffic control.

The FCC allocates radio fre-

See Radio, Page 16

Friday

Movies: In "Serial Mom," Kathleen Turner plays a sort of June Cleaver clone—with a murderous streak. Michael Wilmington's review, **in Take 2.**

Weather

Chicago area: Friday: Thunderstorms possible; high 55 to 60 degrees. Friday night: Occasional showers; low 35 to 40. Saturday: Showers mixed with wet snow possible; high 45 to 50. Details in **Sec. 2, pg. 12.**

Freeway quarrel ends with baby shot

Luxury car driver fires after swapping insults at 70 m.p.h.

By Julie Irwin and Michael Martinez
Tribune Staff Writers

It was an outing perfectly suited for a warm spring day: Richard Mar and Diana Penman of Hanover Park packed up their 7-month-old twins in the family van Thursday and set out for an afternoon at the zoo.

Heading east on the Northwest Tollway, Mar became embroiled in a dispute with the driver of a 1993 Cadillac near the Des Plaines Oasis. Both men maneuvered to cut each other off, and the jockeying gave way to shouts out the window, police said.

But in an instant, shouts led to shooting. The driver of the car pulled out a gun and fired at the van, police said. A bullet passed through one of the van's windows and through an infant's seat, striking Brittany Kaye Strauss in the head.

The infant was fighting for her life Thursday night at Lutheran General Hospital in Park Ridge.

"It's just a sad situation," said Illinois State Police Master Sgt. Bill Schmitt. "It was both their faults. One of them could have backed off."

Police were searching late Thursday for the unidentified driver of the car.

The car is registered to a Wauconda woman who was at work in Elgin at the time of the shooting. Contacted at her home, the woman said the car was with her husband, who was scheduled to be in southern Illinois all week.

The dispute started about 1 p.m. just west of the oasis on the tollway, police said. Mar, 28, was driving a 1965 maroon van with Brittany's mother, Diana Penman, 30, and the baby's twin brother, Timothy Adam Strauss. The babies were in infant seats in the back seat of the van.

Both drivers were traveling about 70 m.p.h. when they rolled down their windows and began cursing at each other, police said.

The driver of the car pulled out

See Shooting, Page 15

Many editors purposely try to counterbalance the hard news, which is usually pessimistic, with feature news, which can give a more realistic, balanced look at our world.

Earlier in this unit, we quoted the legendary feature news reporter Charles Kuralt as saying the news was too negative. Kuralt said he never did have a satisfactory answer for his mother, who frequently threatened to cancel her subscription to the newspaper due to the bad news on the front page.

Throughout his career, however, Kuralt did find a way to answer those who feel the front page and the evening news are too negative. His series of short stories shot on the road, in the quiet corners of the United States, turned the cameras on Americans who weren't the standard clichés of the evening news.

"I think maybe the news was so bad when we started out in the '60s," Kuralt says. "1968 was the first full year of 'On The Road.' It was, as you remember, the year of Martin Luther King's death, Robert Kennedy's murder and the year the Russians invaded Czechoslovakia—and everything else that could go wrong in the world. Cities were burning. And once or twice a week I'd come along with an innocent little feature story . . . something like the last run of the Wabash Cannonball from Detroit to St. Louis. There was some value of reminding people that the whole world wasn't in flames after all. That many people still lived at peace with their neighbors. And perhaps there is a value to that."

Michael Brown, Chicago Defender: "Bottom line: . . . we determine the news."

Roy Peter Clark, Poynter Institute for Media Studies: "News exists in the world; it's not created by journalists. It's conveyed."

The editors of the *Chicago Tribune* published this story on the front page. Would you?

FREEWAY QUARREL ENDS WITH BABY SHOT:
LUXURY CAR DRIVER FIRES AFTER SWAPPING INSULTS AT 70 M.P.H.

By Julie Irwin and Michael Martinez
Chicago Tribune

It was an outing perfectly suited for a warm spring day: Richard Mar and Diana Penman of Hanover Park packed up their 7-month-old twins in the family van Thursday and set out for an afternoon at the zoo.

Heading east on the Northwest Tollway, Mar became embroiled in a dispute with the driver of a 1993 Cadillac near the Des Plaines Oasis. Both men maneuvered to cut each other off, and the jockeying gave way to shouts out the window, police said.

But in an instant, shouts led to shooting. The driver of the car pulled out a gun and fired at the van, police said. A bullet passed through one of the van's windows and through an infant's seat, striking Brittany Kaye Strauss in the head.

The infant was fighting for her life Thursday night at Lutheran General Hospital in Park Ridge.

"It's just a sad situation," said Illinois State Police master Sgt. Bill Schmitt. "It was both their faults. One of them could have backed off."

Police were searching late Thursday for the unidentified driver of the car.

The car is registered to a Wauconda woman who was at work in Elgin at the time of the shooting. Contacted at her home, the woman said the car was with her husband, who was scheduled to be in southern Illinois all week.

The dispute started about 1 p.m. just west of the oasis on the tollway, police said. Mar, 28, was driving a 1985 maroon van with Brittany's mother, Diana Penman, 30, and the baby's twin brother, Timothy Adam Strauss. The babies were in infant seats in the back seat of the van.

Both drivers were traveling about 70 m.p.h. when they rolled down their windows and began cursing at each other, police said.

The driver of the car pulled out a silver automatic pistol and fired one shot at the van, shattering a driver's side window, police said.

The bullet entered the left side of an infant seat and passed through the baby's head. Police found the shell, from a 9 mm or a .45-caliber gun, lodged in the right side of the car seat.

Brittany's brother, sitting in the infant seat next to her, was not injured.

Penman wrote down the driver's license plate number as the driver sped eastbound on the Tri-State Tollway or the Kennedy Expressway, Schmitt said.

"They didn't know the baby had been shot until they turned around," Schmitt said.

When Mar and Penman realized the girl had been injured, they drove about 5 miles to the nearest exit, the O'Hare Toll Plaza.

Schmitt said, "The father came (into the toll plaza) covered in blood," cradling the girl in his arms.

Rosemont paramedics responded to the scene and rushed the baby to Lutheran General, where she was listed in extremely critical condition after undergoing surgery for the gunshot wound. The bullet passed through her head, hospital officials said.

Brittany was breathing on her own after surgery, and doctors said the next 24 hours or so would be critical to her chances for survival.

The family was traveling to Brookfield Zoo when the shooting occurred, said Penman's sister, Rhonda Kemmer of Hanover Park.

"It was just them two and the twins going to the zoo, going to pick up a birthday gift for (Penman's) daughter. Penman's daughter Stephanie turned 7 on Thursday, Kemmer said.

Kemmer's daughter Crystal, $2^1/_2$, had asked to go to the zoo, but Kemmer had refused her request.

"She asked me to go three times, and I told her I wanted her to stay home and hang out and spring clean," Kemmer said as she videotaped the evening news stories about her niece's condition. "That could have been her."

Schmitt said that while feuding drivers occasionally will flash guns at each other, shootings on expressways and tollways remain rare.

Expressway violence has been a nationwide concern since 1987, when at least four people were killed in freeway shootings in Southern California.

CHICO COUNCIL MOVES TOWARD CALLING A TIMEOUT ON NEW BARS DOWNTOWN: ALSO VOTES TO OUST SUCCESSFUL CARD ROOM

By Randy S. Foster
Chico Enterprise-Record

The Chico City Council rejected a proposed land use code change Tuesday that would have legalized a downtown card room, and city officials said they will take immediate steps to shut the business down.

The council also took initial steps to impose an emergency moratorium against new downtown bars and nightclubs.

City Planner Clif Sellers and City Attorney Bob Boehm said it will take about two weeks to close Casino Chico, a card room located inside Team Players below street level in the 300 block of Main Street.

Casino Chico has operated illegally but with city approval, since late 1992.

The bar moratorium is aimed at heading off plans to convert three former retail sites, including the former Clayborne's clothing store at 325 Broadway, into nightspots.

The council will take final action on it at 7 p.m. Tuesday in the council chamber.

If approved, the moratorium would take effect immediately and would remain in place 45 days. The city has the option of extending it 10 months 15 days the first time and a year the second time, after public hearings.

The following story, written by a high school student, is a central part of the first telecourse program "What Is News?" Two professional news organizations considered the story as background for either a daily newspaper follow-up or a story on the television news. After reading this story, what decision would you make about the news value of the alleged incidents?

SPUR POSSE UNCOVERED AT PV: STUDENTS TRY TO SCORE IN SEX-FOR-POINTS CONTEST

By Libby Marks
The Saga — Pleasant
Valley High School

At least 15 senior PV boys are alleged to be members of a spur posse. A spur posse is a group of boys that sleep with girls for points. "This happens so often at schools and has been for some time," said Lori Rice, PV counselor. "Perhaps PV is in the position now to address this issue head-on with information and facts."

At least 15 names—some supplied by members of the alleged group itself—a score system and a tally sheet with the highest scorers were presented to *Saga* reporters by confidential sources. The scoring system indicates that alleged members are keeping track of sexual acts with a competitive point system. For example, one act would equal one point, and virgins were worth more than one point.

"If indeed it is substantiated that this is happening, I would say that if anything being done is not illegal, it is certainly immoral and lowly and immature and speaks of sad lack of personal ethics on the part of a lot of people," commented Vice Principal Mike Morris. "I just hope it is not the case, but I wouldn't be surprised by anything."

Alleged members have refused to make any comments for the record. "If they (the authorities) figure out who is on it, we might all go to jail," explained one senior.

"I don't want you to print this f——— story," said another alleged member.

"This could hurt our personal relationships," said another boy. "By printing this, you'll be saying that I've been cheating on my girlfriend."

A group of six alleged posse members was seen leaving a local dance club with one girl, reported one witness. She watched as alleged members flirted with a "young looking" girl and then left the club with her. No girls have yet come forward to accuse the group of any wrongdoing, and *The Saga* has no evidence of illegal activity by the Pleasant Valley group. Nor does *The Saga* staff have a list of girls' names.

Reprinted by permission.

What is news? Pulitzer Prize–winning humorist Dave Barry has these astute observations on the modern-day role of the newspaper in society.

DUDE, READ ALL ABOUT IT!

By Dave Barry
Miami Herald

Here in the newspaper industry (official motto: "For Official Motto, Please Turn to Section F, Page 37") we are seriously worried. Newspaper readership is declining like crazy. In fact, there's a good chance that nobody is reading this column. I could write a pornographic sex scene here and nobody would notice.

"Oh, Dirk," moaned Camille as she writhed nakedly on the bed. "Yess yes yes YES YES YES YES YESSSSSSS!"

"Wait up!" shouted Dirk. "I'm still in the bathroom!"

It was not always this way. There was a time in America when everybody read newspapers. Big cities had spunky lads standing on every street corner shouting "EXTRA!" These lads weren't selling newspapers: They just shouted "EXTRA!" because they wanted to irritate people, and boomboxes had not been invented yet.

But the point is that in those days, most people read newspapers, whereas today, most people do not. What caused this change?

One big factor, of course, is that people are a lot stupider than they used to be, although we here in the newspaper industry would never say so in print.

Certainly another factor is that many people now get their news from television. This is unfortunate. I do not mean to be the slightest bit critical of TV news people, who do a superb job, considering that they operate under severe time constraints and have the intellectual depth of hamsters. But TV news can only present the "bare bones" of a story: it takes a newspaper, with its capability to present vast amounts of information, to render the story truly boring.

But if we want to identify the "root cause" of the decline in newspaper readership, I believe we have to point the finger of blame at the foolish decision by many newspapers to stop running the comic strip "Henry." Remember Henry? The bald boy who looks like Dwight Eisenhower? I believe that readers liked the "Henry" strip because, in times of change and uncertainty, it always had the same plot:

PANEL ONE: Henry is walking along the street. He is wearing shorts, even if it is winter.

PANEL TWO: Suddenly, Henry spies an object. You can tell he's spying it, because a dotted line is going from his eyeball to the object. Often the object is a pie cooling on a windowsill (pies are always cooling on windowsills on the planet where Henry lives).

PANEL THREE: Things get really wacky as Henry eats the pie.

PANEL FOUR: The woman who baked the pie comes to the window and discovers that—prepare to roll on the floor—the pie is gone. The woman is surprised. You can tell because exclamation points are shooting out of her head.

This timeless humor has been delighting readers for thousands of years ("Henry" strips have been found on prehistoric cave walls), but for some reason, a while back most newspapers stopped running the strip, and readership has been in the toilet ever since. I don't think it's a coincidence.

Whatever the cause, the readership decline is producing major underarm dampness here in the newspaper industry. We're especially concerned about the fact that we're losing young readers—the so-called "Generation X," which gets its name from the fact that it followed the so-called "Generation W." We're desperate to attract these readers. Go to any newspaper today and you'll see herds of editors pacing around, mooing nervously, trying to think up ways to make newspapers more relevant to today's youth culture. This is pretty funny if you know anything about newspaper editors, the vast majority of whom are middle-aged Dockers-wearing white guys who cannot recognize any song recorded after *Yellow Submarine.*

But they're trying. If you read your newspaper carefully, you'll notice that you're seeing fewer stories with uninviting, incomprehensible, newspaper-ese headlines like PANEL NIXES TRADE PACT, and more punchy, "with-it" headlines designed to appeal to today's young people, like PANEL NIXES TRADE PACT, DUDE.

I applaud this effort, and as a middle-aged Dockers-wearing white guy, I want to do my part by making my column more "hep" and appealing to young people. So I'm going to conclude by presenting the views of some students of Daniel Kennedy's English class at Clearfield (Pa.) Area High School. I recently wrote a column in which I said that some young people today have unattractive haircuts and don't know who Davy Crockett was. Mr. Kennedy's class read this column and wrote me letters in

response: here are some unretouched excerpts, which I am not making up:

—"Maybe one of these days, you should look in the mirror, Dave. Dave, you need a new hairstyle man! You have a puff-cut, Dave."

—"Without hair I think every guy in the world would just die of imbarresment (sic). I know I would, but I am a girl."

—"You say that I don't no any thing about Davy Crockett. Well I no that he fought at the Alamo. He also played in several movies."

Let me just say that we in the newspaper industry totally agree with you young people on these points and any other points you wish to make, and if you will please, please, PLEASE start reading the newspaper we'll be your best friend, OK? OK? Young people? Hello?

You're not even reading this, you little twirps.

"Oh, Dirk," moaned Camille, "I am overcome by desire at the sight of your . . . your . . . What do you call those?"

"Dockers," said Dirk.

ALTERNATIVE VIEWS

SENSATIONALISM

Is the prurient interest in gossip and scandal a uniquely American phenomenon, capitalized upon by profit-hungry tabloids like the *National Enquirer*? Perhaps not. Reporter Andrew Loschilin, one of the Russian journalists who replaced the old Soviet propagandists that used to write for the Russian news agency TASS, explains what happened to the press when communism fell in the old Soviet Union and the free press was again allowed to flourish:

"When perestroika started, more and more newspapers appeared in the streets of Moscow or St. Petersburg or Kiev," says Loschilin. "A lot of so-called yellow magazines and yellow newspapers started circulating in Russia and Ukraine and the Baltic States. Even such topics as marital problems, infidelities, and scandals, and lifestyles of rich and famous began to appear on the front pages of Russian and Ukrainian and Baltic States magazines and newspapers. Right now we have a great number of newspapers. I can't name them. Hundreds and hundreds of newspapers, beginning from newspapers for young rockers, punk rockers, and ending with newspapers for homosexuals and pedophiles. It's a crazy situation."

AMERICAN TABLOID JOURNALISM

The *Weekly World News* and *National Enquirer*, two of America's most popular tabloid magazines, are both published under the same roof. Still, they have distinctly different attitudes toward what makes news. But can the average reader tell the difference?

"We'll have to fire everyone that's involved in the front page [if they can't]," says *National Enquirer* General Editor Brian Williams. "That's kind of a scary thought. *Weekly World News* is a black-and-white tabloid that does a lot of fun stories about babies with two heads, and it usually has [President] Clinton meeting a UFO, guardian angels, where you can see the face of God in a tree. And they just do lots of fun wacky-type stories. The *Enquirer*'s a very serious publication that has an emphasis on celebrity journalism and also human interest stories that are all, as far as we know, 100 percent true. I really don't think anybody comes to the newsstand and has a problem telling us apart."

Williams clarifies his magazine's editorial philosophy.

"Every page of the 56 pages is something that somebody wants to read about," Williams says. "That means no stock market reports, very little of what 'mainstream' newspapers call hard news—and a lot of celebrity gossip.

"I think the mainstream press is moving to more personality journalism," Williams says.

There is some evidence to support his claim. Scandals reported first in the pages of the *Enquirer* are more and more frequently ending up on the front pages of formerly staid newspapers such as the *New York Times* and the *Washington Post*.

ADVOCACY JOURNALISM

Michael Tomasky is an advocacy journalist who works for New York's *Village Voice.* His publication also has a different view on what makes news, compared to mainstream news definitions.

"The most important thing I think that I've learned is that objectivity—which is the thing that they teach you to strive for in journalism school—is just a complete myth," Tomasky says. "Objectivity just really doesn't exist, and that's the thing that I would always tell journalism students.

"Everything is based on a subjective decision. The stories that are on the front page of the *New York Times* are a mix of stories selected subjectively by a group of men (and they are all men) who bring a certain bias to what they select and deem to be important. Very often, more interesting stories will be on page A33. I almost always find that to be the case. Those will often be stories that the *New York Times* doesn't want you to know or doesn't at least consider very important for you to know."

GLOSSARY

AGENDA SETTING
Part of the decision-making process of what makes news or what gets published. The process by which politicians, journalists and others determine which topics and events will be the current focus of societal concern. Determining what readers think *about*, but not what they will actually think.

FOCUS METHOD
The method by which the news writer determines what the overall point of a news story is by condensing the elements to one clear sentence.

GATEKEEPING
Part of the decision-making process of what makes news. Gatekeeping is the process by which reporters, editors, news directors and other journalists decide which events and details get reported as news and which events or details do not get reported.

LOCALIZE
Finding a local spin for a national or regional event to communicate to readers or viewers how the event affects things closer to home.

NEED TO KNOW
News that may not be exciting or interesting to the readers or viewers but may affect them in very important ways. (These kinds of news events often affect the health, financial well-being, education or other aspects of the community. Local news agencies feel it's their duty to communicate this kind of news as a service, even if it is not entertaining.)

NEWS MIX
Creating a balanced menu of news for a publication, including good and bad, interesting and important, national and local, hard and soft.

PROXIMITY
How close the news event is to the home.

PUBLIC'S RIGHT TO KNOW
The flip side to an individual's right to privacy. The balance between the two is a constant debate in the court system and the newsroom.

TIME LINES
How fresh or old the news event is.

WANT TO KNOW
News that may not directly affect readers or views but is entertaining and flashy. Most news organizations need this kind of news to grab attention; the *National Enquirer* claims to publish only information the readers want to know.

SUGGESTED WRITING EXERCISES

1 Compare several front pages of a daily newspaper from your home community and the front pages of *USA Today* (or the closest major metropolitan newspaper). What is the balance between international and local news in both papers? What is the balance between negative and positive news in both papers? What is the balance between news the local community needs to know and news the public wants to know?

2 Continue to analyze your local newspaper, but compare it to local broadcast news agencies. How timely is the news? Did you hear the front-page headlines on the television news or radio news before you read the newspaper? How much more than the headline did you hear on the broadcast version of the story? Was the newspaper able to give you a deeper understanding of the story?

3 What are on the topics of the national agenda that are reflected in this week's news? Can you see the agenda-setting process at work?

4 Learn to localize wire service stories. Many local newspapers will take a report from the Associated Press and try to add a few lines that will give the story a hometown angle. For example, if your school newspaper has access to the Associated Press, the editor might need to use a generic story about the state budget to fill up a news hole. By making a few phone calls just before deadline, the editor could get quotes from school administrators about how the budget might directly affect your college or university. Those quotes could be inserted into the wire service story, usually shortly after the lead, to spice the generic news with a local flavor.

Editors at the *Chicago Tribune* used a similar technique when they looked for a Chicago connection to the international news about the helicopter shot down in Iraq.

Look for similar localized pieces in your community newspaper. Often, the byline will read something like "Associated Press and *Daily News* staff writers." How did the community paper localize the wire service story?

If you have access to a wire service through your school newspaper, ask your editor for an assignment to localize one of the stories. If not, take a generic wire service story from the community newspaper and try to localize it. Who would you call for additional information and quotes to give the story more relevance to the readers in your hometown?

5 Pick the most complicated story in today's news. Put the newspaper away, and attempt to reduce the story to one sentence. How similar was your sentence to the lead of the story?

QUIZ

Choose the best answer.

1 A strong understanding of what makes news

    a. can help in defending against a claim of invasion of privacy.
    b. can help a writer sort through a complex story to determine the focus for a lead.
    c. can help an editor decide what stories to put on the front page, to attract more readers.
    d. none of the above
    e. all of the above

2 Jack Winning, editor of the *Chico Enterprise-Record*, did not run the story about the local high school "sex for points" contest in his newspaper because

    a. he felt it was not the kind of story that readers would be interested in.
    b. the paper could not get any solid facts or on-the-record quotes to substantiate that the story was more than rumor.
    c. his paper was "scooped" by the competition.
    d. none of the above
    e. all of the above

3 Kathy Wilson of KHSL television decided to run the story about the local high school "sex for points" contest because

    a. the reporter got close enough to the sources to confirm that the story was based on fact and not pure rumor.
    b. the story could serve an important function to warn teens and parents about a variety of potential problems the practice could cause in the community.
    c. the story would attract the interest of many viewers.
    d. none of the above
    e. all of the above

4 KHSL television news ran a story about breaking news in a nearby Redding murder. Chico's newspaper, the *Chico Enterprise-Record*, did not cover the story. The primary reason for the paper's decision was

    a. there was already too much violence in the news.
    b. the television station had already beaten the newspaper to the story, and it therefore had little appeal.
    c. there was a lack of proximity value to the story.
    d. none of the above
    e. all of the above

5 The *Chicago Tribune*

    a. runs stories about all murders and killings in the city on the front page.
    b. never runs stories about murders on the front page.
    c. prefers to emphasize stories of international importance over stories simply about Chicago on the front page.
    d. none of the above
    e. all of the above

6 The *Chicago Tribune* editors decided to run the story about the shooting on the freeway because

    a. it had significance that might affect relations between different racial and ethnic neighborhoods.
    b. a freeway shooting was something "new" and unusual in the city and therefore of high news value.
    c. most violent occurrences involving shootings and killings end up on the front page.
    d. none of the above
    e. all of the above

7 The *Chicago Tribune* editors, when reporting the international news of the accidental shooting of an American helicopter over Iraq by "friendly fire," were waiting for their own staff members to report on the following angle:

    a. incompetence in the leadership of the army squadron that was responsible for accidentally shooting down the helicopter.
    b. a local connection to the story, by finding out whether any of the servicemen killed or injured were from Chicago.
    c. a connection to Iraqi terrorists.
    d. none of the above
    e. all of the above

8 The following elements are important to determine when a reporter is writing a lead or developing a focus sentence for a news story:

    a. proximity of the story location
    b. timeliness of the event
    c. prominence of subject
    d. unusual nature of the occurrence
    e. all of the above

9 According to the Carole Rich text, *Writing and Reporting News: A Coaching Method*, the primary emphasis of the News 2000 project to revamp the content of the more than 80 newspapers owned by Gannett Co. (which also publishes *USA Today*) is on

    a. providing entertainment.
    b. using information graphics.
    c. making the news relevant to readers in local communities.
    d. none of the above
    e. all of the above

10 At the *National Enquirer*, news is defined as

    a. stories the readers need to know about.
    b. stories the readers want to read about.
    c. stories that none of the mainstream papers would touch.
    d. none of the above
    e. all of the above

SELF·TEST

1 Read the example news stories published at the end of this chapter. Each story is a key part of the televised program for this first unit of the telecourse. For each story, reduce the news value down to one sentence, otherwise known as a "focus sentence." In other words, if you were going to summarize the story for a friend in one sentence, how would you do it?

Write a focus sentence in the space provided for each story. Make sure you use a complete sentence, not a headline.

a. Freeway quarrel

b. Spur posse

c. City council/bars

2 Examine the front page of the *Chicago Tribune* included on page 11. List each story, and capsulize the news value of each story in the space provided. In other words, why did the editors feel the story was worthy of the front page?

3 Dave Barry's column is included for a bit of fun on page 16. But there's more reason than laughs for including it here. Barry has a point. How will the reporters and editors of newspapers successfully compete for readers in the future?

THE
SUMMARY
LEAD

The summary lead is the most basic tool a journalism student should study. Many editors will give an entry-level job applicant a short test that will involve turning raw news information into a brief story. These editors will not even consider hiring interns or rookie reporters unless they can prove an ability to organize information into a summary lead form.

The summary lead style has been with us for more than a century and will likely be a mainstay of journalism hundreds of years from now. The style of writing is so basic and so accepted on the front page of many daily newspapers that readers will often complain if any other kind of story introduction is used.

In a sense, this form of organizing information is a basic model of human communication that has a role in everything from leaving a message before an answering machine cuts you off to writing a public relations press release. A second grader will be asked to include the famous five W's and H—the Who, What, When, Where, Why and How—in that first "How I Spent My Summer Vacation" essay. A scientist from NASA, when submitting his or her "How I Spent My $5 Billion This Summer" report to Congress, must also include the same basic elements.

At first, the summary lead might seem like a dry, rote formula. The most skillful reporters, however, approach the summary lead as an art form. The Japanese poetry form of haiku is certainly a rigid formula. The blueprints for many popular songs are also nearly identical. Certainly, the most talented writers who create within these forms have learned to transcend formulaic composition and achieve true artistry.

Of course, there are hackneyed pop songs. And no doubt there are Japanese poets (and freshman English students) who are churning out bad haiku. The world of journalism is no exception. Often, as many mundane leads appear in a given day's selection of news stories as lively ones.

This program and chapter will instruct you on how to master the summary lead formula and will inspire or challenge you to embrace the form and make it sing.

OBJECTIVES

This unit will teach students how to organize and focus a large amount of information into a succinct and clear sentence that emphasizes the news value of an event, by demonstrating the hard-news writing style known as the summary lead.

**PROGRAM
GUIDE**

BEFORE YOU WATCH

This chapter introduces hard-news style. Listen to the news professionals talk about how they write leads for hard-news stories.

•**Pay close attention to the ways the featured journalists use the following terms:**

Summary lead   Time element
News value   Inverted pyramid
Passive verb   Partial quote
The What   Attribution
Jargon and gobbledygook   The Why

WHILE YOU WATCH

1. Take very close notes. You will be asked to write a lead at the end of the chapter, based on information you hear on the video presentation about the upside-down flag story.

2. Note how different types of journalists, from police reporters to sports reporters, approach leads.

3. Try to notice at least five reasons why mastering the summary lead is important for students.

4. Prepare your own formula for writing a summary lead, and compare it to the formulas other students in the class come up with.

AFTER YOU WATCH

•**Address the following questions in your journal, or, if there's time, discuss them in class:**

1. How can mastery of summary lead styles help you make a deadline?

2. Do advocacy journalists or magazine writers need to master the summary lead? Why?

3. Does the use of the summary lead automatically give way to boring formula writing?

4. If you want to write more "creative" leads—question leads, quote leads or other feature leads—do you still need to understand the summary lead styles? Why?

5. Assuming that you cannot fit the Who, What, When, Where, Why and How in a story, what are the first elements you would leave out? Which of the six elements should be emphasized?

THE
LESSON

A basic journalism class fails if students don't master the summary lead.

The summary lead is simply the most basic building block of news writing.

You probably won't get hired in a public relations job—let alone a television station, radio station or magazine—if you don't at least have a feel for the summary lead. You definitely won't get hired at a newspaper if you haven't conquered the challenges of writing in this style.

Those challenges include a lot more than learning to squeeze a news event down to the Who, What, When, Where, Why and How in 35 words or less. Good summary lead writing transcends learning a mere formula.

"We may have gone wrong in insisting that there was a formula," Carole Rich says about journalism education, in general.

"I think what was tragic, especially for beginning students, is that people got the idea that journalism had to be dull, that journalism or news stories had to be written in only one way, especially in introductory courses. If we give students the opportunity to use variety . . . I know all my students have said 'This is fun!' . . . though, some have said 'This is fun?' as if it was a question, as if it was a surprise."

"There's room for creativity in a summary lead formula," says Bruce Itule. "Not a lot." But enough room so that students and beginning reporters can find a challenge in every news story that requires one. The challenge, according to Itule (formerly a reporter for the *Chicago Tribune* and currently a respected professor at the University of Arizona) is to learn what to leave out and what to emphasize. And how to grab the reader's attention with the fewest words.

Itule and Rich are authors of two widely used textbooks on journalism, and though their approaches differ, both seem to agree on this point.

Rich insists that writing a creative summary—or any news story, for that matter—includes a follow-up to the first unit of this telecourse: learning how to focus the news value of the event you are trying to cover.

Rich, a well-respected teacher who is hired to coach writers at newspapers across the country, says, "I will always teach the focus method first. I don't care if they've been writing for 30 years.

"The first thing that I tell students and writers is . . . just tell me what the story is about. They want to tell you in many sentences, in many paragraphs. And then I say, 'No, tell me what the story's about in one sentence.' What's the story about? One clear sentence. And that's the focus sentence. That one sentence will help crystallize what this story means to you. I believe it's the foundation for writing a news story."

This is exactly what Ed Farrell does with the example story about the upside-down flag in the summary lead unit of the telecourse. According to Farrell, the important thing about the story was not that the mayor "staged a big do-dah" for the media or even that the city council had agreed to let the mayor fly the state flag upside-down and at half mast. The focus of the story was that the state budget decisions had created a state of chaos with the city budget. Farrell leaves the What for later and decides to emphasize the Why of the story at the top of his lead. The rest of his lead is a creative variation of the summary formula.

In writing the lead, Farrell excerpts a partial quote—"the state is in chaos"—from the mayor's statement, to lure the reader into the rest of the piece, while summarizing the news event as succinctly as possible.

Farrell's approach to writing the summary lead emphasizes several basic points made in the telecourse program about summary leads. (The entire story is included for your study in this unit of the book.)

Important quotes or facts must be **attributed** in the lead (though **delayed identification** is a common practice). Notice that Farrell attributes the mayor's partial quote immediately after using it. He also uses strong *active* verbs in his lead (*declaring* and *ordered*) instead of the passive voice.

Good writers rarely stick to the exact Who, What, Where, When, Why and How formula. The Who, for instance, is seldom emphasized in the beginning of a good lead, unless the person making the news is very important. In the story about the upside-down flag, Farrell takes great care to emphasize the most interesting and most important element of the story instead.

It's trendy for students to avoid learning the summary lead and complain that most news organizations now prefer more "creative" alternative styles of leads.

However, you've seen in the telecourse program that journalists from a wide variety of beats and publications depend on this basic journalism tool.

Jeff Chapman, professional basketball beat writer from the *Oakland Tribune*, uses the summary lead to slam a story together when the ball game ends at 10:30 and the presses roll at midnight.

Michael Tomasky, of the *Village Voice*, depends on the summary lead despite the fact that his work appears in an alternative weekly newspaper that practices advocacy journalism.

And Michael Waldholz, from the conservative *Wall Street Journal*, relies on exactly the same tool.

"When I first started as a journalist, I really understood Who, What, Where, When, How and When [sic], because I would constantly be asking myself that question," Waldholz says, "and I would constantly trip up when I wasn't doing it. But now it is so integrated in the way I do my job that I don't think about it. It is like learning the scales to play the instrument. You have to hammer away at answering those questions. It is the most basic thing in reporting and it's why we learn . . . the lead. In this day and age, when there's so much stimulation, so much news, no one is going to get beyond the lead if it's not really interesting."

Will the summary lead survive as a traditional journalism device when even the printed page is no longer dependent on mashed-up trees and delivery boys throwing the morning paper on your doorstep?

Michael Brown, editor of the *Chicago Defender*, America's oldest African-American daily newspaper, thinks it will.

"I am of the opinion that the summary lead will never go out of vogue," Brown says.

Michael Waldholz, Wall Street Journal*: "[The summary lead's] such a rudimentary part of my job, I don't even think about it anymore."*

Michael Tomasky, Village Voice*: "The summary lead is a useful thing, no matter what sort of journalism you do—even 'advocacy.'"*

"For one reason, and that is this: Within the next 10 years, maybe sooner, you're going to be able to take a newspaper—it's going to be an electronic newspaper—in your hand, the size of a pocket calculator. And you're going to be punching what you want to read. And if that information is not tight, it's not going to be read. So we're going to be reading newspapers in the palms of our hands. Therefore, we must learn how to write tight in the concept that we all teach: . . . how to omit needless words. The summary lead is almost just that—omitting needless words, or summarizing what that person's going to read. And if it's going to be on an electronic newspaper . . . summary leads are going to be very important."

Many traditional journalism textbooks start by teaching the student the summary lead. Many journalism teachers believe that students shouldn't be allowed to think about any other kind of lead until they've mastered the summary lead—toward the end of the first semester's course.

Carole Rich waits until the middle of her textbook to fully discuss the summary lead, and then explains it in a chapter that introduces a wide variety of lead styles. That's not to say Rich diminishes the importance of a summary lead—she just trusts her students to understand the importance of this basic journalism tool while learning other more exotic styles.

"I think the summary lead has had a bad rap," Rich says. "As we get more and more into on-line writing, and information overload, there will be more and more use for a summary lead." And, Rich points out, if the story starts with a different kind of lead, a "nut graph"—which summarizes the basic Who, What, When, Where, Why and How—is needed near the top of the story anyway. By any other name, many journalists feel this is still a summary lead in the disguise of "creative writing"—a few inches down from the top of the story. Inevitably, the summary lead is a technique you must master to get a first job and, ultimately, to survive in this business.

Rich first introduces the summary lead with a broader look at the total "Basic News Story," which she describes with a thorough description and numerous examples on pages 33–57 in the second edition of her textbook.

She later fully develops the significance of the summary lead on pages 149–180 in the second edition. Pay close attention to her discussion of attributions in leads and impact of hard-news leads.

You should also read as many daily newspapers as possible while learning to master these concepts, and try to identify the eloquent, as well as the mundane, use of the summary lead.

Finally, many of the example stories included in this textbook have used summary leads—even those which have won Pulitzer Prizes and other awards. Glance through the example stories, and identify the stories that start with summary leads.

Did you know broadcast journalists rarely use the summary lead?

"In radio, it's actually telling a story," says Joyce Davis, of National Public Radio. "I give you a little bit at first, and say, 'Well, you know there was a bad accident today?' and you say, 'Oh, really?' 'Yes, three people were killed.'

"Sometimes you save some of the best for last. You never do that with newspapers, because you always worry about the end getting chopped off. There's a difference between a lead in a newspaper story, and an intro of the radio story."

"Print reporters learn that they have to write a lead sentence, and the lead sentence should employ a number of factors that are explained in the body of the story," says Sam Donaldson of ABC News. "Theoretically someone should be able to read the lead sentence and understand the thrust of the story. Broadcast television— that's not the way it works at all, because we use the pictures. The first words may be, 'The president had a thoughtful and frustrated look on his face as he walked to his helicopter this morning.' You say that's the lead?

"That's the right way to begin a television piece. You wouldn't begin with a headline and then try to back into his walking to his helicopter. The end result is the same; you transmit information. But you don't do it the way the print journalists do it."

UPSIDE-DOWN FLAG SIGNALS CITY DISTRESS OVER STATE FUND RAID

By Ed Farrell
Chico Enterprise-Record

Declaring "the state is in chaos," Chico Mayor Mary Andrews ordered Tuesday that the California state flag be flown upside down on the city hall flagpole beginning this afternoon until the state has finalized its budget negotiations.

An inverted flag is the international symbol of distress, which, she said, aptly expresses the concerns of cities at the prospect of losing upwards of $1 billion in revenues to the state.

Acting on what she termed "mayoral prerogative," Andrews ordered a city crew to lower the state flag to half-staff Tuesday afternoon as a protest suggested by the California League of Cities.

Other communities across the state are making other symbolic protests, Andrews said.

The city of Simi Valley, for example, has sent a truck full of turnips to be delivered to the state Capitol later today, which are to be distributed to Gov. Wilson and members of the legislature.

At Tuesday night's council session, Andrews asked the council for authority to invert the state flag; however, since the matter had not been posted on the agenda, City Attorney Bob Boehm refused to allow the council to vote on the matter.

"Well, then I'll do it myself," Andrews replied.

The mayor then ordered Community Services Director Tom Lando to make arrangements to carry out her instructions.

At a press conference held before the start of Tuesday night's meeting, Andrews was joined by Councilman Ted Hubert, Police Chief Michael Dunbaugh, Parks Director Kevin Cunningham and Fire Marshall Larry Agee.

Noting that the cuts being considered by the legislature would directly impact the city's general fund, Andrews said she wanted the public to realize that the pending state actions would have real, visible impacts on Chico's citizens.

Of utmost importance, Andrews said, was a proposal to abandon the provisions of AB 8, the 1979 legislation by which property taxes were apportioned to cities, counties, schools and special districts.

Legislators, seeking ways to balance the state budget, now refer to the legislation as a "bailout" for local government.

Andrews said the legislature is considering abolishing AB 8, which Assembly Speaker Willie Brown recently said had turned cities into the equivalent of "heroin addicts."

Such action, Andrews said, could cost the city of Chico more than $1 million over a three-year period.

Reprinted by the permission of the publisher.

Consider the following leads in your study of the summary lead style. Look through the other example stories in the study guide to identify summary leads.

Chicago Tribune
Friday, April 15, 1994
By Terry Atlas

WASHINGTON—President Clinton promised a full investigation into the "friendly fire" tragedy in which two American F-15C fighter jets mistakenly shot down two U.S. Army helicopters over northern Iraq on Thursday, killing 26 U.S. and allied personnel.

Defense Secretary William Perry and Gen. John Shalikashvili, chairman of the Joint Chiefs of Staff, could not immediately explain the horrible error.

Record-Searchlight
May 17, 1994
By Adrienne Packer

PALO CEDRO—The owner of a Redding pizzeria killed his ex-wife Monday before shooting himself with a revolver, officials said.

Sharon and Hossein Rostamizadeh died from gunshot wounds at his home in the 7300 block of Chipper Lane in Palo Cedro, Chief Deputy Coroner Lt. John Boyle said today.

Record-Searchlight
November 22, 1994
By Adrienne Packer

A "bomb" that prompted deputies to evacuate 2,000 residents Thursday turned out to be a bundle of road flares wrapped with wiring, a clock and a power source, authorities said Monday.

"It was determined to be a non-explosive device," said Shasta County sheriff's Capt. Larry Jarret.

The device was attached to a pipe linking four 30,000-gallon propane tanks at Campora Wholesale Propane on Eastside Road. Sheriff's bomb specialist Rick Slocum found the device about 8:15 a.m. after three Redding-area businesses received bomb threats from a male caller Thursday morning.

ALTERNATIVE VIEWS

The journalism visionaries who object to the overuse of the summary lead in conventional newspaper work are very vocal these days. They warn against conditioning students to write unreadable formula leads.

"I think summary leads mislead students into thinking that they have to put everything important in the very top of the story," says Don Fry, of the Poynter Institute. "You've got the idiot logic of the inverted pyramid which says that everything heavy floats to the top coupled with the idea that the lead includes the five W's and the H. So you end up with a 35-word sentence with the 5 W's and the H in it. And the sentence is so thick that nobody can read it." Fry's contemporary at the Poynter Institute, Roy Peter Clark, has a similar view.

The problem, Clark says, is that some journalism teachers "suggest that news writing is some kind of fill-in-the-blank kind of thing. Somehow you get the notion that when you write a story, you have to squeeze all of those W's in your lead. We call that the suitcase lead. What do you do when your suitcase is over-flowed? You sit on it until it closes. . . . The cramming of information into a lead is not what contributes to readers' comprehension and understanding."

The solution, according to Fry, Clark and others, is to learn how to emphasize the most compelling information in the lead sentence of the story. The other details are then paced throughout the rest of the reporting.

GLOSSARY

ATTRIBUTION	Giving credit to who said what. The most common attribution verb is *said*. News writers must attribute the sources of all quotes. They must also attribute the source of many facts stated in the news story. Headlines are often also attributed, especially if opinions are stated, as in " 'Taxes to increase,' says President Gingrich."
DELAYED IDENTIFICATION	This is saving the name of a primary news maker for the second or third paragraph of a story. For instance, the summary lead might say, "The mayor announced." In a later paragraph, it would identify him, as in, "Mayor Gomer Pyle."
JARGON OR GOBBLEDYGOOK	Any overly formal, technical or bureaucratic words that would not be used in everyday language.
NUT GRAPH	Essentially a variation of a summary lead in a story in which a lead other than the summary lead has been used. The nut graph (or nut graf) would summarize the important elements of the story—for instance, after a question lead.
PASSIVE VOICE	Any form of the verb *to be*. Examples: "We are"; "I am"; "The book was read"; "When the song is sung by the fat lady."
PROXIMITY	How close to home was the story? Or, where did the event take place?
SUMMARY LEAD	The traditional journalism tool used to start off most hard-news stories. Textbooks and editors vary on how many words (in the telecourse, you heard people say "35 words or less," "25 words or less," "19 words or less"), but all agree the summary lead must be short. And it should summarize the classic news elements, answering the questions readers will want to ask about a news event: Who? What? When? Where? Why? How?
TIME ELEMENT	When the story happened.

Write a summary lead based on the following raw information:

1 News story: Kevin Jurgens, an 18-year-old high school senior from Philo High School, died Tuesday at Urbana's University Hospital. Jurgens was involved in a traffic accident in a heavy rain storm on Tuesday afternoon, riding his bicycle home on River Road, 4 miles east of Urbana.

Students and teachers will be offered grief counseling at the high school on Wednesday.

The teen was struck by a first-year computer science teacher at Philo High— Gary Small, 25, of Urbana. Small told officers he was driving between 50 and 55 m.p.h. on the road and noticed the bicycle well before the accident. The rider, who was not wearing a helmet, turned abruptly in front of the car, according to Small. There were no witnesses. The driver of the car was uninjured.

According to school Vice Principal Mike Ford, "It's terrible both ways. Kevin was here all four years of high school, and Gary is a super guy. He wouldn't hurt a flea."

2 Sports story: The Shasta College men's basketball team played a game against Butte College on Saturday night.

You are writing a story for the Sunday newspaper. Both teams are from the Golden Valley Conference.

Both teams had won six games and lost none in conference play record coming into Saturday's game.

Desmond Smith, of Shasta's Knights, led all players with 33 points. Though he's the tallest player on the team, Smith is only 6 feet, 6 inches tall.

The game was decided in the last two seconds of overtime, when 6' 2" guard Andre Billings hit a three-point shot to put Shasta ahead 79 to 78.

The game was played in the Shasta College gymnasium, in Redding, California.

The Butte College team, the Roadrunners, was led by center Tom "Tree" Treadway, who is 7 feet tall.

With the win, Shasta took sole possession of first place in the conference, at the exact midway point of the season. The two teams are scheduled to meet again, in the final game of the season, which will be at the Roadrunners' home court in Oroville, California.

3 Entertainment story: A band called The Box Tops played at a local nightclub called the Blue Max on Friday night. You are writing a story for the Saturday newspaper.

The Box Tops had several Top 40 hits in the '60s, including "The Letter" and "Neon Rainbow." The nightclub, with a capacity for 300 patrons, sold 121 tickets. By the second set, only 23 people remained to hear the rest of the show.

The only original member of the '60s band was the bass player.

According to one patron, "This band sounded like a lounge act from the Holiday Inn. The drummer was a pregnant woman. I have nothing against women, or pregnant women. But, playing drums in a smoky bar? Absurd!" The band played its two hits in the first set, and then played songs from the current Top 40.

"I guess the bass player owns the rights to the name The Box Tops," said another patron. "But, for my money, this show was a rip-off. How can they sell tickets, when the original lead singer isn't even with the band?"

QUIZ

Choose the best answer.

1 The most important part of a summary lead is the

    a. Who.
    b. What.
    c. When.
    d. Why.
    e. most important, most interesting, most newsworthy element.

2 One element that is seldom emphasized as the first part of the summary lead sentence is the

    a. Who.
    b. What.
    c. How.
    d. Why.
    e. most important, most interesting, most newsworthy element.

3 If an anecdotal lead or some other alternative to the summary lead is used, something very similar to a summary lead is usually included very close to the top of the story. This element of the story is called a

    a. buried lead.
    b. nut graph.
    c. suitcase.
    d. none of the above
    e. all of the above

4 Attribution in a lead

    a. is used to tell the reader who is being quoted.
    b. lets the reader know where the reporter found facts used in the lead.
    c. is needed for an accusatory statement.
    d. none of the above
    e. all of the above

5 Delayed identification in a lead is

    a. a bad idea, because the readers should have a name attached to the Who of a story in the first paragraph of every well-written news report.
    b. standard practice in news writing, even if the story is about the president.
    c. a common practice, unless the Who of a story is a significant member of society known to most of the readers.
    d. none of the above
    e. all of the above

6 The lead for a news story should

    a. be written with a strong active verb, if possible.
    b. avoid using too many flashy adjectives.
    c. use concrete nouns.
    d. none of the above
    e. all of the above

7 The summary lead is

    a. a style used often by writers on a deadline.
    b. a style that most editors expect rookie reporters to know when they apply for a job.
    c. a style that works well with wire service stories.
    d. none of the above
    e. all of the above

8 According to Michael Brown, of the *Chicago Defender*, the summary lead

    a. will die when newspapers are no longer printed on tree pulp paper.
    b. will be an essential part of news, when it is delivered through a palm-sized receiving device that will be much like a cross between an Apple Newton pad and a cordless telephone.
    c. is not important for alternative newspapers.
    d. none of the above
    e. all of the above

9 The summary lead was described as important on which of the following jobs?

    a. the sports beat
    b. the police beat
    c. at advocacy journalism newspapers
    d. none of the above
    e. all of the above

10 Reporters in the telecourse said the summary lead was important because

    a. it helped them organize thoughts on a deadline.
    b. readers often want to know the most important information right at the top of a story.
    c. people often tell personal stories with a summary and feel comfortable reading this conversational style in the newspaper.
    d. none of the above
    e. all of the above

1 In the telecourse program for this unit, an example of a story about the city budget crisis in Chico is given. Several times, the essential elements for the story are given in the videotape. Three important aspects of reporting include observing details, learning to take notes and remembering facts that go by quickly. List as many of the elements of this news story as you can, in the space provided:

The Who:

The What:

The When:

The Where:

The Why:

The How:

2 In the space provided, write a formula Who, What, When, Where, Why and How summary lead for this story, in 35 words or less. This should be a very straightforward, primitive version of the lead in which you simply plug in the elements for the formula. This formula lead should be one sentence.

3 Write a more creative version of the same lead about the budget crisis in Chico, emphasizing the elements that seem most interesting and important to you—and your readers. Since you will probably delay some of the six key elements, write additional sentences for the story until you have listed all ingredients essential to report the full news event.

4 Imagine you have to write a news story about this telecourse being offered at your school. Consider how you would distill what has happened in the first two weeks of the course to tell a friend about it—in one clear sentence. Now, modify the sentence as if it were a lead for a story in the school newspaper about the telecourse being offered on your campus.

NEWS
LANGUAGE
AND STYLE

By this point of the telecourse, you've started to write your own summary leads. However, even before you finish that first sentence, you're likely to run into minor mechanical problems.

How do reporters deal with numbers? Do they spell them out or use numerals? Do journalists spell out state names or abbreviate them? When is a source's job title capitalized, and when is it lowercase? Can the newspaper get sued if you confuse manslaughter, kill and murder? How should you refer to Mayor Jim Smith in the second mention of the story: Smith, Jim or the mayor?

Some of these worries about language use seem pointless, almost trivial. Others, when not addressed properly, can cause great embarrassment, or worse. If nothing else, the newspaper can lose credibility with readers if reporters in the same issue use different spellings for the identical term. At worst, sloppy language use can lead to a lawsuit.

It can be disconcerting to a reader to see his home region referred to as the *northstate*, The *North State*, the *Northstate*, the *north state* and the *North Valley* all in the same day's paper. It can be more than disconcerting if the word *alleged* is used incorrectly.

Journalists working for the same team need to agree on a consistent style.

While you're working on your first summary leads, and as you start to work on developing the rest of the story in next week's lesson, this lesson will help you solve some of the most common language problems encountered by beginning news-writing students and rookie reporters.

Writers who turn in sloppy copy to editors, on the job, often develop a bad newsroom reputation. Journalists who turn in clean copy not only get a good reputation—they tend to get offered the best assignments and more opportunities for advancement.

This unit will help send you down the path to clean copy and inspire you to a work ethic that demands an attention to style details.

OBJECTIVES

After you've started to develop your own news sense and a feeling for how to write a summary lead, this unit will help you learn the basics of news-writing language. From this point on, you should be familiar with the most common oddities, quirks and conventions of journalistic language use. And, if you come across language problems that need solving, you'll know how to look them up in a stylebook and why checking with a stylebook is so important.

PROGRAM GUIDE

BEFORE YOU WATCH

This program will help you understand how reporters view the English language. While good writing in the news business has much in common with other writing styles, a very careful choice of words can help the reporter achieve goals of precision, accuracy, timeliness and credibility that might not be as important in fiction or other kinds of prose.

•**Pay close attention to how the journalists interviewed use the following words:**

AP style	Precision
Attribution	Consistency
Grammar	Credibility
Libel	Clean copy

WHILE YOU WATCH

1. Look for language use rules designed to help keep the reporting balanced, fair and objective.

2. For fun, try to identify elements of journalism style that might run contrary to the lessons taught in a freshman English class.

3. Familiarize yourself with style rules that are meant to protect reporters from getting involved with libel lawsuits.

4. Notice which elements of journalism language use relate directly to newsroom ethics.

5. Identify the aspects of journalism style that make you proud to be part of the business.

AFTER YOU WATCH

•**Address the following questions in your journal, or, if there's time, discuss them in class:**

1. Which aspects of language use in news writing help eliminate bias with regard to gender, race, age, sexual preference or ability?

2. How can sloppy language use lead to loss of credibility, with either your editor or your readers?

3. List examples you picked up from the video presentation of language use that could get you in trouble legally or ethically.

4. Why should a journalist be preoccupied with obscure details such as whether a word should be capitalized or a number should be spelled out or shown as a numeral? Are we being overly picky?

THE LESSON

It's not uncommon for a young reporter to wander over to the editor's desk with a half-finished story to ask about a style rule. Some editors appreciate this.

Since editors are very busy people, however, they are apt to rudely toss the *Associated Press Stylebook* your way and snarl, "Look it up, rookie."

The shrewd employee will quickly learn that the boss appreciates enterprise. If you learn to look up the most common style questions on your own, a keen editor will probably notice that your copy is clean and your stylebook is dog-eared. You can then graduate beyond puppy questions to more learned and scholarly language debates, such as whether a more politically correct term than *manhole cover* is appropriate in a story about the city council's vote to finance replacements for the damaged "sewer entrance protection disc units" on Main Street.

The *Stylebook* is a living, evolving document, and reporters from every type of newspaper imaginable—even alternative weeklies such as New York's *Village Voice*—can eventually affect changes in subsequent editions.

"We have a very particular style," says Michael Tomasky, of the *Voice.* "Which is I guess, in essence very much like the AP's, but slightly different on some things. We have some sort of politically correct style notes, like using *congress member* instead of *congressman* or *congresswoman.* I don't necessarily agree with some of them. I don't see any reason to neuter people just because they're elected to public office."

The editor of the *AP Stylebook*, Norm Goldstein, notices such trends.

"In the journalism business and the newspaper business, we're very aware of how the language changes," Goldstein says. "Editors contact us all the time, make suggestions, ask questions. We revise the book once a year, to update it. A specific example now is the discussion about the use of *Afro-American* or *African-American* as opposed to *black*, as opposed to *Negro*, as opposed to *colored*. And it's one of those major language changes that you could follow even in the past 30 years. In the '60s, *black* became common usage, replacing *colored* or *Negro*. Now it's a question of whether *African-American* or *Afro-American* will replace *black*. AP has decided; we'll wait and see for a while."

The lesson for this unit is relatively short. The best way to familiarize yourself with the *AP Stylebook* is to use it a lot. At first, it will be a bit confusing. Some terms are listed alphabetically; others are listed by category. Sometimes, you'll be sent forward 76 pages, only to be directed to a reference near the front of the book.

Should you write *Fire Captain* John Jones, *fire captain* John Jones, or *Fire Capt.* John Jones? Look up *fire*, and the book will send you to *military titles*.

Look up *larceny*, and you'll be sent to *burglary*.

You might go crazy yourself trying to describe a mental disability. There's no reference under *disability*, *mental illness*, *sanity* or *insanity*. However, the *Stylebook* has specific advice under *handicapped*:

> In general, do not describe an individual as disabled or handicapped unless it is clearly pertinent to a story. If such a description must be used, make it clear what the handicap is and how much the person's physical or mental performance is affected.

We'd like to help you maintain sanity on that first journalism job. Therefore, the emphasis in this unit will be on exercises and self-tests. But, before we get to those, we'll leave you with a last bit of advice from some of the journalists interviewed for the telecourse.

John Katsilometes, a reporter from the Redding *Record-Searchlight*, suggests keeping your *AP Stylebook* with you at all times. Instead of memorizing all the references, learn when you need to look them up.

"Some people can claim to know most of it, but you'll never ever know all of it," he says. "You'll never remember every single AP style for sports, particularly, *goal-line stand*, *free-throw percentage*; hyphenated, not hyphenated—the list is endless. If you don't remember a style [rule] off the top of your head, don't get down. Just go to the stylebook and answer your own question and don't worry about it. Because you're not going to remember everything. Don't be afraid to ask, but try and go to the *Stylebook* before you ask somebody you're working with."

Author's note: *Goal-line stand* is not under the letter *G*. You must look up *football*, in the sports section. Also, under *basketball*, you'll find a list of frequently used words and phrases. Though *free throw* is not hyphenated, *free-throw line* is. *Free-throw percentage* is not listed.

Gene Policinski, of *USA Today*, has this advice for beginning journalism students: "You keep a dictionary and you keep a stylebook, because you know a lot of stuff gets crammed in your head and nobody remembers all of it. So keep them around. Don't think of them as a hurdle. I know it's tough. I never really wanted to listen to people telling me what I'm telling you. Because it sounds boring."

Some students do assume the study of the *Stylebook* will be boring. They usually fail, if they don't find a way to become interested. Others react in panic. In fact, you may be overwhelmed by the volume of information thrown in your direction at a rate beyond note-taking speed in the half-hour telecourse tour of the *Stylebook*. Don't worry! This program was designed with the idea that you should learn how to use the *Stylebook*, not memorize it.

As odd as it might sound, the best advice is to try to have fun with this material. One suggestion that seems to make this portion of your learning more palatable is to approach the *Stylebook* quizzes in this unit as if they were word games. You've all played Scrabble or Hangman or Wheel of Fortune or worked on a crossword puzzle at some point in time. Solving a style problem can actually be a diversion on a slow news night—something that would be entertaining only to a bunch of eccentrics who make their living with words and are waiting for the presses to roll so they can go home.

"We had an interesting incident here at our sports desk the other night," says John Katsilometes.

"How do you spell *jell*? *Jell* is spelled two different ways . . . one way as a noun, one way as a verb. A team can *jell*—that's a really common sports term. It's a common thing for a coach to say, 'This team hasn't jelled; I'm glad we finally jelled; I didn't even know if we would jell; I'm glad we jelled.' We had the spell-check on our computer and it stopped on *jell*, and it all of a sudden became, 'How do you spell *jell*?' It's not hair gel. And it turned into this big discussion . . . took 5 or 10 minutes to finally find out the proper use."

In learning style, attitude is everything. The enterprising reporter looks it up—in a dictionary, stylebook, almanac, book of records or whatever it takes—because accuracy and language in a newspaper are intertwined.

No matter what your attitude, there's no denying mastery of the *Stylebook* will be directly linked to your success. This area of academic study is very different than most collegiate work. Your audience is much larger than the solitary freshman literature teacher who grades your class essays in the privacy of his or her own office. Soon, your writing will be published in the school newspaper for a very critical public to view. If you're successful, your work will be on display for an even larger audience on a daily basis. It's better to have some challenges at this stage of your learning than to irritate those who are going to read your work.

The editor of the *Associated Press Stylebook*, Norm Goldstein, adds this final thought: "Consistency is the basis of style, and I think any time [the reader] stops to think, 'Now didn't I see that spelled differently in the very same paper?' it's the worst thing you could do. Because you lose your audience right away by inconsistencies in style. . . . It takes the reader's mind off what it's supposed to be doing—reading the story."

YOU
SHOULD
READ . . .

The most obvious reading assignment for this unit would be to crack open the *AP Stylebook* and read it from beginning to end. That would be something like trying to read a dictionary or an encyclopedia from cover to cover—it serves little purpose.

One good way to start is to leaf through the book randomly and look for surprises. Another is to familiarize yourself with the different sections, including the Sports, Weather section, Business and Grammar sections and the Libel Manual.

The best way to learn the *Stylebook* is to use it. Over and over. Don't even think about booting up your computer to start a story unless you have the *Stylebook* by your side. Learn the discipline needed to flip through the pages and look up a style rule when you have a question. In the long run, your editors will notice your commitment to clean copy, and your career will prosper from the diligence needed to master this book.

Chapter Eighteen of Carole Rich's textbook (pp. 339–360 in the second edition), "Multicultural Sensitivity," also addresses the language of multiculturalism, which is a hot topic in all stylebooks.

Also recommended: The *UPI Stylebook*, the *Washington Post Stylebook* and the *New York Times Stylebook* are all commercially available, though not as commonly used. Also, most local newspapers and a healthy number of college newspapers have an in-house stylebook that usually contains an emphasis on local references. Ask your editor if one exists. In addition, many broadcast news organizations have their own stylebooks, which contain an emphasis on pronunciation and broadcast language style.

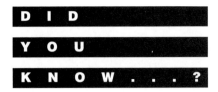

The *AP Stylebook* also contains excellent information on how not to get sued. In fact, the official name is the *Associated Press Stylebook and Libel Manual*.

The back of the book has succinct references on libel, invasion of privacy and other media laws. Much of the same information is covered in Unit Fifteen, "Media Law."

Many of the individual references in the *Stylebook* also can help reporters avoid legal problems, through precise use of specific words.

Covering the police beat, the courts and other stories that involve the law can be complicated, confusing and risky. Sloppy language use can lead to inaccurate reporting and, possibly, libel lawsuits. Many of the references in the *Associated Press Stylebook* are designed to help keep reporters out of trouble as well as to help them get the story straight. Good reporters familiar with these beats still use the *Stylebook*, though infrequently, since they have become familiar with the terms through experience.

Rookie reporters are advised to double-, triple- and quadruple-check even the most common language early on in their careers. A few minutes spent with the editor of the *Stylebook* on just a few of the most common phrases can show why.

The fine points of reporting on a simple arrest require precise language use to avoid confusion and accidental accusation—an important distinction to understand for a journalism student writing his or her first story about a crime-related incident.

Norm Goldstein, the current editor of the *AP Stylebook*, gives this example:

"A phrase such as *accused slayer John Jones* is less accurate than saying *John Jones, who is accused of the slaying*. It may seem like a simple grammatical thing, but it's more than that," Goldstein says. "If you use *accused slayer* as an adjective for the person, you are in effect accusing him rather than saying he is accused of a specific crime. It's a subtle distinction, but an important one.

"Leave the accusations to the courts and to the police. It's not something that you should be doing on your own. Under the entry for *accused*, we say to avoid any suggestion that an individual is being

Excerpts used by permission of Associated Press.

Did you know . . . ? (*continued*)

judged before trial. Do not use a phrase such as *accused slayer*; use *John Jones, accused of the slaying*. It may sound a little picayune, but it's very important to be very accurate about charges of crimes.

"In various criminal cases, it's very important to be accurate about the charge," Goldstein says. "Is someone charged? *Accused* is not a very good word; that's not a legal term you want to get involved with. Wait until someone is charged; otherwise, be very careful how you refer to someone who has been arrested. Just stay with the facts and stay away from loaded words, like *killer* and *murderer*, unless you just say simply that someone is charged with murder or charged with slaying. They best be charged before you use those kinds of adjectives."

Again, Goldstein clarifies the legal jargon necessary for accurate reporting on a story:

"In our entry on *arrest*, we seek to avoid any suggestion that someone is being judged before a trial. Do not use a phrase such as *arrested for killing*. Instead, use *arrested on a charge of killing*. Again, it may seem subtle and small, but it makes a tremendous difference in the use of a phrase.

"I'm not sure you can be overly cautious in those cases. Just stick with the facts. Even the connotation of the word *arrest* can be libelous. If he is eventually not charged with any crime, arrest would involve some legal action by the police."

One common mistake made by rookie reporters is to try to cover a poor understanding of such language use by throwing the word *alleged* in a story to protect themselves from libel charges.

"I would rather err on the side of overusing *alleged* than be sued for not using it," Goldstein says. "Using a word doesn't protect you from anything, but it shows good intent; you're better off with it than without it."

But, Goldstein says, "Simply using the word *alleged* doesn't protect you from any libel possibilities. It's helpful in many cases, but it doesn't mean that it absolves you of any mistakes you've made or any charges you've made that are not supportive."

SENSITIVITY, ACCURACY AND STYLE

Since newspapers are read by members of every conceivable minority or special interest group, unintelligent use of language could easily offend or hurt a segment of society— even when a reporter has no intention to. As often as not, the *Stylebook* rules that govern such language usage involve accuracy as well as sensitivity.

Take, for instance, the *Stylebook* entry on the term *alcoholic*. Society's understanding of the disease can be traced through the evolving stylebook references on this term. Decades ago, it was common to refer to a "reformed alcoholic." But, as editors realized that the word *reformed* implied making amends for committing a crime, the language changed. Editors, realizing that alcoholism is a disease instead of a crime, encouraged their reporters to use the term *recovered alcoholic*.

"We recently had to change that [rule]," Goldstein says.

"AA people wrote to us and said there was no such thing as a recovered alcoholic; it is a recovering alcoholic. There's really no cure for it. So we changed the style based on that information."

Bill Stothers, of *Mainstream* magazine, points out that journalists should be careful when writing about disabilities. If you aren't supposed to say wheelchair bound, what is appropriate?

"Well, wheelchair user works," Stothers suggests. "I've often signed articles that dealt with disability in the mainstream press by saying that 'Bill Stothers is a writer who is liberated by a wheelchair.' A wheelchair does not confine me. This is a liberating piece of assistive technology. Think about the language you use."

ALTERNATIVE VIEWS

The video program about journalism style and language contains its share of journalists poking fun at and complaining about having to use the *Associated Press Stylebook and Libel Manual*.

"It's hard to believe that anybody would say the AP style would be boring," cracks Dave Barry, who admits working for AP himself for a short time—calling the venerable wire service the "Word Army."

"I always argued that any AP person could die in the middle of a story and any other AP person could come up and without having seen what he had written up to that letter, finish the story and you would never know," Barry says. "I loved working for the AP."

But, while many complain about the *AP Stylebook*, they usually admit mastery of the book—considered by many the "journalist's bible"—is essential for an entry-level journalist's employment and survival.

"I don't own an *AP Stylebook*," says Anita Creamer, columnist and feature writer for the *Sacramento Bee*. Then, she reconsiders.

"No, that's wrong. I probably have one from 1975. I bet you it's that out-of-date."

Dave Barry, Miami Herald: "I think that's one of the functions of newspapers. They change their stylebooks every four or five days, just to make sure no one ever gets it."

Gene Policinski, USA Today: "A lot of stuff gets crammed in your head; nobody remembers all of it. So keep the [Stylebook] around. Don't make it a hurdle."

Still, Creamer acknowledges, with a laugh, the importance of mastering style. "I firmly believe that you don't have any business being in this business if you can't spell, if you can't punctuate, if you don't know grammar," she says. "I was very good in all my editing classes in school. I knew my AP style back in the Dark Ages. I knew it. I swear I knew it. But the way it's handled now, we have a copy desk. So shoot me."

"My *Stylebook* is on my desk collecting dust," admits Michael Waldholz of the *Wall Street Journal*. "I don't know if you're going to like what I have to say. I am a firm believer in colloquial use in newspapers. Even a newspaper like the *Wall Street Journal* should be written in conversational style. So I actually have arguments here at the *Journal* in which I argue for the usage of colloquialisms."

Don Fry, of the Poynter Institute, says, "We've got a dynamite stylebook, but it's got things in it that are destructive, like the second-reference rule. In the second-reference rule, you take off all the titles and honorifics on the person the second time you refer to him. So you're writing a trial story and you have Judge Green, defendant Brown, and lawyer Yellow. Forty graphs later, you're not using any honorifics and the reader can't tell these people apart. In other words, it's a bad rule. And there are all sorts of things in the *Stylebook* that are like that. They need to be changed.

"I think the *Stylebook* was invented by people who thought there weren't enough grammar and spelling rules," Fry says. "And they wanted some more stuff to enforce, and so they made it up. And now they've got 5,000 rules instead of 500. And somebody ought to throw it all out and start from scratch. Perhaps."

However, there are many journalists who feel that language use is deteriorating in society and that too many students ignore the *Stylebook*.

Dorothy Rabinowitz, of the *Wall Street Journal*, says we live today in "not only an illiterate age but a proudly illiterate age.

"Most writing of any consequence is written conforming to the rules of grammar. We're talking about the fact that [students] have read very little. No Milton. No Homer. No Keats. No Orwell. So you cannot get a literary population."

LIVING WITH MISTAKES

No matter what your relationship is with the *Stylebook*, here's one last piece of advice: Don't berate yourself when your copy editor catches a style error in one of your stories. Just learn from your mistakes, and learn when to look up phrases you have trouble with.

Even those most familiar with journalism style are exposed to embarrassing errors from time to time. It is inevitable . . . even on the cover of the *Associated Press Stylebook* itself.

Norm Goldstein, the editor, tells this story: "We produced a stylebook, in a trade version for bookstores, and the commercial publishers had a ribbon over the cover of the book saying that it had sold *'Over 700,000 copies.'* We got letters about that. Because somebody realized that our own stylebook says you shouldn't use *over* 700,000. It should be *more than*. And we had to change it."

If you haven't already encountered the following problems writing your first summary lead exercises, it is likely you didn't bother to look up the following rules. Explain, according to the *Associated Press Stylebook*, the style rules for the following common parts of language:

1   The Who: Summarize the style rules for listing titles with names. What kinds of titles are ignored? When are job titles capitalized?

2   The What: Summarize the style rules for *arrested* and *charged.* What is the difference?

3   The When: What is the correct style abbreviation for *three thirty in the afternoon*? What is the correct style abbreviation for *9 in the morning*?

4   The Where: Summarize the style rules for listing an address.

5   The Why: What is the specific difference between burglary and theft?

6   The How: What is the specific difference between murder and killing?

7   How can the word *allege* be used incorrectly?

8   List some examples of redundancies the *Stylebook* cautions against.

9   Are the words *Grim Reaper* and *Mother Nature* capitalized? Why?

10   Find the exact style for the words *teleprompter* and *astroturf.*

Bonus: Why is it a risky idea, stylistically, to say someone was found "not guilty" in a trial?

QUIZ

Which sentence is styled correctly, according to the *AP Stylebook*?

1 The pizza was delivered to the president at

a. 1600 Pennsylvania Avenue.
b. Sixteen Hundred Pennsylvania Avenue.
c. 1600 Pennsylvania Ave.

2 The gun was fired by a

a. seven year old boy.
b. 7 year old boy.
c. 7-year-old boy.

3 The quarterback will make

a. $1.5 million next year.
b. one and a half million dollars next year.
c. 1.5 million dollars next year.

4 Remember to adjust your clocks for

a. daylight saving time.
b. daylight-savings time.
c. daylight-saving time.

5 Reporters and other observers were shocked by the

a. judgment.
b. Judgment.
c. judgement.

6 The dinner will be hosted by

a. U.S. Rep. Wally Herger.
b. U.S. Representative Wally Herger.
c. Congressman Wally Herger.

7 The coldest day on record is

a. Jan. 12, 1993.
b. January 12, 1993.
c. January twelve, 1993.

8 The gun was a clue in identifying the man who committed the

a. robbery.
b. burglary.
c. theft.

9 Cottonwood will welcome a visit next week by the

a. Vice President.
b. vice-president.
c. vice president.

10 Mastery of style

a. could affect your level of success when applying for a job.
b. could effect your level of success when applying for a job.

SELF·TEST

Find and fix the style or accuracy problems in the following sentences. Write a better version of the sentence in the space provided.

1 In order to acommodate the union, the players had to dissasocaite from the team, irregardless of its chances to make the World Series.

2 A 19 year old teenaged boy was injured in the collision.

3 The gentleman who was driving did not see the youth's bicycle in the dark.

4 Michael Jordan made nine field goals and eight free throws for a total of twenty six points.

5 The District Attorney is pursuing a manslaughter charge for John Johnson, who is charged with the vicious slaying of a mini-mart clerk during an armed theft.

6 If you want to insure a good grade on this quiz, look up the rules in the Associated Press Stylebook.

7 The President leaned towards the door.

8 At exactly 12 noon, he set a new record in the 100 with a time of 11.59.

9 The senator, confined to a wheelchair since youth, gave an inspiring speech in spite of his handicap.

10 With visibility half of normal, and winds of 26 m.p.h. the blizzard caused hazardous driving conditions.

NEWS-WRITING
STORY
DEVELOPMENT

By this point in the telecourse, you have started to develop a news sense and have studied language use that is peculiar to news-writing style. You have also learned how to write a summary lead, the beginning journalist's most basic tool.

Many writers are so worried about writing the lead, they can't continue a story until they have finished that first perfect paragraph. This approach to writing is counterproductive toward making a deadline—which is oftentimes just as important in a newsroom as being creative. (In many working environments, making a deadline is quite a bit more important than being creative with the writing—though, hopefully, it is not more important than being accurate.)

In a 12-column-inch story, the lead is often only the first inch, or less. In most daily newspaper work, the writer's job is to organize the rest of the text so that the most important information naturally floats to the top of the story. The theory and practice is, if a page editor decides—just before the paper goes to press—that there is only a nine-inch news hole left for your story, the reader will not notice if the last three inches are cut. Decades of tradition and millions of column inches produced under the pressure of tight deadlines have led to the unique story development style known to journalists as the **inverted pyramid**. Reporters who apply for entry-level jobs today are expected to be well versed within this style, just as musicians who audition for an orchestra are expected to master their major scales or young physicians who start a new practice are expected to know basic anatomy.

Though the inverted pyramid is the industry standard, many respected journalists are successful using other methods to shape the middle and end of a news story. As daily newspapers experience more and more competition from other news sources, these other approaches to presenting a news story are becoming increasingly important. This unit will also explore several alternate story development styles.

OBJECTIVES

This lesson is designed to help you learn—after writing a good news lead—how to organize the rest of your writing, quickly and clearly. The reasons behind and methods of using the inverted pyramid will be explored in detail, and several other popular news story development styles will be considered as alternatives.

PROGRAM GUIDE

BEFORE YOU WATCH

This unit is designed to help you learn how to develop the rest of your story, after you've written the lead. Traditional methods as well as new story development styles are considered.

•**Pay attention to how the journalists interviewed use the following words:**

Inverted pyramid	Circle
Running	News peg
Transition	Cut from the bottom
Hourglass	Breaking news
Nut graph	Background

WHILE YOU WATCH

1. Count the many different reasons the various reporters list for understanding and mastering the inverted pyramid.

2. Imagine what other shapes stories can assume, as the journalists describe story development styles other than the inverted pyramid.

3. Note the other elements of writing—besides story shape—that a writer must consider between the lead and the end of the story.

4. Distinguish between traditional and modern approaches to journalism writing styles.

AFTER YOU WATCH

•**Address the following questions in your journal. Or, if there's time, discuss them in class:**

1. What keeps you reading past the first or second paragraph of a news story? Can you list as many as five news stories you've read from top to bottom in the past week? If you can't, why didn't you finish the stories? If you can, what kept you reading all the way to the end?

2. What elements of story development do good journalism and good fiction have in common?

3. The inverted pyramid has a history that can be traced back for a century. Is this news story development style likely to survive for another century? Why?

4. Why is a long-distance phone call likely to be constructed like an inverted pyramid?

5. Can you think of any other shapes for story development that have not been discussed in the video program?

Dave Barry, the Pulitzer Prize–winning humor columnist from the *Miami Herald*, starts this unit off with a quip about writing in the shape of a "rhombus"—his own twisted version of the inverted pyramid. Barry (who claims to have been a hard-news reporter before he started slinging punch lines in his syndicated column) explains how he approaches story development in his syndicated column:

"It's hard to think of an ending. The beginning is really hard, and the ending is always really hard."

The middle, Barry adds, is pretty hard too, come to think of it. But it is the ending of a column or editorial that can make the difference between a good and a great opinion writer.

"You want to have some clue that it [the column] has an end. And, ideally, if it's a humor column, it should be funny at the end, too. Editorial writers I deeply envy because they can always end with '. . . and somebody should do something about this.' Not us—we're busy writing editorials."

Though you haven't started to study column writing and editorial writing yet, the hard-news writer still has similar challenges to face.

In this course, you've learned how journalists approach the beginning of a news story by developing a focus sentence and writing a summary lead. Now you'll study how to write the middle and the end.

INVERTED PYRAMID

Column writers and editorial writers have the convenience of knowing how much space they have to fill and can craft each piece so that it builds to a satisfying conclusion. The journalists who write hard-news pieces don't often have such a luxury. These stories are often written quickly, on an unforgiving deadline, with the understanding that the editor will have to chop them off and squeeze them into a space called the news hole. (The **news hole** is the space left over after advertisements have been placed on the page.)

Often, the space saved for the story is suddenly, almost randomly, reduced if another, more important story breaks as the editor is deciding what to put on the page. In the fast-breaking world of the daily newspaper, editors don't have time to worry about whether one reporter's feelings are hurt because a story gets cut.

Reporting an incident, without contriving a nifty ending, fits the mentality of a hard-news writer. Many journalists believe that, in a sense, a good hard-news story doesn't have an end. There's always a follow-up to write tomorrow; today's report was simply what could be crammed into the news hole before the deadline. Tomorrow, there may be a whole new set of facts to report and another installment to write. A year from now, there may an anniversary follow-up to write. It is much like writing a chapter a day for a novel that never ends—only, this novel is based on truth instead of fiction.

Imagine covering an earthquake. The event itself might last less than a minute. The first day's coverage will report the hard news of death and destruction. The second day's stories will report how the survivors are coping. A month later, the stories will be about how the city is paying for damages. A year later, reporters will look back to evaluate plans—or lack of plans—to deal with the next earthquake. Five years later, a feature news writer might explore whether the locals had forgotten that a quake could happen again at any time. And so on, until the next quake happens. So, to the journalist, the story never ends.

This kind of thinking has led to the evolution of a story-writing style in which the last paragraph is insignificant—a style in which some editors believe any paragraph can be the last paragraph.

In the telecourse program, you heard a number of explanations about why journalism students and rookie reporters have been coached, forced, compelled, cajoled and urged to write in this style for decades. A recap of those reasons might include the following:

•Some paste-up guy (or gal) in the composing room is likely to cut your bottom paragraphs from the story to fit it in the news hole.
•A cannonball could knock out your telegraph wire at any point during your report from the battlefield.
•Some copy editor is likely to cut your bottom paragraphs from the story to fit it in the news hole.
•Even if your story is on-line with some computer news service, the reader is likely to stop reading at any point and get distracted by some other bit of information.
•Your story may have more than local significance and may go out on a "wire" after you've published it locally.
•Some editor at a newspaper in some town you've never seen is just waiting on the other end of that wire, ready to unceremoniously hack your copy and cram it into whatever space is left, after the advertising has been placed.

WIRE SERVICES

Reporters who write for news services and wire services—such as Reuters, the Associated Press, UPI or the many other news agencies that serve newspaper groups and associations—are almost forced into developing their stories with the inverted pyramid style.

Steve Tetreault, editor of the Donrey News Service, explains: "We find [the inverted pyramid] is very important for what we do, since we produce copy and send it to newspapers that are often thousands of miles away. We have very little idea of the space requirements that newspaper is going to have on a given day. And unless we go inverted pyramid, a lot of times information that we want to get across to the readers is just not going to make it in a newspaper.

"We have, for instance, 55 newspapers that we service here out of Donrey's Washington bureau. And we'll send a story out sometimes to 20, 30 newspapers. It's kind of fun, sometimes, to get the clips back and see where everyone cut us off. Most of our stories do get run in total, but again, we write for some very small newspapers that just don't have the space to run everything that they're given. So it is very important in our circumstances to be able to write tight and to write crisp."

Andrew Loschilin, of the Russian news agency TASS, explained to our video crew, off camera, that mastering the Western journalism traditions of the summary lead and the inverted pyramid was a priority to the young news writers who were reinventing journalism in the new democratic nations that fragmented from the old Soviet Union. TASS serves the newspapers of those new nations (which, for decades, experienced journalism only as state propaganda) in the same way that the Associated Press serves member papers in every state across America. And, like those at any other wire service, the journalists who write for TASS must expect each publication to cut every story from the bottom.

OTHER STORY DEVELOPMENT STYLES: BEYOND THE INVERTED PYRAMID

It's important to master the inverted pyramid, if for no other reason than that you'll be expected to be familiar with the tool when you apply for a news-writing job. Like a sculptor or carpenter or electrician, you'll have the tool that you use most often. But, there are those occasions when the specialty tools in your kit will work better.

News writers have other story shapes that work especially well when the editor (and reader) is willing to accept the reporting in a different form. Page design on computers has eliminated much of the need to cut from the bottom of a story. Still, communication with the editor is essential, if for no other reason than agreement on space limitation can be reached, thus eliminating the need to cut from the bottom.

Don Fry, of the Poynter Institute, is extremely critical of the tradition that demands too much use of the inverted pyramid in high-tech daily newsrooms.

According to Fry, dependence on the inverted pyramid is a human organization problem. He advocates a better system in which writers learn to create a story to the exact length and editors learn to communicate exactly how long the stories need to be. In the computer age, such a system is easier to envision. Much of the dependence on the inverted pyramid is left over from the days of lead type.

"When you start cutting stories from the bottom on the copy desk, often without reading what you're cutting, you're participating in a process that is grossly disorganized," Fry says. "There's no reason, in the computer age, to hack stories from the bottom."

It doesn't hurt to have an editor who is willing to discuss different approaches to developing a story. The use of forms other than the inverted pyramid is expected in magazines and feature departments of daily newspapers, and experimentation with these other forms is becoming more common in the hard-news sections of almost all newspapers—from conservative mainstream stalwarts such as the *Wall Street Journal* to the more trendy daily papers that model their look and feel after *USA Today*.

A BRIEF SURVEY OF PUBLICATION STYLES

NEWSWEEK: A TYPICAL MAGAZINE APPROACH TO STORY DEVELOPMENT

John Leland, of *Newsweek*, describes a typical magazine editor's approach to story development: "A good story would be just killed by removing the last paragraph," he says, "because that's where we're summing up, drawing our conclusions from what we've laid out ahead of time. I think in a [hard-] news story in a newspaper, you've drawn your conclusions at the top and then you lay out your evidence in a sort of descending order after that. I think magazine stories . . . will sort of map out the conflict—or a hypothesis in the beginning of the story—spend the body of the story laying out the evidence . . . and in the conclusion you'll try to weigh your hypothesis, see if it added up in light of the evidence, or draw some conclusions on the evidence."

USA TODAY: SETTING NEW TRENDS

To compete with magazines, radio and television, many modern newspapers are adapting their writing styles to rely more on graphic images and on language that sounds more like everyday speech. Much of this trend was caused by the introduction of a "national newspaper"—in the form of *USA Today*—designed to compete more with television than with local daily newspapers.

According to Gene Policinski, who has edited both the front page and sports section of *USA Today*, "We have to write to our readers, almost as you do in a conversation. You have to be direct; you have to be concise.

"At *USA Today*, you would probably see two or three little boldfaced lines at the bottom of the story that would key you to a graphic explaining a lot more, [for example,] . . . about what else is in a tax program, perhaps a second story about more about the tax and how it came to be . . . to give you some background. So it's a bit different than the inverted pyramid."

WALL STREET JOURNAL: TRADITIONAL BUT BEYOND THE INVERTED PYRAMID

While *USA Today* has pioneered the use of "infographics" to help develop a news piece, the *Wall Street Journal* has taken to using storytelling techniques to make a news report more readable. The *Journal*'s news story style—similar to the **circle** technique described by JoNel Aleccia in Program Four of the telecourse—is so effective, it has become a formula emulated by writers from other publications.

Rich explains: "The *Wall Street Journal* formula almost always begins with an **anecdotal** or a descriptive lead. And it goes to the nut graph, that kernel of 'this is what the story is about,' and then it has substantiation, backup, the statistics and elaboration. It generally comes full circle back to the original anecdote. It was so readable, even though it's called the *Wall Street Journal* formula, you will find this in every good newspaper as a very, very useful structure."

OTHER STORY
DEVELOPMENT SHAPES

HOURGLASS

Certain skills in the craft of storytelling can work well in any medium, whether it's cinematography, journalism or just spinning yarns around a campfire.

One common storytelling technique involves unraveling a plot in chronological order. As Don Fry points out, "Nobody wants to see a movie . . . if you find out who the villain is in the first four minutes." The script writer, instead, uses chronology to reveal plot twists, building to a climax.

However, most editors feel that telling a hard-news story chronologically will frustrate the reader, who doesn't want to wait for a surprise ending. The point of most reporting, after all, is to tell what happened, who did it and why, as close to the top of the story as possible.

Still, the temptation to work **chronological narrative** into news writing is great, especially if the tale can be told naturally, without diluting the integrity or credibility of the news report. Roy Peter Clark, of the Poynter Institute, is credited for putting a name on a form that many writers have been experimenting with: the **hourglass** form.

This form, which Clark describes in a *Washington Journalism Review* article as having a shape similar to an hourglass, still uses a summary lead with a typical inverted pyramid development—up to a point.

Then the writer uses a heavy transition, followed by chronological story-telling, from beginning to end. To wrap up the story, the writer usually uses a **kicker**, or an ending to the dialogue. This story form works well with a news event that profits from being told twice—something that is so complex that the reader is helped by a chronological telling after a traditional telling.

Here's an example:

Lead: Lotta Lapps was acquitted of all counts of murder in the Champaign County Court today, after an extended trial that started three years ago when her estranged husband Jimmy "The Creep" Skierski was found dead, face-down in a pig trough.

Transition: Though much circumstantial evidence was presented at the trial, the prosecution was not able to establish guilt beyond a reasonable doubt.

Chronological Narrative: Lapps met her husband-to-be six years ago, while employed as an exotic dancer at a bar Skierski managed. The two married three years later, in a ceremony held in the same establishment.

Lapps, who was raised on a pig farm, continued to live a lifestyle "more appropriate for a single woman," according to testimony in the courts.

The rest of the sordid tale could be narrated by the writer, almost as if it were from the script of a television courtroom drama.

Roy Peter Clark describes the acceptance by some editors of the hourglass style:

"The inverted pyramid—it's one option, where all the news is at the top and the information is presented in descending order of importance, so that it can be easily sliced from the bottom, and so that readers can stop at any time. Well, now, that's OK. It's served us since the Civil War. But in rebellion to that, and in order to do different kinds of things, you get a sort of a notion that you can tell a story in chronological order. And that stories don't give out the most important piece of information at the beginning. We know that good stories build to some climax."

THE HIGH FIVES FORMULA

Carole Rich describes another alternative to the inverted pyramid as a high fives formula, which is simply a thought process that helps the writer organize the information.

Like the inverted pyramid and most other story organization styles, the *news* must be reported close to the top.

The writer must also communicate the *impact* of the story. In other words: so what? The writer must explain how this story affects the readers.

The *scope* of the story should also be explained. Is it just a local occurrence, or does it affect the entire nation?

Another organizational element is called the *edge*. What does the story mean? Where is it leading? This might be where the writer explains whether the story is an isolated incident or part of a trend.

The *context* of the story is an important element of the high fives formula that can add meaning to the reader. Have other recently reported events affected this story? What is the history that led to this event? Many stories are not isolated incidents, and reporting the context can show where a news event fits in the scheme of things.

Unfortunately, the context is often left for the end of a traditional inverted pyramid news piece and therefore cut out of many news stories. In this kind of writing, the editor and the reporter ideally communicate, and all elements of the piece are left intact.

Unlike the other story development styles listed in this unit, the high fives formula does not emphasize story shape. It is designed to give the reporter flexibility to shape the story in any number of different ways and instead offers a thought process to organize the information.

STORY DEVELOPMENT STYLES: FINAL THOUGHTS

Unit Four of the telecourse and Chapter Twelve of your textbook *Writing and Reporting News: A Coaching Method* both clearly explain several other story development styles, including the **circle** method, the **list technique**, the **foreshadowing** method and the **sections technique**.

These forms are explained as a way to help you get started. They are not meant to be rigid formulas; they are intended to give you insight into how other writers before you have met the same challenges. As you get more experienced, you will no doubt invent story organizational forms of your own.

"Story forms give you a guide," says Carole Rich, "but you have to do some thinking to say, 'Which story form is right for me? Do I need a specific story form at all?'

"Organizing stories is very hard work. I hate when someone says, 'It should write itself.' Some stories get a natural storytelling order and you don't have to struggle. But when you are struggling to visualize whether you are seeing an hourglass, whether you are seeing an inverted pyramid, whether you are seeing the *Wall Street Journal* structure—it's very comforting to have guidelines of things that have worked for people before you, so that you are not [always] reinventing."

OTHER ELEMENTS OF STORY DEVELOPMENT

TRANSITIONS

The best news writers learn how to attract more readers through a story by creating clear transitions from each paragraph to the next.

Don Fry, of the Poynter Institute, recommends the following approach:

"If you want people to read all the way to the bottom of the story, then you have to put things in that encourage them to keep reading. We call those things 'gold coins.' You drop those gold coins in front of the reader as the reader goes down the journey of the story. As the reader picks up each gold coin, the reader assumes there's another one. A gold coin is something like a wonderful quote, or a great turn of phrase, a new interesting character, a terrific **anecdote**, or something like that."

A good writer will find a way to make a story read so that each gold coin appears to be the natural outgrowth from the previous gold coin. This is what reporters mean when they say they work hard at creating good **transitions** in their writing.

Sometimes, literary devices are used consciously to create transitions. Changes of time can work well ("Earlier that day, samples of blood taken from the murder scene had been sent to the lab") and changes of location ("Meanwhile, back at the ranch . . . ") are a novelist's and script writer's stock and trade. They often work for journalists, as well.

The craft of creating smooth transitions from scene to scene or idea to idea is one of the skills that good fiction writers and good news writers have in common. Often, contrived rhetorical devices such as time or location transitions aren't as necessary as a thorough knowledge and understanding of the complex elements that add up to make an event newsworthy. If the writer clearly understands the impact of the news and makes logical connections between each element of the event, transitions between each idea should emerge naturally as the writer narrates the story through the magic of word processing.

If the transitions are not coming easily, the writing technique is not necessarily flawed. Instead, this trouble is often a sign that the writer needs to do more research and ask more questions to gain a more thorough understanding of the news event.

NUT GRAPHS

Journalists who write feature stories for the daily newspaper or who write for "alternative" news weeklies tend to use less conventional organizational styles. However, the readers still desire some sort of organized summary of what the story is all about near the top of the piece. The most common story development tool used to satisfy this need is the **nut graph**, which is, more often than not, a variation on what would have been a summary lead positioned very close to the beginning of the story.

The nut graph is a clear sentence or two that tells the reader what the story is about. It defines the purpose or reason for the story. It can also serve as the transition from a nontraditional lead to the rest of the story.

Even writers who practice advocacy journalism and other unconventional forms of reporting use this tool. No matter how creative or artistic the lead is for the story, the writer needs to let the reader know the focus of the piece as soon as possible.

"You want the reader to know what he or she's reading without having to go farther than three paragraphs into the story," says Michael Tomasky of the *Village Voice*. "If they have to go farther than that, they're certainly going to turn the page. So, if you haven't accomplished that in three paragraphs, and I mean three short paragraphs, not three 200-word paragraphs, . . . unless you're some brilliant stylist . . . people just aren't going to rock with you."

Carole Rich adds, "I think, in addition to a nut graph, which essentially tells the reader 'This is what the story is about,' . . . I think we need to tell readers why they should care. What is the impact? Not every story has an impact on every reader. But if it does, and if you can find it, I think that's a very crucial part of storytelling in reporting today."

ENDINGS

The simple fact that this telecourse and textbook even consider the craft of creating an **ending** for a news story will upset the most traditional of the old-school journalists. Even the process of thinking about a possible ending was deemed counterproductive to those who routinely demanded stories in the inverted pyramid style and cut from the bottom while producing the final page just before deadline.

You've heard that computer page layout has changed the need for this thought process. Perhaps even more important is the fact that newspapers have to compete with television, radio and other news sources. If the readers today demand that reporting also includes a more entertaining approach to writing and storytelling, many editors reason, then newspapers need to address that demand.

Because of this, many editors are considering such radical changes as including endings to hard-news pieces.

Roy Peter Clark says that in normal conversation, most people start "with the notion of a beginning, a middle and an end." If readers expect newspapers to offer a more conversational style, it stands to reason that reporters and editors should take a look at how communication works in other forms of storytelling.

"Three seems to be the magic number in storytelling," Clark says. "Always when we tell a joke, there's always a priest, a rabbi and a minister. And you usually introduce it with a beginning, there's a section on each one of those three characters, and there's a punch line. And I think that, in its own way, is like Shakespeare's five-scene, five-act construction in Elizabethan drama. So, we have to pay more attention; we have to help writers figure out how this works. And I think there's a lot of things we can do, a lot of tools we can give them to help them do it."

Clearly, one of those tools in fiction and play writing—and in some news writing—is the ending. Sadly, according to Rich, many reporters tack on poorly developed endings that read as if the journalist simply ran out of information to report. In these cases, no ending at all is better than one that sounds artificial and contrived.

"Even I, devoted as I am to great endings, have something in my book which I call 'out-of-gas endings,'" Rich says. "There are news stories that don't lend themselves to great endings. You don't have a great quote; you have nothing. Stop. Quit when you have no more to say.

However, if the story does lend itself to an ending, both the reader who finishes the entire piece and the writer who composed it will feel more satisfied.

"I, as a writer, deserve the pleasure of wrapping something up beautifully. I want the reader, and I want myself as a writer, to remember that story on a powerful note," Rich says.

In her textbook, Rich suggests several types of ending styles for news stories. A strong quote is a popular choice. By letting an interesting news maker have the final say, the reader is often left with a strong perspective or flavor of the event.

Introducing a possible future development allows the reader to finish the story on a note of speculation. A story with circular development can use the ending to bring the reader back to the beginning.

You'll hear more about endings for news stories in the unit and program about broadcast news writing—a journalistic form that almost never uses the inverted pyramid and almost always puts heavy emphasis on the story's ending.

To end this section, we'll foreshadow the broadcast news-writing Unit with Charles Kuralt's philosophy about writing endings.

Kuralt, who is one of the most respected broadcast news writers in the history of television, says, "I have given equal attention to the last paragraph and the last sentence. The first one's important. The way the story ends, which is the thought or feeling the viewer's going to take away with him, is just as important."

Kuralt, like many old-school television reporters, found his way to television news through working at a daily newspaper. His perspective on endings in news writing sums up the whole debate.

"It was frustrating working for the *Charlotte News* because," he says, "in the old time, on the newspaper, they would cut from the bottom. Sometimes you'd see your well-thought-out last paragraph cut off. But [today] in feature writing that doesn't [and shouldn't] occur."

In Carole Rich's textbook *Writing and Reporting News: A Coaching Method*, there is an excellent section about story structures that complements Unit Four in this student study guide. In the second edition of the text, this section is Chapter Twelve (pp. 201–223).

In addition to the inverted pyramid, Rich introduces several other possible news story structures, including the high fives formula, the *Wall Street Journal* formula, the hourglass, the list technique, the inverted pyramid, and the sections technique.

In addition, much of the information from Chapter Eleven, "Body Building" (pp. 182–198 in the second edition) and Chapter Thirteen, "Storytelling and Feature Techniques" (pp. 225–250 in the second edition) is connected to the television program in this unit. Students should pay particular attention to Rich's discussion of the "Middles of Stories," "Endings," "Descriptive Techniques" and "Narrative Styles." Almost any story development structure, even the inverted pyramid, will benefit from your learning how to tell a better story.

ALTERNATIVE VIEWS

Forget using the inverted pyramid at the *National Enquirer*. According to general editor Brian Williams, "I think there's always an ending to an *Enquirer* story."

The idea is, Williams says, to leave the reader "even if it's a tragic story, even if it's a death," with an upbeat ending.

It's not just tabloid journalists who eschew the inverted pyramid. Many scholars doubt its effectiveness, too.

"Let's talk about for a second about why copy editors cut from the bottom," suggests Don Fry. "It's because the stories are too long. It's because the writers don't work with the editors before they write, to determine length; it's because the writers are not encouraged to design stories to fit the space. In other words,

Bob Woodward, Washington Post*: "I think there is a tendency in an interesting way, when you're communicating orally, to use the inverted pyramid."*

Helen Thomas, UPI: "I think the inverted pyramid is still very important for news agencies. We're not taking a feature-y approach. If we do, I think our editors will put us on the right road."

because of disorganization. In a properly run organization, where editors work with the writers, the stories will come in at the right length, and you won't have the writers losing control of the bottom by having somebody whack it off. There's no reason in the computer age to have Samurai Editors."

COMPUTER ON-LINE NEWS AND STORY DEVELOPMENT

How will reporters develop stories for computerized news services in the future? Bill Mitchell, of the on-line news service Merc Center, offers this insight:

"One opportunity that you have is to provide additional information beyond the shorter story," Mitchell says. "For example, if a reporter does a 15-inch story about an environmental impact report about expanding the airport, that environmental impact report might be 15 or 20 pages. There is no room for it in a daily newspaper, but there is room for it in the electronic service. We might scan in that entire document, and let the reader get at some of the original documents used to produce the story. To really further empower the reader, let him make up his mind or her mind about what ought to happen at the airport."

This style of story development might be made possible by a technological innovation called "Hypertext." Imagine a news story with a term such as *environmental impact report* in bold highlights. The computer news reader could double-click with a mouse pointer on the bold words on the computer screen. Then, the entire document in question would come up on the computer screen.

Broadcast news writers rarely use a pure inverted pyramid form. The circle form of story development is much more suitable, if for no other reason than the fact that many viewers tune into a radio or television news report in the middle of the piece. They haven't heard the beginning, so the ending is even more important. It makes sense, therefore, that the ending often ties back to the beginning in a classic circle development form.

One occasion when a broadcast journalist might use the inverted pyramid is during a live report. We'll see an example of that in the program about covering natural disasters. The reporter gives the most important information at the top of the story (much like a summary lead) and then rattles off details, in descending order of importance, until he or she can't think of anything else to say. Since this is television, the impact comes from the fact that reporters are telling the story, live, with a remote microwave truck that allows them to stand in front of the forest fire they are reporting about. When the reporters sound like they are running out of things to say, the program director cuts them off (much like an editor cuts the bottom of an inverted pyramid story) and brings the show back to the television studio.

Variations on the tale about how the inverted pyramid evolved center around reporters who covered the Civil War. Most of those stories were sent over telegraph wires, and the telegraph system was even less dependable than an old computer on production night. Some versions of the tale say that journalists got used to cramming the most important information at the top of the story, because the technology was so unreliable. More exotic legends suggest that the gunfire from the battles was apt to destroy the connection.

Whatever the reason, the writing style of a journalist who is sending a story by telegraph is likely to mirror the conversational style of someone who is making an expensive long-distance phone call with a pocket full of change. Considering how expensive the communication is, it makes sense to condense all of the important information for the beginning of the call—before you run out of time, space or dimes.

FOREST SUPERVISOR CALLS FOR CLOSURE OF DEVIL'S GARDEN

By Bobby Calvan
Record-Searchlight

Modoc National Forest Supervisor Diane K. Henderson today formally recommended closure of the Devil's Garden Conservation Camp where paroled serial rapist Melvin Carter has been since March 16.

Henderson made her recommendation in a letter received shortly before 1 p.m. today by U.S. Forest Service Regional Director Ron Stewart in San Francisco.

Henderson's action comes in the wake of an impasse between state prison officials and the U.S. Forest Service over the housing of Carter at the facility near Alturas.

Carter, who served just half of his 25-year sentence for raping 12 Bay Area women, was paroled to Modoc County after being run out of a Bay area community by angry residents.

"It's a serious issue and an important decision," said Matt Mathes, a spokesman for Stewart.

Stewart is expected to decide soon whether he will follow Henderson's recommendation. Before doing so he is expected to consult with federal attorneys and other officials.

"He'll make a decision when he can," Mathes said.

Henderson's letter recommends that Stewart revoke the special use permit granted to the California Department of Forestry and Fire Protection (CDF). The state agency operates Devil's Garden as a work camp for what are described as low-risk prison inmates.

In her letter, Henderson said the housing of Carter at the camp was a direct violation of the use permit's conditions that only low-risk inmates can be housed there.

GLOSSARY

ANECDOTE

An interesting incident or slice of life, usually told as a very brief story, that leads off a news story. Often, the circle development style uses this type of lead.

CHRONOLOGICAL NARRATIVE

Telling a story from the beginning to the end, using a sequence of events in the order they actually unraveled. This is rarely used in news writing, because the most important information (usually the conclusion of your story) is supposed to be part of your lead.

CIRCLE

A story development style that often starts off with an anecdote and then returns to the anecdote, or main character of the anecdote, at the end of the story to "close the circle." This style of story development is popular in the *Wall Street Journal* and broadcast news writing.

ENDING

Unlike many traditional news writers, many modern journalists are starting to consider that good storytelling includes a beginning, middle and end. Many journalists, however, feel a good news story doesn't end—it is "to be continued" in tomorrow's paper. Broadcast journalists and feature writers usually feel the ending is nearly as important as the beginning of a story: it defines the feeling that the reader or listener is left with when the story stops. Newspaper reporters expect the endings of most stories to be cut.

FORESHADOWING

A technique used in cinematography and fiction—and some news writing—in which the storyteller hints at what is to come next to keep the viewer or reader interested.

HOURGLASS

A story development style that combines the inverted pyramid and a chronological narrative. The hourglass uses the summary lead and the inverted pyramid up to a transition in the middle, where the writer brings the reader to the story's beginning and then tells it, in sequence, to the end.

INVERTED PYRAMID

The most traditional style of journalistic story development. The inverted pyramid style of writing assumes that the editor will cut the story from the bottom to fit a news hole or that the reader will stop reading before the end. Therefore, the most important information is revealed as close as possible to the top of the story. The story is developed in a descending order of importance, so that the last paragraphs might be interesting but don't include information essential to the whole story.

KICKER

An ending that finishes a story with a climax, surprise or punch line.

LIST TECHNIQUE   A technique that allows the writer to keep readers interested in a story. For example, the story may include a lot of statistics or facts that would bog down the story. The writer can list those statistics or facts in the middle of the story. Then the reader can look at the list or refer back without being detracted from the story flow.

NEWS HOLE   An important concept introduced in Unit One that is important for inverted pyramid thinking. The news hole is the space left on the page, after advertising has been sold. The news hole is rigid; it is not within the editor's authority to delete an advertisement to make room for a story. Therefore, if a story is too long and does not fit in the news hole, it must be cut. The story is usually shortened to fit, inverted pyramid style, from the bottom.

NUT GRAPH   A paragraph that summarizes the news. This graph is often used after a lead that does not conform to the summary lead style. If any of the important elements (Who, What, When, Where, Why or How) have not been introduced in the lead, the nut graph will round them up. This paragraph is an important concept in story development and often used as a transitional device to bring the reader into the middle of the story.

RUNNING   A development style used in sports. Essentially, the running is the play-by-play narrative of a game, which can be used as the body of the story after the lead has been tacked on. This is especially helpful to have if the game ends near the deadline, and the reporter needs to whip up a story quickly.

TRANSITION   A rhetorical device used in writing to move the story smoothly from one set of ideas to the next by finding a way to logically connect the ideas.

SUGGESTED WRITING EXERCISES

1 Pick any lengthy news story that interests you in today's newspaper. Read the story all the way through. Let's play editor. The story has gone out on the wire, and every newspaper that will use it has a different news hole. Imagine cutting two inches from the bottom of the story. Does the story still work? Imagine cutting four inches. Imagine cutting the story in half. Imagine cutting all but the first two or three paragraphs.

If the basic story works in every variation, the writer has used the inverted pyramid. If important information is saved for the end, the piece might not work as a wire service story.

2 Find a story that is not written in inverted pyramid, and reorganize it so that any newspaper that picks it up on the wire feed can cut at any point.

The same exercise can be applied to any story you have written during this semester for the school newspaper or a homework assignment.

Q U I Z

Choose the best answer.

1 The inverted pyramid is criticized by journalists interviewed in the telecourse program because

  a. the standard newspaper production practice of cutting stories from the bottom might indicate that editors and reporters are not communicating as well as they can.
  b. writers who use the inverted pyramid have the mind-set that "if you think this sentence is boring, the next is even worse."
  c. the inverted pyramid has been the standard journalism story development style since the Civil War, and it is about time to change to something more contemporary.
  d. all of the above
  e. none of the above

2 The inverted pyramid is praised by journalists interviewed in the telecourse program because

  a. it allows the newspaper production process, especially on deadline, to function more smoothly when editors know they can cut a story from the bottom.
  b. the inverted pyramid is a style that pleases many newspaper readers, because it packs the most important information up near the top of the story.
  c. the inverted pyramid is a style that allows a reporter to organize a lot of information quickly, on a stressful deadline.
  d. all of the above
  e. none of the above

3 The circle style of development

  a. is commonly used in hard-news stories.
  b. allows the reporter to tie the end of a story to an anecdote at the beginning of a story.
  c. depends on a narrative, chronological story development.
  d. all of the above
  e. none of the above

4 Miki Turner, of the *Orange County Register*, explains, when sports reporters type in the play-by-play narrative on their portable computers during a game, they are using a story development style called

  a. the hourglass style.
  b. the "running."
  c. foreshadowing.
  d. all of the above
  e. none of the above

5 JoNel Aleccia suggests that one good way a reporter can avoid bogging a story down in a swamp of details and numbers is to

a. use the inverted pyramid.
b. use the hourglass style.
c. incorporate a list, with bullets, into the story.
d. all of the above
e. none of the above

6 The hourglass style, as described by Roy Peter Clark,

a. starts with a circle and ends with foreshadowing.
b. starts with a summary lead and inverted pyramid and then uses a transition to a chronological narrative, or telling of a story.
c. has nothing to do with the inverted pyramid and is therefore a far superior story development style.
d. all of the above
e. none of the above

7 Bill Mitchell, of the *San Jose Mercury News* on-line computer news service Merc Center, says that

a. computer news services will make the inverted pyramid obsolete.
b. it is too early to throw away the inverted pyramid, and even readers who get their news from computers enjoy information organized in a traditional newspaper style.
c. computers will add nothing new to story development styles.
d. all of the above
e. none of the above

8 Andrew Loschilin, of the Russian news agency TASS, says

a. that European newspapers prefer a more entertaining, storytelling style in news accounts.
b. that, since so many different papers pick up his news agency's stories, the inverted pyramid development style is important because each paper cuts in a different place—but from the bottom.
c. that today's Russian newspapers totally reject Western newspaper traditions.
d. all of the above
e. none of the above

9 Story endings in hard news

a. often get cut by the news editor.
b. are often ignored by the readers, especially if the story is jumped to a following page.
c. are often used by the *Wall Street Journal*, tied to the lead as a "circle kicker."
d. all of the above
e. none of the above

10 When writing a news story, the following device can be used as a transition:

a. the nut graph
b. the time element
c. the Where
d. all of the above
e. none of the above

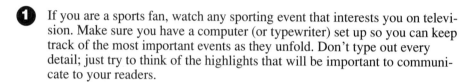

REVIEW: SUMMARY LEAD

In the pressure and haste of calling in a story to the editor over the telephone, Bobby Calvan slapped together a summary lead about his Devil's Garden story with a classic Who, What, When organization. If you were the copy editor and had time to reorganize this lead so that it did not emphasize an obscure Who (how many readers knew who Diane K. Henderson was?), how would you improve upon this lead, while still leaving it in the summary lead style?

PRACTICING THE "RUNNING" STYLE

1 If you are a sports fan, watch any sporting event that interests you on television. Make sure you have a computer (or typewriter) set up so you can keep track of the most important events as they unfold. Don't type out every detail; just try to think of the highlights that will be important to communicate to your readers.

When the sporting event is over, write a summary lead as soon as possible. If participants are interviewed by announcers after the event (as they frequently are), write down a few of the more interesting quotes.

Now, use Miki Turner's formula to write a game story—in less than an hour. Start with a simple summary lead. Then, using your play-by-play notes, tell the story of the event. If at all possible, include a few quotes as transitions. Don't save the final outcome until the end; it should be in your lead, because your story might be cut from the bottom and you have no idea what the news hole will be. Since you want to tell the whole story of the game, keep your writing concise and brief; you'll have a better chance of getting the whole piece into the news hole that way.

This is an excellent reporting exercise, even if you are not a sports fan. Think of this as a way to practice journalistic writing for any other news event. Make sure to check your *AP Stylebook* for any questions about correct language use.

2 If you absolutely abhor sports, apply the same techniques outlined in exercise 1 to a movie review. This time, watch a movie on television, and use the running style of chronological narrative to sketch out the plot of the film. Make sure you have a computer (or typewriter) set up so you can keep track of the most important events as they unfold. Don't type out every detail; try to think of the highlights that will be important to communicate to your readers. When the movie is over, write a summary lead as soon as possible. Be sure to write down a few of the more interesting quotes from the dialogue in the movie as you watch it.

Now, use Miki Turner's formula for writing a game story, as applied to a film review, in less than an hour. Start with a simple summary lead. Since this is a review, include your opinion of whether this is a good or bad movie in the lead. Don't be wishy-washy; take a position one way or the other.

Then, using your chronological narrative notes, summarize the story of the film. Include a few quotes from the dialogue as transitions. Don't save the final outcome until the end—it should be in your lead. Your story might be cut from the bottom, because you have no idea what the news hole will be. Since you want to tell the whole story of the movie, keep your writing concise and brief; you'll have a better chance of getting the whole piece into the news hole that way.

The best way to learn is from practice. Enterprising students will take the time to do both exercises.

INTERVIEWING, QUOTES AND SOURCES

Interviewing is an art form. Yet, the process is so basic, it's just one step beyond learning to have a conversation. The difference is, you must learn to edit and interpret a complex exchange of words—so you can mix the interviewee's voice with your own—while communicating with a large number of readers or viewers. In a well-written news story, this process is repeated several times, with a number of different sources. (Even writers who specialize in personality profiles seek out quotes from friends and peers of the person being profiled. A news story with only one source is generally considered very weak.)

You certainly can't use everything the news maker tells you. Frequently, there's only enough room in your story for one sentence of the interviewee's words.

Just as often, you can paraphrase what your source has said better than he or she can say it. That only makes sense; you are the one who is paid to work with words.

Because you become the medium through which the news maker's words are filtered, many of the people you interview will be nervous. Even worse, novice reporters are also usually tentative and tense during their first interviews.

When it comes to gathering quotes for a news story, experience teaches more than any amount of instruction. The best advice: Grab a reporter's notebook and get to work.

If that advice doesn't satisfy, you can try to absorb the textbook view of how it's done. You can also benefit greatly from listening to the professionals in the telecourse program talk about it and from carefully observing their many different styles in the quest to grab the perfect quote.

OBJECTIVES

By hearing journalists talk about interviews and by watching them practice their craft, you will learn to develop your own style.

PROGRAM GUIDE

BEFORE YOU WATCH

This program is designed to help you get ready for the process of dealing with news sources. This is a process of human interaction, and it can only partially be taught by explaining terms and concepts. The rest must be learned out in the real world, as you attempt your first interviews, grope for the right questions, learn when to listen and discover what makes a great quote. Still, understanding the concepts and terms is very important.

•**Pay close attention to the ways journalists and teachers use the following terms in this program:**

Attribution	Anonymous sources
Direct quote	News tip
Paraphrase	Ground rules
Jargon	Background
Off the record	

WHILE YOU WATCH

1. Observe the reporters as they conduct their interviews. Ask yourself, "What is effective or ineffective about the way the interview was conducted? How would I handle myself in the same situation?"

2. Imagine how each reporter shown in the interviewing process would handle the same story differently.

3. Familiarize yourself with the mechanical aspects of interviewing, including different approaches to taking notes and incorporating quotes from sources into your stories.

4. Consider how you would explain the ground rules of interviewing to an inexperienced source and how you would handle an experienced source differently.

AFTER YOU WATCH

•**Address the following questions in your journal. Or, if there's time, discuss them in class:**

1. What makes the difference between a good quote and a mediocre quote?

2. How would you react to a news source who wanted to tell you something off the record?

3. Can the use of anonymous sources lead to bad journalism? Under what situations is the use of a quote from an anonymous source acceptable or not?

4. How would you handle a source who answered in one- or two-word mutterings and never gave you a good quote? How would you handle the opposite kind of source—one who will never stop talking and meanders off the subject frequently?

5. What is the best method of taking notes during an interview? What are the advantages and disadvantages of using a tape recorder?

THE LESSON

If you are a student reporter, the following series of events probably has happened or will soon happen to you.

You've been given a fresh reporter's notebook and a first story assignment.

Soon, you find yourself in a conversation with a stranger; anything that person says might end up in print. What the news maker says can be the truth or a lie. It could brighten a life or ruin one. If you don't ask the right questions, the editor will complain that there are holes in your story and will send you back.

The person you are interviewing might talk so fast, you can't possibly keep accurate notes on what he or she is saying. Or, even worse, the answers come slowly and painfully, in one- or two-word bursts, and there is nothing to quote.

You could be interviewing people who are so used to talking to the media, they are skilled at manipulating words and avoiding the question.

You might be talking to people who have never interacted with the press and have no idea that portions of what they are saying will actually end up in print. Or, you might be talking to bureaucrats, scientists, lawyers, educators, computer hackers and politicians who talk in jargon so thick, it barely resembles English.

Some people will talk to you for hours; at the end of the conversation, they'll try to tell you it was all **off the record**.

Others want you to print every little nasty thing they have to say, as long as you quote an "**anonymous source**."

The strangers you talk to will make you laugh or fill you with pity. Some will infuriate you so much, you will want to throw down your reporter's notebook and clobber them. Others will make you feel like it's time to shed your reporter's persona and give somebody a big hug. All the while, you must maintain a fairly neutral exterior and somehow capture it all—with 100 percent accuracy—in your own reporter's mock shorthand.

Later, you can sort through all of it and share the best and worst of what you've learned about other human beings through the story that is due in a couple of hours. Your story may rely heavily on quotes, or you might use only one brief statement from all of those hours of interviewing.

Welcome to the world of interviews. It's an unusual way to make a living. Once some of you get a taste of it, you may never want to do anything else.

HOW TO DO IT

To prepare for your introductory interviewing experiences, let's look at the most common problems and give some advice on how to approach your first interviews.

No matter how experienced you become, there will always be a bit of awkwardness that comes with prying into a person's life. This feeling is magnified if you bring a camera for television or a tape recorder for radio. There is little advice we can give that will help, other than to suggest that you simply dive in and start the interview with as much genuine human interest as possible. No academic study can replace experience in this field.

Bob Woodward, of the *Washington Post*, also has this advice: "If you come in and say, 'Look, I'm working on this and I'm not sure where I'm going, I'm not sure what the answers are, I have a lot of questions, I need your help' . . . on that human level, it's like the person trying to carry four arms of groceries when you're coming out of the grocery store. If you just say to somebody, 'Could you help me?' you'll get that [cooperation]."

Here are other simple suggestions:

IF THE PERSON YOU ARE INTERVIEWING TALKS TOO FAST FOR NOTES . . .

Usually, an inexperienced interviewer feels all news makers talk too fast for accurate note taking. Sit back and listen for a while, and stop taking notes. Try to hear and understand what the news maker is telling you; don't spend more time looking at your notebook than at the person you are interviewing.

Don't write *everything* down. Listen.

Listen for the one or two great quotes you need for the story, and write only those down, along with a few general impressions. If appropriate, try asking the person you are talking with if you can read back the quote you plan to use, to verify accuracy. Unless you are afraid of breaking in during a spontaneous, emotional outburst, it is usually OK to slow down the person you are interviewing. Most news makers appreciate a reporter's commitment to accuracy.

Remember: Many editors prefer you to accurately **paraphrase** the news makers. This takes listening and understanding more than rote note taking. It is best to use **direct quotes** only when the news maker's own words are more powerful or interesting than yours—the storyteller's.

BE PREPARED

If you need to, come with a list of questions, but be spontaneous enough to ask new ones that come up as you're interacting with the news maker.

When you wrap up an interview, you should always get a phone number and time you can call to verify a quote or ask a final question. Woodward puts it this way:

"Once you've interviewed somebody, don't hesitate to say 'Can I come back?' That should be at the bottom of your list of questions . . . even if you're not sure why you're coming back."

Consider using a tape recorder, but be aware of the drawbacks.

Batteries die. Background noise often overshadows the words you need. Tapes unravel. If you depend on tapes and don't take good notes, you can almost guarantee something will go wrong at some point during an interview. And, some news makers clam up when they see recording devices. A microphone can ruin spontaneity.

Inexperienced reporters often try to transcribe entire tapes, which usually takes 5 to 10 times longer than the original interview. After wasting 5 hours to transcribe a 1-hour interview, many reporters learn that using a tape recorder only as a backup to find the exact words—for that one great quote—might be the best approach. If the batteries go dead and the great quote is in your notes anyway, you'll probably realize why many of the best reporters don't bother to lug around a tape recorder.

IF THE PERSON YOU ARE INTERVIEWING IS HARDLY SAYING ANYTHING . . .

Some people talk simply and don't elaborate. This is not the same as being unfriendly. Often, people like this are pleasant to be around in everyday life; they drive reporters crazy, however, because after a long interview, there is often nothing of value to quote.

In an interview like this, avoid questions that can be answered with a simple "yes" or "no." Larry King advises, "Ask why. A question that starts with 'why' can't be answered with one word."

Try to warm the news maker up to your interview. If the person you are interviewing is shy, uncomfortable or suspicious, don't take out the reporter's notebook or the tape recorder until later. Start off with a simple, friendly, conversational style. It helps to establish that you, too, are a genuinely interested human being.

If you find the key and your interviewee starts talking freely, take out the notebook (and, if necessary, tape recorder). If this slows things down again, try explaining that you've heard something you really want to use and that you want to quote the person accurately.

DURING THE INTERVIEW . . .

Try to maintain some sort of eye contact. If you spend the whole time frowning into your notebook while you write furiously away, it can take away from the potential human interaction that is essential in any good interview. Many reporters learn to write without seeing the pen or pad.

Most reporters don't know shorthand. However, many make up their own personal set of abbreviations and symbols to help keep track of what the interviewee is saying. Most reporters also have a way of highlighting the quotes that they will probably use in the final news story, so that they can find them easily in the notebook when they're pounding out the final copy into the computer on a deadline.

ⓑEYOND THE QUOTES . . .

During an interview, if the phone rings, don't panic; observe. When the interviewee is on the phone, you can use the time to look around the room and absorb impressions. Note if the news maker is neat or sloppy; look for memorabilia on the walls or desk top; learn what you can from the news maker's working or living environment. By the time the source's phone conversation is finished, you'll have your notebook filled with a lot more than a bunch of quotes.

Roger Ebert, who has published a book of interviews called *A Kiss Is Still a Kiss*, advocates this approach. He gives this example of an interview—that wasn't really an interview—turning into a great story:

"It was a Saturday morning with Lee Marvin out on the beach at Malibu. Marvin was completely hung over—didn't want to do an interview. His publicist is there. Then, his girlfriend comes in. Then his son comes in. Then they decide to send down to the corner for some beer. Then they decide to send out for some pizza. Then they have a long discussion about what kind of car the son should buy—should he get a used BMW, or should he get a new American car? Then there is some discussion about whether he should be drinking so much. Then there's some discussion about whether they want anchovies on the pizza.

"You see," Ebert says, "the unaware interviewers might think that their whole opportunity is just gone down the drain. They wanted to ask questions about [Marvin's movie] 'The Dirty Dozen' or something like that.

"Marvin, who was generous to allow me to stay there for hours while all this was going on, was essentially revealing himself in a very amusing and frank way. And to write that piece is a lot better than to get a nice sober, attentive, polite Lee Marvin who will give you very articulate answers to your questions. Then it will turn out to be just another boring hotel room interview."

Of course, some interview experiences don't focus so much on long observations of a single personality. Still, if a smart reporter is trying to get just one line for a story about a murder, and the homicide detective he or she is attempting to interview is being bombarded by continuous distractions, sharp ears and keen observation can still deliver the one great quote that is needed.

The same skills of listening and observation can come in handy in a press conference or "mob interview." Scott Ostler, of the *San Francisco Chronicle*, is shown in the telecourse program as he interviews Dusty Baker, manager of the San Francisco Giants. While other reporters on the scene were more keenly interested in how the Giants were doing in the season's pennant race, Ostler picked up a detail that others missed: that Baker, as a young player with the Atlanta Braves, had been the next player due up the day that Hank Aaron broke the all-time record for most career home runs. Ostler noticed other details that afternoon and was able to turn them into a fascinating column. (His story is included later in the study guide.)

AFTER THE INTERVIEW . . .

As soon as possible, after each interview, you should write down everything you need to remember. In the case of an interview where you didn't have a chance to get all the quotes down in a notebook, find somewhere to sit down and scribble even before you get back to the office. Many reporters immediately stop somewhere like a coffee shop to write down impressions and sketch out the story. If you didn't get exact quotes, it is easier to accurately paraphrase what the news maker said when the quotes are fresh in your mind. Research shows, the longer you are away from the interview, the less you are apt to recall. And, remember: Many editors prefer paraphrased quotes to direct quotes anyway.

Since you couldn't possibly write down everything that was going on, your notes are likely to be a bit of a mess when you get back to the office. Even if your story isn't due for a couple of days, it is a good idea to translate all the raw notes you'll need into your computer as soon as possible.

INTERVIEW GROUND RULES

WHAT IS ON OR OFF THE RECORD

Politicians and other experienced news makers who have been on the front page a lot know the unwritten **ground rules** for interviews; they understand that anything they might say—no matter how incriminating or embarrassing—could and will end up in print.

However, it is a good idea in any other situation, especially if either the interviewee or interviewer is new to the process, to go over the basic ground rules for what will and will not go into the newspaper.

Essentially, anything the person you are interviewing says is "on the record," which means you can print it. As a reporter, you should identify yourself as a representative of the press and explain the process to an inexperienced news maker at the beginning of any interview. (It is considered unethical by most news organizations to interview and quote sources without letting them know you are with the press.)

After having had these basic ground rules explained, if a news maker tells a reporter something and later says, "Oh, that was off the record," most reporters feel they have the right to print the information or quote anyway.

Some reporters will not run the quote, because it could potentially alienate the news source for future interviews.

If the information is extremely important to the story, the reporter faces an ethical challenge that can usually be resolved by answering these simple questions: Does the public have more of a need or right to know what was just said than the individual has to keep it private? Does the quote have important news value?

"Most people, in fact, talk too much," says Shirley Biagi, a renowned interviewer and teacher. "Sometimes they wish, after they'd said something, that they could take it back. That's the most common situation. They'll talk and talk and talk, and say something rather damaging, or questionable, or maybe not true or potentially libelous, and then they'll say, 'Oh, don't quote me on that' after the fact. In that case, it's a real ethical dilemma. Because they've given you the information, you know it, it was on the record, and supposedly they knew the rules, and you've got to decide whether to use it or not.

"I think each situation has its own ethics," Biagi continues. "If the person was a reluctant interviewee, hadn't ever participated in interviews before, doesn't know the rules of interviews, probably you want to make sure that they meant to say what it is they said, and you want to double-back on that information. But if they've practiced interviews, if they've been interviewed regularly, if they're a public figure and they know the rules—they said it, it's on the record, you've got it, and you can use it on the record."

If the source says that the information is off the record at the beginning of the interview, you have several choices. Some reporters simply end the interview at that point; they feel it is a waste of time if the source is not willing to be quoted. Others will listen, with a high degree of skepticism, after making a point of closing the notebook and putting down the pen. Off-the-record comments can at least point a reporter in the direction of where to look and who to interview next; they can also be lies, which are best ignored.

D EALING WITH LIES

Sources will lie, both on and off the record. If you sense something is not true, trust your instincts and investigate. Many students mistakenly assume, "If someone else said it, I have the right to print it." This is not an adequate defense, if the information is false and libelous. A person who has been libeled may sue the source who originally made the statement but can also sue both the reporter and the newspaper for republication of libel.

Many reporters will not allow sources to give them off-the-record comments, for this very reason. George Thurlow, adviser for the California State University, Chico, *Orion* and a well-recognized reporter himself, says that listening to a source lie about another news maker—even off the record—makes him uneasy. There's always the possibility that hearing the lie will color the reporter's subconscious attitude toward the target of the lie in future encounters.

Bob Woodward adds, "There's a premise in journalism . . . that the truth is hidden. That it's not on the surface." As the "watchdogs" for society, reporters working on investigative reports often have to go back to sources 15 or 20 times to get to the truth, Woodward says.

"Interestingly enough, after being a reporter 20 years, I find I've been lied to infrequently," Woodward says. "People will evade; people will not answer. Sometimes, people will directly lie, but it's rare. I think basically even dishonest people, even criminals, like to think that they're decent and would rather tell the truth if they can find some way to do it."

Steve Kroft, of "60 Minutes," says that television news has one distinct advantage in this situation. An effective "60 Minutes" technique is to let the viewer decide whether the news maker is lying—often with an extreme close-up shot—to emphasize emotion during the quote in question.

ANONYMOUS SOURCES AND BACKGROUND SOURCES

In rare instances, an editor will allow a reporter to run a quote in a news story, attributing it to an anonymous source. This practice is frowned upon as a breach of ethics by many editors. If sources were allowed to anonymously criticize other news makers on a regular basis, the newspaper's credibility would erode. Readers might be led to believe that lazy reporters were simply inventing quotes and sources; certainly, reporters who are willing to put in the extra work often can find a source who is willing to go on the record saying the same thing an anonymous source would say.

Readers and editors will accept anonymous sources in specific circumstances, because protecting the sources' identities can make both good sense and good news stories. Here are some examples:

A local narcotics enforcement agent is interviewed by the newspaper as he flies around the countryside spotting marijuana plots. As a sidebar story, a local marijuana grower is willing to tell what it is like trying to avoid the helicopter—as long as he remains anonymous.

The newspaper is doing a series of stories about the AIDS epidemic. A source, who is gay and HIV positive, is willing to give the reporter an interview about what it is like trying to survive under those circumstances—as long as he remains anonymous.

The paper is doing a series of stories about babies born with drug addictions. The district attorney wants to prosecute addicted mothers after they give birth, but the courts are worried the new policy would cause mothers to attempt dangerous out-of-hospital births. Several addicted and pregnant women approach the newspaper, willing to talk about how they would react to the new policy—as long as they remain anonymous.

ANONYMOUS SOURCES VERSUS CONFIDENTIAL SOURCES

Running quotes from anonymous sources can be dangerous; if a libel suit arises from the quoted material, the judge may demand that the source be named. If the reporter or newspaper refuses to reveal the name of the source, the reporter could end up in jail.

Some newspapers, therefore, differentiate between **anonymous sources** and **confidential sources**. A reporter would go to court, if necessary, to protect a confidential source. In the case of a lawsuit, the name of an anonymous source might be revealed.

Deborah Wilgoren, crime reporter for the *Washington Post*, explains that it is also standard policy for police officers to give out information about arrests, even though department policy might dictate that only the public relations officer can officially make statements to the newspaper. Since the public relations officer is not on duty 24 hours a day and the newspaper reports crimes committed at all hours, editors allow the crime reporters to use **attributions** such as "A police department representative said . . . " without using names. In this case, the reporter and the source have a delicate, ongoing relationship that is protected by the anonymity.

Though some editors simply refuse to publish quotes from anonymous sources, Bob Woodward (who still has yet to identify his anonymous "Deep Throat" source from the Watergate scandal stories that led to the resignation of President Richard Nixon) bridles at the notion.

"I am incredulous that some editor would say, 'Never use an anonymous source—it's not necessary.' I think that is so naive about journalism and about the world," Woodward says. "Who publicly declares their most important secrets regularly? It just doesn't happen. It isn't the way human beings in institutions function."

BACKGROUND AND DEEP BACKGROUND

Sometimes, sources do not even want to be quoted anonymously. A job—or a life—could be in jeopardy. These background interviews may not give the reporter any quotes to use, but valuable information can be revealed. The deep background source may give the reporter information that can lead to documents or other sources who would be willing to go on the record. Woodward's "Deep Throat" source during the Watergate stories would be considered a deep background source.

MECHANICS

ATTRIBUTION VERBS *Said. Said. Said. And, said.*

Sometimes, it is tempting to use other **attribution verbs** for your quotes, simply for variation. Most editors feel that *said* is as easily ignored by a reader as a punctuation mark such as a comma or a period. Therefore, the word is neutral.

The natural urge for a writer is to use different verbs to make the story more interesting. But, if the reporter tries to use attribution verbs such as *complained*, *demanded*, *admitted* or *hinted*, it is possible that the reader or the news source would interpret the attribution as editorializing. Some editors might let reporters get away with an occasional *according to*, whereas others would routinely switch the attribution back to *said*.

Even the verb *stated* has a specific meaning and is overused by writers looking for variation. Good journalism demands precise use of language, and unless your source specifically read a prepared statement, you probably shouldn't use the verb *stated*. With the same precision in mind, it might be possible to say a source *shouted* or *whispered* something, if those verbs precisely describe what happened.

Sources never actually *laugh* or *cry* something; they *say* something. You don't have to take out all of the description, but to be accurate, you could phrase the attributions in the following manner:

Jones said, with a laugh, "It wasn't me."
Smith said, wiping a tear from his nose, "I was to blame."

INSERTING OR DELETING WORDS IN A QUOTE Sources don't usually say things in perfect English, or in ready-to-use phrases that make sense without the rest of the interview. Often, clarification is needed.

Sometimes it is necessary and appropriate to delete words or to add additional words inside of a direct quote. For instance, you could accurately quote the writer of this textbook in the following ways:

> Peter Berkow said, "Sometimes (for clarification) it is necessary and appropriate to delete words or to add additional words inside of a direct quote."

In this case, the **parenthetical phrase** "(for clarification)" indicates something has been added to the direct quote.

> Peter Berkow said, "Sometimes it is necessary . . . to add additional words inside of a direct quote."

In this case, the **ellipses**—three periods—indicate something has been left out of the original quote.

Sometimes a writer will want to use only a few of the source's exact words within direct quotes, to emphasize a point. This works best when the quoted words are very important:

> Berkow said "it is sometimes necessary" to change a quote.

This is called a **partial quote**. Many editors caution against the overuse of partial quotes, because they can make the writing choppy and hard to read.

SOME FINAL TIPS

SHOWING A STORY TO THE PERSON YOU'VE INTERVIEWED, BEFORE PUBLICATION

News makers often ask to see a draft of the story before it is published. This is especially common at the college level, when school administrators and faculty are understandably nervous about being interviewed by inexperienced student reporters.

Keep in mind that reporters at most newspapers are not allowed to show a finished piece to a news maker before the story is printed. The reason for this is simple: Sources almost always will want to ask the reporter to change the story slightly or delete a quote— even if the information is accurate.

At some newspapers, reporters will be fired if they are caught showing a draft of a story to a source before publication. If you are being pressured—perhaps by the president of your college—to bring by the story for an accuracy check before publication, be courteous and explain your school newspaper's policy about showing unpublished work to news makers. (Perhaps you could even bring this book by and point out this passage.) Remember, your relationship with a source like this can be important for future stories.

Some editors, at both the college and professional level, will give permission to a reporter to show a story to a source if the information is highly technical and if translating it from jargon to plain speech is especially difficult. Other editors will allow reporters to read back portions of a story over the telephone—usually just the portions that come directly from the source who wants to see the story before publication—to verify accuracy of quotes.

Obviously, even this policy is not necessary if a tape of the interview is available. But sometimes reading quotes over the phone to a source can provoke additional quotes and observations needed to round out a story.

SPELL THE NAMES RIGHT

As long as we are talking about ways to get fired, let's emphasize spelling. Reporters lose credibility with editors and readers if names are spelled incorrectly. Yes, reporters have been fired for getting a name wrong—or, at least, for habitually not double-checking. Sometimes the most routine names can be spelled differently than you would expect. Just when you get to interview a John Smith, and you don't check the spelling, you'll find—after the story was published—he spelled it *Jonn Smyth*.

In college, no doubt you'll run into several people named Keri, Carrie, Kari, Kerri, Carri and Karry. Beware, and always double-check the spelling, no matter what.

INTERVIEWS: SEVERAL GLIMPSES

Throughout the telecourse program about quotes and sources, you've been given several glimpses into actual news interviews. None of the situations were posed or acted. Each reporter was captured on the job, in circumstances that show the different types of settings and challenges reporters encounter when attempting to gather quotes.

ON BARKER AVENUE

Peter Lundquist, of the *Journal-World*, in Lawrence, Kansas, is shown working on an interview about changes within neighborhoods. His friendly style encourages the people living in the Barker Avenue neighborhood to speak freely, and some of the opinions expressed (especially about minority groups moving into the neighborhood) ran counter to Lundquist's personal feelings. He explains how many reporters deal with similar situations:

"Sources will occasionally say things that are so philosophically different than my personal philosophy," Lundquist admits. "At first she put it in a what I would call a politically correct way . . . then she said the thing that I think was really going through her head, which was, 'I don't want to live in a neighborhood with more than a 50 percent black population.' That bothered me. But, as a reporter, for someone to say that, that is the truth to them. And so you record it, because that's what's really in their minds. And that's part of the story—that these people feel this way. Although you don't philosophically agree with it, you can't leave it out, because it's how she feels. It's difficult when someone says something like that.

"And, what's going through my mind is, 'Should I nod my head here?' Because when you're talking to people and you want to elicit information from them, you'll nod along and keep them talking. But I didn't agree with what she was saying; I didn't want her to think that I was agreeing with what she was saying. It's difficult."

IN THE DUGOUT

Scott Ostler, of the *San Francisco Chronicle*, is shown interviewing Dusty Baker, manager of the San Francisco Giants. Ostler's experience is completely different than Lundquist's. He is in a stadium, filled with 20,000 fans, trying to get an interview while surrounded by a dozen other reporters. Still, Ostler manages to find a unique angle of his own: that Baker was on deck when Hank Aaron broke the all-time home run record. The interview happened near the anniversary of the event, which gave Ostler a news peg for the interview—a glimpse, through Baker's eyes, of a baseball legend whose personal life was rarely revealed.

"I knew nothing about Hank Aaron," Ostler says. "I didn't know all these troubles he had gone through—the racial things, and the pain from the bad back, and all this other stuff, and Dusty was explaining this. To me, it was real touching and poignant; it was obvious to me that Dusty was kind of emotional about it. And that affected me, and so I tried to impart some of that.

"I guess one of the things that struck me was when he was talking about Hank Aaron and how he played through the pain. The constant pain he had from all these various injuries late in his career. And how sometimes he would sit in the clubhouse and observe Aaron. Dusty said, 'You know, I studied him, and I realized he wasn't reading the newspaper. He was focusing away the pain. He was somehow thinking away the pain. And we all thought he was reading the newspaper, and he wasn't really doing that.' And the fact that not only was Aaron doing that but that Dusty was studying him and seeing this and that interplay I thought was really interesting."

ON THE RIVER

Reporter Bobby Calvan, of the Redding *Record-Searchlight*, is pretty far from a big stadium in the middle of a city. He's walking through the trees, along the scenic upper Sacramento River. And he looks like he is barely doing anything. He nods in assent every 10 or 15 seconds and mumbles, 'Uh-huh.' He asks about one question every 5 or 10 minutes, and scribbles a line or two in his notebook about twice as often. It may not seem like it, but Calvan is working quite hard. He is carefully listening to the naturalists explain the effects of herbicide poison in the local environment. Calvan doesn't need to fire a list of questions. He needs to understand everything. And, when he knows 10 times more than he needs to write, he'll interpret the story so his readers can understand, with a glance at the daily newspaper, what he took all day to research.

IN THE CONGRESSMAN'S OFFICE

Steve Tetreault, editor for the Donrey News Service, is shown interviewing Congressman Wally Herger in his Washington, D.C., office. The congressman understands the interviewing process and how to handle reporters who ask tough questions. Tetreault understands how to handle his role, also.

"I will save my tough questions for the middle or end of an interview," he says. "Instead of going into an interview with guns blazing, where more than likely you'll get your subject to just clam up and not tell you a thing, you can establish some sort of rapport—and then once you're into the interview, you can kind of slip in your tough questions. A lot of it has to do with how you ask the questions, too. You don't want to be accusatory when you're asking questions. Because what you want, bottom line, is a response to your questions. So there's a way that you can ask questions that are tough questions without appearing to nag or to badger."

Tetreault listens to the congressman but questions some of his answers.

"A reporter's job is not to be that pipeline of unfiltered information," he explains. "If I, as a reporter, was just taking stuff that a congressman tells me as gospel, you really wouldn't need me here; you could just run his press releases verbatim in the newspaper.

"On that particular interview I didn't find a lot that was out of the ordinary or unexpected," Tetreault says. "The congressman did a good job keeping it along the lines that he wanted to keep it on. And at some point on the bus home tonight I'll probably kick myself in the fanny and say to myself, 'Gee you should have taken it another direction or you should have done something differently.'"

For instance, during the excerpt of the interview on the telecourse program, Herger states that only about five or six million Americans are not covered by health insurance. Tetreault explains that, rather than confronting the congressman in his office, his approach was to check around the next day. Other statistics showed that the actual number was anywhere from 5 to 10 times greater than the congressman's estimate. Often, Tetreault and others point out, the follow-up is the most important part of the interview.

ON THE SIDELINES

Sports reporter John Katsilometes is so amiable and offhanded in his approach to interviewing coaches, athletes and trainers, it is not unusual for him to receive off-the-record tips—as we captured on tape, when a trainer casually mentioned that a football player on an opposing team was using illegal steroids to gain weight and muscle.

Though the source did not say officially that the comment was off the record, Katsilometes would not use the information in a story for several reasons. The source would assume that the remark was made in an informal, nonquotable situation. Also, Katsilometes would need further substantiation to avoid a libel suit before using such a comment. The best approach would be to log the information in the back of the brain, accumulating the knowledge as background for a possible future story about steroids. Many beat reporters gather information about their specialty areas in a similar manner. We'll join Katsilometes for a more in-depth look at beat reporting in Unit Seven.

YOU

SHOULD

READ . . .

The Carole Rich textbook *Writing and Reporting News: A Coaching Method* has a very complete discussion of the issues covered in this unit. Chapter Six, on "Sources of Information" (pp. 87–107 in the second edition), has an excellent look at how to find sources before you even start the interview process. This chapter includes topics seldom discussed in textbooks, including how to use telephone directories, cross directories, public records and databases to track down sources. The chapter also presents another point of view on the topics of anonymous and off-the-record sources, which was introduced in this unit of the telecourse.

Chapter Seven, on "Listening and Note-Taking Skills" (pp. 109–115 in the second edition) contains excellent advice for beginning reporters about basics such as using tape recorders and note pads.

Chapter Eight, "Interviewing Techniques" (pp. 117–131 in the second edition), continues with a discussion of aspects such as telephone use and planning as well as tips and approaches to take in dealing with sources during an interview.

Chapter Twenty-One, "Speeches, Press Conferences and Meetings" (pp. 396–420 in the second edition) describes situations in which reporters are not dealing with sources in a one-on-one situation.

ON THE PHONE

You'll join Monica Davey at length in the ethics unit of the telecourse, as she works on this same controversial story about adult entertainment in the city of St. Petersburg, Florida. In this program, you get a brief glimpse of her aggressive interviewing style, as she first grills the owner of a strip joint. Davey later gets the owner of another adult entertainment establishment on the phone, but this source is reluctant to cooperate. Davey's approach is to engage the owner in polite conversation, and the result is a lengthy interview and several valuable quotes.

"I pretty much went into each interview with very easy, easy questions and, depending on how things were going, worked my way into some of the tougher questions, like, 'Would you want your kids to be working in a place like this? Are there prostitutes there? Wouldn't this offend you if it was happening in your home?'

Linda Ellerbee, "Nick News": "'What is it like to be you?' That's what an interview is."

Joyce Davis, National Public Radio: "It is amazing when you shut up how much you get. People don't like silences."

"Those types of questions I definitely saved until I felt a little more comfortable," Davey says, "because these people are not required to speak with me. And there's no law that says they can't hang up on me; plenty of them did."

GATHERING THE SOUND BITE

Television reporters have an unusual challenge, as Charles Kuralt points out. The quotes gathered from news sources are rarely as spontaneous or fresh on the second take. They somehow sound rehearsed or stilted. We'll join reporter Karen Reuter, from Reno, Nevada, station KOLO, in Unit Thirteen, and she fully develops an interview with fire-fighting safety officers. Here, we see just a glimpse of the interview, as she stretches out a question while the camera operator quickly adjusts the tripod. Reuter's instincts are the same as Kuralt's: Don't let the source start talking until the camera is rolling.

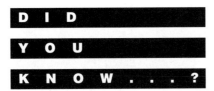

In spite of all the hard work you do collecting quotes, your editors will warn you against using too many quotes in a story. This is hard, since it is easy to fall in love with the words you have gathered from the news makers you have met. The usual advice is, use only the best quotes, and tell the rest of the story in your own words.

"I am using fewer quotes in stories now than when I came here," says Debbie Wilgoren, of the *Washington Post*. "That's something that my editors here have taught me. I think younger journalists rely more on full quotes. Paraphrasing takes a certain amount of confidence that you understand exactly what this person was trying to say, and, in fact, you have a better way to say it.

"In high school and college my rule was basically like lead, quote, a couple paragraphs more, quote—you know, lots of quotes. Now, in a 15-inch story, I might have three quotes, maybe four. And they have to be good quotes, and they more often than not are going to be single sentences. People don't speak the way that you write; they don't take time to craft their sentences when they're speaking the way a reporter does sitting at the computer. So chances are your paraphrase is going to read better."

Jack Cappon of the Associated Press agrees. "I think our tendency is to believe that anything between quotation marks is thereby made interesting," he says. "That's insane. You have to be very selective about quotes. Quotes are intended to advance a story, not retard it. Not to repeat, for example, what the lead says. Quotes are supposed to crystallize a situation. An emotion. Give a different slant on a news subject's outlook. And if they don't do that, they're no good. We tend as a profession vastly to overquote."

"The number one disease in journalism is the quotation," says Joel Achenbach, of the *Washington Post*. "We use them so much because they're easy."

AARON A BIG HIT AS BAKER'S MENTOR

By Scott Ostler
San Francisco Chronicle

Hank Aaron had a major impact on Dusty Baker's baseball career, and life, but you really have to work Dusty to get him to talk about Aaron.

You have to do something like, say, mention a topic related to baseball or life.

In Baker's informal dugout press chat before yesterday's gem, the subject was the Braves, and first baseman Fred McGriff, and how McGriff hits a ton of home runs but gets relatively little publicity.

"He reminds me of Aaron," Baker said. "Doesn't say a lot, just does his job."

A lot of players just do their jobs, but the jobs they do seldom involve hitting 755 home runs.

Professor Hank

Baker studied under Professor Aaron, graduated with honors from Hammer U.

When Baker made it to the big leagues in 1972, Aaron befriended him, helped him become a big-leaguer, taught him things he still uses every day, on the field and off.

So it will be special for Baker when the Giants play in Atlanta tomorrow night, the Braves' home opener, which will feature a ceremony honoring the 20th anniversary of Aaron breaking Babe Ruth's career home run record.

Baker was on deck April 8 of '74 when Aaron went to bat against Al Downing. It was Aaron's second at bat of the night. First time, he walked on four pitches.

"He told me, 'I'm gonna get it over with right now,'" Baker said.

"I thought, 'OK, Hank.'"

Hank did, thus becoming the answer to the famous trivia question, "Who hit a home run on April 8, 1974, to set the table for Dusty Baker's ringing double off All Downing?"

It was one of three occasions when Baker heard Aaron call his shot. The year before, after an hour rain delay, Aaron went to bat in the bottom of the ninth, a runner on, two out and the Braves down by a run.

Aaron told Baker, "I'm gonna hit the next pitch over the right-center field fence." And he did.

Aaron Knew the Game

A lot of us who saw Aaron play in his prime never really knew anything about him, except that he never seemed to say anything remarkable in public, that he seemed bland, and years after he retired he started coming off as a tormented soul, bitter over racial injustices, to the point that he almost made you forget the 755 home runs and assorted ball glories.

For instance, I've read a lot of baseball stuff over the last several decades, and I don't recall one word about Aaron as a cerebral ballplayer.

But listen to Baker.

"He knew the game better than anyone," Baker said. "He's the reason I moved to left field [from center]. He told me, 'Let the young boys run. You move to left and save your legs for hitting.'

"He knew everything. Everything. He knew the umps, which ones were high-strike umps and which were low; he knew every pitcher's sequence, knew where to play every hitter, different on every pitch. One night in the dugout he said, 'Watch their left fielder. He puts his head down a little early every time fielding ground balls. If I hit one to him, I'm going to take off fast, slow down, then sprint.' That night Hank hit a routine single to left, and I look up and he's on second base.

"He was amazing. I probably saw 100 of his home runs and I never saw him hit a tape-measure homer. Not once. The ball always went just far enough, no matter what park. I swear, he must have had a gauge in his bat."

Under His Wing

When Baker was a high school kid deciding whether to go to college or sign a baseball contract, his mother asked the veteran Aaron if he would take care of her son. Aaron promised he would, and he did. He opened his home to Dusty and another rookie, Ralph Garr. Aaron befriended them, let them drive his cars, study his veteran sophistication and style. Baker and Garr called him Hammer, or Ham, or Supe, short for Superstar.

In '71, Aaron was going through a wrenching divorce. On plane flights, he would make Baker and Garr sit on either side of him and goof off, joke, make him laugh. It was the only way Aaron could relax, and Baker and Garr would laugh Aaron to sleep, as if singing a lullaby.

Aaron taught Baker what to eat, and how to stay in shape. Baker says Aaron was a fanatically dedicated conditioner, another thing I never heard or read. Apparently the hard work is what made Aaron the natural athlete he was always said to be.

Lessons in Survival

Mostly what Hammer taught Baker was how to be tough enough to survive.

"He had a bad back, and a sciatic nerve problem; he was really beat up. He would sit at his locker reading a newspaper, but I studied him and I realized he wasn't reading at all. He was thinking away the pain. He would come to the clubhouse looking like he was 50 years old, go out and play like he was 25, then come back in the trainer's room looking like 50.

"My greatest accomplishment as a ballplayer was never going on the DL. Hank always told me, 'The best way to keep your job is to keep the next guy on the bench.' One year he cut his hand real bad, was in a lot of pain, but played anyway and hit three homers in three games. That's why in the '81 World Series, my hand was real messed up, I should have been out, but I played anyway.

"Last year I got some racist letters, but I thought back to the ones Hank used to get, and I would think, 'This ain't nothin'. What I got all year, he got every day.'"

So when Aaron takes a bow tomorrow night in Atlanta, Dusty Baker will be in the visitors' dug-out, applauding, and wiping away any eye perspiration, because Hammer taught Dusty you never let 'em see you sweat.

ALTERNATIVE VIEWS

PARAPHRASE

Many editors prefer paraphrased quotes over direct quotes. The reason? Reporters are paid to work with words; you are the professional storyteller. And, unfortunately, many news makers are not eloquent when they speak.

Mitch Stephens, of New York University, expresses a slightly different point of view.

"A good quote is always better than a paraphrase," he says. "Readers would rather read the words of the news maker than hear your version of those words. But there are going to be times when you're going to have to paraphrase. One of those times is if the news maker didn't say things all that clearly. Sometimes, under the pressure of being interviewed by a reporter, the right words aren't necessarily going to pop into their heads. They may be making a point but doing it in such a long-winded and dry fashion, that you'd be doing your reader a disservice quoting that whole long-winded and dry quote. You're better off paraphrasing it, putting it in your own words, getting across that point in words that you can make clearer, more efficient, more engaging, sitting at your computer than they could when they were being interviewed by you."

BUYING A QUOTE

Tabloid journalists have a completely different attitude about gathering quotes in news stories—an attitude that disturbs many mainstream journalists.

"We do pay sources," says Brian Williams, of the *National Enquirer*. "It depends on what the information is and depends on the story. The range could be from a hundred dollars to thousands of dollars. There are some stories you're going to get, somebody's going to talk to you only because you're going to pay them. You're going to get information that (you) wouldn't get otherwise."

This issue is explored in more depth in the unit about journalism ethics.

GLOSSARY

ALLEGE	According to the dictionary: "To assert without proof." *Allegedly* has a similar meaning to *supposedly*. This word is a qualifier used often in journalism to protect the writer, as in "The mayor allegedly used the city credit card for his own personal gain." Sometimes used as an attribution verb, but editors caution against this. The *AP Stylebook* warns: Use with great care. Avoid implication that the writer is alleging.
ANONYMOUS SOURCE	If a reporter quotes a source and purposely does not name the source, that source is called an anonymous source. Usually, the reporter is trying to protect the source by not including the name with the attribution.
ATTRIBUTION	Giving credit to the person who is being quoted. Facts and opinions should be attributed in a news story.
ATTRIBUTION VERB	The most common attribution verb in journalism is *said*. Most other attribution verbs—*complained, griped, sighed, cried, asserted, claimed, admitted*, etc.—are discouraged, because they tend to reflect the reporter's opinion rather than the news maker's actual intent.
BACKGROUND	A background source usually gives information that is not intended for publication. Often, a source would be jeopardized if the information was published—even without attribution.
CONFIDENTIAL SOURCE	A source who will give information, with the understanding that the reporter will never reveal the identity of the source—even under the threat of a lawsuit.
DIRECT QUOTE	When reporters use a direct quote in a story, they are indicating that they are reproducing the exact words the news maker said. The exact reproduction of the source's words are indicated mechanically with quotation marks.
ELLIPSES	Ellipses (three periods) are used in a direct quote to indicate that the writer has left out some words to shorten the quote.

GROUND RULES   When a reporter interviews a source who is not experienced with the media, the ground rules for attribution should be explained. Basically, anything the source says may be reproduced in a news story (unless the source asks to go off the record during the interview).

OFF THE RECORD   When a source tells a reporter something that he or she does not wish to be repeated, that comment is said to be "off the record." In most situations, people who are being interviewed know that everything they say may end up in the news story. That information is on the record.

PARAPHRASE   When reporters use an indirect quote, or paraphrase, in a story, they are indicating that they are summarizing (and rephrasing) the words the news maker said. Ethically, the reporter is bound to maintain the spirit and intent of the quote when paraphrasing. Mechanically, the quotation marks are omitted, to show that the reporter has slightly changed the words.

PARENTHETICAL PHRASE   When a reporter inserts his or her own words into a direct quote to clarify the quote, the reporter's words are indicated in parentheses. (You may have noticed that brackets have been used instead of parentheses in this study guide—that's following *book* publishing style. As the *AP Stylebook* explains, parentheses are used in newspaper journalism because brackets can't get transmitted over the AP wires.)

PARTIAL QUOTE   A partial quote is used when a reporter wants to use only a few of the words actually said by the news maker. The words that were actually said by the source are indicated with quotation marks.

SOURCE   A person who talks to a reporter on the record, for attribution in a news story, is also called a source.

1. Pick a person in the class you don't know very well, and take turns interviewing each other. Your goal will be to write a personality profile—a style of writing that will be discussed in the unit on feature writing. As you talk to the new friend in the class, think of Linda Ellerbee's advice: All interviews are based on the same question: "What is it like to be you?"

Students who are taking news writing as a distance-learning class can pick somebody in the community to interview. It is best, for the sake of this exercise, not to pick a family member or somebody you know well. An important part of the learning process is to discover what it is like to ask questions of somebody you don't know.

If several distance-learning students are taking the class, ask the instructor of record to help you contact each other. If you can't arrange to meet in person, try conducting the interviews over the telephone.

2 Read a copy of today's daily newspaper.

    a.   Pick out five direct quotes that really grab you, and write them down in this space. What makes each of these quotes strong?

    b.   Pick out five direct quotes that are really boring and do not add to the story. Write them down in this space. Why did the writer include these quotes in the story? Would the story work without the quotes?

c. Pick out five indirect quotes, and write them down in this space. Why did the writer decide to paraphrase the news source, instead of quoting the source directly?

3 Talking and studying about how to conduct an interview will get you only so far. The best way to learn how to interview is to write something for the school newspaper. Contact editors in each department (News, Sports, Entertainment, etc.), and ask for a story assignment. If you are a distance-learning student, there is a good chance the school newspaper could use you as a stringer to cover a part of the campus community that might otherwise get ignored. If your school does not have a newspaper, see if you can get an assignment from a small community magazine or newspaper.

Q U I Z

Choose the best answer.

1 Direct quotes

a. should be the unaltered words said by the news maker.
b. are always preferred by editors over paraphrased or indirect quotes.
c. should make up at least half of any well-written hard-news story.
d. all of the above
e. none of the above

2 An indirect quote

a. is often preferred by editors over direct quotes, because sources often don't speak as clearly as reporters write.
b. is usually discouraged, because the writer is not using the source's exact words.
c. is never used in a news story, because indirect quotes show the reporter was too lazy to get the exact words.
d. all of the above
e. none of the above

3 A parenthetical phrase inserted into a direct quote means

    a. the words in parentheses were said as a joke or in jest.
    b. the words within the parentheses were said as an "aside" by the source.
    c. the author has added words to clarify the words of a source in the direct quote.
    d. all of the above
    e. none of the above

4 Ellipses (or three periods) inserted into a direct quote mean

    a. the person being quoted trailed off before finishing a sentence.
    b. some of the words said by the source were left out to shorten a direct quote included in a story.
    c. "to be continued."
    d. all of the above
    e. none of the above

5 An off-the-record comment

    a. is something told to a reporter by a source who does not want to be quoted in a story.
    b. can be used as a tip to find additional information or to find a source who will speak on the record.
    c. may be something included in a story if it can be established as true, though the writer will probably not attribute the source.
    d. all of the above
    e. none of the above

6 An anonymous source

    a. should never be used in a solid news story.
    b. can be attributed in a news story, in selected circumstances, with your editor's permission.
    c. should be used only for deep background.
    d. all of the above
    e. none of the above

7 When a journalist interviews a source, a list of questions made before the interview

    a. can be a helpful tool to help the reporter organize thoughts.
    b. can be a distraction, if the reporter is more worried about sticking to the list of questions than listening to the answers.
    c. is forgotten by some good reporters, until the end of the interview—as a sort of checklist—when a connection is made with the news source, and the interview becomes more like a conversation.
    d. all of the above
    e. none of the above

8 Reporters who take notes with a notebook and no tape recorder

    a. usually know shorthand and write down almost everything the source says.
    b. are taking a great risk by not using a tape recorder.
    c. usually write down observations, important facts and the most important quotes.
    d. all of the above
    e. none of the above

9 According to Bob Woodward, an important question a reporter can ask is

    a. how to spell the news source's name.
    b. when you can call back to ask follow-up questions.
    c. "Who's responsible?"
    d. all of the above
    e. none of the above

10 In an adversarial interview, reporters are advised to

    a. take the offensive and attack back when the news source gets nasty.
    b. get into the interview slowly, remain polite and build up to the tough questions.
    c. avoid embarrassing questions.
    d. all of the above
    e. none of the above

SELF-TEST

1 List several differences between broadcast and print news interviews.

2 List two reasons why a tape recorder could help with an interview.

3 List four reasons why depending on a tape recorder is not a good idea.

4 Give two examples of stories in which the readers might accept quotes from an anonymous source.

5 In the space below, write down an explanation of the ground rules for on-the-record and off-the-record comments you would give to a person who is not experienced at being interviewed by the media.

6 Using the rules for partial quotes, shortening (with ellipses, or three periods) and clarifying (with parenthetical phrases) that you learned in Unit Three (study of the *Associated Press Stylebook*), take the following rather wordy passage by a blowhard news source and find a quote:

Transcript from interview with Peter Berkow, producer of the Annenberg/CPB telecourse "News Writing:"

"This course was intended to supplement, not replace, journalism teachers—or, rather, supplement the work they do. The video section, in a way, is a modern equivalent of a textbook. Can you imagine? There were teachers who objected to textbooks when they were first introduced. Their gripe was, the textbook would replace the method of mentor-student learning—or, the old sage-on-the-stage routine. So, the telecourse is similar to a textbook. Actually, it does one other thing. It can allow us to change the role of the teacher. Instead of some professor lecturing as the expert all semester long—pushing his or her attitudes and opinions at you—you get to listen to about 180 of the best journalists in the country express their different views. The new role of the teacher, then, is to spend more time working shoulder to shoulder with the student—coaching, reading, editing, giving feedback, writing red marks—and maybe some blue ones, to indicate positive feedback, and giving that one-on-one attention that they don't have time for when they're so busy with lecture preps."

a. Pick an interesting part of the quote and use ellipses in the correct way to shorten the quote.

b. Pick an interesting part of the quote and use a parenthetical phrase to clarify the quote.

c. Paraphrase, with accuracy, a section of the quote in your own words.

WRITING VERSUS REPORTING

Linda Ellerbee's opening for the video portion of this unit in the telecourse sums up the intent perfectly. Writing and reporting are separate skills. Students must learn to combine fluent writing with accurate reporting to create good journalism. Journalists must conquer the language even more forcefully than fiction writers. Reporters can't make up plot twists or characters. Instead, they must capture the people and events precisely and quickly—without exaggeration—relating through a news report: what happened, why it happened, who it happened to and (sometimes) how it felt.

On top of that, they must do it with as few words as possible. And, they must often try to grab the attention of readers or viewers who could care less.

Because of those challenges, journalists have a much different feeling for rhetoric than other writers. Language professors commonly complain that students from the school newspaper who are also taking their college English classes write too much like journalists: Their sentences are short and to the point. They break back paragraphs too often. They don't use enough pretty sounding-adjectives and adverbs. And, they favor workman-like verbs and nouns over $50 schoolteacher words that make you run for the dictionary.

Of course, it could be argued that a significantly higher percentage of journalism majors than English majors actually get a job that requires them to write. A surprising number of those move on to be successful essayists, novelists or script writers.

It has something to do with learning eloquence.

Eloquence without truth, however, is of no value in reporting. A news writer must learn to be exact while discovering his or her writer's "**voice**." This takes persistence, stubbornness and a fanatical attention to detail. Sometimes the elusive fact can be found only via monotonous digging through piles of musty documents or tedious drudging through forgotten databases. Other times, the missing quote or verification can be obtained only by wringing it out of stubborn, evasive sources. Good reporters learn to do this with tact, with forcefulness bordering on irascibility or (sometimes) with threat of legal action—whatever it takes, within ethical boundaries.

More commonly, the essential facts are easily accessible. Reporting skills should never become routine. Sometimes the truth is so effortless to come by, the sloppy writer blows it by simply failing to double-check the obvious—as in when the source spells his name "Jonn Smyth."

In the unlikely event that all of the requisite elements of good writing and good reporting come together, Terry Armour of the *Chicago Tribune* jokes, you've reached perfection. You're the Michael Jordan of journalism; it's time to retire and find something more challenging.

OBJECTIVES

Students will learn about the similarities and differences between good writing and good reporting. By working to combine the two, they'll start on the path toward good journalism.

BEFORE YOU WATCH

This program is created to provoke you into thinking about essential aspects of journalism that are not emphasized in other writing courses you may have taken in college. Though the traditions of good reporting are emphasized, elements of good communication common to all writing are also considered:

•**Pay close attention to the ways writers and reporters use the following terms in this program:**

Accuracy   Voice/style
Active verbs   Sunshine laws
Passive verbs   Detail
Concrete nouns   Freedom of Information Act
Second draft/rewrite

WHILE YOU WATCH

1. Look for the similarities between good writing and good reporting.

2. Think about how you can adapt specific bits of advice about good writing to your own work.

3. Notice which aspects of good writing are intricately intertwined with good reporting.

4. Notice which aspects of good writing, in disciplines other than journalism, can lead to bad reporting.

5. Decide what makes the difference between a great reporter and one who is just adequate.

AFTER YOU WATCH

•**Address the following questions in your journal. Or, if there's time, discuss them in class.**

1. What leads to bad or mediocre reporting?

2. Why have so many journalists made the transition from writing news to becoming good fiction writers? Can fiction writers make a similar transition to news writing? Why?

3. Bobby Calvan has a reputation as a reporter committed to accuracy, yet his work was chosen to illustrate principles of writing. What principles mentioned by other writers did you notice in the description of Calvan's story?

4. Tom Philp has a reputation at the *Sacramento Bee* for turning in clear copy, and his story has been chosen in this study guide as an example of good reporting. What aspects of his reporting style can you adapt to your own work?

THE
LESSON

Some schools call this introductory journalism course "Reporting." Others call it "News Writing." Which is the most important skill to study at this point of your education?

"I always counsel my students to work on the skill in which they're weakest," says Shirley Biagi, of California State University, Sacramento.

"If they're not particularly excited about going out and getting the information, spending a lot of time in the library, on the phone, with people, interviewing people, I say, 'That's what you've got to do more of while you're in college and while you're training to be a journalist. Because that's your weakest point.'

"If, on the other hand, they walk around the desk 50 times before they sit down and start writing a story, then maybe they love the research . . . but actually physically sitting down and organizing their thoughts into a good story is something that's difficult for them. So then I say, 'You have to work more on your writing.' Work on your weakness. And play to your strengths."

The journalists interviewed for the telecourse seemed to be split on which skill is the easiest to learn.

"Reporting is something you're born with or not," says Monica Davey, of the *St. Petersburg Times*.

"I think writers are born. Reporters can be made," says Kurt Loder, of *Rolling Stone* and MTV news.

Probably neither is accurate. Some students have aptitudes for language skills or stubborn, persistent personalities suited for fact gathering. But these traits are more likely linked to upbringing and disposition than genetics. Both skills can be learned through hard work. And lazy students with natural aptitudes often never progress beyond the high school newspaper.

"I think a good writer's going to make it interesting," says Loder. "Just work at it and work at it and work at it. There shouldn't be anything in there that doesn't belong in there—that's dull. You should cut it out. And the most important thing you can do is learn to edit yourself. And then go back and rewrite. Rewriting is a large part of the whole job. Get rid of stuff that's not working. Just pare it down until it's a beautiful thing."

"Reporting is having the energy to get out there and talk to who you don't particularly want to talk to, and deal with things you don't particularly want to deal with—that may or may not be fun," says Davey. "I never start writing until I've completely finished reporting and I know the answer to every question in my mind."

"The biggest skill that I think a reporter needs is adaptability," says Biagi. "You have to be adaptable to each situation and be able to analyze the situation and say, 'What does this particular story need the most? Does it need my reporting skills? Does it need my writing skills? Does it need my interviewing skills? Does it need my listening skills? Which of those skills can I pull from to make this the best story it can possibly be?' Each person comes to that task differently. Each person has different things to add to the skill of story writing and the skill of reporting."

GOOD WRITING

In Unit Three, you studied the *Associated Press Stylebook*. Clearly, the language use of journalism is different from other forms of literature. Journalists have an aversion to adjectives and adverbs and a special rapport with **active verbs** and **concrete nouns**. Their attitudes toward sentences, voice, paragraph structures, transitional phrases, attributions, jargon and other elements of style are also often different.

The following sections are a survey of some of the points journalists made, when interviewed for the telecourse about good writing.

VERBS

"Verbs are better than adjectives," says humor columnist Dave Barry. "Things should happen rather than be described. All the clichés about writing always turn out to be true. Show me; don't tell me. Who is going to read a sentence 'He was very angry' when you could have read what he actually said or did that made the writer observe the anger? The writer obviously saw something to make him say that, to draw that conclusion. But, rather than let the reader see it and draw the conclusion, the writer tells the reader 'Here's what I know. I'm a journalist!'"

Barry's example—"He was very angry"—is less effective than "He threw the chair at the referee." The first statement is built with a passive verb (*was*) and adjective (*very*). The second uses an active verb and needs no adjective.

Almost all the journalists surveyed avoid passive verbs and favor active verbs.

"One of the best things writers can do is read it aloud, so that you hear not only cadence but also the word choice," Carole Rich says. "Are you using too many 'to be' verbs?

"'He is.' *Is* is not a strong action word. It's important to be selective about language."

For example, a passive "to be" sentence would read:

Clemens *was throwing* the ball to first, just to keep Henderson from stealing.

The passive "to be" form of the verb—*was throwing*—does not communicate as much as an active verb. Notice how different the meaning becomes, if the writer selects the following verbs:

Clemens *lobbed* the ball to first, just to keep Henderson from stealing.
Clemens *fired* the ball to first, just to keep Henderson from stealing.
Clemens *tossed* the ball to first, just to keep Henderson from stealing.

Ted Clark, of National Public Radio, says, "If you choose just the right verb, it makes the sentence clear and powerful. Instead of saying 'criticized' you could say 'condemned.' Instead of saying 'praised' you could say 'extolled.' It just takes a little extra time to find the verb that communicates the feeling more powerfully than the one that comes first to mind."

"The verb is what drives a sentence," says Jack Cappon, of the Associated Press. "It makes a sentence act. For example, if you say, 'They experienced hunger and great cold,' . . . that's a sentence of sorts, but what you've got is a weak verb and abstract nouns. If you say instead, 'They starved and they froze,' which is exactly what this other sentence said, it's much better."

Cappon also warns students to watch out for passive verbs that creep into writing through government press releases. "It serves a purpose to obscure things. That's why I think [bureaucrats] will use a passive verb so often. 'It is believed.' Who believes it? 'It is said.' Who says it? Everything is made as vague as possible."

NOUNS

"Nouns and verbs are what count," says Richard Aregood, editorial writer for the *Philadelphia Daily News*. "The rest of it is decoration. If you can't say it with nouns and verbs, and the odd adjectives, . . . then you're not quite doing it. Because you're putting too much weight on the adjectives. They weren't designed to tell the story. They're not the muscle of the thing. They're kind of like hair; they're not the basic part of what you're trying to do."

Many journalists prefer concrete nouns to abstract nouns. Abstract nouns usually involve ideas, traits or characteristics. Examples include *wealth* and *ugliness*. Concrete nouns name something tangible: *dollars* and *grime*. The more abstract nouns included in a news story, the more the writer teeters on vagueness or editorializing. Instead of writing about ugliness, the writer can show specifics: the grime, the warts, the blemish, the smudge. The readers can then make personal judgments to the degree of ugliness or beauty from the pictures painted by the writer's (hopefully) accurate portrayal.

ADJECTIVES AND ADVERBS

"We have a very tight line at *USA Today*, so adjectives have to be very carefully placed," says Gene Policinski, sports editor. "They shouldn't be there just to liven up a story, and many times, particularly in sports writing, I find them added on because you sort of feel obligated to throw an adjective in every eighth or ninth word. Use them only when they're very appropriate. I would prefer you be specific.

"It's not a 'big' tax bill. It's a bill that would force you to pay an extra $25 a month on your heating bill. Adjectives can be lazy writers' tools because they haven't gotten the facts, and they try to cover it up. They say an 'important' thing. They haven't asked why; they aren't going to tell you what's 'important' in the story. So I use adjectives very judiciously. I think that facts are much better than adjectives."

Ted Clark, of National Public Radio, agrees. "Any adjective that simply augments the power of the word, I would be suspicious of," he says. "This is a particular problem for broadcast reporters. You have to keep your stories fairly short; time is limited. Every unnecessary adjective is a word that takes time away from the story."

SENTENCES

"Keep it simple. Keep the sentences declarative," says John DeNatele of PBS. "You learn pretty quickly about not saving something for the bottom of your sentence—rearranging the sentence so that it's clear what you're going to talk about right at the top of that sentence. Put the noun close to the top, so that we can take the viewer along in a very linear fashion."

Roy Peter Clark, of the Poynter Institute, gives this example sentence:

> The executive vice president of one of the chain of companies that did business with Florida Power during the 1996 oil embargo was indicted Thursday.

"The verb disconnected from the subject violates our whole sense of predictability," Clark says. "Don Fry calls it 'steady advance'—the ability to move through the sentence without ever having to turn back. Perhaps if this is a line of poetry, maybe I want to turn back and sort of make some connection between the beginning and the end of the sentence, but not in journalism. In journalism we want it straight through. Not only through the sentence, but through the paragraph and through the story."

Notice how subject and verb are disconnected by a string of descriptions and titles:

> The executive *vice president* of one of the chain of companies that did business with Florida Power during the 1996 oil embargo *was indicted* Thursday.

The readers might be better served if some of the details were delayed for a second sentence:

> Key West Rigging's *executive vice president was indicted* Thursday.
> The drilling outfit was one of the chain of companies that did business with Florida Power during the 1996 oil embargo.

Such sentences can also be improved by using common words (vernacular, in schoolteacher talk) instead of the high-priced language that spills from the lips of lawyers, scientists, bureaucrats or elected government officials. In our example, "drilling outfit" communicates more to the average newspaper reader than terms such as "oil futures consortium" or "petroleum exploration enterprise."

JARGON AND GOBBLEDYGOOK

"Gobbledygook is as old as mankind," says Jack Cappon. "Referring to bad weather as 'adverse weather conditions.' Gobbledygook is using an elegant word or **jargon** word in preference to saying something simple. Something having a 'negative impact on the economy'—that's pure gobbledygook. What you want to say is 'something is hurting the economy.' There's corporate talk: 'Downsizing,' for example, . . . or the 'streamlining of entire divisions.' This is gobbledygook for saying, 'We're going to lay off 10,000 people.' There's a less innocent aspect of this."

Richard Aregood expresses a similar attitude. "Official bodies speak in a language that is designed to disguise what they're doing," he says. "You find if you're covering, say, a school board, that you'll end up writing in a language other than English, because that's what these people speak. I think you could probably save maybe a fifth of the poundage of a given administrative or education story just by throwing out the damn jargon . . . because none of it makes any sense to anybody. That's the reason for it; nobody understands it."

Attorneys use a form of jargon, or legal talk, that is nearly impossible for the average person to understand. Physicians and scientists also have a language of their own. Reporters must be careful to translate quotes from these sources into plain English that readers can understand—not only for comprehension but for an interesting story.

Lawyers, doctors and bureaucrats are not the only people who use a language of their own that can obscure meaning to the common person. Reporters are also often guilty.

JOURNALESE

"**Journalese** is an actual horror," says Cappon. "It's our own fault; nobody else invented this. It's not gobbledygook. It's contrived excitement. And it's fake. It's hype. You have these action verbs (as opposed to active verbs), which I hope to God we hardly ever use anymore—*rip*, *spawned*, *sparked*—this sort of thing. You have those terrible adjectives—hype adjectives as much as a 'violent explosion.' What's a 'gentle explosion'? The 'brutal murder.' What's a 'gentle murder'? This is journalese. It has the exact opposite effect on the reader that's intended. It just lulls them to sleep."

Journalese also leads to exaggeration, which substitutes poor reporting for a style some writers mistake for good writing. Most writers fall into this trap, from time to time. The good ones learn to edit out the journalese on the second draft, before the editor gets a whack at it.

GOOD WRITING: REWRITE

"You have to be willing to throw out your best line, no matter how proud of it you are—even if it feels like killing your children," says Richard Aregood. "You've got to really believe that the most important thing is making the story work."

"With computers, you can edit as you write now, in a way that you never could on paper. If I've got in my mind this editorial has to be 10 inches long, while I'm writing it, I can scroll back and I can fool around with it. I take a line here, I can justify it, and maybe bite a little **widow** off—the little tiggy part at the end of a paragraph—to save a line. There are all kinds of things you can do in the process of writing with a computer that were abysmally difficult to do on paper."

Roy Peter Clark says students could drive themselves insane worrying about a list of language rules during the first draft. He recommends getting a rough version of the story down first, and then editing as Aregood suggests.

"Don't think about the rules or tools in the drafting process necessarily," Clark says. "Apply them as soon as you can in the period of revision. That's when you literally turn to your metaphorical workshop and say, 'I need to work on this sentence. It doesn't ring true. It doesn't sound right. It doesn't feel right. It's unclear. What can I do to correct it? Put subjects and verbs at the beginning of sentences. Use active verbs. Cut out all clutter, especially unnecessary adverbs and adjectives. You'll have to develop 20 or 30 such tools which will be reliable to you over the course of time."

GOOD WRITING VERSUS GOOD REPORTING

"There's a big difference," says Jane Kirtley, of the Reporters Committee for Freedom of the Press. "I've known a lot of journalists who are excellent fact gatherers, who have the proverbial nose for news and can go out and get the story, yet they can't write worth a darn. I think good writing—developing a **voice** of your own—depends upon having heard and absorbed a lot of other voices, by reading. You can be a very good fact gatherer and a terrible writer. By the same token, the good writer may not be a very good fact gatherer."

Kirtley and others interviewed for the telecourse point out that good reporting is not worth much without good writing—or good storytelling—added to the raw facts.

Susan Antilla, of the *New York Times*, adds, "If I have trouble with the writing, it's an indication I need to make more phone calls." The reporting process isn't complete.

Clearly, you can't have one without the other.

GOOD REPORTING

In journalism, there's no room for fiction.

"Be very precise," says Steve Tetreault, editor of the Donrey News Service. "Find out exact times, exact dates. Be very detailed. Be very observant. Observe colors, how tall people are, what they're wearing, anything that can flesh out a story. The bottom line is to know what you're writing about. The best reporters know about three times more than what they put in their stories.

"Readers aren't stupid. They can tell when a reporter knows what he or she is talking about. Sweat over your stories. Go over every line, every word. From what I've read, and the seminars that I've been to, the best writers are the writers who are really slaves to their copy . . . really agonize over it. The one thing I hate to see as an editor is reporters who throw something on a computer screen, send it to me and say, 'OK, here's my story. Fix it.' That's ridiculous. . . . That reporter's not going to get too far. The best reporters are the ones who take responsibility and make sure the copy is the best as it can be before it leaves their terminal."

"I've had a lot of experience with people who write fluidly," says Jane Kirtley, "but there will be gaps in the story that they won't see. There'll be facts that they don't think are important enough to double-check. That is something that drives me mad. And it drives readers crazy. If you look at letters to the editor, . . . a very high percentage of those contain readers pointing out mistakes. Our credibility is only as good as our accuracy."

Commitment to accuracy of even the most minor of details is the bedrock of good reporting.

"If your mother says she loves you, check it out," says Terry Armour, of the *Chicago Tribune*. "It's very trite, but that's the first thing I ever heard when I was working on the city desk. Which means, even the most mundane thing, you need to check out . . . even if it means double-checking a name like Joe Smith."

Or Jo Smythe.

Sometimes, getting accurate information isn't as easy as asking the spelling of a name. Many facts are obscured, on purpose, by people who would rather hide them from the public. Some of these people even work for the public, at the local, state or federal level. For this reason, the federal government, and most states, have two separate sets of statutes—one governing documents and one governing meetings.

"There is a tremendous resistance on the part of government officials," says attorney Jane Kirtley, "to open the doors to the public. Open records, or meeting laws, are often referred to as **sunshine laws**, and it's based on a notion that government should be done in the 'sunshine,' in the open for the public to see and participate to the extent that that's possible.

"You so often hear from government bureaucrats, 'Government's business cannot be done in a goldfish bowl.' And that means, to their mind, that there are certain kinds of discussion that have to take place behind closed doors, for the public good, of course."

Lazy reporters give up when officials tell them information is not available. Enterprising reporters apply the pressure needed to get the facts. And they often

The Carole Rich textbook *Writing and Reporting News: A Coaching Method* has several sections that are relevant to this chapter of the telecourse, though they are not all packaged together in the same area. One chapter is called "Curiosity and Observation"—two traits that are essential in good reporting (pp. 77–84 in the second edition). The emphasis on accuracy in reporting as the best defense against libel cannot be overemphasized, and a bit of reading ahead to Rich's media law chapter (pp. 303–318 in the second edition) is also an important read in the study of good reporting.

"The Writing Process" (Chapter 9 in the first edition) reviews many of the same concepts introduced in the televised portion of this unit, and introduces a few new concepts, including an intriguing summary of tips on good writing from Mark Twain, William Strunk, Robert Southey, William Zinsser and others.

discover closed doors and locked document cabinets that protect the people in the government, who have something to hide.

In the telecourse program on writing and reporting, reporter Tom Philp of the *Sacramento Bee* is shown in action as he presses to get documents about money wasted by state agencies on fighting fires. Though the public officials involved resisted the release of the documents, Philp obtained the information with gentle pressure—by pointing out the reports he needed were covered by the California Public Records Act. Sometimes lawsuits aren't necessary; reporters often find that the mere existence of such laws makes obtaining some information easier.

"One of the wonderful legacies of the 1960s, the Watergate era, is freedom of information laws," says Jane Kirtley. "On the state and federal levels, governments are required to make their documents available to the public and to the press. This is an invaluable source for a journalist. As a matter of practice, when you go down to the police station to look at the docket book of the day, you don't have to file a formal **Freedom of Information Act (FOIA)** request because the police know they've got to make it available to you. I've heard reporters say, 'I never use freedom of information or records laws—they're too cumbersome.' But the fact is, they use them every day, in that informal way."

Of particular note to student journalists is the Family Educational Rights and Privacy Act, also known as FERPA. This law is often used by college administrators as a ruse to obscure information needed for school newspaper stories.

If you were one of those kids in grade school or high school who had a hard time respecting authority, journalism might be a good profession for you. Some of the same traits that might have gotten you in trouble with your teachers might make you a good reporter.

"One of the things that I see in young journalists is what I consider to be a dangerous respect for authority," says Jane Kirtley. "When record keepers say, 'No, you can't have this record,' that becomes the end of the discussion. Journalists, if nothing else, should be iconoclasts. They should be people who are always questioning and always wondering.

"If you're willing to take no for an answer the first time around, you're not doing your job. I always remind reporters who have complained to me about government officials that won't give out documents that when they as a reporter are denied documents, their readers or viewers are also being denied the documents. If you won't do it for yourself, do it for the people out there who are depending upon you to get the information."

"It was originally intended to protect students' private files," explains Kirtley. "Grades, evaluations—academic records, in other words—and that type of thing. The statute has been misused by many universities as a justification to withhold information on everything from campus crime, to campus judicial proceedings, to any kind of disciplinary proceedings that go on on campus. They claim that these are not matters of public interest or concern."

Most proceedings and documents involving state-supported campuses, however, should be available to your college newspaper through local sunshine laws.

Student reporters who are experiencing problems obtaining such information may obtain guidance by calling the Student Press Law Center (703-807-1904) or the Reporters' Committee for Freedom of the Press (703-807-2100). The Student Press Law Center is designed specifically to offer basic advice to school newspapers on a no-cost or low-cost basis.

Terry Armour, Chicago Tribune*: "In a perfect world, when good writing and reporting meet, and you find your own voice, . . . you can't top that. Then, it's time to retire."*

Richard Aregood, Philadelphia Daily News*: "If you can't say it with nouns and verbs and the odd adjective, . . . then you're not quite doing it."*

PLANTS, TREES STILL DYING ALONG UPPER SACRAMENTO RIVER: THREE YEARS LATER, EFFECT OF HERBICIDE IS A CONCERN

By Bobby Calvan
Redding
Record-Searchlight

DUNSMUIR—Plants and trees continue to die along the scenic banks of the upper Sacramento River nearly three years after the spill of a potent herbicide, according to scientists.

And it may take many years more before some species of trees begin showing improvement, according to Beth Vining, a Department of Fish and Game plant biologist taking part in a river vegetation study.

In some places, the damage is obvious. Bare trunks poke out of the river's edge, while in other areas the usual thick canopies of leaves are markedly thinner.

"We've seen continued mortality," Vining said. "It's been only a small group of trees that are showing some improvement."

While public attention has been mostly focused on the recovery of fish populations, important work is also taking place to catalog the extent of riparian damage caused by some 19,000 gallons of the herbicide metam sodium, which spilled from a de-railed train tanker on July 14, 1991.

The chemical drifted through a 42-mile stretch of the river, from Cantara Loop six miles north of Dunsmuir to Lake Shasta. During its course, the blob swirled over algae-covered rocks, eddied through pools and poisoned the water. All the while, scientists believe, plant and tree roots soaked in the herbicide and leaves absorbed the wind-driven gasses that wafted from the toxic brew.

Wildlife mortality—particularly among fish—was immediate. More than a million fish carcasses gave almost instant proof of the harm.

The full extent of damage to plants and trees, however, wasn't nearly as immediate and visible. Much of the damage may be hidden underground, in root systems and in the soil, according to Vining.

"If the roots of trees are killed," she said, "then the next year when the tree goes to foliate itself, it won't have enough roots to sustain its canopy."

It is a tree's canopy of leaves that collects the sunlight and the carbon dioxide needed to complete photosynthesis—the life-sustaining process that allows plants to grow and produces the oxygen animals need.

Plants along the river contribute to a complex—and delicate—web of life. Foliage provides habitat for critters and forage for insects, and it contributes to a long food chain.

"People should understand that the system is really fragile right now. It hasn't fully recovered," Vining said.

Cottonwoods and willows have been particularly hard hit, she said.

"Even when the chemical dissipates from the environment, trees don't immediately recover," said Craig Martz, leader of the Cantara vegetation team.

Many trees, however, weren't substantially damaged and have fully recovered.

"[Some] large trees were injured so severely that they're not going to recover. But that's not the case for all riparian species," Martz said.

To help nature along, the Department of Fish and Game is launching a massive planting of cottonwoods and willows along the river, as part of a five-year monitoring and re-vegetation program to boost the river's recovery.

As many as 3,000 trees will be planted along a 22-mile stretch of the river, from the spill site to Sims Flat campground, according to Martz.

Much of what Vining and her colleagues are doing along the upper Sacramento has never been done before.

"There's no precedent for vegetation assessment," she said. At least nothing on the scale of the upper Sacramento. "We've learned a lot of things along the way."

Vegetation monitoring is costing the Department of Fish and Game about $150,000.

The DFG, however, is still assessing how much it will cost to re-vegetate the river's banks.

With the state's lawsuit against Southern Pacific Transportation Co. already settled, attention is shifting toward restoration programs. Much of the settlement money will pay for wildlife programs, including restoration of the fishery.

FROM HOTELS TO HONEY: IT ALL ADDS UP

By Tom Philp
Sacramento Bee

For government, a big fire means bills. Lots of bills. In the 1992 Fountain fire in Shasta County, state officials cut nearly 5,000 checks.

In 1992, the California Department of Forestry and Fire Protection dutifully added the bills up (more that $22 million), filled out some forms and sent the tab to Washington, D.C. Because the Fountain fire was bad enough to be declared an official federal disaster, Uncle Sam got to pick up the costs.

When state auditors a year later decided to go through the bureaucratic remnants of the 64,000-acre Fountain fire—boxes of invoices and payments—they found that little bills added up to bigger problems.

Here's a sampling of the kinds of bills that a big fire sends floating back to government agencies behind the fire lines.

• The average American consumes about a pound of honey a year, according to the National Honey Board. Auditors would not have been surprised to find perhaps a few dozen pounds of the sticky sweet among the bills for feeding Fountain fire warriors.

But 1,810 pounds of honey?

There it was, in Special Purchase Order No. 769806.

Nearly a ton of honey.

For $7,223.57.

"The audit team could not determine reasons for the purchase," said the reviewers.

That was the first mystery.

The second was whether the honey was ever delivered and eaten after being purchased.

"The only evidence of receiving the items is the receipt itself," said the audit. There was no mention of the honey in any food inventory.

• Coffee is the elixir for fatigued fire commanders. When a purchase of 80 cans of coffee appeared as part of the Fountain fire's food bill, auditors weren't surprised.

What raised eyebrows was the timing of Special Purchase Order No. 882450—in mid-September, when almost all the fire-fighters were back home.

Forestry department staff members took exception to the coffee criticism.

"Suppression operations were not concluded until mid-November," almost three months after the first flames, the staff responded to the auditor.

• Capt. Gary Poole was perhaps the most expensive firefighter at the Fountain blaze. The Los Angeles County Fire Department billed the state $90.24 for every hour that Poole was away from home.

Poole's bill reached $21,206.40. About half went to Poole, according to the Fire Department. The rest went to the department for "overhead."

Poole was in Shasta County under a unique arrangement.

In the rest of California, state prison inmates on fire duty are supervised by the state forestry department and correctional officer. Not so in Los Angeles County, where local firefighters supervise the inmates and bill the state for all the overtime.

Los Angeles County sets its own rates. The state forestry agency and the federal government under their joint agreements have to pay them.

"For L.A. County what they pay their people is astronomically high compared to what we pay our people for a fire," said Russ Greenlee, a state forestry department accounting administrator.

How high?

While Poole was costing taxpayers $90.24 an hour, a similar rank of state forestry ranger was making $36.06 an hour, according to auditors. A Los Angeles crew foreman—$58.83. A state forestry foreman—$18.20.

Poole was there to supervise his department's supervision of the inmates.

The Los Angeles county billing rate "is prepared by our department and blessed by the county auditor-controller," said Debby

Prouty, an assistant chief of financial management for the fire department.

• Bought for the Fountain fire and now missing:

Two walkie-talkies ($399.80). Telephones ($1,005.73). Calculators ($264.90). A labeling machine ($595.94).

"It would seem proper to make sure such items are fully accounted for after the incident is over," the auditor opined.

Firefighting may conjure images of makeshift camps with tents and mess halls. but consider these Fountain fire bills: The Charm Motel in Burney—$19,520. Days Hotel—$36,079.44. Holiday Inn—$17,062.74.

• Usually in the world of government and industry, employees have to submit detailed forms to justify the expense and duration of such accommodations. but when auditors tried to figure out the hotel bills, they ran into a gap in the paperwork. In many cases, they had no idea which firefighters stayed where or for how long. "It was difficult to determine whether occupied rooms were used in accordance with policy," said the audit.

It was a direct violation of Section 7557.1 of the forestry department's Logistics Handbook. Fountain fire leaders have an explanation: "CDF currently has a lack of depth in trained and experienced Motel Technical specialists."

Translation: The department needs to teach staff members how to fill out motel forms.

That means training.

"Nobody wants to spring money for training," said forestry department chief Richard Wilson. "That is not something that the Legislature or anybody is keen on."

• Meet "Eager Beaver."

His name is Ed Brown. He was once a fire logistician for the U.S. Forest Service.

Now he is retired from the government and is a fire entrepreneur.

Equipped with a travel trailer, fax machine, personal computer and monstrous copier, Eager Beaver Mobile Officer Service heads to fires in the United States from the Canadian to Mexican borders. The rental rate for Brown to make copies and faxes in his trailer—about $900 a day. For the first 11,000 copies, that is, according to the California forestry agency.

And in the world of firefighting, 11,000 copies can be churned out before lunch.

The so-called Coffee fire this summer in Siskiyou County, for example, required about 70,000 pieces of paper a day for all the incident updates and logistics orders, said Kate Graham, a forestry department cost unit leader.

The Barkley fire in Tehama County in August was a paper lightweight in comparison—about 13,000 copies a day, said Graham. That translates into about $1,100 a day for Eager Beaver.

"I recognized the need," said Brown, who has only one known competitor—in Red Bluff. "This summer has been good to us. We have been out 30 days so far this year."

• A man hired at the scene billed the government for 244 hours of firefighting on a state forestry department fire engine. The only problem, noted auditors, was that the engine was off duty for 72 of those hours.

The explanation: The volunteer's FC-42 form didn't correspond to the CDF 61 form for the engine, whose respective instructions are outlined in Sections 3836.5 and 3836.5.1 of the *Incident Fiscal Management Handbook*.

Translation: A bloated paycheck slipped through the cracks.

PAUL SIMON IN NEW YORK: THE SINGER'S CENTRAL PARK CONCERT WAS A TRUE BIG APPLE EVENT

By Anthony DeCurtis
Rolling Stone

Paul Simon's free concert in Central Park on August 15th was one of those events that both entirely captured the imagination of New Yorkers and gave expression to all of the contradictory emotional currents that run like electricity through this city. During the weeks preceding the show, the local media unraveled the Byzantine economics of the concert, speculated about the possibility of a guest appearance by Art Garfunkel, reminisced about the success or the failure of previous free shows in the park, recapitulated Simon's lengthy and distinguished career and, as the day itself drew to a close, tracked the construction of the stage and shifts in the weather with an obsessiveness perhaps more appropriate to an impending space-shuttle launch or military strike.

That Simon's performance drew 750,000 people—an estimated figure that in all likelihood reflects the desire of even the New York City police to enshrine this as the mother of all concerts—and came off without a hitch is attributable to luck, the sheer force of Simon's will and the much-vaunted, if merely occasional, ability of New Yorkers to quit luxuriating in their problems for a moment and have a good time. And a good time was had by all.

In announcing the concert, Simon spoke of wanting to present a gift to New York City—and indeed, the perennially beleaguered Big Apple hopes to clear $175,000 once the municipal costs of the concert are subtracted from a $400,000 donation made by the Time Warner company. It shouldn't bespeak a lack of appreciation for Simon's generosity, however, to suggest that both he and Time Warner—which owns both Warner Bros. Records, the label to which Simon is signed, and HBO, which broadcast the concert live—ultimately stand to make a considerable profit from the Central Park concert. In addition to the hundreds of thousands of people who attended the show, mil-lions more saw it on HBO or heard it on the Westwood One radio network. Those numbers, along with all the publicity surrounding the performance, should ensure increased sales for Simon's current album, *The Rhythm of the Saints*—which, thus far, has failed to make anything like the commercial impact of Simon's 1986 blockbuster *Graceland*—as well as his extensive back catalog. A home-video release of the concert and a live album are also possible, according to Simon.

On a more personal level, the Central Park show, somewhat predictably, became the latest episode in the ongoing bickering "friendship" between Paul Simon and Art Garfunkel. In planning the show, Simon seemed determined, as a solo artist, to re-create, and possibly to supersede, the spectacular triumph of the Simon and Garfunkel reunion concert in September of 1981. Simon made it painfully clear from the very first that he would not be inviting Garfunkel to perform with him this time.

For his part, in a startling display of narcissistic self-abasement, Garfunkel gave a number of interviews in which he bared the psychic wounds inflicted by Simon's refusal to ask him to perform. "I'm not good enough to be invited," Garfunkel inexplicably told reporter Douglas Martin of the *New York Times* a few days before the concert, adding that Simon might feel diminished by having to share the spotlight with his former collaborator: "My guess is that it would hurt his sense of stature."

Garfunkel had visited Simon the previous weekend, but the concert apparently never came up in conversation between the two men, despite its unavoidable prominence in the news. "Paul and I communicate as if we almost know what the other one's thinking, and there's just the occasional need to clarify," Garfunkel explained in the *Times*. "I just sensed he wasn't going to ask me to sing in the show." The article went on to note that among the other activities in which he is engaged, Garfunkel is currently "reading a 1664-page dictionary from cover to cover, backward, and has reached the letter c." Garfunkel eventually went to Europe in order to avoid being in New York, or his Fifth Avenue apartment along the eastern edge of the park, the night of Simon's appearance.

Marketing ambitions, urban desperation and interpersonal rivalries aside, the concert was a delight. Backed by a supple seventeen-piece band, Simon cruised confidently through a twenty-four-song, two-hour-and-fifteen-minute set that emphasized the *Rhythm of the Saints* and *Graceland* but that also drew intelligently from his earlier solo work and his records with Garfunkel. The set was the same one Simon has been performing on his current tour, which began last November and is still underway.

Simon appeared nervous but typically in control during his opening number, "The Obvious Child," on which his band was joined by Olodum, a propulsive ten-piece percussion group from Brazil. The buoyant rhythms of "The Boy in the Bubble" loosened Simon up some, and by his next song, the dreamy "She Moves On," he seemed fully confident and at ease. Simon effectively reworked his older songs to suit the international flavor and rhythmic sophistication of his current band: "Kodachrome" was propelled by a lighthearted, rolling groove; "Bridge over Troubled Water" was souped up and given a hearty reggae bounce during the "Sail on, silver girl" section; and "Cecilia," essentially an Everly Brothers homage in the original Simon and Garfunkel

version, was completely overhauled and treated in a jauntier, more knowing fashion.

After a rollicking rendition of "Graceland" got the crowd dancing, an ebullient "You Can Call Me Al" proved the show's energetic high point. As he has throughout his tour, Simon acknowledged the song's audience appeal by performing it twice in a row rather than, say, letting his band cut loose on one extended version. Still, the musicians locked into an irresistible groove, and seeing hundreds of thousands of people shaking it up and singing the song's chorus, waving banners and smiling, spinning umbrellas and tossing balloons, was wonderfully uplifting. Simon closed the show with an impressive run of Simon and Garfunkel songs: "America," "The Boxer," "Cecilia" and "The Sounds of Silence." That Simon brought off the quieter material with such emotional power—"The Sound of Silence," in particular, became a stark, melancholy meditation—was a testament both to the superb quality of his performance and to the extraordinary respect his work can command from even this large a group of his fans.

The mutual respect Simon inspired overwhelmed even the deep-seated tensions of life in New York. Late in the show, as Simon was turning in a lovely, delicate reading of "Hearts and Bones," a large object flew out of the crowd toward the line of police officers in the front of the stage. One policeman instinctively ducked and then bent down to pick up what turned out to be a bouquet of flowers. Obviously relieved—and touched—he smiled gently and blew a kiss to the crowd. It was that kind of summer night in New York City.

ALTERNATIVE VIEWS

Brian Williams, from the *National Enquirer*, doesn't consider the writing or reporting from tabloid magazines that much different than mainstream publications. He doesn't consider it art, either. "I think there's a difference between writing and reporting," Williams says. "I think there are some people who are very good writers who can take information and polish it and form it, and there are people who get information. I think reporters are people who get information. It can always be fixed in terms of the writing. Especially for what we do. It's not meant to be art."

The approach to language use at *Enquirer* is also different.

"We're probably more Anglo-Saxon," he says. "We probably use more adverbs. We probably lead the world in using the word *wacky*. We do use more adjectives; it's more descriptive. You get into more detail. If the writing is so beautiful, if you're concentrating on the writing, we failed."

GLOSSARY

ACTIVE VERB	Any verb that is not a passive verb—not a form of "to be" (*am, are, is, were, will be*, etc.). Not to be confused with action verbs, or verbs that contrive action.
CONCRETE NOUNS	Concrete nouns are tangible objects, as opposed to abstract nouns, which indicate concepts. Example: *money* = concrete; *wealth* = abstract.
FREEDOM OF INFORMATION ACT (FOIA)	An act established by Congress in 1966 that guarantees the public (and, therefore, journalists) information to most federal government documents. Most states have similar acts that cover access to both government documents and meetings.
JARGON	Language (used by bureaucrats, scientists, politicians and other news sources) that is too specialized for the average reader to understand.
JOURNALESE	A type of jargon used by newspaper writers. Language used by journalists that would almost never be used in everyday speech.
STYLE	Style, in a journalism sense, usually means conformity of language use with the other writers in your publication. AP style is conformity to the rules of language, according to the Associated Press. Not to be confused with *style* as it is commonly used to indicate individuality.
SUNSHINE LAWS	A general term for the laws that guarantee the public access to government documents and meetings.

VOICE

A writer's development of distinctive characteristics and idiosyncrasies of language use that make his or her own writing as easily recognizable as the inflections, tone and pronunciation of speech that normally make a person's vocalized speech patterns distinctive.

WIDOW

A typesetting term that describes a situation in which one extra word of copy requires an extra line of type. In newspaper journalism, where every line is precious, a widow is considered a waste of space. If a writer edits every one-word widow from a 12-to 15-inch story, as much as an inch of copy (or an entire paragraph of space) can be saved.

SUGGESTED WRITING EXERCISES

All writers, not just students, can benefit from a steady diet of writing exercises that will improve their mastery of language and reporting. Richard Aregood, a Pulitzer Prize–winning editorial writer for the *Philadelphia Daily News*, describes an activity he participated in at a workshop for professional writers.

"I love one that Don Fry used at the Poynter Institute," Aregood says. "He would take this class of professionals (in the sense that they're getting paid for journalism), . . . assign them to go outside, pick something out and describe it in 250 words. I did that exercise; it was an eye opener. Poynter is right on the Bay with the Salvador Dali museum across the street. I picked out this abandoned union hall . . . and just set my mind to describing it without editorial input. It was really a mind-clearing kind of experience. What is this building? What does it look like? . . . And then reduce that to 250 words. It's a valuable exercise. I think about it often. I must have done that 10 years ago, but it still comes back to me when I get stuck on trying to say something in a hurry."

Telecourse students should attempt the same exercise. If your first draft uses too many words, learn to edit and prune and pluck out every unnecessary adjective and adverb. Shorten sentences by using active verbs instead of passive verbs. Use concrete nouns, and make sure that your strong writing also includes elements of strong reporting. Observe the object you are describing, and portray it accurately, without exaggeration.

QUIZ

Choose the best answer.

1 According to the writers interviewed, the prevailing attitude toward adjectives in journalism is

   a. reporters should use a lot of really strong adjectives and adverbs to describe situations with words that readers cannot see with their own eyes.
   b. reporters should be very selective and precise about adjective use.
   c. reporters should never use adjectives.
   d. none of the above
   e. all of the above

2 Passive verbs

   a. are variations of the verb *to be*.
   b. are avoided in much journalistic writing.
   c. tend to make a sentence longer and less precise.
   d. none of the above
   e. all of the above

3 Active verbs

   a. always show the news maker doing something vigorous, causing excitement much like an action/thriller movie.
   b. allow the reporter to be more specific with fewer words.
   c. are a reflection of good writing but not necessarily good reporting.
   d. none of the above
   e. all of the above

4 According to Richard Aregood, Pulitzer Prize–winning editorial writer,

   a. cutting words from a sentence should be avoided, because too much editing can hurt the accuracy of reporting.
   b. verbs and adjectives are like the muscle of a sentence, while nouns are like the hair.
   c. stronger journalistic writing comes from tight editing and brevity with words.
   d. none of the above
   e. all of the above

5 According to Peter Berkow, author of this *Student Study Guide* and producer of the telecourse,

   a. good writers are born, not made.
   b. good reporters are born, not made.
   c. both writing and reporting are skills that can be learned with hard work.
   d. none of the above
   e. all of the above

6 According to journalists interviewed for this telecourse,

   a. the best writing comes during the first draft, when the reporter feels inspired.
   b. the best writing comes under deadline pressure, when the reporter has only a few minutes to crank out a story.
   c. the best writing comes from constant rewriting and self-editing.
   d. none of the above
   e. all of the above

7 Good reporting includes

    a. attention to details, such as the spelling of names.
    b. careful checking of statistics.
    c. the willingness to be aggressive and persistent when information is hard to get.
    d. none of the above
    e. all of the above

8 According to Tom Philp, of the *Sacramento Bee*,

    a. writers who are not getting the information they want should fill out a Freedom of Information Act request immediately and pressure to receive the information.
    b. writers who know they are being avoided by government officials who have information they want should simply be polite and seek out another source.
    c. writers who are not getting the information they want should try a persistent, polite approach first, then fill out an FOIA request (or local equivalent) if that doesn't work.
    d. none of the above
    e. all of the above

9 According to Tom Philp, of the *Sacramento Bee*,

    a. government officials who try to obscure information from journalists usually inspire them to report harder and dig deeper.
    b. government officials who want to hide information are protected by so many loopholes in the law, Freedom of Information Act requests and sunshine laws are weak and meaningless.
    c. government officials almost never have anything to hide from reporters.
    d. none of the above
    e. all of the above

10 In the movie "All the President's Men,"

    a. both Bob Woodward and Carl Bernstein are portrayed as good reporters and weak writers.
    b. Carl Bernstein is portrayed as a stronger writer who helps Bob Woodward improve the style of his crackerjack reporting.
    c. both Bob Woodward and Carl Bernstein are portrayed as good writers and weak reporters who stumble on a story dished out by an anonymous source.
    d. none of the above
    e. all of the above

SELF·TEST

1 Look at the example stories in this unit and do a survey of how many passive verbs each writer uses. Which writers use the most passive verbs? Give some examples in the space provided.

2 Read the example stories in this unit and do a survey of how many active verbs each writer uses. Which writers use the most active verbs? Give some examples in the space provided.

3 Look at the example stories in this unit and do a survey of how many concrete nouns and adjectives each writer uses. Give some examples in the space provided. What do journalists think about these elements of the English language?

4 Identify the elements of strong reporting in the Tom Philp piece that less experienced and less aggressive reporters might have missed. Are there similar qualities in Bobby Calvan's reporting?

5 Though the review of Paul Simon's concert by Anthony DeCurtis of *Rolling Stone* magazine might have been included in the telecourse unit about opinion writing, it is instead included in this chapter about good writing and good reporting. Read the piece, and answer the following questions:

a. How does DeCurtis mix in solid reporting with his opinion piece?

b. Why is DeCurtis considered one of the best writers in his genre?

c. Identify elements of good writing in this piece, and compare his work to that of a mainstream daily newspaper.

BEAT
REPORTING

John Katsilometes and Adrienne Packer both work for the same newspaper. They're pretty good friends but have very different types of personalities.

John is the kind of guy who needs at least two television sets. One for ESPN, the other for ESPN2. A third would be preferable, so he could channel surf in search of ball games without missing a moment of the Japanese ice hockey and the middle-aged boxers on his other two sets.

Adrienne brings her work home too. The police radio scanner is often propped up in the room as she subliminally tracks the crime activity in her hometown. She knows the secret cop codes, and if a big arrest is going down, she's often out the door and at the scene before the subject is even handcuffed and placed in the police car. Packer is ambitious, assertive and prolific. It's not uncommon for her to have three stories on a given day's front page. If the local television reporters scoop her, she broods for days. She's even less happy if another writer at her own paper grabs a story from her beat because a bank robbery or narcotics bust broke before she arrived at work.

Katsilometes is a bit more laid-back. He sleeps late, sort of clears the pizza leftovers and empty beverage containers from the television area and saunters into work some time in the afternoon. He'll catch an evening ball game at one of the high schools and finish writing his story in time to make the midnight run. His shift will likely keep him up until the early morning hours, as he helps lay out sports pages of box scores and line items about college and pro games from around the country. After 10 hours of hard work, he'll go home to catch a few more hours of ESPN before collapsing "for a drooler" on the couch.

Though John's not as ambitious, he's fun to work with and has a knack for humor. The boss realizes this and has rewarded him with a column that allows him to express opinions once a week. It's hard to read one of John's essays without busting out with a laugh or two, even if you're not a sports fan. Other editors have noticed this, and, though he's not yet 30, his work is being picked up on the wire services by a healthy number of other newspapers. His witticisms are much needed. The sports section was once thought of as a recreational section in the paper. Today, coverage of athlete drug addiction, labor strikes and million-dollar business deals coat the sports pages with a slimy gloss of cynicism.

Adrienne's work often involves morbid news. She's written about decapitations, abandoned infants, corruption and racism. The beat covers the bizarre (an emergency room patient who swallowed ag chemicals and gassed doctors with the putrid odor) to the pathetic (drug-addicted babies)—and Packer has a reputation for covering all of it with taste and reporting excellence. Somehow, she maintains a sense of sanity and humor through it all.

Both reporters use the same techniques that you have studied so far in this course. They have good news judgment and know how to write a tight lead. Both have written so many stories, they instinctively compose copy with correct Associated Press style and classic journalistic form. Both handle interviews with confidence and know how to blend precise reporting with compelling writing.

You'll meet John and Adrienne in this unit of the telecourse, along with beat reporters who cover business, the environment, entertainment, government and health. Each has found a niche in the newsroom uniquely suited to his or her own personality.

O B J E C T I V E S

This unit is designed to show how reporters at every beat of the newspaper apply the skills learned in the first six units of the telecourse. It will also help you start thinking about which newsroom niche best suits your own personality.

B E F O R E Y O U W A T C H

This program will help you get a feeling for the different opportunities for specialization within the newsroom.

•Pay close attention to the ways journalists and teachers use the following terms in this program:

General assignment reporter	Summary lead
Police beat	Inverted pyramid
Sports beat	AP style
Environment beat	Hard news/feature news
Government beat	Ethics

W H I L E Y O U W A T C H

1. Observe the wide variation of environments and experiences that the reporters on different beats cover. Notice the glimpses you receive into the personalities of the various reporters—and see whether the personalities and the beats somehow match up.

2. Look for similarities and differences in the needs for reporting and writing skills on the different beats.

3. Imagine yourself as a general assignment reporter. Think about the different types of stories you would write about your own community, if you were given the opportunity to write about something different every day.

AFTER YOU WATCH

•**Address the following questions in your journal. Or, if there's time, discuss them in class.**

1. Assume a police beat reporter and a general assignment reporter are both given an assignment to write a series of stories about the county jail. What advantages and disadvantages would each reporter have in covering this story?

2. How would you describe the effect that the covering of a police beat on a daily basis might have on a reporter? Would working on this beat necessarily be a negative experience? How would you personally respond to the challenges of this beat?

3. What is the function of a sports page? Is there more to a sports reporter's job than writing about fun and games?

4. Which beat would be most ideally suited for your personality? Why?

5. Which of the skills addressed in this course are universal for all beat writers, no matter what their specialization?

THE LESSON

"I'm a political reporter," says Sam Donaldson. "I mainly interview politicians who serve in public office or want to serve in public office. I think these public figures who have the public trust ought to be interviewed aggressively. I believe that when public figures are interviewed on important public questions, the interviewer . . . has to press that person. Not just ask a question, and accept the answer—particularly if the interviewer is smart enough to understand the answer isn't quite right. I think the interviewer has an obligation to press that person down the line. It doesn't serve people to have a nice friendly interview with someone who holds a public office, a public trust, and not press that person fully to explain how they're managing that public trust."

Donaldson defines himself by his beat, and so does his audience. When you're channel surfing through television stations and Donaldson's face appears on the screen, you can be fairly certain some politician is getting a thorough grilling.

If you catch Larry King's face on another network, you're more likely to encounter a friendly conversation, with a politician or movie star or celebrity athlete.

"I'm innately curious; I ask what comes to mind," King says. "I listen to the answers, and follow up. That's all I've ever done my whole life. There are no rules that I know of. I've never worked with prepared questions. Never."

King describes personalities such as Donaldson and his ABC news late night counterpart Ted Koppel as news writers who do interviews.

"I'm an interviewer who affects the news," he says. "If two of us covered a fire, and the fireman came out of the fire, the first thing [the news writer] would ask that fireman is, 'What caused that fire?' The first thing I would ask the fireman is, 'Why do you want to fight fires?' The trained newsman, he's interested in why the fireman wants to fight fires, too, but he's more interested in what caused the fire. So I would describe myself, if I were in the newspaper, as the style page. The style page asks the fireman why do you want to fight fires; page one asks what caused the fire."

The same politician interviewed by both Donaldson and King would reveal completely different emotions for the viewers. King might cozy up to the interviewee and get him to admit surprisingly personal revelations; Donaldson might confront the same person, badgering him into a confession. Either show would be entertaining as well as enlightening—completely mirroring the journalist's personality. The difference between King and Donaldson illustrates the main theme of this unit in the telecourse.

Each personality can cover the news from a different perspective. And, the newsroom—broadcast or print—seems to have a niche for every type of personality.

APPLYING THE LESSONS: REVIEW

The other main purpose of this unit is to review the concepts taught in the entire course, showing how they are applied to actual work situations.

NEWS JUDGMENT

Adrienne Packer has a strong sense of what will make a front-page news story. While other reporters might ignore an incident, Packer has the instinct to identify the unusual.

"It's the best feeling in the world to get that little piece of news that nobody knows about," she says.

"An example of that is an older woman who recently wandered from a retirement home here. She was found dead outside the home something like three hours after she disappeared. The press release said, 'An elderly woman with Alzheimer's disease wandered from the retirement center. Police searched and found her two hours later and believe she died of'—I think they said a heart attack.

"But, she was found right outside the building. Which didn't make sense to me. And after talking to the investigators I called, I found out that she'd been out of the building for about three hours. The employees of the building said they'd searched for an hour before calling search and rescue, and the police department reported her missing. The police, assuming they had searched the immediate grounds, expanded the search with helicopters and all. And then came back and found her right on the back porch. Dead. So it was obvious nobody looked for her. So I called down to the Department of Health Services, which looks over the facility, and I said, 'How many other complaints have been filed against this place?' They said, 'About 17.'"

Packer's news sense said to keep investigating.

"It turns out the door this woman left through was supposed to be unlocked. She should have been able to get out, but she should have also been able to get in. It was locked. She tried to get in, and she was found dead outside the door. She couldn't get in."

Packer ended up with an important story, while "all the other news agencies had just simply said this woman had left the building and was found dead."

On the sports beat, John Katsilometes has no less of a need for a keen news sense. His stories are interesting as well as important to readers.

"I've covered two events where a fatality occurred," he says. "One was a football game. Then, last spring at a rodeo, a bull rider was killed while I was on assignment. That happened right in front of me. You make the adjustments that are necessary. It was tough because I wasn't used to asking a lot of hard questions of people who had seen somebody die, and I needed to get information out of people who were going through a lot of emotional trauma. That was new to me. It was tough, but I think the fundamentals are the same."

A more typical story for Katsilometes would be his coverage of the San Francisco '49ers football team as it prepared for an upcoming season in the 110-degree heat of summer training camp at Rocklin Community College, in rural Northern California. While all of the other reporters were competing for an interview with superstar quarterback Joe Montana, Katsilometes's news sense led him to seek out an interview with backup quarterback Steve Young. Katsilometes was rewarded with an exclusive, personal, in-depth conversation with the man who would eventually dethrone Montana, earn two NFL Most Valuable Player awards and lead the '49ers to their fifth Super Bowl victory.

The rest of the reporters in the camp ended up with nearly identical, cliché stories pieced together from mob interviews with Montana—lauding him as a future hall of famer ready to lead the team to another championship season.

The next day, Montana ripped a tendon in his throwing arm. Montana ended up sitting out the next two years with injuries. He was eventually traded to the Kansas City Chiefs, and Young became the heir apparent.

Katsilometes's story moved out on the wire and was picked up by the newspapers whose sports reporters lacked the news instincts to seek out their own interviews with Young.

Summary Lead

Hard news is the domain of the summary lead. And certainly, police reporters are expected to report many stories in a straightforward fashion. "I like having a straight lead," says Packer. But the 35 words or under, that's way too many. You don't necessarily need to include the who, what, when, where and why all in the first graph."

Sports writers need to know the summary lead style, but they use it less frequently.

"You know when you're going to be writing a feature lead for a story, and you know when you're going to be writing a summary lead for a story," says Katsilometes. "When I'm taking information over the phone, like if we have a coach who's out of town at a game calling in the results—which happens frequently on weekends—then you just take summary lead mentality. You go 'who, what, where, when, why' and do it that way. If you're on assignment in person, covering an event, the feature lead comes into play, because you're there. . . . The less insight he receives, the more likely he'll use a summary lead," Katsilometes says.

A P STYLE

"When I was in school, I always referred to the *Stylebook* on things like *AstroTurf*. Is this a brand name? Is it capitalized? But I never ever thought of using it for *burglary* and *robbery*. I used those words interchangeably," Packer says, "and it's wrong. I wasn't in the business very long before I learned that. I'm always learning things about the *AP Stylebook*. Plus the newspaper also has its own stylebook, so there's two you need to learn. I refer to it all the time."

First-time reporters on the sports desk often have to refer to the *Stylebook* even more often. "One thing that is continual with all of our interns is numbers," says Katsilometes. "When to use numerals or write out the word for the number. How not to use a number figure in a quote. In a track and field story, it's not the hundred—it's the hundred-meter dash. And in 12.34 seconds instead of 12 point three four. You'll never learn every reference in the sports section of the *Stylebook*," he says.

The best approach is to learn how to look things up. If you don't, you could lose a lot of credibility. Katsilometes gives this example.

"I was reading a magazine . . . a kind of lower-grade NFL preview. They had their 'Superbowl predictions.' It was one word all the way through—'Superbowl predictions.' They're going to tell me who's going to be in the Super Bowl, and they don't even know how to spell it?"

S TORY DEVELOPMENT/INVERTED PYRAMID

"It's important to think about the inverted pyramid and get your facts up in the news story, and not simply because the editor's going to lop off the last 3 inches," Packer says. "Because the readers need to know. And you're challenged with luring them into your story. You can't start off with fluff and then get into the facts because your readers are gone—you're going to lose them."

In the sports department, Katsilometes says, "The inverted pyramid is a concept we don't talk about very often, but it's sort of a given that you naturally write in inverted pyramid . . . especially if you're taking a phone call on it. You take the most important information and bring out the less, the more trivial, the more extraneous information at the bottom. That's a natural.

"But, if you're writing a feature story we're going to have time to lay out the story with some artwork, in advance. I think the inverted pyramid might not even be a consideration. You make the story flow. . . . You might want to end that story with some amusing anecdote that might be pertinent and can't be cut."

INTERVIEWS, QUOTES AND SOURCES

The interview situations on the police beat are often starkly different than those on other reporters' beats. They're often filled with tension and emotion.

"Calling somebody on the phone whose family member may have died in a traffic accident—I used to hate doing that," says Packer. "It's not a pleasant job. But it's surprising how many people don't mind. A lot of times they are relieved to talk to you; a lot of times they say, 'I don't want to talk to you right now.' In that case, I don't panic. I say, 'I understand. Here's my number. If you think of something to say, please call.' I'd say 80 percent of the time they call back. Sometimes they tell you to screw off. It's my job, and it stinks sometimes, but you have to do it."

Sports reporters have a completely different challenge with interviews—getting players and coaches to say something original you haven't heard in hundreds of other nearly identical stories.

John Katsilometes has heard just about every cliché sports quote imaginable.

"'Rise to the occasion' comes to mind," he says. "'We're going to crank it up a notch.' 'Play 'em one game at a time' is a classic. 'Go-to guy' is a new one. I wrote a column about my favorite cliché over the calendar year; 'Go-to guy' was the top one. It's the coming cliché. 'He's giving 110 percent'—probably the first time it was uttered, it was really a clever thing to say."

The 99th time, it's not so clever. And the 9,999th time the same cliché quote is included in a story, the readers will use the sports section to line the cat box before even reading it. Why bother? They've heard it all before.

REPORTING VERSUS WRITING

A sports beat writer sometimes has to use the same techniques of hard-news reporting as a police reporter, though perhaps not as frequently.

"A great example is a story that came out today actually on page A1—it could have been a sports story," says Katsilometes. "It was about a former basketball coach in our area who was involved in a lawsuit over his job. Turned out he had taken essentially some hush money to get out of his position because some students had filed claims with the counselor for sexual harassment.

"It required a lot of time . . . it required a lot of interviews with the students who had made allegations of sexual harassment, trying to get them to talk on the record. It also took a lot of talking to the one coach who was going to go on the record, and the accused, who wasn't. We had to go through all the lawsuit documents, and there's just layers and layers of reporting. There are times when, honestly, a news reporter is more qualified to do that—simply because they have the experience of doing it."

Packer's police beat job routinely requires investigative reporting. In the telecourse program about beat reporting, she is shown linking two apparently unrelated press releases: one about a local resident who received a gunshot wound in a remote wooded area and one about a marijuana-farm bust in the same neighborhood.

In this case, Packer pieced together the news article using information gleaned from police documents and by politely and persistently badgering the (somewhat evasive) officers on duty into admitting the two incidents were related. It was all part of a typical day's work on her beat.

APPLYING THE LESSONS: PREVIEW

Your look at the life of a sports beat writer and a police beat writer will also preview several of the topics we'll cover in the remaining chapters of the telecourse, including feature writing, special leads, news-writing ethics and media law.

FEATURE WRITING

"On a hard-news story you're set for the facts—the who, what, when, where, why," says Packer. It's too easy, she says, to lose the human aspect of it.

"When you write a feature story, you always put a little of yourself in it. You're obviously not editorializing, but your personality directs a story. You have to pick out what's important to you. What strikes you as the most devastating, or the funniest, or the most ironic. And that's your own personal decision.

"A feature story isn't all fluff," Packer adds. "You can mix news facts, and it makes it a better story. I think you have the freedom when you're doing a feature, to explain things, to give background, to describe the person. It's like a movie, how you're developing a character. But it's more challenging, because you don't have that much room to do it."

Packer remembers a particular story—about a woman murdered by her husband—that would have lost much of the human aspect if it had been reported as another dry, formula homicide hard-news story. Instead, Packer was given the opportunity to develop the woman's character for the newspaper's readers.

"This woman died, and she was a person and she had family," Packer says. "I think the feature story allows you to go back and describe who this woman is, where she grew up, what she liked to do. And it humanizes her. It's not just, 'She was beaten by her husband and now she's dead.' It was, 'This woman liked to get up in the morning, go jogging, go hang out with her friends, go take a walk on the river trail, ride her bike, go to movies, take her kids out, and then she had this problem with her husband that ultimately ended her life.'"

Katsilometes also enjoys working on feature stories. "Deadline writing is a necessity in hard-news coverage, and game stories are a necessity," he says. "If you can't do that, you're not going to get to the point where you're going to be able to be given a chance to write a lot of features.

"But, I look forward more to writing a feature because you get to spend some time getting to know your subject instead of just going out to a site, watching something happen for two hours and coming back and writing a story under a real hard deadline. I like interviewing multiple sources and getting the texture of the story to come out.

"Getting somebody who isn't usually a good quote to open up is a real challenge. You're not going to get that in a game story, because you're only going to have about a minute and a half after the game sometimes. Your questions are going to be 'Why did you call that play?' as opposed to 'What was the defining moment of your youth?' It's the nature of the questions you're asking that's going to get the information that you want. I would much rather do a feature anytime now than a game story."

OTHER KINDS OF LEADS

"The summary lead—it's for your hard-news story," Packer says. "Your feature story gives you an opportunity to experiment with different leads."

She gives this example of a mundane story that was given life by a creative lead.

"Everybody gets stuck with weather stories. And they're awful; they're boring. Well, I went out in a hail storm last year and talked to this guy. He was driving a big Budweiser truck, and he's leaning out his window, and the hail's all piled up on his windshield, and my lead said, 'Mark Hanson looked out his window guiding his way through Redding's worst hail storm,' and it went on and talked about how he made it down this hill with a truck full of beer, sliding and slipping—and what a mess it would have been if he crashed. And then I went into what brought the storm on. It was a little more interesting. Your lead is the most important part of the story. Once you get people lured in, it's a little easier to keep people into it."

Katsilometes is considered by his peers as one of the best lead writers in the newsroom. But his approach is far from academic or analytical about the process.

"You list the types of leads to me, and I recognize them, but I don't consciously think about it when I'm writing," he says. "I never do think, 'Oh, I'll do an anecdotal lead this time' or 'I will go with a gee-whiz lead' or whatever. I do consciously think about what grabbed me about what I covered. If I'm at a game story, what caught my attention, what will catch the reader's attention, what will get them into the story. And that's the best way to explain it. What will get them to read three graphs into it from the first graph. And it might be an anecdote. A lot of people don't like using quotes as a lead, but I'll do it, if I think it will work. But, I never consciously think about the various definitions of writing techniques—ever."

ETHICAL CHALLENGES

"With the police beat, there are plenty of ethical challenges," says Packer. "Dealing with the cops themselves can present a challenge, because you tend to develop a relationship with them. You talk to them every day.

"There was a sergeant at the police department that I was not friends with, but he was always really helpful and we had a pretty good relationship. He screwed up on a case."

The hard part of the job, Packer says, is knowing you're going to have to write that story about the friendly policeman who went wrong.

It's nearly identical to the ethical challenge that faces most small sports beat writers.

"Our problem has always been one of being too chummy with our sources," says Katsilometes. "I do like most of the people I deal with personally a lot, and it's hard not to become socially connected in some way. You might have to turn around and report about this serious legal problem this guy has, and he's also part of your inner circle of friends. So that I think might be more prevalent in sports than it would be on the cop beat.

"I know Adrienne is always talking about trying to fight being too close with your sources. But if you're not . . . . You know, we have the same problem here too. If you totally distance yourself from them personally and make it just completely a business arrangement, you're going to risk not being given information you would be given otherwise. I'm sure I get information because I'm personable with them and they like me more than I would be if I were just a reporting robot."

Ⓜ E D I A L A W

As a police reporter, Packer writes many stories a year that require investigative journalism. Often, her reporting makes the people she writes about look very bad—as in the example she gave earlier about the Alzheimer's patient who died locked outside of her own nursing home.

"I worry about being sued when I do stories like that," Packer says.

"I'm extremely careful about getting all the information accurate. Everything is in a report. I can go back and say, 'Look it said it here; this is public information.' I'm really careful with that. I let the editors decide if something is libel. And then they come talk to me and they ask me where I got it, and I can say 'Right here.' I rely on them; they rely on me."

"As long as everything is true, you're fine," she says. "And I go over things two, three times. If I have a touchy story where I could get sued, I'll go over it again and again. . . . People can sue newspapers pretty easily. Or at least try to."

The final unit of this telecourse will give you a thorough introduction to media law, to elaborate on Packer's introductory statements on the topic.

FINAL THOUGHTS

"The police beat can be draining because of all the tragedy," Packer says. "I used to be a really sensitive person. In my family, I was the most timid or sensitive. I was always thinking about other people's feelings. I have, in a way, become demented. My job is to write about tragedy. I don't want anybody to be seriously injured, but at the same time it's like I'm bored if nothing bad happens.

"I remember my first fatal accident. I had a hard time sleeping that night. A kid . . . he was 17 years old, was drunk, and he took a curve too fast, and rolled his car and died. When I got there he was still out on the pavement. I couldn't sleep at

The Carole Rich textbook *Writing and Reporting News: A Coaching Method* introduces beat reporting in the chapter titled "Sources of Information," with a description of how beat reporters cultivate a special rapport with the news makers in their specialty areas (pp. 87–107 in the second edition).

The Rich textbook also discusses crime and court beat reporting ("Crime and Punishment," pp. 445–477 in the second edition).

all that night. And then I talked to a police reporter friend [at another paper], and she said, 'You have to remember one thing. When people die, it's not your fault.'"

"I think any of our sports reporters could handle the cop beat," Katsilometes says. "We've had people who have worked both beats, who have gone from sports to the cop beat and back to sports and to the news desk. So it would take a little adjustment, but I think gathering information and things like that are something we're all used to.

"I think my beat is more fun," says Katsilometes. "Adrienne . . . kind of enjoys catastrophic events, natural disasters, hostage situations, bank robberies. . . . I like to cover games. We just get interested in different types of things."

In spite of the blood and tragedy, Packer thrives on her beat—and probably wouldn't have it any other way.

"If I ever get burned out on this, I don't want to be shoved off on the features beat or business," she says. "I'm not interested in that. It's too boring. I like action. I like my beat because every day I come to work, I don't know what's going to happen. I don't know if a guy's going to rob a bank and paddle down the river, or somebody is going to be shot, or if there's going to be a fire. . . . That's the challenge."

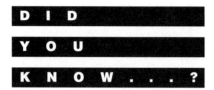

DID YOU KNOW . . . ?

Did you know that Bob Woodward was a rookie police beat reporter when he broke the stories about the infamous Watergate scandal, which eventually led to President Richard Nixon's resignation?

"In the fall of 1971, I came to work at the *Post*," Woodward says. "My first job was the night police beat. That was working from 6:30 at night to 2:30 in the morning. It was a great beat. Great example of seeing the real city, having to work fast, having to deal in facts, having to know when you don't have a fact.

"I don't really think there's investigative reporting and then reporting. I think they're all the same. And investigative reporting just means spending more time, talking to more people, going back again and again, working on this premise: 'The truth is not right on the surface.'

"In fact, the truth is often deeply buried beneath the surface. What I did was cover the police beat at night, and then go home and sleep a while, and come in in the morning and work on stories I would develop or stories that were assigned to me, and found out you could talk to almost anyone. That a great deal of records were available whenever there was a story that people were talking about. . . . I became a great believer in documents. They don't always tell the truth, but they will give you some idea of where the truth might lie.

"Certainly the crimes of Watergate were a constitutional crime of unparalleled magnitude. And what I find interesting in continuing to cover the government, is the government has changed. The people, though by no means perfect—they have their flaws—but I think they incorporated the lessons of Vietnam and Watergate."

ALTERNATIVE VIEWS

There's one job in the newsroom that's designed to be an opposite to beat reporting. The position is usually described as a general assignment reporter.

The general assignment reporter comes into the newsroom every day expecting almost anything to happen. This reporter could be assigned to work on a feature story for a week or sent immediately out in the field to cover an important breaking story.

Miki Turner, Orange County Register*:*
"Parents want to read about their kids in the
newspaper. That's why I always go above the
call of duty to try and cover high school
sports as accurately and as closely as possi-
ble—because I know that's going to sell
papers."

Debbie Wilgoren, Washington Post*: "By the*
time you finish a stint on night police, you can
cover anything quickly. From there you can
get into more sophisticated assignments, but
you've got the basics down."

The general assignment reporter can expect to overlap and even compete with the territory usually covered by a beat reporter—and for good reason.

The beat reporter could be too close to his or her sources. Sometimes, seeing the big picture is easier for somebody who doesn't look at the individual parts so closely each day.

Here's an example:

The newspaper gets a call about an all-girl's hardball baseball team that is playing in the local Little League circuit. Nobody on the sports department staff is interested in the story. Girls playing hardball? Who cares? The professional baseball team down the road is a contender, and everybody wants to read about it.

The editor assigns the story to the general assignment reporter, instead. It turns out that this is the only all-girl team to play hardball in the history of Little League—in the whole country. An additional angle is that Little League is celebrating its 50th anniversary. Though the girls win only one game all season (their last), the team gets its picture in the Little League Hall of Fame. The general assignment reporter's resulting feature story goes out on the wire to papers all over the country.

His next assignment is to write about why so many prisoners are escaping from the county jail.

YOUNG AND RESTLESS: MONTANA'S HEIR ALMOST 30 AND STILL WAITING

SAN FRANCISCO'S STEVE YOUNG CONTINUES TO BE ONE OF THE NFL'S BEST NO. 2 QUARTERBACKS, BUT HE STILL COVETS JOE MONTANA'S STARTING POSITION.

By John Katsilometes
Record-Searchlight

ROCKLIN—Tuesday was an atypical day for the San Francisco 49ers at their Sierra College training camp.

Known for its oppressive August heat, Rocklin was unseasonably cool after morning showers tempered the temperature. Since sweltering players have been losing their cool and throwing punches in earlier sessions, the lowered temperature was a welcome change.

Other training camp oddities . . .

Bubba Paris, appearing much less ponderous than at the end of last season, is being complimented on his physique. Paris is a "svelte" 320 pounds.

Bubba's pounds aren't all that is missing. Two of the team's most vocal leaders, Roger Craig and Ronnie Lott, are absent.

Keena Turner and Eric Wright are still around, but their playing days are over. Turner is an assistant in the public relations department. Wright has an undefined position which involves yelling at the defensive backs.

Even Joe Montana isn't right. Nursing a sore right elbow, Montana's passes are on target but lack zip. They wobble. Even Ralph Martini, a rookie free agent out of San Jose State, throws prettier passes.

At this point, Super Joe looks all of his 35 years and very ordinary.

Not everything is out of whack, though. Steve Young, 29 years old, is still a frustrated backup quarterback.

Some things never change.

Young is returning to the 49ers after signing a two-year contract in the offseason. Last year it was widely assumed, as he continued to languish in a backup role, Young would choose free agency and a chance to start for another team over more pine time with the 49ers.

In truth, Young says the compelling reason he stayed with the club was because team management assured him more playing time, regardless of Montana's age or health.

Also, his new two-year, $4.5-million contract is the highest of any NFL backup. But Young is more competitive-minded than financially driven.

"Obviously, I want to play more, so something had to be done," Young said following Tuesday morning's workout. "I had to know that I would be more of a part of the team."

If the 49ers' three preseason games are any indication, management's promise will be kept.

Young has played extensively in the exhibition schedule. He started San Francisco's 24–6 win over Denver, completing 9 of 12 passes for 76 yards and a touchdown. Overall, he's 26-for-33 for 234 yards and two touchdowns. He hasn't thrown an interception and has also rushed for 38 yards on four attempts.

Still, without question Montana will be the starter when the team opens its season Monday, Sept. 2, against the New York Giants.

"Everyone knows we're in a unique situation, because Joe is so great. He's almost irreplaceable," Young said. "I just have to be patient."

Young's signing put to rest talk of free agency, but perhaps only temporarily. Young will be a free agent again in 1993 and may yet choose that route.

"You can't rule anything out," he says. "If my role hasn't been defined by then, I'd have to do what's best for my career."

At this stage of his career, Young might be the 49ers' best quarterback— physically. He's more mobile than Montana and is more of a running threat. He has a stronger arm, he's younger, and more durable.

Reprinted by permission of the publisher.

But intangibles like reading defenses, performing under pressure and big-game experience still favor Montana. And, as a lock for the Hall of Fame and the team's resident living legend, Montana has as secure a hold on his position as any quarterback in the league.

Young realizes it, but continues to persevere.

"When you're in this type of a situation, you just try to keep improving and let everything else take care of itself," he said.

The flaw in that theory is there isn't much more room for Young to improve.

"Off the field, Steve doesn't have anything to improve on," 49ers offensive coordinator Mike Holmgren said. "He knows the system and he's beyond the point of working on technique and things like that."

The key is game experience.

"We'd like to see Steve in game situations over a period of time and work with him on things like recognizing alignments, picking up certain things that a defense likes to do in specific situations," Holmgren said. "But he has to start a number of games before we'd do that."

The number of games Young has started with the 49ers is precisely the issue.

He has started 10 games in four years with the team, and just one last year, a 13–10 loss to New Orleans. His finest performance was a relief effort at Minnesota in the last regular season game. He played the entire second half, completing six of seven passes for 88 yards, in a 20–17 come-from-behind win.

His overall season statistics were equally impressive. He completed 38 passes in 62 attempts (61 percent) for 427 yards with two touchdowns and no interceptions. His quarterback rating of 92.6 was better than Montana's 89.0.

Young also played in the postseason, taking over after Montana was ransacked by the New York Giants' Leonard Marshall late in the NFC Championship game. He completed one pass for 25 yards. If the 49ers had held on to win, Young would have been the starting quarterback in the Super Bowl because Marshall's hit broke Montana's left hand.

"I hope that wasn't my last chance [to play in the Super Bowl," Young says.

What keeps Young's frustration from boiling over in a Tim McKyeresque display of discontent is the parallel between Young and his hero, Roger Staubach.

"He's my idol," Young says. "I liked the way he played. He had a great command of the game and played with a lot of heart. And he didn't start for the Cowboys until he was 29."

It is a valid comparison. On October 11, two days before the 49ers play their sixth regular-season game at Atlanta, Steve Young turns 30.

BOMB SCARE DEFUSED: FUEL BLAST THREAT FORCES EVACUATION

BUSINESSES SUCH AS THE UNITED PARCEL SERVICE DISTRIBUTION CENTER WERE DISRUPTED THURSDAY BY THE BOMB THREAT THAT SHUT DOWN HIGHWAY 273.

By Adrienne Packer
Record-Searchlight

An explosive device strapped to a pipe linking four 30,000-gallon propane tanks in south Redding prompted authorities to evacuate 2,000 people for about 11 hours Thursday.

An area within a one-mile radius of where the bomb was found on Eastside Road was evacuated until bomb technicians from the Butte County and Shasta County sheriff's departments safely removed the explosive device from Campora Wholesale Propane property.

Shasta County sheriff's bomb specialist Rick Slocum found the bomb—a device about 1½ feet long wrapped with wire and rigged with a clock—after an anonymous male caller warned dispatchers of the explosive about 8:20 a.m.

The call to the sheriff's dispatchers came after three Eastside Road businesses received bomb threats early Thursday morning, according to the Sheriff's Department.

The bomb, which authorities said was "genuine," was taped to a pipeline connecting the four propane tanks that were each about 30 percent full, said sheriff's Sgt. Arlin Markham. Three more 30,000-gallon rail cars filled with propane sat on tracks only yards away.

"If these things exploded, they'd take off like rockets," Sheriff's Lt. Herb Davidson said.

Shasta County Sheriff Jim Pope said Slocum told him, "Boss, I ran from this one," after locating the bomb shortly after 8:30 a.m.

Emergency personnel from 12 agencies, including the Butte County sheriff's bomb unit, crowded a command post set up in the Sky Ranch Airport parking lot on Highway 273.

Firefighters, state Department of Transportation workers, police officers, sheriff's deputies, FBI, and Alcohol, Tobacco, and Firearms agents were served coffee and food by a Salvation Army truck while they waited for information on the status of the bomb.

While Deborah Russell, an Office of Emergency Services coordinator, appraised Gov. Pete Wilson of the situation, sheriff's deputies began evacuation of residents and businesses.

Jesse Road resident Barbara Goble said she was watching television when sheriff's deputies knocked on her door and told her to evacuate. Deputies took her to the command post and she rode a bus to the Shasta District Fairgrounds in Anderson, one of two evacuation centers.

"It doesn't bother me as long as they give me a ride back home," Goble said.

More than 50 people went to the fairgrounds, while about 10 went to the Senior Citizens Hall in Redding.

Mary Clancy remained in her home on Virginia Avenue in Anderson about a mile south of the propane tanks.

"I'm a little worried, yeah, but we're going to stay," she said.

Employees at the United Parcel Service distribution center in the 6600 block of Eastside Road abandoned a fleet of trucks and rented vans used to pick up and deliver packages to businesses.

UPS employee David Altermatt said some 8,000 packages were not delivered Thursday because of the evacuation.

Redding police helped the California Highway Patrol by directing motorists traveling south on Highway 273 to Interstate 5 from the Girvan Road intersection. California Highway Patrol Lt. Bob Hubbell worked with sheriff's deputies to divert traffic.

The bomb scare also closed Southern Pacific Transportation Co. railroad tracks.

After a six-hour search for special bomb

suits, two U.S. fire marshall suits were flown into Redding from Sacramento about 4 p.m. Slocum and Butte County sheriff's Sgt. Tom Handy met with Shasta county officials and discussed how to disarm the bomb.

The two met briefly with police chaplain Lupe Phillips to pray before making the two-mile trip from the Sky Ranch Airport to the Campara Propane site.

Firefighters staging at Canyon Road and Ox Yoke Road prepared to race to the business in case of an explosion.

After two failed attempts to knock the bomb from the pipeline by a remote-control device, Slocum and Handy removed the explosive by hand about 6:30 p.m. and placed it in the Sheriff's Department bomb trailer.

Slocum declined to discuss details of the bomb, the equipment used or how the bomb specialists finally disarmed the device.

"The more you know about what I do, the more you can circumvent what I do," Slocum said.

Davidson said sheriff's detectives will examine the bomb and conduct interviews to try to determine who set the device and why.

"By [today] they should be able to tell whether the bomb was live," Davidson said.

The Sheriff's Department is looking into whether the bomb threat was used to divert authorities while a Redding bank was robbed Thursday morning.

Propane is stored in its liquid form in subzero temperatures because it turns to gas at 44 degrees below zero. If a tank ruptures, the violently released gas ignites in an explosion and fireball, according to "Chemical Data Notebook: A User's Manual."

If that happens to a 30,000-gallon tank, "Everything within 500 feet of the tank car is in danger of being incinerated instantly, and the danger zone for the radiated heat of the fireball and the concussion from the explosion extends out another 2,000 feet," the manual states.

SPORTS BARS SEEM TO HAVE A LITTLE TROUBLE LIVING UP TO THEIR NAMES

IF A PLACE SAYS IT'S A SPORTS BAR, THEN IT SHOULD BE SHOWING EVENTS SUCH AS THE RAIDERS VS. 49ERS AND THE NCAA TOURNAMENT. THAT'S ALL WE ASK.

By John Katsilometes
Record-Searchlight

Greetings from the local newspaper, where this week we wined and dined free agent defensive lineman Reggie White in hopes that we can hire him in time for the all-employee flag football season.

We'll find something for him to do down here. Maybe a Dear Reggie advice column for affluent young pro athletes in Shasta County.

Maybe not.

It is now time for our semi-annual personal anecdote session. Pull up a stool and listen intently.

A few years ago, when I lived in the far-off land of Chico and worked for the newspaper there, I was sent on an overnight assignment to Redding. Another reporter from another town was also up here, and we arranged to meet the following day to watch the 49ers play the Raiders on television.

We ended up shooting someone, robbing the place and . . . wait, that wasn't us.

Actually, we decided to watch the game at one of Redding's self-styled "sports bars." In fact, the place claimed to be one of Redding's best sports bars.

Ha.

The place was closed. The 49ers and Raiders were playing and one of Redding's best sports bars was not open for business.

If a sports bar is not open for the Raiders-49ers, what is it open for? The collegiate lacrosse championships on SportsChannel?

Nonplused, we went to another establishment. This one even had Raiders and 49ers pennants hanging all over on the walls. There was an inflated Otis Sistrunk doll in the corner. But no game.

We walked in and stared at the big screen. Staring back was Kristy McNichol. It was some 15-year-old movie where McNichol and Tatum O'Neal had placed a bet on who would be the first to lose her virginity.

There were three people present after we walked in. Two stupefied sports fans and a beer tendress who was transfixed by the movie. The only raider on the TV was the movie's co-star, Matt Dillon, who ended up winning the bet for O'Neal.

We didn't ask to change the channel. It was best for all involved that we just leave and never come back.

I thought to that incident last week, when a few of us sporty boys went on a junket to watch the NCAA tournament game between Cal and LSU. We went to another of Redding's reputed sports bars.

The NCAA tournament was nowhere to be found.

Instead, we were greeted by a big screen carrying the Florida state high school basketball tournament.

("You're kidding! Boca Raton beat Kissemee? That was my upset special in the office pool.")

We asked the man in command if he could please switch to the NCAA tournament. I swear, he said, "Is that on?"

Yes, everywhere in the free world. Except here.

We told him what station it was on, and he said he'd try to find it. This is a local television station, he has a satellite that picks up C-Span from Iraq, and he's going to TRY and find the network carrying the NCAA tournament game.

"I have to pick up the feed from Denver," he said.

He finally finds the feed from Denver. Denver, which is about 1,000 miles away. He puts the game on the smallest screen in the house and wipes his brow. A job well done.

A woman in Wranglers walks by on her way to the jukebox.

"They'd better have Garth Brooks here," she said.

Finally, we leave.

The intent here is not to belittle the place just because it plays Garth Brooks, or because it didn't have the NCAA tournament on the mega jumbo screen, or even because it decided to show a totally meaningless high school basketball game from Florida.

All that stuff is fine, whatever. But be honest about it. Instead of trumpeting itself as one of Redding's finest sports bars, there should be some truth in advertising.

The place should be known as "Redding's Headquarters for Florida High School State Basketball and Canned Top 40 Music."

And for establishments serious about becoming a real sports bar, let's set a few guidelines:

Have a satellite dish, but also have regular cable so you can pick up feeds from around the world and cross the street.

Provide munchies. Popcorn, pretzels, trail mix, chinchilla jerky, even stale Lucky Charms will work. We get nervous watching games and have to have something to chew on other than the corner of a table.

Have games. Not just video games, but FoosBall, table tennis, shuffleboard, billiards, an Olympic-sized swimming pool, a boxing ring . . . something we can compete in at half-time or after the game. Otherwise, our competitive urges will go dangerously unchecked.

Mute the music. It's hard to enjoy the finer subtleties of an NFL game with Mariah Carey warbling in the background. John Madden is in; Casey Kasem is out.

Have a little stand filled with sports pages and sports magazines. That way we can check facts, read up on the game we're watching, scan box scores or swat our neighbor.

Of course, after this, I know of a couple places that probably won't be passing out newspapers.

SUGGESTED WRITING EXERCISES

In the first six weeks of this course, you studied the rudimentary skills needed to become a beat reporter. Now, let's work on those skills in a real-life setting and compare your work to that of the pros. Pick one of the beat reporting assignments listed here, attend the event and write up a real story. If possible, get an assignment from your school newspaper or local community newspaper to match up with this exercise. Your goal should be to actually get published as often as possible. The realities of deadline pressure and public feedback on your work can't be duplicated with mere homework.

Environment 1: Pick a local sporting event, and attend in person. Your assignment is to write a story about the outcome. Be sure to include quotes from the participants, fans and anybody who could add insight and interest to the story. Compare the results of your story to the story about the event published by the local newspaper. (It's best to pick an event that is likely to be covered by other media—your college football, basketball, baseball, track, swimming, hockey or volleyball team might make a good choice. If you can't stand sports, try something different, like Special Olympics or a body-building contest.)

Environment 2: Select a local government meeting, and attend in person. Your assignment is to write a story about the outcome. Be sure to include quotes from the participants, including government officials and those in the audience who spoke up. Often, these meetings are dull until a public hearing comes up on the agenda. If the hearing is about a controversial issue, the participants will be quote machines. Don't be shy about approaching them after the meeting, to get better quotes. Compare the results of your story to the story about the meeting published by the local newspaper. For best results, pick the kind of meeting (city council, board of supervisors, school board, etc.) that your newspaper covers regularly. Other good alternatives would be student government or college board of trustees meetings (if they don't have a history and reputation of being exceedingly dull and uneventful).

Q U I Z

Choose the best answer.

1 According to Helen Thomas, UPI White House reporter, on her beat

   a. a reporter learns how to treat an important person like the president with respect.
   b. it is the duty of a reporter to ask tough questions, to keep the president honest.
   c. the feature lead and feature story work the best.
   d. all of the above
   e. none of the above

2 If Larry King and Sam Donaldson were to interview the same news maker on different nights,

   a. Donaldson would probably press the news maker with tough, probing questions.
   b. King would probably try to bring the personality of the news maker out with softer, more indirect questions.
   c. both interviewers would probably be able to get interesting interviews from different angles.
   d. all of the above
   e. none of the above

3 The summary lead

   a. is used as a staple for hard-news stories on the police beat.
   b. is used in sports, especially when the game results are called in on the phone.
   c. would probably not be used in a sports feature story.
   d. all of the above
   e. none of the above

4 According to the *AP Stylebook*,

   a. burglary is the same as a robbery.
   b. a robbery is theft with violence.
   c. a burglary is a theft with violence.
   d. all of the above
   e. none of the above

5 According to the *AP Stylebook*, the following is correct:

   a. The '49ers are the *Super Bowl* champs.
   b. The '49ers are the *Superbowl* champs.
   c. The '49ers are the *super bowl* champs.
   d. all of the above
   e. none of the above

6 Sports reporter John Katsilometes said that writers on his beat

   a. should beware of the cliché quotes delivered by coaches and players.
   b. often have to deal with grief.
   c. never have to deal with hard news, such as death or drugs.
   d. all of the above
   e. none of the above

7 According to police beat reporter Adrienne Packer,

a. "It's important to think about the inverted pyramid and get your facts up in the news story."
b. when talking to grieving news sources, "A lot of times they are relieved to talk to you; a lot of times they say, 'I don't want to talk to you right now.'"
c. "Dealing with the cops themselves can present a challenge, because you tend to develop a relationship with them."
d. all of the above
e. none of the above

8 Feature stories were characterized by reporter Adrienne Packer in the following way:

a. "A feature story is a rare event on the police beat. You have to convince your editor."
b. "Feature stories are considered fluff on this beat."
c. "A feature story isn't all fluff—you can mix news facts, and it makes it a better story."
d. all of the above
e. none of the above

9 Police beat reporter Adrienne Packer characterized her job in the following way:

a. "The police beat can be draining because of all the tragedy."
b. "I like action. I like my beat because every day I come to work, I don't know what's going to happen."
c. "I don't want anybody to be seriously injured, but at the same time it's like I'm bored if nothing bad happens."
d. all of the above
e. none of the above

10 Sports Reporter John Katsilometes characterized his job in the following way:

a. "There's never any stress."
b. "Pro sports is fun; prep sports are boring."
c. "I could never handle the police beat; I wouldn't know where to start. It requires completely different skills."
d. all of the above
e. none of the above

BROADCAST NEWS WRITING

By this point in the telecourse, you've studied traditional techniques of newspaper journalism, including such basics as hard-news leads and the inverted pyramid style of story development. You've also been introduced to newspaper language use and interviewing techniques. By now, you probably have your first assignments for hard-news stories to be written for class or (if you're lucky) for the school newspaper.

While you're working on those first story assignments, we'll take a detour in the next couple of chapters to introduce writing styles for broadcast news and public relations. Much of what you see and hear will be a review of what you learned in the first seven weeks. Both broadcast news writing and public relations writing use many of the techniques we've already studied, though each career track requires specialized writing skills.

Broadcast news writing is affected by the technology that accompanies the words. The most successful writers are well aware of this. In Unit Eight, we've interviewed several broadcasting industry legends as well as a number of younger, rising stars. Though a half-hour program can only introduce this writing style, it can also show how this entire course will eventually help you build necessary skills, should broadcast news become your career choice.

Any frank discussion of broadcast news, even one that primarily exists to introduce you to the writing style, will include some criticism of the medium. We conclude Unit Eight with a very brief section that touches on what the industry's toughest critics have to say about broadcast news writing. Those of you who are taking the course with a group can use this topic as a starting point for a class discussion; those of you taking the telecourse at home are encouraged to address the strengths and weaknesses of broadcast news in your journals.

OBJECTIVES

Now that you have had seven weeks of being trained to be a newspaper journalist, this lesson will help you view a news story from a broadcast news writer's point of view. If you are contemplating a career in broadcast news writing, this chapter will help you adapt the lessons learned in this telecourse to that writing style. The program can also help you become a better—and perhaps more demanding—consumer of broadcast news.

BEFORE YOU WATCH

Television and radio newsrooms are full of jargon. It will help to at least understand the concepts, if not the technical terms, if you some day apply for an internship or job in broadcast news.

•Pay close attention to the ways the featured broadcast journalists use these terms:

Actuality	SOT (sound on tape)
Sound bite/Head bite	Stand-up
Ambient sound	Reader
Nat sound	Package
Intro-lead	Tape

WHILE YOU WATCH

1. Think about ways you can apply what you have already learned in this course if you were to adapt an already written newspaper story for a radio or television news report.

2. Look for ways television news writing differs from radio news writing.

3. Listen for ways radio news writing differs from print news writing.

4. Watch for differences in reporting techniques, as expressed by journalists who work for local versus network news organizations.

5. Notice how the concept of the news peg or nut graph in print journalism shows up with a new name in broadcast journalism.

6. Notice the subtle differences in attitudes toward news writing expressed by reporters who work for commercial versus non-profit news organizations.

AFTER YOU WATCH

•Address the following questions in your journal, or, if there's time, discuss them in class:

1. Can a television or radio story communicate as much as a newspaper story? Why or why not? How do well written and poorly written broadcast news stories differ?

2. What are the advantages and disadvantages of gathering and editing quotes in print versus broadcast journalism? What do you think about Bruce Lang's statement that quotes in television news can't be edited without the viewer noticing? Did you notice that Lang's statement was edited on the video?

3. Do you agree with Dorothy Rabinowitz and Neil Postman that dependence on broadcast news adds to a growing national illiteracy problem? Why or why not? Are there ways broadcast journalism can enhance literacy? What is your feeling about their other criticisms?

THE LESSON

INTRODUCTION

Talk show host Larry King, of Cable News Network television and the Mutual Broadcast radio network, has been the interviewer of choice for presidential candidates through several elections. He posed the following question to students:

How is television news different from print?

American newspaper traditions such as the summary lead and the inverted pyramid evolved during the Civil War era. But, King asks, "How would the Lincoln/Douglas debates have played on television?

"To me, Lincoln was starkly handsome," King says. "But . . . he had a mole on his face and was tall and thin. If the camera doesn't like him, he doesn't get elected."

Whether we like it or not, broadcast journalism has changed the world. In many ways, it has even changed the way journalists write for newspapers.

CBS television news correspondent Russ Mitchell suggests that a television reporter can only highlight the news of the day and cannot compete with newspaper journalists when it comes to thoroughness. In Mitchell's opinion, national newspaper *USA Today* "is a newspaper for the TV generation," serving a similar function.

Gene Policinski, an editor for *USA Today*, agrees, noting the national newspaper has influenced many smaller regional dailies to write short, punchy stories that don't jump from one page to another—while newspapers like the *New York Times* and the *Wall Street Journal* endorse a more traditional approach. "Newspapers have to learn to compete with television news," he says.

WRITING FOR BROADCAST

Mitchell Stephens, author of the textbook *Broadcast News*, says, "I've done both kinds of writing—print and broadcast—and I find in some ways, broadcast writing is more exciting. First, you're sort of stunned at the thought of only having four or five sentences to tell a really important story. But when you get it right, it's a satisfying discipline. It forces you to think about what the most important part of that story is. And, your language has to be perfectly efficient.

Larry King: "I love reporters, and the printed word will never leave us. I love the feel of the newspaper, the texture. I like to pick it up in the morning. But, because of CNN and C-SPAN . . . there's no headline . . . no 'EXTRA.' The biggest problem a newspaper faces today is getting young people to read it."

"A story that might be told in 400 to 700 words in a newspaper might be reduced to 20 seconds, which is 50 to 75 words in a broadcast story. In newspaper stories, you have to whittle down vast collections of facts to ensure efficient stories. But in broadcast journalism, you have to whittle away a lot more, because those stories have to be even shorter to fit in air time. In newspaper, stories are measured in column inches. In broadcast, they're measured in seconds, and you don't get a lot of seconds to tell the news."

Skillful broadcast writers allow pictures and sounds to compensate for the shortage of words.

LEADS IN BROADCAST NEWS

Both print and broadcast journalists must capture the attention of the news consumer as quickly as possible. Print journalists traditionally have tried to do so by cramming the "Who, What, When, Where, Why and How" of a story as close to the top as possible.

Broadcast journalists have less time and fewer words, and often compensate by focusing on the most important element of the five W's and the H. The other elements follow, often giving the reporter the bulk of the material necessary for what little time there is to complete the story.

Elizabeth Arnold, of National Public Radio, explains: "In print, the writers tend to top load it . . . trying to put everything in the first paragraph, and to section out each thought in following graphs. In radio, you don't have to do that. Instead, you're pulling listeners along. Introducing new thoughts is a good way to hold them, instead of trailing off. In radio, you can surprise the listener and introduce questions."

You should read the accompanying chapter in Rich's book, *Writing and Reporting News: A Coaching Method* about broadcast news writing (Chapter 15) when you view this unit of the video program. Anything you can learn about editing or shortening your sentences to make them communicate the most with the fewest words will help when writing broadcast news.

Pay special attention to the section on story development in Chapter 15. Notice that circular development is a lot more popular in broadcast journalism than it is in print journalism. Finally, read Chapter 13, "Storytelling and Feature Techniques." As Bernard Goldberg of CBS News said, in television a reporter is looking at his audience "telling them something . . . and it has to be a story, or they won't stay interested." This is very similar to the "tell-a-friend" technique advocated by Carole Rich, author of the textbook.

The textbook also has some very effective examples of active and passive verbs. Reading these examples will help reinforce why broadcast journalists prefer using active verbs and avoid using passive verbs.

Television news writers tend to agree. Notice that Harry Smith's "give a darn" line bears a lot of resemblance to another technique in print journalism—the "nut graph." The lead sentence in broadcast news is quite similar to the feature lead, which we will study in Unit Ten.

STORY DEVELOPMENT IN BROADCAST NEWS

The inverted pyramid is out; circular development is in.

Often, sound bites, ambient sounds or taped packages take the place of transitional phrases in the text of newspaper journalism. The "reveal," as explained by Bernard Goldberg, was originally a phrase used for development of story lines in plays and movie scripts. In a way, this phrase illustrates how television news borrowed from show business and the industry of "moving pictures," as well as the traditions of print journalism.

Joyce Davis, of National Public Radio:
"When print journalists first try radio,
they use way too many words."

STORY ENDINGS IN BROADCAST NEWS

Hard-news stories in newspapers are written as if they don't have an ending. In a sense, they don't; most important stories could simply end with the phrase "To be continued." The next day's newspaper almost always includes a follow-up. As experienced print journalists know, writing with the inverted pyramid makes a lot of sense for other reasons, too. The newspaper writer who labors over a clever ending rarely sees it get to print.

But writers who originally worked in print journalism such as Joyce Davis, of National Public Radio, have to retrain themselves to think about endings. Davis says, "Sometimes (in radio) you save some of the best for last; you never do that with newspapers, because you always worry about the end getting chopped off. That's the first thing you learn. But with radio you have the luxury of . . . doing a complete circle if you'd like."

Charles Kuralt, the legendary and now-retired writer, reporter and anchor for CBS, says he gives equal attention to the first sentence and last sentence of each story, because the last sentence is the one that television reporters leave the viewer thinking about.

Bernard Goldberg, also of CBS, has a similar approach. "I pace throughout the story, because," he says, "I think of it as if I'm sitting around a campfire, and I'm telling a story and I want to give the punch line of the story at the end, not the beginning."

Most broadcast news writers agree. In this style, the ending is as important as the beginning. And, if possible, it should be connected to the beginning, in case the viewer tuned in during the middle of the story.

WRITING WITH IMAGES

Charles Kuralt advises students, "Never write a sentence that would fight the picture. The picture is so strong, you should always write the sentence so it

Sound bites allow viewers to see the source's emotions, according to Steve Kroft, of "60 Minutes." Extreme close-ups emphasize this effect.

Good television reporters never write news copy that will fight the picture, according to Charles Kuralt, recently retired from "CBS Sunday Morning."

complements rather than struggles with picture. Ideally, the viewer shouldn't notice writing at all if the reporter is doing his or her job correctly."

Watch a television newscast with the sound turned off and see if the broadcast still communicates the essence of the news without the use of words.

Many skillful television reporters believe that the words should only supplement the video images. They consider it redundant to waste words describing what the viewer is already seeing.

"The difference between television and print is we're a visual medium," says Sam Donaldson, of ABC. "The pictures are what drive us. They ought to. Sometimes people say to me, meaning to be derogatory, 'Ah, this is nothing but captioned pictures.' Right. That's my job. If I wanted to write and be a great writer . . . I would try in print. If I wanted to write a script that had nothing to do with pictures, I'd be on radio. But television is bringing people into the event as if they were there."

There are alternate points of view, especially from broadcast journalists who specialize in "magazine" style television pieces or investigative journalism.

Steve Kroft, correspondent for the immensely successful "60 Minutes," says writing to the pictures is a "standard way of approaching television news. Ideally, you would write to the pictures and you don't have to say whatever the pictures are saying."

Kroft says that, in writing for his show, the emphasis is on the words, not on pictures: "You could listen on the radio and you would understand (the stories) as clearly as you would without the pictures. It's a very distinctive '60 Minutes' style."

However, Kroft also says that television journalism has a big advantage over newspapers, because the camera can let the viewer see, with tight face shots, whether the news maker is lying or uncomfortable, whereas print journalists are just "stuck with the words."

One distinctive "60 Minutes" production trademark, the extreme close-up shot, is reserved for the most emotional part of an interview. This technique is often used when the "anti-hero" of an investigative piece confesses or denies guilt. The show also uses the same "emotion shot" when celebrities or "good guys" in news stories reveal their innermost feelings.

WRITING WITH SOUND

The best radio journalists use sounds to create images for listeners. But Claudio Sanchez, of National Public Radio, warns, "It is too easy for beginning radio news writers to use ambient sound gratuitously." If a news situation does not present natural sound to help communicate the event, words alone will have to suffice.

Though tempting and easy, it is also considered unethical to use stock sound effects recordings to stage the sounds of a news event.

Beginning radio reporters should heed these warnings about overuse or mis-use of natural sound. Still, a skillful radio journalist must learn to capture atmosphere for a news story with a microphone, recording ambient sounds, as a television journalist can with a camera, recording images. Also, taped quotes or "actualities" from the news makers themselves often communicate much more emotion than the same words printed on paper.

INTERVIEWS IN BROADCAST NEWS

Though this telecourse has an entire program on conducting interviews, we should point out that broadcast interviews pose a unique set of problems. Spontaneous answers usually result in the best news stories, but the simple act of inserting a microphone or a camera between the reporter and the news maker can inhibit a news source.

Charles Kuralt, perhaps the best-traveled interviewer in broadcasting history, has this advice:

"It is important not to rehearse, even slightly. When you pull up into the yard of a man who has a windmill collection, he knows why you're there. And natural-ly, he comes out of his house and starts talking about windmills. I finally got to the point of saying, 'Look, let's not talk about it yet. Because, I don't even know you yet. I don't even know what the weather's been like around here for the last week.' So get off on the weather, or his family life, or how long he's lived in this neigh-borhood or just anything except the subject of the story for that short time that it takes the camera crew to get ready to really go to work. Because, if you talk about the subject of the story before the camera's rolling, he's gonna tell you all the good stuff. And it's never quite as rich or as eloquent, as fresh, the second time.

There should never be a second time; you should always be sure you're rolling the first time that the guy tells you. The essence of a good interview is that the reporter is genuinely curious about it."

In all fairness, it should be pointed out that many of the broadcast journalists interviewed for this program—especially those working for National Public Radio or "60 Minutes"—have the luxury of creating the television and radio equivalent of newspaper feature stories. In most broadcast hard-news pieces, the quotes are limited to very brief "sound bites." Many reporters would consider a 10-second quote too lengthy. Some networks—notably, during elections—are trying to avoid reducing important news events into sawed-off, slogan-like quips. Still, broadcast news quotes tend to be very short.

Recorded quotes in radio are called "actualities," and Elizabeth Arnold admits the use of the sources' words at National Public Radio is very different from commercial radio and television. "I don't call them sound bites," Arnold says. "In fact, when I go to an interview and they say to me 'How long do you want the sound bite?' I go 'Wait a minute. Remember, this is NPR. Please ramble on.' Because, I don't like them to give their sound bite. After a while it just becomes so old and overused, and you turn on the news, and there he is saying the same thing on Ted Koppel, or ABC News in the cab when you're going home. So I tend to dissuade people I interview from giving me quotes as sound bites.

"After I do an interview, I come back with all my tapes, and I listen to it. And if there's something that absolutely knocks my socks off, that really makes the point well, I will use that. If there's something that is generally a trite soundbitey kind of thing, I generally don't use it. I'm looking for the people to tell the story and not me. So even if something is 60 seconds long—which is unheard-of in television or commercial radio—say it's an anecdote, or it's just a better explanation than I myself could give . . . I'll generally take that."

Joyce Davis has one final suggestion for getting a great quote: "I had to learn one technique, and that is keeping your mouth shut! It is amazing when you shut up how much you get. My normal way of interviewing someone would be to sit down, and ask you a question, and as soon as you shut up, give you another one. I tried with the radio . . . to let you answer, and then say absolutely nothing. That was very hard. The person will come out with the deepest thing if you just let them fill those silences."

LANGUAGE USE IN BROADCAST NEWS

DEVELOPING A VOICE

Almost every broadcast journalist interviewed for this program emphasized that language in broadcast news has to be conversational. Somewhere along the line, somebody has to read the words out loud. If the words don't roll off the tongue gracefully, listeners will simply hit the channel changer.

Elizabeth Arnold, of National Public Radio, says that the first thing a writer notices when switching from print to radio "is that you can only say so much without taking a deep breath." The result, Arnold explains, is that radio news writers have a tendency to write shorter sentences. She also says most of the best broadcast writers read the copy aloud as it is being composed. "That way, you can hear and sense where you've got long sentences, where things should be broken up and where you get into sort of a pattern. You learn how to mix it up more when you're writing for radio. Because, you can lose your beat and you'll lose a listener."

Print writers often talk about developing a "voice" that readers can recognize in text. This concept is even more important in radio or television news, because the writers are literally composing for voices on the air—either their own or the voices of the anchors who will read their news copy.

"In radio especially, or any of the semi-performance types of medium, you have to develop your own style," says Joyce Davis, of National Public Radio. "I can sit down with a reporter and write a wonderful script . . . and when they go to read it, it's not them. The best people in this business develop something that will let them express themselves. If you can't allow yourself the freedom to be yourself, and to write for yourself, and to develop your own voice, I don't think it's going to translate to the listener."

Bernard Goldberg, of CBS News, believes that developing a voice is just as important in television news writing. "You have to be a free spirit," Goldberg says, "if you're going to be a good writer. And on television, that's very difficult. What you wind up doing, is you say, 'I can't talk too long, it's going to be boring, so I'll talk just for 10 seconds and then I'll throw in an interview. And then I'll talk for seven more seconds and throw in some natural sound.' It's not what a writer should be doing. A writer should be able to let him- or herself go."

Reporters who are not part of the dominant culture—those who might be members of a minority group or have a regional accent—all work out different ways of developing a broadcast voice.

Joyce Davis, of National Public Radio, offers this somewhat controversial advice to other African-American journalists: "We still have to learn to use the mainstream language. That's what I want to tell you African-American listeners. Yes, you have to learn to communicate through the mainstream language. We all know there's another way; we all know there's another language. If you're going to fit into this business . . . you've got to find a way to express yourself so that everybody will understand you. Because, the audience is primarily white America here."

This is not a unique phenomenon for African-American reporters. Larry King, of CNN, had to do essentially the same thing with the Jewish-Brooklyn accent of his youth. Other broadcast reporters interviewed for the program said it was a challenge to temper southern and East Coast accents while still developing or maintaining a personal on-air "voice."

LANGUAGE STYLE

Time constraints in broadcast news typically require that the equivalent to a 400-word newspaper story be reduced to about 40 words. This requires an economy of style that demands precise verbs, concrete nouns and fewer adjectives.

Bernard Goldberg, CBS News: "You have to be a free spirit if you're going to be a good writer."

Ted Clark, of National Public Radio, says, "I think that adjectives often diminish the pure meaning of the word, especially if it's a powerful word. High hope? Hope is already high. Time is limited. Every unnecessary adjective is a word that takes time away from the story. I would leave almost all of the adjectives out."

Bernard Goldberg, of CBS News, says the same holds true for television. "I find that understatement is better than overstatement. Less is more. The best writing is elegant. It's simple. It's clean. You don't need a lot of adjectives. You just want to say something simply and get people to think about it."

Broadcast reporters avoid unnecessary adjectives or adverbs by using concrete nouns and active verbs.

Charles Kuralt says, "Try to avoid the passive voice. Provide short, active sentences. I try to keep my writing as simple as I can. Just plain old declarative sentences seem to serve best in this field. I don't mean that it has to be without feeling or without emotion. But it shouldn't ever be scholarly sounding, or complicated."

Ted Clark, of NPR, says, "I think the verb is the neglected part of the English language. We focus so much on concepts, and nouns and adjectives that if you choose just the right verb, it makes the sentence clear and powerful. Instead of saying 'criticized' you could say 'condemned.' Instead of saying 'praise' you could say 'extoll.' It just takes a little extra time to find the verb that communicates the feeling more powerfully than the one that comes first to mind."

Joyce Davis adds one last piece of advice, which might be the only point ever universally accepted by English teachers, print journalists, broadcast journalists and news consumers: "No clichés. Just get rid of them. Don't even try. Forget it; it doesn't work."

WRITING AND REPORTING

Rick Kaplan, executive producer of ABC television's "World News Tonight," says, "Good writing is good writing . . . whether it's newspapers or television. But, you have to be factual . . . your pieces have to be substantive and eye opening."

Kaplan and others who care about the credibility of television and radio news work toward using colorful language and gathering eye-catching images.

However, they also feel a responsibility to ensure that the language is accurate and precise and that the images tell a true story.

"It's the difference," Kaplan says, "between solid reporting and nonsensical television."

THE JARGON
OF BROADCAST NEWS

Understanding the various terms for broadcast news stories will come in handy at this point. News departments in different markets may have different names for the same things, but most of this jargon is universally applicable. Don't worry too much about memorizing a list of fancy terms; understanding the concepts is more important.

QUOTES IN BROADCAST

In broadcast journalism, you'll have video or audio of a news source's exact words. Most radio stations refer to their audiotape quotes as **actualities.** In television, these quotes are known as **sound bites**. Some stations call them **head bites**, because what you see is a "talking head." Essentially, all of these are terms for what print journalists call direct quotes. Because of the technology involved, broadcast journalists seldom use indirect quotes; when they do, the attribution ("Mayor Smith said") comes before the quote.

STORIES FOR ANCHORS

A **reader** is simply a written news story that the news anchor reads without moving video images to accompany it. Often, a still graphic that illustrates the topic of the story is shown over the anchor's shoulder.

A VO (or voice over) is usually a short story (approximately 30 seconds) that the news anchor reads over video. The pictures must match the copy, so, prior to the newscast, the reporter must edit the video in time with the words. Often, the person who writes the script is not the anchor, so the writer must take care to pace the words to fit the reader's style.

SELF-CONTAINED STORIES

Reporters also appear in their own stories, usually on tape. These stories are edited before the news show airs and played after a brief introduction by the anchor. The edited stories include narration by the reporter—the reporter track—over video images. The images are often called **B-roll**, a television production term that refers to the tape on a second videotape recorder (the "B" deck) used in editing two sources to a final master tape.

SOT (short for sound on tape) can refer to ambient sounds or the words spoken by a news maker. **Ambient sound** (also called **nat sound**, short for "natural

DID YOU KNOW . . . ?

Did you know that broadcast journalists prefer to use present-tense verbs? These verbs simply make the report seem more immediate. Broadcast journalism can be live, from the scene. If it isn't, the story is usually only a few hours old. By contrast, print journalists almost always write in the past tense, because the event usually happens many hours—or days—before the newspaper or magazine is published. (One exception would be an advance story.)

Did you know that if a reporter must quote a source, and no tape of the quote is available, the attribution verb is used first? Otherwise, the listener might get confused, thinking that the quoted material was actually the reporter's words.

Did you know that the practice of avoiding the "stutter quote" in print has a counterpart in broadcast journalism? It is considered bad writing—and a waste of time—for the reporter's script to say what a source is going to say, or to repeat what a source has said before or after the sound bite is used.

Did you know that many broadcast news writers have to be careful to avoid using too many words containing the letter "s" in the same passage? Sibilant sentences sound suspiciously sizzley in small-sized stereo speakers.

Did you know that broadcast news writers often try to place the subject and verb as close together as possible? Such placement helps prevent confusion when the listener hears a sentence.

sound") is especially important in radio, but it is also used in television. This can be the sound of anything—from sirens to breaking surf to chanting protesters—to illustrate what was going on around the news event. Radio news reporters use sounds to paint the pictures the listener can't see; skillful television reporters supplement their video images using the same techniques.

A **package** is a complete story on tape, where the reporter has assembled all the elements—the reporter track, head bites, the B-roll and the SOT. Often, the reporter also appears on tape in the story, talking into a microphone—usually at the scene of the event. This is called a **stand-up**. If the story ends with the reporter talking, the reporter uses a **standard out-cue** (**SOC**), usually something along the lines of, "Reporting live from East Biggs, this is Mike Donnelly from KHSL." The SOC alerts the anchor to start reading the next story. In breaking news, the reporter may be live on the scene; in this case, the stand-up is more spontaneous and often gives the viewer a glimpse of the news as it unfolds behind the reporter.

Mike Donnelly, KHSL: "It's an art, getting a source to be comfortable on camera."

A **VOSOT** or a **VSV** is a combination of a VO and a package, where an anchor reads over video and then gives way to an SOT, which is usually a head bite or a piece of an interview. The timing of the anchor's script is essential in this type of story, because if it is too long, the anchor's final words could be buried under the sound of the SOT.

EXAMPLE STORY

The following three pages contain the actual raw copy for Mike Donnelly's Farm City Week story, which was the example used in Program 8 to show how television news reporters write for a "package."

Note the points in the script where Donnelly has written copy for the anchor to read. Donnelly's rough copy for the ad-lib, live stand-up includes a cue for the studio crew to roll the package (PKG IN on the script). Note that the times for various points on the package are indicated on the script. The TAG means Donnelly comes back in, live, with a final ad-libbed stand-up, which ends with a standard out-cue. (Donnelly's rough notes for the package are included. Because reporters usually edit their own packages, nobody else usually has to be able to read this script. Spelling, typing and neatness are not too important.)

Donnelly allowed us to use the rough copy to illustrate how he conceived the story discussed in the program. Notice that Donnelly's script calls for his own words to read as voice-overs with B-roll images of cows and other generic agricultural B-roll images pulled from the television station's farm news file tapes. In between the voiceovers, Donnelly indicates several SOT sections (sound on tape quotes) that feature talking head shots of a Farm Bureau "lady" and a Farm Credit "dude." Total time (TT) is indicated as 1:53, which allows the producer to fit the package into the rest of the news broadcast.

Slug __FARM CITY__ Writer __M.D.__

Date __1/7/94__ Show __6:30__

LIVE/PKG

Anchor's script ↗

THE NORTHSTATE'S MOST
IMPORTANT INDUSTRY COULD BE
FACING A DRAMATIC TURN FOR
THE BETTER THIS FARM CITY
WEEK.

AFTER SIX YEARS OF
DROUGHT, AND THEN A PAINFUL
RECESSION...THE AGRICULTURAL
INDUSTRY COULD REBOUND WITH
THE HELP OF INTERNATIONAL
TRADE AGREEMENTS.

SPLIT SCREEN IN _____

CHANNEL 12'S MIKE DONNELLY
IS AT A FARM/CITY WEEK
CELEBRATION IN CHICO RIGHT
NOW.

HE JOINS US WITH A LIVE
REPORT...MIKE?

TAKE LIVE VAN _____

12 LIVE/MIKE DONNELLY
CHICO

(AD LIB)

(MORE)

Page _____
Talent _____

⊕ Channel 12 News/ KHSL-TV 12 Chico, CA 95927

```
                      2222
  Slug FARM CITY ____ Writer M.D. ____
  Date _____ Show _____        ...BUT IT CERTAINLY IS        Page _____
                                                                          Talent _____
        Roll cue      ⟶                 GOOD NEWS, FOR NORTHSTATE

                                             FARMERS.
             PKG IN _____

  12 BUTTE COUNTY/NEWSFILE  :00

  MARGE TAYLOR/BUTTE COUNTY FARM BUREAU :28

  JIM GRIZZWOLD/FARM CREDIT UNION 1:14

  O.C...COMMUNITY CONCERNS."

  TT 1:53

                TAG _____           (AD LIB)

                                             DEAN, TRACY...BACK TO YOU

                                             IN THE STUDIO.

                                                        #####
```

◉ Channel 12 News / KHSL-TV 12 Chico, CA 95927

⬛ REPORTER'S VOICE FOR PACKAGE

COWS
↓

XX THE NORTH AMERICAN FREE TRADE AGREEMENT AND THE RICE INDUSTRY BREAKING
INTO THE JAPANES MARKET ARE JUST TWO REASONS WHY FARM CITY WEEK IS MORE *(Farm*
IMPORTANT THAN EVER. THE UPS AND DOWNS OF AGRICULTURE ARE NOT JUST FELT *Newsfile)*
IN THE FIELDS. THE NORTHSTATE'S MOST IMPORTANT INDUSTRY AFFECTS US ALL.
↑
SOT FARM BUREA LADY   *AG B-Roll*

NORTHSTATE FARMERS HAVE ████X█X███ FACED MANY HARDSHIPS AND OBSTACLES
IN RECENT YEARS. THE DROUGHT, THE POOR ECONOMY, ████████ CHANGES IN
REGULATIONS...BUT AGRICULTURAL LEADERS SAY THE INDUSTRY IS STILL THRIVING.

SOT FARM CREDIT DUDE

STAND UP

SOT GUARINO

SOT ANYONE ELSE ON N.A.F.T.A.   *(Farm city* ↓*Generic B-Roll)*

THE GOAL OF FARM CITY WEEK IS TO XX█X█X SHOW HOW ALL THESE ISSUES AFFECT
AGRICULTURE, WHICH IN TURN AFFECTS THE LOCAL ECONOMY. IT ALSO ALLOWS THE
AGRICULTUR█L INDUSTRY TO RESPOND TO COMMUNITY CONCERNS.

SOT NAT SOUND

MORE SOT'S

:00   12   B.C *Newsfile*

:28   *Marol*

1:14   *Grizzwold*

              TT 1:53

BROADCAST NEWS: ALTERNATIVE VIEWS AND FINAL THOUGHTS

Writers in general—and print journalists in particular—are often critical of television. This is understandable. Reading, as a whole, is on the decline in our society, and the publishers of newspapers feel the effect more than anybody. Many of the journalists interviewed for the telecourse had strong feelings about this issue.

Dorothy Rabinowitz, media critic for the *Wall Street Journal*, says, "Time is everything in television. Half of the junk you see on television news has to do with the fact that you've got 30 minutes. Yes, it tests you to say something you can sometimes do in an epigrammatic 30 seconds; it's not easy. You have to be able to finish a sentence. And you can't do it. You can't think in that kind of sound bite."

Interestingly, Rabinowitz is less critical of television itself than of the time constraints that network programming puts on packaging the news broadcasts.

"I think that the best kind of broadcast journalism is the kind you get on C-SPAN now," she says. "A lot of people live for C-SPAN because they cover everything, and they cover as much as you want of it and they just let the camera go.

"I'll give you a good example. During the recent march on Washington, the homosexual march, every network camera, every network report carefully deleted what was really going on in terms of the great extravaganza, you know, lesbians who were talking about how they wanted to screw Hillary (Clinton), and all the rest of that. All of this was going on at a great rate. C-SPAN put the cameras on and just let them roll.

"The unedited C-SPAN tapes, compared to the network tapes . . . (the networks) cut out all of this tremendous, bizarre scene that no one wanted, that would have been politically very bad to be seen in America. But C-SPAN had it."

Neil Postman, who is the author of several best-selling books that heavily criticize television, is concerned about the thin line that exists between information and entertainment in televised news.

"Television is all about raising a large audience," Postman says.

"You don't want people to switch the dial. And so news directors do remember at all times that people watch television. What they like to watch are dynamic, exciting, even exotic images. That's what keeps them rooted and so this will determine, to a considerable extent, what will be defined as news on television.

"Now we mustn't be naive," Postman adds, "because newspapers are also interested in gathering an audience. But I don't think they've got the same sort of problem, for this reason. In a newspaper, we know that people do not read everything in the newspaper. They pick out different things to read. . . . (On television), you can't say to them, 'Look, we put this on because there are some people interested in this. Hang with us for another seven minutes, and then you'll see we'll get to something that you're interested in.' "

For the very same reason Postman criticizes television news, many of the print journalists interviewed for the telecourse praised it.

According to Jack Winning, of the *Chico Enterprise-Record*, it is the daily newspaper's stock-in-trade to provide 20-inch stories on items that few readers will read from top to bottom.

"Television (and radio, even) kind of whet the appetite of people," Winning says. " They create a market with their visual stuff . . . for what we do.

"We can't be the first with the news anymore, but we can fill in the gaps. And if television and radio can get people hungry for more news, and we can provide it, more power to them. I think that's great. And I think that's the key to how community journalism is going to function in the future. And, that's the reason why I think its future's pretty bright."

Kathy Wilson, producer for KHSL-Television news in the same market, agrees with Winning.

"The newspaper has its function," Wilson says, "which is different than television. In television, we can get maybe five or six facts on a story out in the brief time that we have. At the newspaper, they can go into all the nuances. . . . They can tell the whole story. And that's where it's frustrating, sometimes, in television, because you often don't have the luxury of the time to tell the whole story. You have to get a big part of it out. Then, they can go to the newspaper and get the details of that story the next day. So, I don't see us as any competition. I think, in some respects, we complement each other."

GLOSSARY

ACTUALITY	The "audio sound bite" or tape-recorded quote used in radio news.
AMBIENT SOUND	Also called "nat sound"—the natural sound surrounding a news event. This is important in creating the atmosphere of a radio news story and is important in television news.
B-ROLL	Video images shot specifically to be used over a reporter's words to illustrate the news event or story. The reporter's words are narrated over B-roll. Sometimes, B-roll images are edited over a source's words, after the source's face has been established talking for a few seconds. Among other things, B-roll can be used to cover up audio edits of quotes (to avoid the jerking head effect) or to cover up bad shots (out of focus, poorly lighted and so on) of a source talking.
PACKAGE	A completed television news story on tape, which is edited before a news show goes on the air. The package contains the reporter's stand-ups as well as narration over images and an out-cue for the anchor to start speaking at the end of the tape.
READER	A news story with no moving video images, read on television news broadcasts by the anchor.

REVEAL   A type of transition used in broadcast journalism and related directly to cinematic plot development. The story is developed by "revealing" bits of information that tease the viewer into listening until the end.

SOUND BITE   Also know as a "head bite"—the videotaped quote in television news.

STANDARD OUT-CUE The phrase used to close a package—for example: "This is Jimmy Olsen reporting live for KSUP, Metropolis."

STAND-UP   A reporter's appearance in a news story, usually a head-and-shoulders shot, which features the reporter talking into a microphone at the scene of the news event. The stand-up is used as a transition in a television news piece and often as a beginning or ending.

SUPER   A video effect that allows the television station to print and superimpose the name of a news source over his or her image when the source is shown talking in a news story.

TELEPROMPTER   The piece of technology that allows an anchor to see and read words of script while looking directly into a camera. The unusual spelling and odd uppercase letters come from the brand name.

SUGGESTED WRITING EXERCISES

Hearing broadcast journalists talking about their news-writing styles can be of some help in learning the style, but practical application of the principles (doing it) is the key to learning to write effectively in broadcast news style. Many of you taking this course will not have access to the tape recorders, cameras and editing equipment necessary to complete an actual broadcast news piece. However, you can learn more about the actual writing process through work at your typewriter or computer—away from all of the electronic toys associated with broadcast news.

As KHSL News Director Bruce Lang says, "Many of the students who apply here for jobs have had some exposure to cameras and editing equipment. But I'm more interested in three things—someone who can write, someone who can write and someone who can write." Charles Kuralt, formerly of CBS News, adds, "A new reporter on the staff who can really write is a rare find. . . . You hear whispers in the hallway behind his or her back, 'That one's really a writer.'"

Bruce Lang, of KHSL television: "When I hire a reporter, I look for someone who can write, someone who can write, and someone who can write."

Here are a few exercises that can help you better understand broadcast news-writing styles:

1 Make an audiotape of a quality radio news broadcast. (We recommend National Public Radio's "Morning Edition" or "All Things Considered.") Pick out the story that makes the biggest impact on you, and transcribe the tape. Then, outline the story, identifying the reporter's use of ambient sound (or nat sound), taped quotes (actualities) and his or her own words. Identify the reporter's lead, use of transitional phrases and ending. Critique the reporter's effectiveness in using language—with sounds—to communicate the news story. Finally, try to find newspaper accounts of the same news event, and compare similarities and differences in the way the radio stations and newspapers portray the event.

2 If you have access to a VCR, videotape a television news broadcast. Pick out the story that has the biggest impact on you. Outline the story, identifying the reporter's use of video images (B-roll), nat sound, taped interviews and his or her own words. Identify the reporter's lead, use of transitional phrases and ending. Critique the reporter's effectiveness in using language—with images—to communicate the news story. Finally, try to find a newspaper account of the same news event, and compare similarities and differences in the way television stations and newspapers portray the event.

3 Take the first print news story you have written for your class assignment and show how you would hypothetically cover the same story for a television or radio newscast. Make a thorough outline; be sure to show what sounds and images you would include with your words. Be sure to adapt what you have learned about leads, transitions, endings and other forms of language use in broadcast news to this new version of your story. You may use the sample scripts for television and radio news stories shown in this study guide as models for your own outlines.

QUIZ

Choose the best answer.

1 Story development style in broadcast news writing

    a. has much in common with the inverted pyramid.
    b. is often similar to the "circle" style discussed in Unit Four, with an emphasis on an ending that connects with the lead.
    c. is similar to the sports writing style called "running."
    d. all of the above
    e. none of the above

2 Though radio news does not have the advantage of television's video images

    a. radio news writers usually compensate with many colorful, descriptive adjectives that can "paint" the missing pictures.
    b. radio news writers usually compensate by giving personal impressions of the news scene.
    c. radio news writers usually compensate by editing in ambient sounds to create the feel of a news scene.
    d. all of the above
    e. none of the above

3 Radio news reporters usually call taped quotes used in news stories

    a. sound bites.
    b. actualities.
    c. direct quotes.
    d. all of the above
    e. none of the above

4 If a newspaper has covered a story with 10 to 12 column inches, the equivalent story on the evening news must be edited down to approximately

    a. half the number of words used in the news story.
    b. 30 to 90 seconds.
    c. 8 seconds.
    d. all of the above
    e. none of the above

5 Videotaped quotes in hard-news stories on television evening news broadcasts

    a. are usually less than 10 seconds.
    b. are always sound bites and are never read by the reporter or anchor.
    c. can't be used if the camera goes out of focus while the source is talking.
    d. all of the above
    e. none of the above

6 Leads in television and radio news stories

    a. are similar to the summary leads in newspapers.
    b. often leave out details such as names, dates or addresses.
    c. must have most of the classic news elements such as Who, What, When, Where, Why and How.
    d. all of the above
    e. none of the above

7 The reporters interviewed on the telecourse program about broadcast news agreed that language use in television

a. places less emphasis on colorful adjectives.
b. is more effective when active rather than passive verbs are used.
c. has more impact when concrete nouns are used.
d. all of the above
e. none of the above

8 Interviews in television and radio news

a. are more believable to the news consumers, because they can never be edited without the listener or viewer noticing.
b. often take up more than half of the entire news story.
c. are easier to gather than print news quotes, because the reporter has recording devices such as cameras and tape recorders.
d. all of the above
e. none of the above

9 Interviews in television and radio news

a. can often show the news consumer more than a print interview can because the listener can hear emotions in the source's voice.
b. can often show the news consumer more than a print interview can because the viewer can see emotions in the source's face.
c. can often be very powerful if conducted live.
d. all of the above
e. none of the above

10 A television news "package"

a. often includes the sound and image of a reporter reading words, also known as a "stand-up."
b. often includes the reporter's voice dubbed over "B-roll," or images of the news event.
c. often includes a standard out-cue to the news anchors.
d. all of the above
e. none of the above

STYLE AND DICTION SELF-TEST

Instructions: Figure out the correct style use and diction for each word pair by using your style book and dictionary. After you have analyzed each sentence, read all of the sentences into a cassette tape recorder. Be sure to enunciate each word correctly. Present the tape to your instructor for evaluation. Alternate exercise: Circle the correct word choices in each sentence.

1 The odor from the septic tank's (**effluent/affluent**) leak had the (**effluent/affluent**) suburbanites complaining to the authorities.

2 The stockholders' (**biannual/biennial**) meetings were held in July and December.

The Olympic events, which had been staged every four years for centuries, were changed to (**biannual/biennial**) competitions in even-numbered years.

3 The unusual (**climatic/climactic**) extremes have led to several disasters that cost hundreds of lives.

The (**climatic/climactic**) meeting between Superman and Godzilla was a smash in the movie theaters.

4 The army was successful because it learned to adapt camels and horses to the (**dessert/desert**) conditions.

5 After the April Fools' issue, the newspaper adviser wanted to (**dissociate/disassociate**) himself from the reporters and editors.

6 This style study will (**affect/effect**) journalism students in a positive way.

7 The space probe went (**farther/further**) into the galaxy than any other.

8 The editor urged her reporter to investigate (**farther/further**) into the senator's questionable dealings.

9 The restaurant owners were nervous, because the (**gourmand/gourmet**) from the daily newspaper was evaluating their establishment on a busy night.

10 Though the suspect was convicted of (**homicide/manslaughter/murder**), no evidence of premeditation or malice was offered at the trial.

11 The journalism teacher wanted to (**ensure/insure**) his students understood the importance of precise language use and correct diction.

12 The football coach was detained in the city (**jail/prison**) while on trial for misdemeanor charges filed involving a car accident.

13 The president met with 25 (**kindergartners/kindergardeners**) and talked about education.

14 The coach was held (**libel/liable**) for the team's behavior.

15 Of the seven running for mayor, Smith received the highest, with 40 percent; the top two candidates, Smith and Jones, must run against each other, because neither received a (**majority/plurality**).

16 The jury gave its verdict; the accused was (**innocent/not guilty/acquitted**).

17 The compass needle was (**oriented/orientated**) toward the North Pole.

18 The National Football League has reached such (**parity/parody**), any team can beat any other team on any given Sunday.

19 It was a simple (**question/inquiry/enquiry**) from a driver, who asked a police officer for directions to the nearest bank; the question led to an (**inquiry/enquiry**) by the suspicious officer, and the eventual discovery of drugs in the driver's car.

20 The (**restaurateurs/restauranteurs**) were nervous, because the food critic from the daily newspaper was eating at their establishment on a busy night.

21 Bands (**such as/like**) Led Zeppelin had no keyboard players.

Today, there just aren't any cool bands that can play (**as/like**) Led Zeppelin did.

22 Joe Montana pointed (**toward/towards**) the goal line.

23 Broadcast journalists are encouraged to (**utilize/use**) the style book, just as in print journalism.

24 A smile can express emotions (**verbal/oral/aural**) communication cannot.

25 The president understood (**that/which**) he must circumvent the Congress and take his case directly to the voters.

26 The county court charged a fee to discourage journalists from (**Xeroxing/photocopying**) too many legal documents.

27 The 15-year-old (**youth/man**) was detained for questioning by authorities.

28 Children should send letters asking for special gifts to the address on your television screen:
Santa Claus
North Pole
(**zip code/ZIP code**) 00001

PUBLIC
RELATIONS
WRITING

To some, the skills needed to be a reporter and a public relations person might seem identical. At one point in this unit's video presentation, David Hatfield from the media relations department for the Golden State Warriors describes a scene after a game in which "there's a huge crowd in the locker room and I'm just one other reporter trying to find my way through the crowd to get the quotes we need."

Hatfield, a former journalist, still thinks of himself as a reporter. After the game, he's gathering quotes right along with the sports reporters from the local newspapers, television stations and radio stations. He has to recognize news value, work on a deadline and type fast. He even has to have some broadcast writing skills to put together radio pieces at the end of a game.

Hatfield is successful working with the San Francisco and Bay Area media, partially because of his experience. When he writes a press release, he is familiar with the AP Stylebook. He can easily craft his writing to fit summary lead and inverted pyramid formulas. He knows about good writing and good reporting and takes care to dish out accurate statistics and facts about his team.

Hatfield also understands the attitudes and values of his counterparts. Therefore, sports beat reporters at Bay Area newspapers, radio stations and television stations feel comfortable accepting his information.

Reporters in every niche—from the police beat to the entertainment beat to the government beat—have similar relationships with public relations professionals in their fields. Many of these journalists feel comfortable accepting information for a story from public relations professionals—up to a point.

"All reporters need to be careful of falling for the spin," explains Steve Tetreault, editor for the Donrey News Service. "Where the flacks give you information but present it in a way that serves a purpose. It's one of the fun challenges to being a journalist . . . to dissect the information that comes over to you and be able to pick out the spin, and take it out of the material and then see what's left."

Journalists and press agents have other differences. For instance, it is considered unethical for a news writer to manufacture a quote. In a public relations job, it is common to make up a quote, call the boss to verify it is something he or she probably would have said and include it in a press release.

The public relations business has also learned how to use broadcast journalism techniques to produce video press releases. Many television stations are tempted to use the sounds and images presented in these releases, knowing that it would cost much in time, money and resources to create virtually identical sounds or images that could be valuable in a news story. But, again, these images come with a spin, and therefore a credibility gap.

In spite of the different attitudes, journalists know they often need the public relations people to help them fill up the space in a newspaper or the time on television and radio stations. The creative tension between the two fields can often lead to good journalism.

Bringing journalism students and public relations students together in a news-writing class is the start of this process.

OBJECTIVES

This unit is designed to provoke thought—by both public relations students and journalism students—on how the two professions can coexist. Future reporters will be introduced to the value (and some of the pitfalls) of obtaining information from press releases. Public relations majors will learn how the skills taught in this course will apply toward their future jobs.

PROGRAM GUIDE

BEFORE YOU WATCH

This program will help future reporters better understand how public relations people think; it will also give an idea of how information that comes from public relations sources is regarded in a newsroom. The program is important for public relations majors who wish to understand the function of journalistic writing in the preparation of news releases and other aspects of the public relations process.

•Pay close attention to the ways journalists and teachers use the following terms in this program:

Public affairs	Press release
Media relations	Facts sheet
Flack	Free advertising
Propaganda	Plug
News release	News tip

WHILE YOU WATCH

1. Observe the different attitudes that journalists express about people who work in public relations.

2. Notice how public relations professionals handle newsroom attitudes toward their jobs.

3. Look for similarities and differences in public relations writing and news-writing styles.

4. Watch for different types of public relations jobs and the kinds of people who work in them.

AFTER YOU WATCH

•**Address the following questions in your journal. Or, if there's time, discuss them in class.**

1. Are there times when unedited press releases can be used, verbatim, to fill up a news hole in a daily newspaper? When might this be appropriate or inappropriate?

2. Is it a good idea for journalism and public relations students to be mixed in the same classroom? Why?

3. What aspects of journalism writing style, studied in this course already, can be applied directly toward public relations writing style? What is different about public relations writing?

4. Should television stations allow portions of video press releases to be used as part of a news package? Why?

5. What aspects of public relations work appeal to you, as a writer and student? What aspects of public relations work do not appeal to you? Try to list several types of public relations jobs that you could enjoy working in. What types of public relations jobs might make you feel uncomfortable?

THE LESSON

In the opening scene of the telecourse program about public relations, Andy Rooney seems enraged. According to Rooney, the world would be better without **press agents**, **flacks**, public information officers, **media relations representatives** and any other kind of public relations practitioner.

In the next scene, Linda Ellerbee admits it is probably a good idea that public relations students study news-writing techniques; she just wishes that they were in another classroom.

This might seem like a poor choice of sound bites to start a unit on public relations. Certainly, these comments could be depressing as a career introduction for a PR major. But no matter what the niche you work in—be it as a press agent for a fire-fighting agency or a media relations representative for a sports franchise or a publicity department head for a recording company—the attitudes expressed by Rooney and Ellerbee come with the turf.

It's a reality you might as well be aware of early on. It's just part of the job.

"There are certain publications that deal with you as a necessary evil, which is an uncomfortable feeling," says Dominique Leomporra, a public relations representative for Capitol Records.

Still, many journalists fully value the hard work that PR people put into their jobs and appreciate the information they give out—data that can be used as tips for stories, supplementary research information or even unedited padding for a magazine or newspaper with a large news hole to fill.

"One thing that journalists never have is time," says Ellerbee. "Any time you can save a journalist some of those precious minutes, you're going to get their attention." That's when a PR person's services start to become valuable.

Anthony DeCurtis, music editor of *Rolling Stone*, is often on the receiving end of Leomporra's press releases.

"They're just people doing their jobs, and they can get you important information," he says.

It's amusing, at best (and irritating, at worst), DeCurtis says, when a press agent tries to deal with a reporter as if he or she is simply part of a publicity machine. The publicists in the music industry who have a real respect for journalists also have something valuable to add to rock and roll, he says.

It's those public relations people that DeCurtis and writers in other newsrooms actually look forward to hearing from.

Judy VanSlyke-Turk, author of *This Is PR: The Realities of Public Relations*, a former journalist and dean of the journalism department at the University of South Carolina, has had quite a bit of experience with the symbiotic relationship between news writers and public relations professionals.

"In order to help students and even practitioners who are already working in the business understand that [negative] attitude, they need to understand where it's coming from," VanSlyke-Turk says. "Some of it comes from reality. Some journalists have had very bad experiences with particular PR people. And, as is the case in almost anything, one bad apple spoils the barrel. If the only PR people you have had contact with have been people who have treated you with less than professional respect, who were less than honest with you, who tried to pretend that something was important when it really wasn't, then of course you're going to have a negative opinion."

There is a solution to the problem, VanSlyke-Turk says.

"I think it all comes down to standards of professionalism in both journalism and public relations. Professional disciplines are trying very hard through their professional organizations, through their educational process, to kind of inculcate the right values. It's a very slow process. There are a lot of journalists out there who didn't go to journalism school; there are a lot of PR people out there who didn't go to PR school."

Educating public relations majors about journalism practices—including ethics, news values and reporting techniques—is the first step of that education process.

"I wish all public information officers had been newspaper reporters or had taken those courses," says Debbie Wilgoren, police reporter from the *Washington*

Post. "Because sometimes they just have no idea how you function, what news is, what their role ought to be. A good public information officer is the greatest thing in the world. A bad one is like the biggest handicap."

Wilgoren says, as a police reporter, it is essential to maintain a good relationship with the police department's public information officers. For her beat, they are essential sources.

"The same rules apply as do other sources," Wilgoren says. "Don't screw around with them. If they say, 'I'm not supposed to give you this information but, I think that decision is wrong, and I'm going to give it to you anyway,' you just can't say it came from the public relations office. Then you have to say, 'An internal police document obtained by the *Washington Post* said, "Blah blah blah."' You can't say, 'A department spokesman released these figures.' It's not playing around. Their jobs are really on the line. So is your ability to get additional information in the future."

Miki Turner, a sports writer for the *Orange County Register*, has a similar attitude. "I've worked in PR and in newsrooms," she says. "And I think that it's important for PR majors to have a journalism background, because it helps to prepare you . . . because when you send releases to newspapers, you know what style to write it in. You can pretty much make sure they're not going to toss it out the window."

Turner also says her brief stint as a PR person also helps her news-writing career. "I know where they're coming from," she says, "because I've been there and I'm able to work with them [PR people] a lot better than some other reporters."

This complex interrelationship between public relations people and news writers exists at every level, from the smallest local publications to the largest international news magazines.

Barrett Seamann, a senior editor at *Time* magazine, says, "A good PR person really has to know the mechanics of journalism, know the philosophy of journalism . . . what we're trying to convey. So I think it's very important for people in public relations to have had some experience in journalism themselves. And a lot of the good ones do have that experience."

"The writing skills and the ability to organize information and distill it down to its most significant essence and then pass that along with clarity is just a universally necessary skill," says VanSlyke-Turk. "Especially at the entry level, when people are just getting started in their PR careers. When you're writing a press release . . . I say to students, 'You are in fact a journalist in residence within your organization. And you should be approaching it the same way a journalist does.'"

George Thurlow, a teacher at California State University and former editor of the small weekly paper, the *Chico News and Review*, adds, "The first thing I tell people who are going into PR as a career is that they ought to go into journalism first. Most of the people that I encounter who are very successful in the PR field are former journalists. I find very few people who are successful in the PR field, or are at least way up in the PR field, who have just done PR all their lives. What you tell the PR student is, 'If you don't understand how journalism works, you're never going to be able to understand how to get a message through on the media.'"

A REVIEW OF
WRITING SKILLS

Though this public relations unit is designed to acquaint students with the basic techniques needed for press release writing, it can also be viewed as a review and reinforcement of the news-writing concepts introduced during the first half of the telecourse.

NEWS VALUE

The first program and unit in this telecourse were designed to help students start creating a personal definition of news. Careful attention to this program will reveal that each of the public relations professionals interviewed had his or her own unique relationship with the news.

The public relations practitioners featured in the television program all have their clients—whether the Golden State Warriors, Capitol Records or the Forest Service—in mind when writing a press release. But they also understand that they should limit press releases, **facts sheets** and even promotional materials to information that journalists would consider newsworthy. All three public relations professionals are familiar with the reporters who work their beats and therefore have a strong feeling for the kind of news they would find useful. All three also understand that part of their primary mission is to "**spin**" the information so that it is favorable to clients.

"Nobody minds a good PR person trying to put a spin on the story that puts their organization in the most favorable light," says Barrett Seamann, of *Time* magazine.

"You expect them to do that. But you expect it to be an honest spin. People who are misleading, people who hide, people . . . who are protecting their masters, do no good to the trade.

"I think the value of public relations people [to reporters] depends entirely on how useful those people are in getting reporters the information they need, accurate [newsworthy] information . . . or getting them access to the people who are going to tell them what it is reporters need."

Though Dominique Leomporra's function at Capitol Records is mostly to gain free publicity for the bands the company is promoting, she still needs this basic news sense.

"To be a good publicist, you could probably have a lot of different backgrounds. But I think the most solid background is a background in journalism," she says.

"You have to understand what they need . . . what is newsworthy about it. You have to pretty much put that in their face . . . separate it from all the other newsworthy things that are coming at them a mile a minute."

Peggi Lawrence, the fire information officer for the Forest Service, has a slightly different attitude about the relationship of her job and the news value it conveys. Lawrence is not necessarily promoting a client; her mission is to help journalists get vital information out to the community about a dangerous fire—through any branch of the media possible. In this type of situation, the public relations job is more like reporting and less like a sales pitch. Even the job title is likely to be different in a position like Lawrence's—something official sounding, such as public information officer or public information technician—as opposed to press agent, flack or client representative.

The press is actively seeking out the information and dependent on the public relations contact for accurate news that could inform residents about evacuation procedures or help deliver other essential survival information to the public.

At the command center, where reporters are allowed to gather information about the disaster, Lawrence told reporters, "The information we're currently giving out gives the status of the fire, how many people are involved, how many acres, what kind of equipment we're using and, then, any cautionary things that we want to convey to the public.

"For instance, we need to tell people [in some areas] that they need to consider moving out of their homes until the danger period is over."

Lawrence still had to have her client's best interests in mind, though, when reporters discovered the blaze might have been started by a worker directly employed by the Forest Service. Ironically, the person in question was hired to clear brush as a method to prevent fires.

Lawrence explains:

"When we have some touchy subjects, and there are quite a few of them that can come up in any fire type situations—such as a private contractor who was working for us—if the investigation comes up that way, that he was partially or totally at fault for the fire starting, we have to be very careful about what we release and who we release it to.

"It's a delicate balance to try to convey all that I know without misdirecting people. Without betraying a confidence or something that needs to be held for a good reason, for a while, until we have more facts. I appreciate honesty in the people I deal with, and I'd like to give it to them in the same way. So when I can tell them something, I'll just tell them straight out what's going on."

LEADS

The summary lead, introduced in Unit Two, clearly has a role in public relations writing. Essentially, the first paragraph of most press releases is written in this traditional journalism style. If it isn't, the basic raw information required for a reporter to turn a press release into a quick hard-news lead should be easily accessible in the press release.

"You want to always include who, what, where, when and why immediately," says David Hatfield, PR rep for the Golden State Warriors. "Because that's what people want to know. They don't want to read your ability to write flowing verses. They want to read what you're trying to tell them. And you want them to read what you're trying to tell them. So you're better off to get it done in the first paragraph than you are to get it in there in the last paragraph because most of the people won't get to the last paragraph."

JOURNALISM STYLE

Even the *Associated Press Stylebook*, introduced in Unit Three, has a place in the press agent's office.

David Hatfield notes each public relations department has its own special style concerns. "*First-round draft pick* is hyphenated," he says. "And *free-throw* is hyphenated. *Warriors* is a perfect example. Is there an apostrophe? Is it possessive? Where does the apostrophe go . . . beginning or end or between the *s*?"

STORY DEVELOPMENT

Traditional journalism writing techniques again are reinforced when press release development style is examined. Press releases are usually written with breaking news or the most important information packed toward the top of the page. The least important information is saved for the end of the release. This aspect of press release writing bears a striking resemblance to the classic inverted pyramid style of news story development, which was introduced in Unit Four.

Fire Information Officer Lawrence says, "The same things that I learned in my basic journalism classes, Journalism 1-A or the equivalent nowadays—using the most important items as your lead-in and gradually moving the story down so that the least important items that you wish to convey—are still important. I know that in the print media, which is where I was working, that if you didn't have enough space, the least important parts of the story got cut off at the end, and you only saw the very most critical things that we were trying to convey to the public about what was going on. It's the same story with public relations information."

QUOTES AND INTERVIEWS

Unit Five focused on sources and gathering quotes. Journalists are often wary of quotes found in a press release, and for good reason. As David Hatfield, of the Warriors, points out, "In the best-case scenario you'll interview whoever it is you want to write the quote for. Because obviously you want to put it in their own words. That's best-case scenario."

However, Hatfield also says, "Any media relations person who tells you that they've never created a quote is not telling you the truth. What you must do is always get it approved. You'd be making a large mistake to issue a quote from your president without getting his approval first. So in fact you may actually be writing the words, but he or she has definitely approved them if you're a smart media relations coordinator."

Judy VanSlyke-Turk says, if the CEO of the company is in China, "I might 'make up' or '**manufacture**' a sentence or two that would be attributed to him. If I'm a good PR person, he's going to see it. I'm going to fax it to him in China. He's going to see it and he's going to say, 'Yes. I'm comfortable with that. That's what I would say if I were there to actually be interviewed by the reporter.'

"So that quote made up in the news release—he actually never uttered those words. But the PR person, because of a close working relationship with him, can kind of second-guess and say, 'What would Chairman Jones say in this situation? Ah, something like this' . . . run it by him, he says, 'Yeah, that's what I would have said.' I think that's the ethical way to approach it, as a PR person. You may not actually have a chance to stick the microphone in his or her face and ask the person 'What would you say?'"

Good reporters prefer to get their quotes directly from their sources, to make their stories more credible and more original. Too often, if a quote is taken from a press release and incorporated into a news story, the writer will find the identical quote in the competition's report.

Still, sometimes the news maker is simply too busy or is bombarded with more requests for interviews than it is possible to handle. In these situations, reporters will sometimes resort to using a quote from a public relations representative or a press release, instead of the original source.

The best journalists take care with attribution of a quote taken from a press release, introducing it with a statement such as "In a statement released by the publicity department, the governor said, 'Yadda yadda.'"

Still, if it is a **manufactured quote** and the reporter uses it in a story, the readers are getting information of questionable credibility.

WRITING VERSUS REPORTING

Unit Six is about the relationship between good writing and good reporting.

Though it would seem that the writing opportunities for public relations practitioners are limited to formula press releases, Judy VanSlyke-Turk points out that some get to flex their writing muscles in certain situations.

"I think if a public relations person is approaching a story from a feature angle as opposed to a news angle, they have more of an opportunity to focus on what's in it for the company they represent and to tease out some of the self-interest that we can't afford to mess with in a news release," she says.

"You're still putting yourself in the place of the journalist or the ultimate consumer of the information and saying what would be interesting. But I think you can play a little bit more with how you frame that message and do a little bit more self-serving promotion of the organization, its products, its view of a situation perhaps, than you would in a straight news story. Opinion and subjectivity don't belong in a news story, but they are acceptable in a feature story as long as they are kind of linked to something that is newsworthy to begin with."

BEATS

The different beats introduced in Unit Seven each have a unique relationship with the public relations professionals who intersect those beats.

"You have to remember that they represent the police department," Debbie Wilgoren says, of the public information officers in the Washington, D.C., police department. "You are reporting objectively on that agency that they represent. It's difficult because, again, you don't want to get frozen out. But you can't let that affect the way that you cover something. You just always have to be honest and fair."

When necessary, Wilgoren finds a way to work around the PIO. "We use anonymous sources all the time. I probably use them too much. The unfortunate thing is the district's metropolitan police department and their fire department basically have very strict rules about who can speak for attribution. And basically both offices want any interviews to be cleared through their public information office before they take place. If I'm out at a murder [scene] at 11 o'clock at night speaking to a homicide detective, well, there's no PIO officer to call up and say, 'Would you mind if Detective So-and-So talked about the nature of this crime?'

"So, basically, what we're left with is getting to know a detective who we trust and then using them. We don't always say in a police story that they were an anonymous source. I will say, 'A homicide detective said' and since there were four homicide detectives on the scene, a person can't get caught."

At the highest levels of government, Helen Thomas, UPI White House correspondent, must deal with public relations professionals from a very specialized beat.

"There's PR here every day," Thomas says. "They have a press spokesman—he is the press secretary at the White House, spokesman for the president of the United States. They're very circumscribed in what they can say."

Still, Thomas says, "They have to have as much credibility as we do. They should believe in what they're selling, and if they don't, it comes through—one way or another. You know, you have to have a certain sincerity about whatever you're trying to peddle. And I think that it can be a profession of high integrity and ethics. But it doesn't have that reputation, and I think that you have to overcome that immediately by establishing real confidence. And public relations people can be very good sources if they tell you the truth."

Nancy Vogel, who covers forest fires for the *Sacramento Bee*, finds a similar relationship with the PR people at the low levels of government.

"I think most reporters naturally tend to want to stay away from public information officers," she says. "But, when on a fire, those are the people you need to talk to first just to get the basic facts because they've already done the work."

Often, Vogel says, "They're the backbone of our stories."

Sports reporter Miki Turner expresses a parallel point of view. "Sports information directors are our lifeline," she says. "Without them, we don't have stats, we don't have people to write about. We need that information terribly. . . . [Often] that's how you find out what's going on."

The Carole Rich textbook *Writing and Reporting News: A Coaching Method* features a complementary chapter for this unit, also titled "Public Relations Writing" (pp. 253–266 in the second edition). A code of ethics from the Public Relations Society of America is included in Rich's ethics chapter.

BROADCAST NEWS AND PR

When the relationship between the public relations industry and broadcast news is examined, the hottest topic is the video press release. Like newspapers, which sometimes include a verbatim sentence, paragraph or even an entire press release as part of the news hole, some television news departments are starting to incorporate video images and sounds—presented by public relations firms—into news stories. Most producers and news directors are quite squeamish about the practice.

Linda Ellerbee, of Nick News, expresses a typical point of view with this scenario:

"You're out on a story, and some guy comes up and hands you a piece of videotape. He says, 'You're doing a story about tuna [fishing] . . . dolphins that get caught in the net? Here's some video of dolphins getting caught in the net you can use in your story.' And you say, 'Well, hey, thank you, because that's surely some video I couldn't go out and shoot today.'

"What guarantee do you have that that's exactly what it is?" Ellerbee asks. "Where was it shot, and when was it shot, and under what circumstances? It's very dangerous stuff. And yet it was so easy. That is why so many PR people are using that now—because it is so easy and they know that journalists will very often fall for what's easy; we're a lazy lot."

Many public relations professionals, however, feel video promos aren't much different than press releases on paper.

"I think deep down, most of us who have spent some time as working journalists would like to think . . . that we really are independent, that we don't need help from PR people to do our jobs," says Judy VanSlyke-Turk.

"The reality is, we can't be in all the different places we need to be. Our budgets have shrunk. And reality is, we need PR people and the information they provide to help us do our job better. I think there's kind of this ego resentment there. 'I

Public relations representatives are often hired to coach politicians on how to talk to the media. During campaigns, many candidates are actually trained to talk in perfect eight-second sound bites, so that the television reporters have nothing but slogans for their news pieces.

Government officials use public relations for other practices that don't make a reporter's job any easier.

"People in government have learned that it's very dangerous for midlevel bureaucrats to talk to the media," says George Thurlow. "So almost all large public agencies now deal through public information officers. It's extremely difficult to get information out of them because they don't know anything. They're essentially PR people. You're either calling them because you need an answer to a question about—say, a hazardous spill in the lake—and you want to know what kind of chemical it was. What does it do? How fast does it break down? The PIOs, the public information officers, don't have a clue. They have to go call a government scientist. Now it would have been just as easy for you to go call the scientist, but these government bureaucracies are scared to death the scientist is going to tell you something that they don't want you to know. It's a really frustrating situation."

really wish I could do it without you folks.' And I think that's probably more pronounced in the case of video news releases, where it's more obvious that you've had help, than in a written news story where you could put a new lead on it, you can add some quotes and you can get some reaction. Then it becomes your story, and it's not recognizable to the public that you've had help from the PR person."

ALTERNATIVE VIEWS

"I'm sure that there are very good PR people who are former news writers," says Steve Tetreault, of the Donrey Media News Service. "It may be helpful for reporters to go on that side of the fence for a little bit, to get an idea of how PR agencies—say, for instance, for congressmen or senators—put out their information. And then come back and say, 'OK, here's what it looks like coming over;

David Hatfield, Golden State Warriors: "There's a huge crowd in the locker room, and I'm just one reporter . . . trying to get the quotes we need."

Judy VanSlyke-Turk, author and PR instructor at the University of South Carolina: "You have to put yourself in the shoes of the rep and say, 'If I ran across this information covering my beat, would I go to my editor and say, "Hey, I think we ought to do a story on this?"'"

now I know what went into putting it in.' When you're a reporter, I'm convinced that you only see the tiny tip of the iceberg—that is what agencies or politicians, what public relations people want you to see."

Barrett Seamann warns journalists, however, that "there's a kind of feeling . . . that once you've gone over to the other side, once you've been in public relations, it's very difficult to come back again and be considered an objective journalist. Somehow, you've sullied yourself; somehow you've kind of sold out. I spent a lot of time interviewing prospective candidates here for jobs . . . and I feel I know the prejudice is there in myself. I just see somebody who is now working as a PR person but anxious to try to get back into journalism. I ask myself questions. 'What made this person leave journalism in the first place?' I don't think that's fair, but I think [the feeling] is out there."

CRYSTAL FIRE INFORMATION

Fire Cause Briefing Sheet

The Crystal Fire began Thursday afternoon (8/4/94) just west of the
Stampede Reservoir where a private contractor was doing site preparation
work for a Forest Service tree planting project.

The Contractor was using a piece of machinery with large blades which
shear and break down the brush into smaller pieces. The Contractor
looked away momentarily to obtain more fuel for the equipment; when
he looked back, the fire had started. The Contractor tried to
put out the fire, and when he could not, called the Forest Service on
a cellular phone to report the fire.

The investigation is continuing. If the investigation shows the
Contractor was negligent, the Contractor could be liable for the
suppression costs of the fire.

The Contractor is from out of the area.

FIRE INFORMATION CENTER   Telephones
August 6, 1994   345-1754
10:00 am   345-1756
                                                   345-1758

FOR IMMEDIATE RELEASE

CONTACT: Dan Finnane
(510) 382-2306

WARRIORS TO STAY WITH OWN ARENA PLANS

OAKLAND, CALIF., June 16, 1994 -- Golden State Warriors President Dan Finnane said today the organization's efforts to develop a new arena remain focused exclusively on two sites, the Oakland Coliseum complex and the Rincon site located at Folsom and Main streets near downtown San Francisco. The Warriors plans do not include the Mission Bay "entertainment complex" idea being floated by the Giants, Catellus and the Cow Palace.

According to Finnane, a San Francisco arena must be as close to downtown as possible for three very important reasons:

1. - "The arena needs to be located near the major Bay Area transportation links. The Rincon site is ideally located in proximity to BART, MUNI, the proposed CalTrain station, and the TransBay Terminal.

2. - "Many of our fans and sponsors are located in downtown San Francisco and would desire to walk to the arena without having to relocate their cars.

3. - "Since virtually all of our events take place at night, we would want to be located close to the existing downtown parking structures which empty out at the conclusion of the business day. It would be very convenient for out-of-town fans to use these parking facilities for our evening events.

"We view our arena project as a neat, small, manageable project and we would like to avoid getting involved in a mega-project with many problems which include traffic, parking and other unknown issues," Finnane said. "In 1995, the Warriors will have the smallest arena in the NBA and are anxious to occupy a new arena by 1998."

-30-

GLOSSARY *

ANGLE
Particular emphasis of a media presentation; sometimes called a *slant*.

COMMUNITY RELATIONS
A function of public relations that involves dealing and communicating with the citizens and groups within an organization's geographic operation area.

COPY
(1) Any broadcast writing, including commercials; (2) any written material intended for publication, including advertising.

DEMOGRAPHICS
Certain characteristics in the audience for any medium—sex, age, family, education, economics.

FACTS SHEET
Page of significant information prepared by PR people to help news media in covering a special event.

FILL COPY
Pad copy. Relatively minor material used to "fill out" a broadcast or page.

FLACK
Slang for a press agent or publicist, primarily those in the entertainment fields.

GOVERNMENT RELATIONS
A function of public relations that involves dealing and communicating with legislatures and government agencies on behalf of an organization.

LEAD ("LEDE")
(1) The introductory sentence or paragraph of a news story; (2) a tip that may develop into a story.

MANUFACTURED QUOTE
A quote "created" by a PR person intended to be similar to words the boss would speak, if he or she was available.

MEDIA RELATIONS
A function of public relations that involves dealing with the communications media in seeking publicity for, or responding to media interest in, an organization.

NEWS RELEASE
A news story written in print or broadcast style for use by a news medium.

NEWS TIP
A news story idea not in story format given to a news medium for that medium's staff to write if the story idea is deemed to have merit.

PRESS AGENTRY
A function of public relations that involves creating news events of a transient, often flighty sort.

PRESS RELEASE
A brief document prepared by a public relations professional for the purpose of communicating information to the news media.

PROPAGANDA
A function of public relations that involves efforts to influence the opinions of a public in order to propagate a doctrine.

*These glossary terms have been adopted from *This Is PR: The Realities of Public Relations*, by Doug Newsom, Judy VanSlyke Turk, and Dean Kruckeburg.

PUBLIC AFFAIRS	The various activities and communications that organizations undertake to monitor, evaluate, influence and adjust to the attitudes, opinions and behaviors of groups or individuals who constitute their publics.
PUBLICITY	A function of public relations that involves dissemination purposefully planned and executed messages through selected media, without payment to the media, to further the particular interest of an organization or a person.
SPIN	The hidden slant of a press release, which usually casts the client in a positive light.
VIDEO PRESS RELEASE	A press release for television, prepared on tape—complete with images and sound which can be used by the news media, without additional permission.

SUGGESTED WRITING EXERCISES

Most of the journalists interviewed for this telecourse said they received hundreds of press releases a week—from very professionally assembled releases and facts sheets to completely amateur pieces that routinely end up in the garbage. Here is a summary of tips press release writers should always remember:

Remember to include a phone number.

Reporters might be intrigued by your press release, but they have a lot of different ways of using it. Some might use it as a story idea, and they'll want to chat about angles and get ideas about who to interview. Also, journalists are reluctant to publish your press release verbatim, even as a calendar item. They may want to add a few facts, clarify or double-check details, verify spellings or gather additional quotes. If you haven't included a phone number, the press release—and your story—will likely land in the trash. Remember to keep it simple.

A wordy press release takes time to read, and journalists are very busy.

Include important details.

•Prepare a facts sheet.

Sometimes, a simple facts sheet included with your press release is the best way to inform reporters of the basic information needed to write a story. It's a great way to create a checklist, in case they don't have time to call for important details you might have left out. Here's a blank form you can use for all your facts sheets. It will probably look pretty familiar:

Press Release Facts Sheet Form
Who
What
When
Where
Why
How

The skills needed for writing different kinds of press releases vary almost as much as those for different kinds of news writing. Following, you will find three raw blocks of information. Take each block, and write a one-page press release as if you were

1. working as a fire information officer;

2. working as a public relations employee of a major record company; and

3. working as a public relations employee for a professional basketball team.

1 **Fire information officer:** The Redwood Valley Estates subdivision, five miles north of Zeppo, California, is on the edge of a fire that has consumed 2,000 acres of timber and brush in the Sierra Nevada hills outside of Zeppo. Approximately 600 people live in 200 homes in this development. The city of Zeppo has 45,000 residents. The southern edge of the fire has completely destroyed six homes. There have been two fatalities. One was a fire fighter, who was trapped in a canyon near Redwood Valley Estates during the first day of the fire, on Wednesday, August 12. The other was an elderly man, who was caught in his home, which was consumed by fire on Friday, August 14. You are writing the press release for Friday afternoon.

The disaster started Wednesday, when a trash fire in a local resident's back yard burned out of control. Prevailing winds pushed the fire north of town and beyond containment by local fire departments. Drought conditions, caused by a low rainfall pattern for three years, added to the problems. The windy, dry conditions have created a situation that could accurately be described as a fire storm; fire fighters have been able to reach only 20 percent containment and expect the conditions to get worse before they get better. The city of Zeppo is not expected to be threatened unless the winds shift directions.

Write a press release for the California Department of Forestry, fire prevention unit. The release is for use by all news organizations interested in reporting on the fire. The press release should be a straightforward presentation of the relevant news.

Quotes you may use: "We've established a barrier on the south end of the fire, and I don't expect anything but northward movement into virtually uninhabited territory. But, if the winds change, anything can happen." Attribute the quote to Fire Capt. Richard Alverado.

2 **Public relations employee of a major record company:** A new band, Coffee Jag, has released its first compact disc, titled "Jag-Jag-A-Laggin." The CD, released on the Fleeting Fad label, was self-produced by the band. Several songs have received heavy airplay at college radio stations, including "Peel Down My Eyelids," "Legalized Middle-Class High" and "Don't Talk to Me in the Morning Till I've Had My Fix." A more mainstream song, "I'll Love You Through Our Highs and Our Low, Low, Lows," has received some Top 40 airplay but has remained at number 98 on the Billboard Charts for three weeks in a row.

Coffee Jag has been touring colleges to promote the new disc and is scheduled to appear in your college's student center this coming Friday the 13th [pick a month]. The concert is being billed as a benefit, with 20 percent of the proceeds (after expenses) going to local 12-step addiction programs.

Write a press release as if you worked for Fleeting Fad Records. The release will be sent to any media organization that might help promote the concert. Your task is to drum up as much free publicity as possible and to help student organizations attract large crowds for the concerts.

Quotes you may use: "I use caffeine as an inspiration for the lyrics to my songs. In the mornings, before I have my first cup of joe, I can barely think, let alone play my guitar or relate to my girlfriend. But, one espresso, I'm groovin'. I kiss my gal. I plug in. I start jammin'. Next thing you know, I've got a new song. Recently, on a trip to New Orleans, I wrote a dozen new songs in a week. They've got some strong java there." Attribute the quote to Steve Slovenly, lead guitarist and vocalist.

3 **Public relations employee for a professional basketball team:** You are working as the sports information director for the Houston Hoopsters, a professional basketball team in the United Basketball Association. Houston is entering the third week of a 20-week season as defending national champions. However, the star center—a 7-foot, 300-pound all-pro known as Greg "The Gorilla" Goreman—broke the little toe on his left foot in a freak accident in the training room when a 50-pound weight slipped and fell on his foot.

Goreman, who averages 40 minutes, 31.5 points, 15.4 rebounds and 10.1 assists per game, has been placed on the injured-reserve list and is expected to be out of action for 10 weeks. He will be replaced for 10 weeks by second-string center Steve Stiffman, a journeyman veteran who has survived in the UBA as the ultimate backup man, playing for 10 teams in 6 years, averaging 5 minutes, 2.1 points, 5 rebounds and 1.3 assists per game.

In a surprise move, the team has used an available 1-year, $2.1 million salary slot to sign the legendary center from the Olympic Silver Medal–winning Sudanese national team—a 7-foot, 9-inch, 185-pound Dinka tribesman named Inte Llat. Llat, known mostly for his defensive abilities and shot blocking, had retired from organized basketball to work for charitable organizations in his native Sudan.

He agreed to play professional basketball with the understanding that $1 million of his salary would be paid in advance, immediately, to help hungry children in his native land.

Your job, as sports information director for the basketball team, is to write a press release that will put a positive spin on a potentially disastrous situation. The local press corps for the daily newspapers in Houston have only heard rumors of the injury to Goreman. Your press release, which will be delivered in time for stories to be written for the Friday paper, will confirm the injury and the team's attempts to compensate.

Quotes you may use: Goreman: "Scooter [5-foot, 5-inch point guard Justin "Scooter" Womack] and Pick-Man [forward John Pickens] are going to have to step things up for half a season. But no team depends completely on one man. We'll win enough games to make the play-offs, and I'll take my frustrations out on the other teams in the second half of the season. Besides, I like the idea of going into the play-offs with Inte Llat on the team. I hear he's been working on a three-point shot."

Llat: "I am privileged to play for God and the children of my country. I thank, very much, the management of the Hoopsters for helping the children of Sudan to survive the drought and famine. I have much to learn from American players. Mr. Womack is teaching me to shoot a three-point basket."

QUIZ

Choose the best answer.

1 To communicate better with mainstream journalists, a press release should

   a. emphasize the most sensational aspect of the potential news value, so the journalists can come up with a flashy headline.

   b. push only the most positive aspects of your client's message, so that the journalists will not find out about potential negative information.

   c. deliver the news value of the message, with the Who, What, When, Where, Why and How easily identifiable, so the reporter can easily rewrite the story in journalism style.

   d. all of the above

   e. none of the above

2 Journalism students are often mixed in with public relations students to take a news-writing class. One good reason for this is that

   a. journalism students should learn how public relations people think, so they can be better prepared to understand the value—and drawbacks—of using information from press releases.

   b. public relations students should learn how news writers think, so they can communicate their messages with an understanding of journalism ethics, writing styles and news values.

   c. public relations students can benefit from learning news-writing style, so that their press releases will be written in a journalistic style—possibly to the point where the newspaper can use the information, unedited, as a news hole filler.

   d. all of the above

   e. none of the above

3 Information from a press release can be used

   a. in some circumstances, as a news hole filler, if the facts are checked.

   b. as a tip for a good news story.

   c. as supplementary information for a story that is already being written.

   d. all of the above

   e. none of the above

4 Video press releases

   a. include much visual information that is difficult and expensive for a television station to gather but can make a news story look very good.

   b. have caused much controversy in the news business, because some stations and networks have incorporated images from the press release without citing the source.

   c. could put a "spin" on a story that is desired by the people who produced the video.

   d. all of the above

   e. none of the above

5 According to Dominique Leomporra, who works with the public relations department of Capitol Records,

    a. learning to type quickly, while still thinking at the same time, is an invaluable writing tool.
    b. a public relations professional should not "push" his or her client.
    c. the public relations business does not have a code of ethics.
    d. all of the above
    e. none of the above

6 According to Peggi Lawrence, fire information officer,

    a. unlike the kinds of public relations people who function mainly to promote a client or product, a public information officer never has to cover for a boss or organization after an embarrassing mistake has been made.
    b. her job is to give reporters the basic information so they can ask intelligent questions—depending on which direction they want the story to read for their readership.
    c. her job is completely unlike a news reporter's.
    d. all of the above
    e. none of the above

7 According to Bob Woodward, of the *Washington Post*,

    a. many military public relations representatives are professionals who "don't lie."
    b. military public relations representatives, in his experience, are the worst.
    c. a good reporter never gets information from a "public relations hack."
    d. all of the above
    e. none of the above

8 According to Debbie Wilgoren, police reporter for the *Washington Post*, and Miki Turner, sports reporter for the *Orange County Register*,

    a. reporters often depend on public relations professionals for information essential for a news story.
    b. reporters never depend on public relations professionals for information essential for a news story.
    c. reporters should not depend on public relations professionals for information essential for a news story, unless they are desperate.
    d. all of the above
    e. none of the above

9 According to David Hatfield, who works with the public relations department of the Golden State Warriors,

    a. the summary lead and inverted pyramid are essential tools in press release writing.
    b. in the ideal world, a public relations person would prefer to interview people in the organization he or she represents, avoiding the necessity to manufacture quotes.
    c. public relations people sometimes manufacture quotes, though the good ones check with the boss to make sure the quote sounds like something he or she would have said.
    d. all of the above
    e. none of the above

10 A basic mistake many public relations students make when first writing a press release is

a. making the release too wordy.
b. forgetting to include a phone number for additional information.
c. forgetting basic information, such as a date or time of an event.
d. all of the above
e. none of the above

SELF-TEST

1 Compare the approach of public relations writers and newspaper journalists with respect to gathering quotes. What are the differences? What are the similarities?

2 Compare the approach of public relations writers and newspaper journalists with respect to writing leads. What are the differences? What are the similarities?

3 Compare the approach of public relations writers and newspaper journalists with respect to news value judgment. What are the differences? What are the similarities?

4 Compare the approach of public relations writers and newspaper journalists with respect to the difference between advertising and news. What are the differences? What are the similarities?

5 What are the differences and the similarities in the jobs of a public information officer working for the government (e.g., Peggi Lawrence of the Forest Service) and a media relations person (e.g., David Hatfield of the Golden State Warriors)?

WRITING BEYOND THE SUMMARY LEAD

The second unit of this telecourse makes a pretty strong sales pitch for learning, mastering and loving the summary lead. It is a style of writing you almost certainly must acquire to get hired in a newsroom.

The summary lead will help you kick-start a story when you're on a deadline and have little time to think or get fancy. And, in certain situations, news consumers simply demand that you cram all the facts into the first sentence of your story.

There are other ways of starting a news story.

Historians say we live in the Information Age. This means that there is an explosion in the amount of raw data, hearsay, scuttlebutt, gossip, rumor, trivia, unedited reports and other forms of news for every consumer to muddle through.

There is an abundance of competition for each reader, and if you want to write a story that demands attention all the way to the end, it takes some cunning and literary seductiveness. Often, that means starting your story with vigor and using every language trick you can borrow from script writers, storytellers and other word magicians.

We must remember to be journalists, never losing sight of the fact that our primary task is to get the facts straight and report them accurately. But that doesn't mean we have to be dull. We can mix great writing and strong storytelling with good reporting to fashion a compelling news story. To move to that next level of journalism, we will start studying innovative ways to create more powerful news leads.

However, in the process of learning more potent ways of starting news stories, we must not forget our old friend, the summary lead. As tempting as it is to leave the more traditional techniques of news writing behind, the summary lead is a style that will always have a place in news writing—even in a story that starts off with the most impressive, dazzling, magnificent lead ever written.

Don't forget that your ever-present stubborn readers will demand that the old Who, What, Where, When, Why and How be explained somewhere in the story—hopefully somewhere pretty high up, within a few sentences of your splendid introduction.

OBJECTIVES

This program will present you with alternative ways to start a news story and inspire you to attempt a number of elegant and innovative writing techniques to capture the news consumer's attention.

PROGRAM GUIDE

BEFORE YOU WATCH

This program should inspire students to think beyond traditional and rudimentary news-writing styles by challenging them to consider new approaches. In hard-news writing, that often means starting the story with something other than a summary lead.

•**Pay close attention to the ways journalists and teachers use the following terms in this program:**

Question lead   *Wall Street Journal* lead

Quote lead   Direct address lead

Anecdotal lead   Scene setting lead

Narrative lead   Summary lead

WHILE YOU WATCH

1. Consider why journalists would prefer to use leads other than summary leads. Consider why summary leads are still the mainstay of hard-news writing.

2. Compare and contrast the different lead writing styles, and note the strengths and weaknesses of each.

3. Notice how the discussion of leads differs when hard-news reporters and feature writers talk about the same subject.

4. Observe the trends of mass media that affect newspaper writing styles.

AFTER YOU WATCH

•**Address the following questions in your journal. Or, if there's time, discuss them in class:**

1. Why would some editors object to the use of question leads? When might the use of a question lead inspire the reader to read the rest of your story?

2. Why would some editors object to the use of quote leads? When might the use of a quote lead inspire the reader to read the rest of your story?

3. Which of these alternative lead styles work best in broadcast journalism stories? Which of the lead styles work best in press release writing? Why?

4. What kind of lead would work best with an on-line computer news service that the reader could access through a telecommunications information system such as CompuServe or America On-Line? Why?

5. How do the alternative leads discussed in this chapter relate to the competition for readers' attention between newspapers and magazines?

THE LESSON

Let's assume you're writing a story that more than half your readers are familiar with already. They've seen it on the television news or heard about it on the radio. They know most of the basics. Starting your story with the summary lead might interest somebody who was hibernating. But for those who already know about the story, your lead will just sound like another rehashing of the same old Who, What, When, Where, Why and How.

The challenge is to tempt readers into reading your version of the story. Think of the 40-word broadcast account as a mere advertisement for your 500-word epic. The relationship between broadcast and print is natural—the radio or television version of the news event will make readers vaguely aware of your story's essence. Your job is to lure them into reading about the details.

"A lead ought to entice rather than try to put the whole gist of the story before the reader," says Jack Cappon, author of *The Word*, a widely appreciated book among professional reporters.

"A lead should give the reader an hors d'oeuvre rather than the whole seven-course dinner," Cappon says. "Summary leads, for that very reason, are somewhat less effective."

Cappon and most of the other writers interviewed for the telecourse all suggested that one good alternative to the summary formula would be a lead that focused on the most compelling aspect of the story—usually the What or the Why of the news event.

Another option is to tease the reader with word play.

Cappon offers this example from his book:

Local school boards in Kentucky are being caught in the middle of a controversy over posting copies of the Ten Commandments in the classroom.

"Now, that's pedestrian," he says. Then, Cappon suggests this livelier example:

"Thou shalt post the Ten Commandments on the classroom wall," says a 1978 Kentucky law. "Thou shalt not," says the U.S. Supreme Court. "Help!" say confused local school boards.

A MENU OF LEAD STYLES

The rest of this chapter offers a menu of different types of leads. An inventory of alternatives offers some guidance to a student who strives to write beyond the summary lead—but it is only a list. The best advice is to let your lead grow out of the story itself. If you've researched the story thoroughly and have interviewed enough sources, the lead will emerge from the raw data. If you don't have enough information, it might be time to hit the phones or the streets once again.

"The biggest problem that writers have, whether they're students or professionals, is they think they should try to create leads, especially when they want to be great writers," says Carole Rich. "That's when they get into clichés. So I always say, 'Don't pull from your head—pull from the story.' What struck you as most interesting? What hit you? What did you like? What image did you see? What did somebody say that was most important? You base your lead build on that."

ANECDOTAL LEAD

> Doni Chamberlain was not the typical journalism student just out of high school. She was a single mom, raising three children and holding on to a part-time job. But she had the one thing going for her that would guarantee success in her quest to become a good journalist.

If that anecdote works to keep you reading this section, it works as a lead. If it bores you, it doesn't work.

"A lead is a work of art," says Jack Winning, of the *Chico Enterprise-Record*.

"And it can take any fashion. I get a kick out of reading the *Wall Street Journal*. It's almost a formula, and it's a wonderful formula. It's all narrative-style stuff. You start off with Joe Blow and he's doing something in the first two paragraphs . . . , and these two paragraphs are very interesting. In the third paragraph . . . you're going to find out what that story is all about."

"The *Journal* is famous for making use of what's called the anecdotal lead," says Michael Waldholz, health beat reporter for the *Wall Street Journal*. "You tell one person's story very briefly, to draw the reader in, and then very soon afterward, say, 'This is one of a million such stories in America.' It works wonderfully, if you have a very powerful anecdote that you can tell very succinctly."

Waldholz warns against forcing or contriving an anecdotal lead. "Often, I'll get into a story where I wish I had that kind of an anecdote. My reporting just didn't turn it up. And I can keep reporting from now until hell freezes over, and I might not get one. You know, I've got a deadline. At that point, write as compelling a news lead as you can.

"Sometimes, I write anecdotal leads and realize some time into writing the story that I need a news lead. And sometimes—into the story, as I'm writing it— the anecdote will surface. And I realize, 'Aha! I just wrote the lead.'"

SCENE-SETTING LEAD

> The journalism instructor surveyed the newspaper lab full of freshman and sophomore reporters. Studying their behaviors, he could already observe traits—invisible to the eyes of anyone else—that could predict which ones would succeed and which ones would fail.

Has this scene captivated your attention? Read on.

"The sort of scene-setting lead. That's always a good one to use," says Michael Tomasky, of New York's *Village Voice*. "Particularly if you can pick out some peculiar observation. If you've been somewhere to a meeting or you've been to a political event of some kind, and you see something peculiar or makes a nice contradiction or juxtaposition or something that kind of serves as metaphor for the larger point you're trying to make in the whole piece. That works well."

The leads discussed in this program are just as important for broadcast news as they are for print news. Bernard Goldberg, of CBS, gives this example from one of his own stories:

> You've heard of the middle of nowhere? Well, this is it. The Nevada Desert. Nothing here but the sand, the mountains, and the juvenile delinquents.

"Are you interested in what that means?" Goldberg asks. "If the answer is yes, it worked. Because it was a story about a boot camp in the middle of nowhere where they send juvenile delinquents. So what I tried to do was have the audience say, 'The sand I understand. The mountains I understand. The juvenile delinquents! What are you talking about?'

"Then, boom! An edit right to the juvenile delinquents marching like marines and counting off. You have to take your audience seriously. In other words, if you just write, and you don't think of your audience, you're wasting everybody's time. I want you to pay attention, and I want you to say, 'What the . . . ?' If I tell you too much too soon, you won't."

QUOTE LEAD

> "I know the secret to being a successful journalist," said Peter Berkow.

If you are willing to read more about writing catchy leads because of that statement, the quote might make a good lead for this section.

You can sometimes tempt the reader into the story with a great quote. However, if the quote doesn't intrigue, the reader may lose interest in the rest of the story.

"The quote lead can be effective," says Cappon. "But it hardly ever is, because people don't sum things up the way we [journalists] do."

"Quote leads are very tough," says Gene Policinski, of *USA Today*. "Because the quote had better be a harpoon. It had better spear the heart of the story. If you don't do that, the quote can just blather, blather, blather, and people will doze. Use quote leads only when you've got something like, 'I rob banks, because they're there.'"

Sometimes, the writer can break off part of a quote to incorporate the most interesting words into a summary lead or other style of lead. Notice the lead in Unit Two—Ed Farrell's piece about the upside-down flag—depended heavily on the mayor's partial quote "a state of chaos."

QUESTION LEAD

How much are you willing to sacrifice to become a successful journalist?

If you are provoked to read more about becoming a successful journalist because of that question, the question might make a good lead for this section. A good reporter with a strong question lead can sometimes convince even the most skeptical editor to experiment.

Most editors feel, however, that question leads are too easy. Often, the use of a question lead on a story is an indication that the reporter is either inexperienced or lazy.

"Question leads are very questionable," Cappon says. "You're not supposed to interrogate the readers. You're supposed to tell them something. It's extremely tiresome if a paper has two or three question leads in one page."

"Question leads?" asks Policinski. "My response to that? Why?

"I think you're better off not asking a question, because the reader may answer, 'Who cares?' I really avoid them; we avoid them here at the newspaper. Readers are a little uncomfortable with question leads too, because they come to you expecting answers, not questions. Question leads don't convey information. You've lost one or two precious lines at the start of your story. I might use a question lead once in my life. Every time I was tempted to, I would ask myself, 'Is this the one story I really want to use it on, or do I want to save it for a better situation?' I could probably die without ever using one."

DIRECT ADDRESS LEAD

You have what it takes to become a successful reporter. The secret is hidden inside of you. Your journalism instructor can unlock the door that hides the secret, if you will only read on.

Are you lured into reading on? If so, this lead might work for you. But it might not work for others.

The direct address lead talks directly to the reader, using the second-person voice—leaning on the pronoun *you*.

"The direct address lead—I'm not crazy about," says Steve Tetreault, of the Donrey News Service. "I like to stay in the third person and tell the story of other people rather than convey myself directly to the reader."

Other reporters believe that this type of lead will demand that a precisely defined audience read on. For example, the following lead would probably grab a very specific group of readers in the April 16 issue of any newspaper:

If you missed the tax deadline yesterday, the IRS will likely be knocking at your door next week. To avoid going to jail, you should read the rest of this article.

SOME MORE LEADS

Carole Rich lists a large number of successful and unsuccessful lead ideas in her textbook *Writing and Reporting News: A Coaching Method*.

Here is a sampling of a few she mentioned in her interview for the telecourse.

THE WOW LEAD

According to Rich, this is a lead based on information so interesting, the reader will say, "Wow! Give me the news. Give it to me straight. That's interesting!" A simple summary lead will do.

> A candidate for public office is convicted of child molesting in the middle of an election.

THE CRYSTAL BALL LEAD

Rich gives this example:

> If only David Johnson had known when he boarded the plane it was going to crash.

"Well, if he had any brains, he wouldn't have gotten on the plane if he knew it was going to crash," Rich says. "I don't know why writers do that, but we do it all the time. These kinds of leads are such fun because they're so stupid.

THE GOOD NEWS/BAD NEWS LEAD

"People speak that way," Rich says. "'First, let me tell you the good news. Then I'll tell you the bad news.'" The lead can work, since it sounds so conversational. The problem is, this lead style has become as much of a cliché in news writing as it is in everyday conversation.

THE NIGHTMARE LEAD

According to Rich, "I have said to students, 'You are allowed one nightmare lead for your whole life.' So last year we were working on this wonderful story as a class project. Everybody was writing the same story, and one of the students began this story about this mother whose child was missing. He said, 'It was her worst nightmare.' I looked at him and I said, 'You are 22 years old. Do you want to use up your one nightmare at this early stage of your career?' If you read newspapers as much as I do, you will not get through a week without getting at least a few nightmare leads. Everything bad that happens is a nightmare. You think people are sleeping their whole lives, dreaming everything. The reality is, you have a great wow lead, not a nightmare."

THE PLOP-A-PERSON LEAD

This is an anecdotal lead gone astray. "It's become such a popular lead to start a story with a person and then say hello, nut graph, good-bye," complains Rich. "We never hear from this person again. That's my idea of plop-a-person. When you start a story with a person—an anecdotal lead—that person needs to have some role in that story. Very often it's a cheap trick to say, 'Well, look at me, I can write a soft lead too.'"

THE CHAIR SITTER LEAD

"Too often we try just for the sake of description to say, 'He sits in his chair and rocks.' If that's the most interesting thing that somebody does, you're off to a boring start," Rich says. "Beware of anyone who starts a speech and says 'I'm so pleased to be here. Thank you for inviting me.' You know you're in for a boring speech. I think of the chair sitter lead almost in the same vein."

THE NARRATIVE LEAD

"This narrative lead is truly my favorite and the most underused in newspapers," says Rich.

"It's a lead where you just tell a story and hook the reader because the story is so wonderful. It can be the most compelling wonderful lead. We can make so many stories fascinating. Particularly court stories. They have so much drama and we dull them to death by saying something like, 'A 32-year-old friend testified yesterday that his roommate stabbed his girlfriend'—instead of saying, 'He was convinced that he had seen the murder. He saw a man in the shadows take a knife.'"

FORESHADOWING

"This is one of the techniques in narrative writing that is just so much fun," says Rich. "Even if it has to be as bad as, 'He got the feeling it was going to be a bad day.' Something that tells the reader some drama or suspense is coming. Foreshadowing is a wonderful technique that will work if you want to postpone the nut graph."

THE NUT GRAPH

No matter what your lead might be, the story still needs to be summarized. A paragraph is usually included to accomplish this task very close to the top of your story.

"You want the reader to know what he or she's reading without having to go farther than three paragraphs into the story," says Michael Tomasky. "If they have to go farther than that, they're certainly going to turn the page. So, if you haven't accomplished that in three paragraphs, and I mean three short paragraphs—not three 200-word paragraphs—people just aren't going to rock with you."

That paragraph is usually called the nut graph. The graph will probably wrap up any of the key Who, What, When, Where, Why or How elements that have not already been introduced through your lead.

Does this paragraph sound suspiciously like a summary lead? Surprise! Even if your whole point of trying to write a more "clever" lead is to avoid the summary

Chapter Ten in Carole Rich's textbook, "Leads and Nut Graphs" (pp. 148–180 in the second edition), starts with a review of the hard-news summary lead. The rest of the chapter introduces many of the leads covered in this unit of the telecourse, including anecdotal leads, descriptive leads, narrative leads, quote leads, build-on-a-quote leads and question leads. Rich also introduces several more leads, including contrast leads, teaser leads, mystery leads and list leads. More importantly, the textbook includes an excellent discussion of how to find the perfect lead for your story—and a look at leads to avoid.

lead formula, the reader is going to demand that you identify all of the key news elements in your story.

A well-written combination of a creative lead that introduces key points of the news and a nut graph that helps focus the story can help the writer avoid a common problem: The need to cram all six of the basic news elements into a typical summary lead/nut graph style that is, as Richard Aregood says, usually dense enough "to gag a mule."

AUTHOR'S NOTE

I have one final point to make in this chapter.

Forgive me for promising the secret to success to journalism. It's really quite boring—probably something you've already figured out.

Did my anecdotal lead, question lead, quote lead or scene-setting lead make you want to read this far?

Consider the following summary lead:

Reporters interviewed for this telecourse overwhelmingly agreed that a solid work ethic is the key to a successful journalism career, because a natural gift for writing is not enough by itself.

Yep. That's the secret. Pretty boring, but I've got my basic Who, What, When, Where, Why and How here.

How many journalism students are willing to read on if I tell them the equivalent of "All it takes is hard work?" Probably not many. My job as a writer is to keep them reading the textbook, not scare them off.

Guess what answer you'd get if you asked one of the only people on the planet who had won the Pulitzer Prize twice (the journalism equivalent of being struck by lightning twice while holding a winning lottery ticket each time), "How do you write a good lead?"

The answer? Be yourself, and stay simple.

"Don't make it sound like something that was in the paper yesterday," says Tom Knudson, of the *Sacramento Bee*. "Don't make it sound like something Bob Woodward did; make it new. Make it you. Let Bob Woodward be Bob Woodward. I should be myself. I think we reflect our culture—we reflect our society when we do that. And it makes for better reading. I think people read papers not just for facts, or figures, or the weather, for the sports and last night's basketball game—they read to be entertained and to learn.

"Another thing I try to remember—always try to remember the acronym KISS: keep it simple, stupid. You're not impressing anybody by using big words, by using acronyms, by throwing in every single fact into a lead. You may be impressing yourself; you may be impressing your editor; you may be impressing your professor. But, you're not impressing your reader. You're putting your readers to sleep. So I try to remember: Keep it simple, stupid."

That's your job as a news writer, too. If the summary lead says, "Wow! Read me," then use it. If you can think of something more potent to get the reader to the nut graph, then go for it.

However, if any of the other "more creative" leads had tempted you as the student to read this far—and I had not included the basic information (either in a nut graph or scattered throughout the essay)—I could expect a fairly angry reaction at the end of the piece. It would be the literary equivalent of claiming to know the secret of success, and then not revealing it.

Leave your readers satisfied.

Don't forget the nut graph.

Work hard.

Gene Policinski, USA Today*: "My response to question leads: Why?"*

Tom Knudson, Sacramento Bee*: "Anybody can wham, bam, slam an inverted pyramid lead onto a story, and sort of lag-bolt seven or eight more paragraphs. The challenge is . . . (whether) somebody (is) going to read that story and be moved by it."*

HOTTER, ANGRIER, DEADLIER: TODAY'S BREED OF FIRES

By Tom Knudson
Sacramento Bee

BOISE, IDAHO—The Rabbit Creek fire had just turned nasty.

Sluggish all morning, it swept up the north fork of the Boise River with a fury Kevin Brown will not soon forget.

"It is very difficult to put into words," said Brown, who was monitoring air traffic from a helicopter over the Idaho forest fire, which grew into the nation's second-largest this year.

"Awesome seems understated," he said. "Nothing was going to stop it. There wasn't anything we could do but watch."

HOLE BURNS IN PUBLIC'S WALLET: WHEN FORESTS IGNITE, FIREFIGHTING COSTS ROAR UNCHECKED

By Tom Philp
Sacramento Bee

As any major wild-land blaze dies to a smolder, firefighters head home and public attention shifts elsewhere, bills like these come in:

More than $90 an hour to borrow a fire captain from a Los Angeles department. More than $105 an hour for a state prison lieutenant, a sergeant and a guard to watch the $1-an-hour inmate laborers. And more than $7,800 an hour to rent a single big helicopter.

In an era of budget cuts and demands for fiscal restraint, there remain few bills as unsupervised and as big as those for fires. The millions spent on the ground and in the air explain a saying among some firefighters—"Black trees. Green wallets."

FROM HOTELS TO HONEY: IT ALL ADDS UP

By Tom Philp
Sacramento Bee

For government, a big fire means bills. Lots of bills. In the 1992 Fountain fire in Shasta County, state officials cut nearly 5,000 checks.

In 1992, the California Department of Forestry and Fire Protection dutifully added the bills up (more that $22 million), filled out some forms and sent the tab to Washington, D.C. Because the Fountain fire was bad enough to be declared an official federal disaster, Uncle Sam got to pick up the costs.

When state auditors a year later decided to go through the bureaucratic remnants of the 64,000-acre Fountain fire—boxes of invoices and payments—they found that little bills added up to bigger problems.

Here's a sampling of the kinds of bills that a big fire sends floating back to government agencies behind the fire lines.

The average American consumes about a pound of honey a year, according to the National Honey Board. Auditors would not have been surprised to find perhaps a few dozen pounds of the sticky sweet among the bills for feeding Fountain fire warriors.

But 1,810 pounds of honey?

There it was, in Special Purchase Order No. 769806.

Nearly a ton of honey.

For $7,223.57.

"The audit team could not determine reasons for the purchase," said the reviewers.

That was the first mystery.

The second was whether the honey was ever delivered and eaten after being purchased.

"The only evidence of receiving the items is the receipt itself," said the audit. There was no mention of the honey in any food inventory.

Coffee is the elixir for fatigued fire commanders. When a purchase of 80 cans of coffee appeared as part of the Fountain fire's food bill, auditors weren't surprised.

What raised eyebrows was the timing of Special Purchase Order No. 882450—in mid-September, when almost all the firefighters were back home.

AS HOMEOWNERS HEAD FOR THE HILLS, DANGER'S HOT ON THE TRAIL

By Tom Knudson
Sacramento Bee

PLACERVILLE—The narrow road winds along the edge of town, through a lovely wooded section of the Sierra Nevada foothills. Thick stands of manzanita, toyon and coyote brush line the sides of the road. Overhead, oak, pine and fir trees form a shadowy veil of vegetation. Half-hidden in the greenery are beautiful country homes, some worth $250,000 and more. To many, this is the dream of a lifetime—a house in the woods, outside the city's shadow.

But today's dream is also tomorrow's nightmare. For just as homes in a floodplain are threatened by disaster, so, too, are these homes in the path of danger.

The danger, though, is not a river's fury. It is fury of another kind: the uncontrolled combustion of carbon, oxygen and volatile gases, the whoosh, roar and blinding orange light of wildfire.

"It makes me shudder," said Doug Leisz, a fire safety specialist in Placerville. "The risk of people losing their homes, their lives in this situation is so apparent."

SMOKEY'S LEGACY: MOONSCAPES
FOREST FIRE SUPPRESSION LEADS TO ALL-KILLING INFERNOS

By Tom Knudson
Sacramento Bee

IDAHO CITY, IDAHO—John Thornton couldn't believe it.

Just ahead, on the side of Rattlesnake Mountain in central Idaho, was an environmental disaster.

Across 250 acres, nothing was growing, not even grass or brush. Gullies zigzagged across steep, unstable slopes.

"It was a moonscape," said Thornton, a hydrologist for the Boise National Forest.

FIRE RACES TOWARD TINY SIERRA TOWN: FIVE BUILDINGS BURNED IN BLAZE NEAR I-80

By Nancy Vogel
Sacramento Bee

A raging, out-of-control wildfire shot flames more than 100 feet into the air Thursday after exploding in sick, dry forest northeast of Truckee. It burned at least 3,000 acres, destroyed at least five buildings and threatened the small Nevada town of Verdi.

While hundreds of firefighters assaulted the inferno from hillsides and aircraft, struggling to save million-dollar homes, curiosity-seekers gathered in droves beside roads to gawk at the reddened sky and shoot souvenir photographs.

"It looks like they're watching the Fourth of July," said Jimbo Cronon, general manager of the Gold Ranch Casino in Verdi. "The first thing I sold out at my store is film."

EAST BAY HILLS REBUILD—WITH NEW VIGILANCE

By Nancy Vogel
Sacramento Bee

In 1976, fire ecology professor Harold Biswell armed a few former students with chain saws and took them to the Oakland hills.

"He said, 'There's going to be a catastrophic fire up here,'" recalled Elliott Menashe, who studied under Biswell at the University of California, Berkeley.

"'We have to start now.'"

They cut firewood from thick groves of Monterey pine and eucalyptus.

"It didn't last more than a week," said Menashe. "People called the university and said, 'What are you doing? Get these people out of here.'"

In the East Bay hills—as in much of California—it took a disaster to inspire people to prepare for a disaster.

On Oct. 20, 1991, the elements that Biswell feared converged: Hot gusts, called Diablo winds, twisting over the hills at 25 mph. A cache of freeze-killed and drought-baked debris in the hills' mini-forests. And a spark.

The nation's costliest single fire wrought most of its damage within a few hours—25 people were killed, more than 2,700 structures destroyed, more than $1 billion in property damage. So hot that it boiled asphalt, the fire also wiped out any notion that city dwellers need not fear wildfire.

Biswell, who died two years ago, "saw it all," said Menashe. "He just didn't have any PR."

PRESCRIBED BURNS: AVOIDING THE INFERNO

By Nancy Vogel
Sacramento Bee

BUCKS BARR—On a steep El Dorado County hillside, a firefighter dips his torch over dry grass. A necklace of fire crackles to life and begins to creep. The firefighter watches idly. A pair of wild turkeys step gingerly through the smoke. The man whose home sits a few feet from the flames smiles with satisfaction.

This, firefighters hope, is the fire of the future.

U.S. TEAM WILL SEEK WAYS TO PREVENT INFERNOS

By Tom Knudson
Sacramento Bee

Stunned by the cost and severity of the 1994 fire season, the federal government has assembled a team of specialists to find a way to avoid expensive and deadly fire seasons, officials said Wednesday.

The group, made up of representatives of several federal agencies, is expected to consider many prominent issues, including the tremendous buildup of fuel in Western forests, the surge of home building in fire-prone areas and the role of fire in maintaining healthy forests.

ALTERNATIVE VIEWS

Though much of this unit has been spent discussing different categories of leads, some journalists and scholars believe that the story should dictate the lead—the kind of lead shouldn't dictate the story.

Roy Peter Clark, of the Poynter Institute, says, "I don't think it's very helpful for reporters to have a list of 12 different kinds of leads—the surprise lead, the question lead, the summary lead or the direct lead. I think the process works in a different way. I think the best reporters and writers are looking for the best possible way to begin the story. They have on their metaphorical workbench . . . a number of different kinds of tools that they use. This is determined not by the kind of lead they're looking for, but their sense of how the story should be told. Does it need to be told quickly? Does it need to have a slower pace? Does it need to take advantage of information which is new and urgent? Does it need to focus on a character or an individual whom we're going to follow through some kind of a chronology? Those are the kind of overriding conditions that help determine how you'll begin.

"I also think that one of the problems in the way that we think about leads," Clark says, "is that we invest too much hope in them, which is to say that we think if we just craft the perfect lead, that we can fool the readers by dumping all the rest of the toxic waste in our notebooks into the stories. I think too much time and energy goes into the sort of crafting of the perfect lead. I think it would really help us, in fact, to lower our standards a little bit and to give us some time and energy to pay attention to the rest of the story."

SUGGESTED WRITING EXERCISES

Raw data from an actual story appear on page 213. In the space provided, write a lead for the story in each different style. Some leads will work better than others, but this exercise will at least help you get an idea of how the different leads work.

1 Summary lead

2 Anecdotal lead

3 Foreshadowing lead

4 Scene-setting lead

5 Question lead

6 Quote lead

7 Direct address lead

8 Narrative lead

9 Other type of lead

10 Pick up a daily newspaper, and find as many examples of the different types of leads listed in this chapter as you can. Rate the leads on effectiveness on a scale of 1–10. Did they make you want to read on? Why?

Raw Data for Writing Exercise

Directions: Use the raw data below to write your assigned leads and nut graphs.

Saturday, June 1, at noon, a large group of disgruntled water sports enthusiasts gathered at Lake Oroville, near the north end of the dam. Oroville Police Department estimated the crowd at 1,053. Butte County Sheriff's department accounted for 1,110 participants. The crowd was there to protest a number of problems at the lake. These included:

•**Sharply increased boating fees, which went into effect last September 1. (The annual day use passes went from $50 to $75 and annual boat/day use passes rose from $75 to $125. It also now costs $11 a day to put a boat in the water. Before September, the cost was $6 a day.)**

•**The closure of Loafer Creek boat launching area and picnic ground.**

•**The alleged failure of the state to live up to conditions imposed by the Federal Energy Regulatory Commission (FERC) when it approved the application by the state Department of Water Resources in the 1960s for construction of Oroville Dam.**

The crowd was very tense and angry. One boat flew a Jolly Roger (black skull and crossbones) flag. It was almost impossible to approach the demonstration site, because the road was clogged with vehicles. Dozens of protestors carried signs and placards. Most had messages that read, "Lower the Fees!"

One visibly enraged man, Bob Caldwell, shouted at the crowd and peace officers, repeatedly (and loud enough that he didn't need a bullhorn),

"Let them know we're not going to stand for it any more and that we're going to start today!"

Caldwell, of Paradise, represented United Fund for Outdoorsmen, one of many groups participating in the rally. Also represented were the Oroville Chamber of Commerce and the Oroville City Council. Mayor Susan Sears also supported the rally and was in attendance.

In a calmer moment, Caldwell told reporters, "We are here, because we can't afford to use the lake anymore. What about our senior citizens? They have paid and paid through the years."

Mayor Sears criticized the state's decision to raise fees and said that the tourism industry in the area would suffer because of the new fees.

Sears complained, "We are selling a way of life, a lifestyle. We are using the lake to promote Oroville and bring companies here. This will hurt more than tourism. This means less jobs in the area, because we may not attract new businesses.

"It just breaks our hearts to see the State of California turn around and take it away from us. We are here today to ask the state to stop selling us down the river."

Sears cited a recent survey that showed a drop in 20–40 percent of revenues for those local businesses that depended on the lake traffic. The drop was since the fees went into effect.

Original agreements between the state of California and the federal government promised "Free and reasonable access to facilities" when the lake was originally constructed. No arrests were made, and the protestors disbanded between 2 and 3 p.m.

The protests are under review, and public comments are being accepted by FERC. No state officials accepted an invitation to address the rally. According to one man, Rupert R. Roberts (of United Anglers of California), "When I look out there, I don't see a lake. I don't see foothills. I see 30 years of broken promises by the federal government and the state Fish and Game."

QUIZ

Choose the best answer.

1 A nut graph is

   a. a summary lead–style paragraph that capsulizes the news shortly after a nontraditional lead.

   b. a paragraph that turns the story, in a transition, to a new point.

   c. a paragraph that grabs the reader's attention directly after a quote lead.

   d. a paragraph at the end of the story, which summarizes the news value.

   e. a paragraph written by a slightly crazed reporter suffering from deadline stress.

2 Reporters seemed to feel the following about questions in leads:

   a. Questions often provoke the reader into wanting to finish the story.

   b. Questions frequently make a good lead.

   c. Questions rarely make a good lead.

   d. none of the above

   e. all of the above

3 The anecdotal lead is a creative alternative to the summary lead, made famous by

   a. progressive, alternative weekly newspapers such as New York's *Village Voice*.

   b. the staid, conservative *Wall Street Journal*.

   c. the Poynter Institute for Media Studies.

   d. none of the above

   e. all of the above

4 Alternatives to the summary lead are popular with some journalists because

   a. with so many information sources, the reporter needs to find a way to lure readers into a story.

   b. many readers have already heard the news on television or radio, and do not need summaries.

   c. feature news stories need a more creative introduction than the typical formula lead.

   d. none of the above

   e. all of the above

5 Andrew Loschilin, of the Russian news agency TASS, says that as many as 80 percent of his wire service stories start with

   a. a summary lead.

   b. a question lead.

   c. a narrative lead.

   d. a quote in the lead.

   e. an anecdotal lead.

6 Reporters seemed to feel the following about quotes in leads:

   a. Starting with a quote is sometimes a creative alternative to the summary lead.

   b. A creative way to use a strong quote near the top of the story would be to build up to the news maker's words—perhaps with a summary, anecdote or scene-setting lead.

   c. reporters should rarely use a quote in a lead—news makers rarely sum up the story well enough with a good quote.

   d. none of the above

   e. all of the above

7 According to Carole Rich, the following lead style should be avoided:

    a. the plop-a-person lead
    b. the chair sitter lead
    c. the nightmare lead
    d. none of the above
    e. all of the above

8 In their series about wild fires, Tom Philp, Tom Knudson and Nancy Vogel of the *Sacramento Bee*

    a. used scene-setting leads.
    b. used anecdotal leads.
    c. used summary leads.
    d. none of the above
    e. all of the above

9 According to Roy Peter Clark, of the Poynter Institute, and Carole Rich, of the University of Kansas,

    a. reporters should memorize a list of different types of leads and pick from one of them.
    b. reporters should alternate between summary, anecdotal, scene-setting and other leads for variety.
    c. reporters should let the content of the story dictate the style of the lead.
    d. none of the above
    e. all of the above

10 After a scene-setting, anecdotal or quote lead, a reporter needs

    a. to immediately identify the news makers, to avoid libel.
    b. a nut graph to focus the news value of the story.
    c. to tell the rest of the story chronologically.
    d. none of the above
    e. all of the above

SELF·TEST

This textbook contains some excellent examples of lead writing—in all chapters, not just in the examples featured at the back of this chapter. Read the introduction to each of the stories in each chapter, and categorize them as to style of lead:

1 Summary lead

2 Anecdotal lead

3 Foreshadowing lead

4 Scene-setting lead

5 Question lead

6 Quote lead

7 Direct address lead

8 Other type of lead

9 For each of the stories, find the nut graph. In the space provided here, write out the first sentence for the nut graph for at least five of the stories that do not use summary leads:

a.

b.

c.

d.

e.

10 This is your space to be a critic or an editor. Take any five of the leads given as examples in this book and rewrite them in a different style, using the space provided. For instance, if the story starts with a summary lead, use something more creative. If the story uses an anecdotal lead, try a direct address or a quote lead or some other type of lead as an alternative.

a.

b.

c.

d.

e.

FEATURE
NEWS
WRITING

You've studied hard-news style throughout this course, with a brief detour to compare the writing styles of newspaper work to those of broadcast and public relations writing. Next, we'll expand your newspaper writing abilities to include feature writing.

But, what is feature writing?

Some journalists think it's **fluff**: Soft news with no point.

Others confuse feature writing with **advocacy** journalism.

The best feature writing, however, is rooted in the same traditions of hard news that we have emphasized throughout the course. It avoids bias and often exhibits great reporting by allowing the writer (and thus the reader) to observe events from a different angle.

There is plenty of fluff printed in newspapers today; much of it has little or no news value. This space filler should not be confused with good feature news writing, which usually has some solid news judgment at its core.

Advocacy journalism has its place in our society (some would say America was founded on advocacy journalism), and often it has some of the same qualities and characteristics as the feature writing found in mainstream daily newspapers. Ultimately, though, advocacy journalism pushes the writer's opinion; it has much more in common with editorial writing.

Good feature news writing does not need to push the writer's point of view. It does, however, give the writer the license to stir up emotions and show the human side of the news. Good feature writing can provoke curiosity, call forth a laugh, evoke a tear or boil up anger—without overtly displaying the writer's prejudices.

Journalism students are usually trained to write hard news first. Since hard news is a dry, unemotional style, these students often have a difficult time making the transition to the demands of good feature writing.

OBJECTIVES

After 10 weeks of focusing on hard news, this unit will encourage you to think about and start writing feature news stories. Seeing how the best feature writing is built around the traditions of hard news will inspire you to make the transition to feature news writing by building and expanding upon the writing techniques you have already learned.

BEFORE YOU WATCH

This program is created to offer the beginning journalism student a perspective of the news other than covering it with a hard-news story. The term *feature writing* means different things to different reporters and editors, and this program will introduce the variations on covering the news which fall under the broad category of "features."

•Pay close attention to the ways journalists and teachers use the following terms in this program:

Profile	Human interest
Soft news	Investigative journalism
Trend story	Advocacy journalism
Background story	Mainstream journalism
News angle	Broadcast feature

WHILE YOU WATCH

1. Consider the relationship between hard news and feature news.

2. Notice the debate about advocacy journalism—a style of writing that is often confused with feature news writing.

3. Observe how Sam Donaldson's feature news story expands on a hard-news event.

4. Watch how Debbie Cobb's "bright" is designed to add a smile on an otherwise negative news day.

AFTER YOU WATCH

•Address the following questions in your journal. Or, if there's time, discuss them in class:

1. What elements of hard-news writing carry over to good feature writing? What can be accomplished with feature writing that cannot be accomplished by hard-news writing?

2. What similarities do feature writing and fiction writing have? What similarities do feature writing and editorial/opinion writing have?

3. Does feature writing have any relationship to advocacy journalism? Where does advocacy journalism fit in with our society?

4. Can a good feature story exist without some element of hard news in it?

5. Sam Donaldson talks about developing a point of view. How does he achieve this in his featured piece in the television program? How would a tabloid journalist or advocacy journalist approach the same story differently?

6. Is there any news value at all to the Debbie Cobb pumpkin patch story? If so, what is it?

In this program, several journalists explain the difference between writing feature news stories and writing hard-news stories. Through their narratives, several themes emerge:

•**Feature news is not just "fluff."**

•**The best feature writing reports the news just as well as a traditional news story, with added literary devices of suspense, human interest and emotion that make the telling of the event—or series of events—more interesting to read, watch or listen to.**

•**No matter what style of feature writing the reporter is using, the most successful pieces are built around some nugget of hard news.**

Those themes are reinforced by the following comments, most of which didn't make the final edits for the telecourse program on feature writing.

Claudio Sanchez, of National Public Radio, says most of his best pieces would be considered feature writing by "the normal definition of the word," but he prefers to call them "explanatory stories."

"I'd like to believe that I'm explaining things beyond the headlines," Sanchez says. "Things that we otherwise would not be able to hear or listen to."

Sanchez says that NPR reporters usually file shorter spot news stories—or hard-news condensations of their longer pieces—before working on the feature versions.

"I usually like to do those first before I do my feature story or before I do my longer story, because it allows me to condense precisely what the story is," he says.

"Once we have filed the obligatory story . . . then we're able to say, 'Well, here's the rest of the story,' as Paul Harvey would say. Here's why it's meaningful to you. You can't do that in 30, 45 seconds."

The longer versions of the stories, Sanchez says, allow him to have more fun with words and with the creative writing techniques usually associated with features.

Mitchell Stephens, a successful feature writer as well as a teacher at New York University, says newspapers could benefit from the additional topics—as well as the different writing techniques—that good feature stories bring to a publication.

"They're all journalism," Stephens says. "There's no line that says somehow if you report how kids are hanging out at a mall in the evenings, that is somehow not news. If you do a story that happened in Congress, that somehow is news. There are people in my journalism department who think it's absurd even to have a course called 'feature writing,' because it's all journalism; it's all ways of reporting on things.

"You don't have to start, certainly, with the summary news lead," Stephens says.

"You might start by telling a little story, an anecdote. You might start with some clever statement. A little snappy, zinger lead, they're often called. As the story progresses, you can also loosen up a bit on the rules. Your story certainly doesn't have to peter out [inverted pyramid style]. You can write a real solid end for the story. Maybe coming back to where you were at the start. Borrowing from the literary technique, the 'rondo' technique, of returning to the beginning. You can use much more description in your writing.

"I don't buy this thing that serious stuff is news, and feature is this little fluff stuff. In some ways, writing feature stories is a more serious journalistic activity than writing a news story.

"You still have to be clear, you still have to be efficient, and you still have to be engaging in your writing. There's no time to get super fancy. But you can be clever, maybe even make the occasional pun. You can loosen up in your style. You can play with words in interesting ways."

Joel Achenbach, a feature writer for the *Washington Post*, is a great example of a writer who brings both offbeat topics and a creative writing style to his newspaper. (Achenbach's unusual and humorous feature pieces have been combined into several successful books. Recommended reading: *Why Things Are,* published by Ballantine Books.)

"I've done both kinds of reporting," Achenbach says. "I've done hard-news reporting, where you have half an hour to pull together a story about a homicide that happened at 11:30 at night, and you have 500,000 newspapers that are about to go to press, and you're phoning in to the city editor [saying], 'We know where the body is.' I think that every reporter should do that kind of reporting. Should learn how to write and report on deadline, spell names right, figure out quickly, 'What is the news here; who are the players?' You have to learn how to do that at some point in your career."

Achenbach, like most of the other feature writers interviewed for the program, says it is important to have a news angle for a feature story. Writing hard news gives the reporter more experience in finding a "news peg" to focus the feature. It doesn't necessarily make the writing of a feature any easier.

"Having done both kinds of reporting, I think writing a feature story is harder because you have to think more. You have to tell a story that has a narrative arc to it, that takes you someplace, that has a shape to it," Achenbach says.

Anita Creamer, a successful feature writer and columnist from the *Sacramento Bee*, says that feature writing allows the news writer to put feeling into a publication that usually discourages the reporter from including emotion.

"Of course there's emotion in feature stories," Creamer says.

"How much depends on what the subject of the story is and what's appropriate to the story. I think there's nothing worse than reading a story that's flat and dull in the feature section. I, as a reader, expect more from a feature section.

"Finding a way to do that as a writer is what writing features is all about . . . the fun part of it. That and playing with language. You have a lot more leeway and a lot more freedom to do that than you do in news writing. What we do is not different from what is done in news. It's how we do it. And how we do it makes all the difference. Because of that emotion; because of the freedom of language."

ADVOCACY AND POINT OF VIEW: WHERE DO YOU DRAW THE LINE?

A point of view is an important element in feature reporting, with the writer tapping into the best techniques of narrative storytelling.

Beware! You should exercise caution when first attempting to incorporate these elements of feature writing into your work for the newspaper. Many students confuse having the permission to incorporate emotion, freedom of language and point of view into a feature story with getting the license to editorialize. For that reason, a dialogue about advocacy journalism is included in the lesson about feature writing.

Writers such as Michael Tomasky, of the *Village Voice*, practice a clever writing style that combines classic techniques of feature writing with clear opinion writing. While most mainstream journalists admit that these publications add a valuable perspective to our society (some would say that without advocacy journalists such as Samuel Adams and Thomas Paine, there would never have been an American Revolution), they would prefer to keep this kind of writing out of today's modern daily newspapers.

Peter Bhatia, managing editor of the Portland *Oregonian*, says that he respects certain aspects of advocacy journalism but has trouble with it in his—or any other—mainstream daily newspaper.

Jack Winning, the managing editor of the *Chico Enterprise-Record*, a small newspaper in northern California, agrees. "The question of whether or not we can keep our opinions on the editorial page has been with newspaper since day one," he says.

"Is it my job to make the news report unbiased? The answer is yes," Winning says. "If the question is 'Do I always do it?' The answer is, 'Probably not.' If the question is 'Can anybody do it?' I think the answer is 'Probably not.' This is not a robot talking; this is a subjective judgment. And to that extent we are subject to slanting the news. However, . . . if it turns into just an advocacy sheet, that's going to be recognized. We're not selling our paper to dumb people. They'll recognize it for what it is and they won't buy it. The front page is entirely different than the editorial page."

The tradition of advocacy journalism is practiced today mostly by independent publications such as the *San Francisco Bay Guardian* and New York's *Village Voice* and many other excellent news publications. Most of these newspapers publish on a weekly basis. Michael Tomasky explains his approach to advocacy journalism:

"I wouldn't reject everything that traditional journalism school teaches you," he says. "You still very much have to get facts out there. You have to be accurate. You have to be on target. You have to be fair. I see a slight difference between balance and fairness. If I think somebody is dead wrong on one story, and somebody else is dead right on the story, then I'll say that, and I'll concentrate maybe on the person who I think is dead right. Because that's what advocacy journalism is. And that's what I can get away with, and that's what I'm supposed to do."

Tomasky gives an example of advocacy reporting seeping into the mainstream press. "I as a reporter for the *New York Times* or any mainstream paper could put whatever spin I wanted on it simply by not saying, 'I think it means X' myself, or by calling up somebody who I know is going to say, 'I think it means X' and putting their quote in the third paragraph.

"If I want to downplay another particular spin, I can call up another person, who I know is going to say 'Y,' and I can play his quote or her quote in the 12th paragraph. Any journalist can construct a story in such a way that it has some of the reporter's biases. It's their job at the *New York Times* and the *Wall Street Journal* to take them out. It's our job here, to leave them in. And instead of having to call a person to say 'I think it means X,' I just myself say 'I think it means X.'"

An example of advocacy journalism that uses the techniques of feature writing is included at the end of the unit. The piece was published in the *Village Voice* and was written by Tomasky.

TABLOID-STYLE FEATURES

Much of the writing that is published in the *National Enquirer* could be classified as feature writing, and some of it is very entertaining and humorous. Sensational stories—about how somebody made a quick million, or narrowly escaped death, or caught a wanted felon, or discovered an astonishing cure for a disease—are staple goods for the inside pages of such publications.

But, show business gossip is the mainstay of the front pages. The *Enquirer* is also famous for breaking political scandals, such as the precedent-setting series of stories about what showed up in ambassador Henry Kissinger's garbage. Though the stories predated editor Brian Williams's presence at the *Enquirer*, he relates how the reporters and editors approached the story.

"They decided to see what Henry threw away," Williams says. "They checked the law to see what the property rights were on that. It was legal; his trash was out on the street. So they went and got Henry's trash and saw what was in the trash.

And as I remember there were some things that Henry shouldn't have been throwing away. That's clever. That goes beyond what a [typical] reporter would do. Would I go through the trash today? If the story called for it, sure."

BROADCAST
FEATURE STORIES

Many newspapers and television stations feel that, with the amount of information becoming available through mass media, a higher percentage of news stories should be packaged in one of the feature forms discussed in this program. Newspapers can compete better with television by featurizing news events. Television news teams rely on newsmagazine shows to elaborate on the basic reporting of the evening news to draw viewers away from other networks.

Rick Kaplan, former executive producer for Sam Donaldson's show "Prime Time Live" and current executive producer for ABC's "World News Tonight," explains his take on incorporating feature or "magazine style" reporting into television news:

"*U.S. News and World Report* is a magazine, but it isn't exactly a comic book," Kaplan says. "The same goes for television programs. 'Prime Time Live' is a program that does a lot of hidden camera work, that does a lot of investigative journalism, that does solid profiles, that does a lot of topical news. But there's all kinds of programs on the air [called magazine news shows]. If you listen to viewers, they think 'Oprah Winfrey' is a news program, 'Geraldo Rivera' is a news program, 'Phil Donahue' is a news program. 'Hard Copy,' 'Current Affair,' 'Inside Edition'. . . they're all on the air, and some would think they are suffocating the viewers. I'm not sure that's the case. We all do different things."

Those shows, Kaplan says, bear more in common with advocacy journalism or the tabloid journalism of *National Enquirer* than they do with mainstream newspaper feature writing styles.

"I think we do [our magazine-style stories] with a certain degree of dignity and integrity that isn't necessarily the rule at other programs on the nonnetwork places," Kaplan says.

Sam Donaldson explains his approach to broadcast feature news writing:

"If all you can do as a reporter on a magazine show is spend 14 minutes of someone's time out there and at the end of it say, 'And so, we can't figure out who's telling the truth here' or 'We don't know whether there's really a problem here or not,' you've wasted everyone's time. If we investigate a condition, an individual, a system for 'Prime Time Live,' we're going to come up with a point of view. And we're going to say to the audience, 'Look at these people scamming you. You see—through our hidden camera—them doing it.' At the same time, we can't go beyond our information, we can't go beyond the fact we have developed, and we must give the people who we think are the scammers a right to rebut and a right to reply."

Charles Kuralt, of CBS—who many consider to be the best television feature news writer of all time—has a completely different approach to feature news writing than Sam Donaldson. Donaldson specializes in feature news with a hard-news, investigative edge. Kuralt's "magazine television pieces" bear more in common with the profiles and human interest feature stories described by Mitchell Stephens in the telecourse program.

Kuralt explains his view of feature news:

"I've always assumed that if it was a story that interested or amused me, that it would have the same impact on other people. And it is true that people remember these feature stories. Hardly a day passes that somebody on the street or on an airplane doesn't say, 'I'll never forget that story you did about the man who built a yacht in his barnyard—the farmer who always hated farming, and decided to go out by sea to see the world.'

"That fellow couldn't tell you what the lead story was that day, has no idea what important event might have happened. The story he remembers is the farmer who built a yacht in his barnyard. So those stories do have impact; at least, people remember them for a long time. Sometimes for an absurdly long time. I have had people ask me about stories I did 30 years ago, that somehow stuck in their heads. The reason is that it was a story that somehow affected them. It reminded them of something that happened in their own lives, or they were just struck by the eccentricity of the subject.

"I wanted 'On The Road' stories to be an alternative to everything else that was on the news that night. A reminder that even in the midst of great events, in Washington and Moscow, that out here in Kansas, people still have to get the kids off to school in time, and life goes on. The life that never makes it to the front page.

"America seems, on the surface, to be homogenized. But, if you get off the interstate highway and drive on past the McDonald's, where, sure enough, a Big Mac tastes the same in California as it does in Maine, then you find a country that is rich and varied and full of fascinating people."

TYPES OF
FEATURE STORIES

Feature news stories have a number of qualities in common that can also work in hard news.

"Actually, there's no difference between good writing, whether it's good feature writing or good news writing," says Carole Rich, of the University of Kansas.

"I think we differentiate too much and so people think if there's a soft lead on a major news story, well, is this a feature. I don't see why we have to classify things. Why can't we just make it interesting writing?"

Rich's observations are accurate; the best writers rarely limit themselves to rigid forms. Still, beginning news-writing students might benefit from writing in several commonly recognized forms—before inventing their own.

"The whole thing in teaching journalism and doing a course like this is you do break things down into categories; all these categories to some extent are artificial," says Mitchell Stephens. "There aren't hard lines between them, but they're good ways of thinking about things. When I teach, I do that as much as I can. Try to separate things out. There are a bunch of different categories that feature stories seem to fall in."

The following list is a brief tour through the types of feature stories journalism teachers such as Rich and Stephens and successful feature writers such as Achenbach, Creamer, Donaldson, Kuralt, Sanchez and Tomasky mentioned when interviewed for the telecourse:

•**Trend story**—A trend story details what's changing. It explains what is new, where people are choosing to live, what sort of restaurants they are going to or what jobs seem to be trendy. Current fads of music or fashion are common trend stories. So are more mundane issues such as the stock market and health care. Readers often find these stories fascinating and important because the trends change their lives.

•**Background story**—A good background story can shed light on a breaking news event. What events in history led up to the event? How did it start? Who are the people who set the series of events into motion? Where are they now? What are they going to do? If the front page today is filled with bad news about an airline crash, tomorrow's paper might be filled with background stories about the captain, the passengers, the airline company or air traffic control issues. A detailed analysis of other disasters involving similar weather conditions or the same type of airplane would also make good background stories.

•**Bright**—A bright is a shorter, livelier story than newspapers usually run. It might be a cute thing that is happening somewhere obscure or a heartwarming story. The bizarre, eccentric, strange or odd bit of news that varies drastically from the hard-news formula story makes a good bright. A noisy kitten saving a family from a fire would make a good bright. Brights are designed to give readers a laugh or smile on an otherwise bleak and depressing news day.

•**Sidebar**—Sidebars are accessory stories to larger news stories. If the larger story is about a devastating earthquake, the following subjects might make good sidebars: Plans for future quake protection, effects of the earthquake on local roads, the role of the local Red Cross in relief efforts.

•**Localization**—A localization is bringing a bigger story closer to home. If you're doing a story on statewide tuition increases, for example, you might do a localized story on how the tuition increases directly affect attendance at your school. Often, well-written wire service stories can be localized with a few quick phone calls. The bylines are usually something like "AP story and staff writers."

•**Profile**—The challenge of this type of feature story is to paint an individual—with words—the way an artist would with oil and canvas. The writer must bring out what's interesting about the subject of the profile. Sometimes, the subject is involved in some sort of newsworthy activity: Arts, sports or politics. Often, the best features are written about the quiet people in the community—individuals whom readers know nothing about. The good profile writer is adept at eliciting quotes from the subject (and his or her friends, family and peers) as well as observing descriptive details about the person. The goal is to communicate more than what's on the surface about that person—giving the reader an opportunity to look beneath the surface to find out what makes the profile's subject different from all other human beings.

•**Human interest story**—The best human interest stories find news value in everyday events. Charles Kuralt's brand of journalism specialized in human interest stories. While the rest of the world seems to be in chaos on the front page, a human interest story might remind the reader that humans are still engaged in living normal, pleasant, worthwhile lives. These events are as worthy of news coverage as traffic accidents, bank robberies and courtroom battles. While the Congress is threatening to impeach the president, fiddle players from 8 to 80 might be playing bluegrass music in a mountain music festival, oblivious to the political drama. While a nation is on the verge of civil war, the preschool children may be inventing new games with dolls and toy soldiers. Human interest stories go one step beyond the profile, finding the value not only in the individual but in human interactions as well.

•**Investigative journalism**—An in-depth investigative piece allows a reporter to dig deeper into a potential wrongdoing than the customary and perfunctory glance a short daily news piece would give the same topic. Investigative reporters are often given weeks or even months to fight for the information to make an investigative piece work. Two-time Pulitzer Prize–winning reporter Tom Knudson, of the *Sacramento Bee*, specializes in investigative pieces about the environment. Sam Donaldson, of "Prime Time Live," and Steve Kroft, of "60 Minutes," specialize in investigative pieces for broadcast television. Bob Woodward's writing about the drug abuse of John Belushi, the campaign strategies of Bill Clinton and the political intrigues of Richard Nixon are all examples of investigative journalism. The investigative story takes a lot of hard work to pry information out of sources who don't want to talk. It takes hours of digging through dusty files and disorganized databases. Sometimes, the reporter must file Freedom of Information Act requests to force bureaucrats to give out documents they would prefer to hide. Often, the hours of work lead to nothing worth publishing. But, the stories that meet with success fulfill the ultimate reporter's responsibility: to function as the watchdog for society or as the unofficial fourth branch of government, also known as the "Fourth Estate."

TWO EXAMPLES

More than just theory and discussion, Unit Eleven of the telecourse focuses on two feature stories that illustrate the principles you have studied in this unit of the news-writing telecourse.

SAM DONALDSON'S STORY ON THE 5:33 TRAIN TO HICKSVILLE

Sam Donaldson's story in the telecourse program is an example of how journalists attempt to humanize a hard-news piece that might otherwise be reported only as a mere incident. A straightforward account of the event—with a summary lead and inverted pyramid—might be exactly what many editors (and readers or viewers) demand.

But, by reducing random acts of violence to an unemotional account of the number of people murdered (or injured), location, time and date, a news writer could miss many opportunities to bring out the human interest angles—the courageous acts, the sadness, the pain, the brutality, and the suffering—of the event.

Donaldson's account of the mass murder on the Long Island train dramatizes the events as well as reports the basic facts. It's a news feature approach that would work in news print as well as on television.

YOU
SHOULD
READ . . .

The Carole Rich textbook *Writing and Reporting News: A Coaching Method* has an entire chapter dedicated to writing profiles (pp. 515–534 in the second edition).

Profiles, however, are just one small part of feature writing. This would be a good point to review the chapter on "Storytelling and Feature Techniques." Many newspapers assume that hard-news stories simply deliver the facts; feature stories are the opportunities to use the more creative literary devices described in this part of Rich's text. Of course, as Rich points out throughout the book, attitudes in newsrooms are changing, and the once rigid distinction between hard-news and feature news writing styles is breaking down.

An additional reading exercise would be to pick up as many daily newspapers as possible in one day. Identify the stories that are features and the stories that are strictly hard news. Try to distinguish between the two different styles. Also, it would be good to look for stories that don't fit rigidly into either category.

As Carole Rich points out, the best feature writing often overlaps the artificial boundaries set up to categorize writing styles. Donaldson's piece blends human interest angles with a harder, investigative journalism for a powerful effect.

Which approach would you prefer as a reader or as a news writer?

DEBBIE COBB'S "BOOK'S PUMPKIN PATCH" STORY

Some editors, writers and readers might consider this a piece a light bit of fluff. But others would point out that the human interest angles of a story about the children at the pumpkin patch adds a smile and a bit of light news to an otherwise negative and violent menu of standard news items. Notice, also, that this light and easy story does have the important details of a "news nugget" that could otherwise be reported as a rather dull informational piece—the basic Who, What, When, Where, Why and How—to explain to parents that a wholesome, pre-Halloween

Claudio Sanchez, National Public Radio: "I'd like to believe that I'm explaining things beyond the headlines."

Joel Achenbach, Washington Post*: "The dirty little secret about journalism is that you have to do more reporting when you do a feature story."*

activity is available near the town for the youngsters and parents who could enjoy it. By presenting the piece as a feature story with a number of human interest angles, Cobb is able to communicate much more than just the raw information.

As Cobb points out in her close, except for the price of the pumpkin, the afternoon's entertainment for the whole family is free.

For Cobb, a good feature story "never starts with an agenda. The message evolves with the story." If you leave the viewer or reader with a smile, you've succeeded, she says.

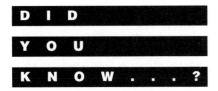

Many formerly conservative daily newspapers are leaning more toward feature writing—even on the front page. Weekly magazines, such as *Time* and *Newsweek*, also depend on feature writing for a high percentage of the content.

"Every story, to a certain extent, should be a 'feature' in that it's not just a news story," says Barrett Seamann, a senior editor at *Time*. "So that . . . had you been watching television, and reading your daily newspaper, and following a subject from day to day, we want to come out with a story the following week that's going to tell you yet something else you didn't know about that. Or maybe even change your mind about it.

"I suppose the word *feature* could be applied to that kind of journalism, and if so, then we are a feature magazine," Seamann says. "You look at daily journalism now, and television journalism and they're all going that route. Look at the *New York Times* . . . even the stodgy old *Wall Street Journal* does some of the best sidebar or feature stuff in the business. Their front-page lead, on a regular basis, is one of the highlights of daily journalism."

AFFIRMATIVE REACTION

By Michael Tomasky
Village Voice

The first expression of the notion that American society is, or should be, color-blind is generally accepted to have found voice in 1896. Dissenting from *Plessy v. Ferguson*, Supreme Court justice John Harlan, striking an early blow for integration (but a blow that Harlan did not strike consistently during his tenure), wrote that the Constitution "is colorblind, and neither knows nor tolerates classes among citizens." That "classes" means, of course, legal ones. Economic ones, Harlan knew as well as anyone else, are not merely tolerated by the Constitution but are a crucial basis of its design.

Time passed, and the nation saw more than its share of behavior that was indeed unconstitutional, but more to the point, malicious and murderous. Through it all, the color-blind society remained the goal and the catch phrase of the leaders of the mainstream civil rights movement and their defenders in government. Hubert Humphrey is noted for having said that civil rights legislation, as it was crafted back in the mid 1960s, would foster color-blindness—and that he'd "eat my hat" if it led to racial preferences. A few Supreme Court decisions later, it did just that, and the right, ever alert to such openings, saw that it could now present itself as the champion of color-blindness, and that some people would even fall for it. I recall being appalled at hearing—of all people—Ed Meese earnestly employ the phrase during—of all things—a defense of the Reagan administration's attempt to grant tax-exempt status to the openly discriminatory Bob Jones University!

The next two years will find affirmative action programs a central target of conservative attacks. Last week, the Supreme Court heard arguments in the case involving the white Colorado contractor who lost a state contract to a Latino-owned company even though his bid came in lower. The court will rule according to its own inscrutable calendar, but the odds are strong that the current court has five votes against such preferences, which usually require states to accept a minority-owned firm's bid if it is within 5 percent of the lowest overall bid.

But the heavy action, as is often the case these days, is in California. The 1996 March presidential primary ballot will likely carry something its proponents call the California Civil Rights Initiative, the main paragraph of which reads as follows: "Neither the State of California nor any of its political subdivisions or agents shall use race, sex, color, ethnicity or national origin as a criterion for either discriminating against, or granting preferential treatment to, any individual or group in the operation of the State's system of public employment, public education or public contracting." It will, in other words, strike down racial preferences in state hiring, admissions to state-run colleges and universities, and the awarding of state contracts.

To say the initiative will be controversial is rather like saying the Simpson trial will get some media attention. Nevertheless, based on readings of opinion polls and taking into account the fact that turnout for the presidential primary will probably be more heavily Republican than Democratic—since there will probably be several Republican presidential candidates on the ballot and only one Democrat, and he isn't expected to inspire much enthusiasm—the initiative is today rated a surefire winner at the polls.

It's the baby of Glynn Custred and Tom Wood, two academics who, according to Wood, "had the idea independently" at about the same time. Wood, while acknowledging that the initiative was likely to win big, poor-mouthed the operation as well, noting that the drive was not launched with the sort of massive outside support one might expect and saying that they're still not sure if the funding will come through to get the thing on the March '96 ballot (if Humphrey were still alive, I imagine he'd eat his hat if the funding didn't materialize).

Used by permission.

"People think we're some colossus that bestrides the world," Wood says. "Right now, we're just a very grassroots group of people." A 12-member advisory board is in place, which includes a few big names (Bruce Herschensohn, the GOP candidate against Barbara Boxer for U.S. Senate in 1992, and William Rusher, the former publisher of the *National Review*), one Democrat, one woman, and one minority (black businessman Errol Smith).

Wood seemed to spend as much time on the phone describing the things that CCRI wouldn't affect as the things it would. To be sure, the brochure his group sends out to prospective backers assures that "CCRI would leave all existing federal and state civil rights protections intact. The burden of proof that California's public employers, contraction agencies and educational institutions must meet when facing civil rights challenges to their practices would also remain unchanged." For good measure, the pamphlet also notes that CCRI would not restrict preferential treatment "on the basis of other criteria, including socioeconomic disadvantage."

The opposition? As usual, our side lags a little behind, but in the forefront are Willie Brown, the assemblyman who seems at this moment to be holding on as speaker of the state house (Democrats lost their majority last November, but one moderate Republican voted for Brown over his GOP challenger), and the California Teachers Association, which played a large role in the fight against Prop. 187.

That initiative, needless to say, is seen as having given rise to CCRI. Wood refutes this, but it's hard to deny that at the very least 187's victory sketches the outline of the coalition that's expected to lift the CCRI to victory (although black voters, half of whom backed 187, will surely be less enthusiastic about this one).

Will the opposition to CCRI be any more successful than the opposition to 187? Brown, appearing on "Crossfire" on January 12, stressed the points that, though not without moral merit, aren't likely to persuade many fence-sitters. In not so many words, he argued that the color-blind society is all well and good, but that we're a long way from it,

and until we get there, preferences are a needed tonic.

To make headway against the tide of opinion that made CCRI possible, liberals have to come up with some better ideas. For example: The conservatives argue that they're against preferences because preferences dictate "outcomes," whereas non preferential civil rights measures merely ensure "equality of opportunity," which Pat Buchanan said on the same "Crossfire" program he's entirely for. It's the attempt to manipulate outcomes that gets their goat. Very well; after all, who can be against equality of opportunity? Further, conservatives insist, as the CCRI pamphlet quoted above demonstrates, that they have no problem with preferences based on economic disadvantage.

Consider some obvious implications of supporting these two elements of affirmative action. It stands to reason, from a desire to ensure equality of opportunity, that you think state spending on pupils from school district to school district should achieve at least rough parity, if not be exactly the same per pupil. After all, how can you say you're for equality of opportunity and tolerate a public education system that spends two or three times the money on a child in Sherman Oaks than it spends on a child in Compton? Likewise, it stands to reason from support for preferences based on economic condition that, if parity does not exist, then you endorse preferences for students on whom less is spent.

Logical, no? Of course, conservatives would never in a million years support real equality of opportunity, because that would mean they'd be the ones leading the fight for equalization of school spending and for equal opportunity in general. It's always been the central contradiction in their argument. Making this the issue, rather than retreating to the usual emotional appeals about the rolling back of the clock and other clichés that too many people tired of long ago, may or may not win. But at least it forces the conservatives' hand. You want equality of opportunity, Governor Wilson, Speaker Gingrich, Governor Pataki? Then by all means, let's have it.

The following is just one story from environmental beat reporter Tom Knudson's series of feature stories about the Sierra Nevadas. The series—which filled an entire 16-page broadsheet edition when reprinted in its entirety—won a Pulitzer Prize in 1992.

COMFY WOODSTOVE FIRES BRING CLOUD OF ILL HEALTH

By Tom Knudson
Sacramento Bee

TRUCKEE—As a real estate agent, Lois Nisporic has heard a lot of talk about the joys of mountain life—the spectacular scenery, the clean air and so on.

The other day in Reno, she heard a different story.

"I had met this woman," Nisporic said. "When I told here I was from Truckee, she said, 'Truckee! I hate to go through that town in the winter—the smell from the woodstoves just knocks you out."

Truckee, a picturesque mountain town that clings to the east side of Donner Pass about 100 miles northeast of Sacramento, is hardly unusual. Today, air pollution from woodstoves is fouling mountain skies from one end of the Sierra Nevada to the other.

At Mammoth Lakes, about 160 miles southeast of Sacramento, the glorious eastern wall of the Sierra is no longer so glorious, obscured by a foul-smelling layer of wood smoke. Step outdoors in Quincy, Nevada City or South Lake Tahoe on a winter morning, take a deep breath—and gag.

The problem is more than an inconvenience and a stain on the majesty of the Sierra. Today, many officials believe wood smoke is bringing a cloud of ill health to the mountains.

"The old statement that wood smoke is good smoke isn't really true," said Thomas Cahill, head of the Crocker Nuclear Laboratory's air quality group at the University of California, Davis.

"You're looking at some mild carcinogens—cancer-causing chemicals—in enormous quantities. You've got to be concerned about the health effects."

Clearing the air is not going to be simple. Few things are more sacrosanct in the mountains than a cozy wood fire on a cold winter night. Some towns, though, have started to take action. Mammoth Lakes, for example, now bans wood burning when air quality is poor. But other communities, such as Truckee, have done little or nothing.

"Basically, the majority of days we sample in winter in Truckee are violations of the state health standard," said Russell Roberts, air pollution control officer for the Northern Sierra Air Quality Management District.

"And it's not a borderline situation. In December, Truckee had a reading of 112 micrograms per cubic meter. That's more than twice the state standard."

Scientists have yet to pursue actual field-work that might link wood smoke to a rise in respiratory disease in the mountains. In fact, scientific knowledge about wood smoke in general is limited, in part because government agencies and universities tend to worry more about urban air pollution.

Today, though, mountain skies often are filthier than city skies. Consider:

- Levels of benzo(a)pyrene—a cancer-causing compound found in wood smoke, automobile exhaust and elsewhere—are 25 times higher in Mammoth Lakes in the winter than along the freeways of suburban Los Angeles, according to a California Air Resources Board study.

- The amount of respirable dust—dust so small you breathe it into your lungs—in mountain towns routinely exceeds the state health standard of 50 micrograms per cubic meter, often by two to three times. In February 1990, Truckee and Mammoth Lakes had higher average respirable dust levels than Los Angeles or Sacramento. Most of the dust comes from wood smoke.

"It's very striking," Roberts said. "You start with this brilliant white filter and at the end of 24 hours, it's black. And it smells like wood smoke. And everything on that filter you are breathing into your lungs."

The list of pollutants in wood smoke is long and worrisome. It includes carbon monoxide, benzene, dioxin, formaldehyde, arsenic, sulfur dioxide and a complex family of chemicals called PAHs—short for poly-cyclic aromatic hydrocarbons—many of which are carcinogens.

On top of that you have billions of air-borne dust particles, ranging from visible chunks of ash to microscopic specs of dust.

"The smallest particles are the biggest threat," said Bill Sessa, a spokesman for the Air Resources Board. "We're talking about particles smaller in diameter by several times than a human hair—small enough they can bypass your body's natural filtering system and cause problems deep in the lung.

"In many cases, these small particles are carriers for other compounds, the PAHs and things like benzene and dioxin."

Just how concerned should one be?

"If you live in one of these mountain areas, it makes sense to try to avoid being exposed," Sessa said.

"Anytime anyone is exposed to these pollutants above the health standard, there is ample reason for concern. But the people we are most concerned about are those who have existing respiratory problems and heart disease—and young children and the elderly."

In October 1989, the Air Resources Board approved a list of suggested reforms, from requiring more efficient woodstoves in new homes to establishing voluntary no-burn days when air quality is poor.

In December, Mammoth Lakes went a step further, adopting a mandatory ban on wood burning when air quality is bad.

"Most people agreed we have an air quality problem," said William Taylor, asso-ciate planner for Mammoth Lakes. "You can see it and you can smell it. And they were willing to cooperate."

In Truckee, progress has been slower.

"What I hear is an unwillingness, a ner-vousness to proceed until the technical facts are in," said Roberts of the Northern Sierra air quality district. "There are demands we do more monitoring. The fact is people are voting with their woodstoves. Very clearly, they want to burn wood. How we deal with that desire and solve the air quality problem at the same time is going to be a very diffi-cult proposition."

ALTERNATIVE VIEWS

Many journalists feel feature writing gives them an excuse to write more column inches. Joel Achenbach, of the *Washington Post*, feels that's a mistake.

"The biggest problem with feature writing is that we do ourselves a disfavor and we write too long," he says. "We think we're writing in a beautiful way—you know, 'I write so well.' In fact, it's not really that good. If people really wanted to read good writing they should pick up Dostoyevsky or something. We bury the significance of the story sometimes amid this big clutter of words. That's one of the nice things about a news story; sometimes you cut to the chase."

GLOSSARY

ADVOCACY   A style of journalism in which a reporter is expected to take sides in controversial issues. Advocacy journalists assume their role is to interject a personal bias into a story—the opposite of mainstream journalism, in which reporters are expected to be as objective as possible. Though mainstream feature writers are often allowed to develop a point of view, they are encouraged to remain as objective and balanced as possible—to stop short of advocacy, which also often employs techniques of feature writing.

BACKGROUND STORY   A feature story that gives the reader a behind-the-scenes look at a major news event. A backgrounder can give historical, political or personal context to a hard-news story that might ordinarily not be reported with much depth.

BROADCAST FEATURE   Also known as a "television magazine piece" or radio feature, this is a longer than usual broadcast news story that gives the reporter 5–25 minutes (compared to the usual 30–60 seconds) to develop a deeper look at a news event, trend or individual. The broadcast equivalent of a newspaper feature story.

FLUFF   A feature story of absolutely no substance. A story with little or no news value, worth little more than filler for the space between ads.

HUMAN INTEREST   The emotional angle of an event or occurrence.

INVESTIGATIVE JOURNALISM   A news piece that requires a great amount of research and hard work to come up with facts that might be hidden, buried or obscured by people who have a vested interest in keeping those facts from being published.

MAINSTREAM JOURNALISM   The style of journalism practiced by most daily newspapers that embraces the traditional journalism values of objective and balanced news coverage. A style of journalism designed to appeal to the widest cross-section of American society.

NEWS ANGLE   The aspect, twist or detail of a feature story (no matter how fluffy it might seem) that pegs it to a news event or gives it news value for the reader.

PROFILE   A feature story that focuses on one individual, painting a word picture of the attributes that make that individual unusual or interesting.

SOFT NEWS   A story that is not necessarily built around a breaking news event.

TREND STORY   A feature story that focuses on the current fads, directions, tendencies and inclinations of society.

Pick a major current event happening near your town right now. (If you can't think of one, imagine that there has been a big forest fire or earthquake near your town.)

Explain, in the space provided, how you would develop each of these different types of feature stories:

1 Human interest story

2 Background story

3 Investigative report

4 Profile

5 Trend story

Bonus: Develop a feature angle that is not listed for the same event.

QUIZ

Choose the best answer.

1 Sam Donaldson's feature story used in the telecourse

   a. was designed to bring out the emotional consequences and human interest angles of a mass murder that had been reported by hard-news accounts as a dispassionate collection of facts and numbers.
   b. was created by Donaldson to editorialize, in classic advocacy journalism style, against gun control laws.
   c. was a typical soft feature news story, with almost no hard-news element visible in the writing and editing.
   d. none of the above
   e. all of the above

2 Donaldson's feature story

   a. could not be adapted for a newspaper-style feature story.
   b. is an example of a background story.
   c. is an example of a personality profile.
   d. is an example of a trend story.
   e. is an example of typical hard-news coverage.

3 Debbie Cobb's feature story about the pumpkin patch

   a. has absolutely no news value.
   b. is an example of typical hard-news coverage.
   c. was designed as a foil to the standard bad news, to bring a smile to viewers.
   d. none of the above
   e. all of the above

4 Jim Nicholson, who won the Distinguished Writing Award from the American Society of Newspaper Editors for his writing in the *Philadelphia Daily News*, compares well-written obituaries to

   a. a dirge.
   b. a feature profile story.
   c. a hard-news, summary lead, inverted pyramid story.
   d. a painting.
   e. a nail in the coffin.

5 According to Joel Achenbach of the *Washington Post*, the "dirty little secret" about journalism is

   a. feature story writers work harder than hard-news reporters.
   b. feature story writers often make up quotes to color the story.
   c. feature story writers are allowed to use more adjectives than regular reporters.
   d. feature story writers never worry about deadlines.
   e. feature story writing is easier than hard-news writing.

6 Sound bites from the first five writers featured in this unit of the telecourse revealed the following theme:

   a. Feature writing allows reporters to relax and write fluff pieces.
   b. Feature writing belongs on what used to be called the "woman's page" and is now relegated to the "focus" or "lifestyle" page.
   c. Most good feature writing focuses on one person.
   d. Most good feature writing contains at least some news value.
   e. The only good feature writing is an elaboration of hard-news events.

7 Feature writing for television is similar to newspaper feature writing, in that

a. it often involves a writer's point of view.
b. it brings out emotion in an event that might be just reported as dry facts in a hard-news piece.
c. it can better highlight major news events by reporting about background information, personalities or trends represented by the events.
d. none of the above
e. all of the above

8 Advocacy journalism

a. is designed to promote a cause.
b. is common and appropriate in mainstream, daily newspapers.
c. is essentially the same as feature news writing, since it allows the reporter to ignore objectivity and balance.
d. none of the above
e. all of the above

9 Which of the following could never be considered a feature story?

a. an obituary
b. a game story
c. a sidebar
d. a human interest story
e. none of the above

10 Some of the devices that Sam Donaldson used in his television feature piece about the subway shooting include

a. dramatization.
b. music.
c. special video effects.
d. background reporting.
e. all of the above

SELF·TEST

Compare the differences in the Sam Donaldson story on "The 5:33 Train to Hicksville" with Debbie Cobb's "Book's Pumpkin Patch" story in the space provided.

1 Many of the writers interviewed in the television program said that good feature writing can bring out the emotion in a story. What emotions are these stories designed to evoke in the viewers?

2 How would these stories be treated differently in a newspaper feature story? A magazine feature story? What would be the same?

3 Many of the writers interviewed in the television program said that most feature writing still contains a bit of "hard news." Is the "Book's Pumpkin Patch" story pure fluff—meaningless "soft news" space filler? Or is there some news value to the story?

4 Is there a hard-news element to "The 5:33 Train to Hicksville" story, or are Donaldson and ABC just sensationalizing a tragic event?

5 How would an advocacy journalist handle "The 5:33 Train to Hicksville" story differently than Donaldson did? How would a tabloid journalist handle the story differently?

EDITORIAL, OPINION AND COLUMN WRITING

This course has spent 11 weeks encouraging students to write news stories that show the maximum of objectivity and minimum of bias. Now you will be asked to write in a style that has no other point than to promote your opinion.

Is this schizophrenic?

Perhaps. Many journalism instructors won't touch opinion and editorial writing within a basic news-writing course. They feel that students might get confused and start mixing opinion in with hard news.

However, it can be quite instructive and therapeutic to write in a style that gives you an excuse to flaunt your convictions. By purposely writing in this style, it is easier to see when your own bias might be accidentally creeping into a news story that should ideally avoid opinions. Learning to tell the difference can make your basic reporting more credible.

There are other reasons to study opinion writing at this point in the course.

Perhaps the most important reason is that there is a direct connection between the best editorial writing and traditional hard-news writing styles. Most successful editorial writers have earned the right to write opinion pieces for their newspaper through years of working as beat reporters. They apply the critical thinking and fact-finding skills of basic journalism to their arguments, which usually makes their writing more persuasive.

The same can usually be said about critical review, column writing and other kinds of opinion articles featured regularly in the newspaper. Within the most powerful of these pieces, you'll usually find a solid bit of hard-news reporting.

There is one final reason for introducing editorial/opinion/column writing at this stage. Soon, many of you will be asked to write **editorials** for the school newspaper. You'll be given the opportunity to write **critical reviews** of local music or theater presentations or even asked to write your own **column**.

If you don't get the opportunity to study opinion writing in an editing class, this is the point where you'll learn to make the connection between the basics of news writing and journalistic opinion writing.

OBJECTIVES

This unit in the news-writing class will show how you can apply basic journalistic skills (which have been presented for the past 11 weeks) toward effective editorial, critical review, column and opinion writing.

This program contrasts the writing style of editorial, opinion and column writing with the writing styles of hard-news and feature news writing, which usually have the mission to cover events from an unbiased and objective point of view. In the process, the program prepares students to write their own opinion pieces.

•**Pay close attention to the ways editorial writers, column writers and other opinion writers use the following terms in this program:**

Bias	Emotion
Objectivity	Voice
Balance	Reporting
Point of view	Humor

WHILE YOU WATCH

1. Look for techniques of news writing that are still important for successful editorial and column writing.

2. Notice the subtle differences in attitudes expressed by editorial writers and column writers.

3. Recognize which aspects of opinion writing are in direct contrast to news writing.

4. Observe the qualities that these great opinion writers have in common.

AFTER YOU WATCH

•**Address the following questions in your journal. Or, if there's time, discuss them in class:**

1. What makes readers laugh at a humor column?

2. Several of the writers interviewed in this program (Dave Barry, Roger Ebert, Richard Aregood) have won the Pulitzer Prize—the most prestigious award given to journalists. What attributes do these great opinion writers have in common?

3. Many beginning journalism courses do not address opinion writing. Some instructors feel that it might be counterproductive to teach young journalists how to report the news objectively in one part of the semester while encouraging them to write editorials or columns in another. What do you think about this dilemma?

4. Objectivity is emphasized in basic hard-news writing. How does a reporter earn the right to write columns and editorials that express opinions?

5. What makes Fahizah Alim's column about black Vietnam veterans so powerful?

THE
LESSON

Roger Ebert's Pulitzer Prize–winning criticism of movies in the *Chicago Sun-Times*. Dorothy Rabinowitz's conservative editorials in the *Wall Street Journal*. Dave Barry's goofy humor in the *Miami Herald*. Richard Aregood's Pulitzer Prize–winning columns on the politically liberal editorial page of the *Philadelphia Daily News*. Fahizah Alim's emotionally powerful columns in the *Sacramento Bee*. Scott Ostler's knee-slapping sports columns in the *San Francisco Chronicle*.

What do they all have in common?

These writers have earned the privilege to express personal opinions in a mainstream daily newspaper—the kind of publication that usually requires writers to remove any vestige of personal bias in the normal reporting of the news. The kind of publication where the worst insult a reporter can get is to have the boss send back a story, complaining, "It sounds like you're editorializing."

How do these journalists earn the right to editorialize?

The answer is, they usually master the reporting process—all of the things you've studied so far in this course. They know the summary lead and the inverted pyramid better than the midnight path to the refrigerator. They've progressed beyond journalism rudiments to write engaging feature stories. They've learned how the community works—grinding out formula hard-news pieces on the courts and the cops or in the gymnasiums and the ballparks. They've assimilated the quirks of journalism language and conquered the *Associated Press Stylebook*.

Perhaps they've reached some sort of journalism Utopia—that place sports reporter and columnist Terry Armour, of the *Chicago Tribune*, jests about in Unit Six of the telecourse—when all the elements of good writing and good reporting align in perfection. When a reporter reaches that point, Armour jokes, it's time to retire.

Or to graduate to the opinion or column section of the newspaper. "I get letters sometimes from college students who want to become columnists," says Dave Barry. "They make it very clear that they don't want to be reporters first. They want to skip that nasty phase and just go right to telling everybody what wonderful ideas they have. And I tell them, 'I don't think you should do that; I don't think you can do it.' Very few papers are just going to hire somebody to be a columnist. I think it's a mistake to miss the experience of trying to be a journalist first."

EDITORIAL WRITING

Somewhere between the basic freshman news-writing and reporting class and working at a newspaper, the best students become editors of the college newspaper. Often, this job comes with the responsibility of writing editorials. But where do we teach editorial writing? Many teachers avoid the topic in the reporting class. The justification: Never shall opinion and reporting mix! Student reporters must learn to be objective, and we can't confuse them by introducing editorial writing so early in their education process.

In editing class, we teach headline writing and copy editing and page design. There's rarely a moment spent talking about writing editorials. The closest we might come to actually discussing this kind of writing in school is not in the journalism curriculum but in the argument and persuasion unit of a freshman English class. Perhaps that is why so many editorials in school newspapers read like rhetoric essays.

The editorial writers interviewed for the news-writing telecourse all agreed: The very best editorials usually exhibit strong opinion, built around a bit of hard-news reporting.

Here's an example: An editorial could be written anytime about the pros or cons of nuclear weapons. But the day the president announces that America's missiles will stay armed and ready although they will no longer be aimed at a specific target, editors have a news nugget to build an opinion piece around.

An opinion piece must take a stand. It is not enough to just complain about events. Advocate getting rid of nuclear weapons completely, or advocate building more and aiming them at communists in China instead of the Soviet Union. Report the news, take a side and defend your stance with the rest of your editorial.

"Pick something you care about," says Richard Aregood. "If all you care about is whether Butthead really likes Beavis, write about that. And if you really desperately care about Bosnia, write about that. Make sure you know what you're talking about, and you add the component of passion. Make sure you back it up, . . . and you've got one hell of an editorial if you do it right. It's that simple."

The first part of the editorial is based on much of what we have already learned in this course. The news nugget must contain all of the important basic elements—including the old standbys Who, What, When, Where, Why and How. Your story needs a lead that will entice the reader to read the entire editorial. The copy must conform to newspaper style. You still have the same ethical and legal obligations to honor as you did while writing hard news.

"Any editorial has to have some kind of news element," Aregood says. "You have that news element as the hook."

The rest of the writing will bear much resemblance to the aforementioned English paper.

PREMISE

Classic argumentation is usually built around a premise. (In English, it is called a thesis sentence.) Some writers state the premise early and defend it; others build up a case for the premise, and then state it at the end of the editorial. In almost every case, the editorial must have a point to prove or disprove.

Aregood puts it this way: "We try to have every editorial say one thing. Just one thing. Not everything that we know on the subject, not everything we think everybody should know, but one thing. The most important thing. Which we then pound into the ground."

P URPOSE

The best editorials usually have a purpose. Here are a few that might help you focus:

Convince readers to vote one way or another.
Persuade readers to act on something.
Convince readers to spend money on something (taxes, charitable causes, etc.).
Persuade readers to change their views.
Convince readers to join a cause.
Persuade readers to fight an injustice.

Notice that there is a lot of persuasion and convincing going on in the list of purposes for writing editorials, and not a lot of arguing. Many students feel that simply expressing anger is plenty of purpose for an op/ed piece. Most readers find this kind of writing boring or offensive.

A UDIENCE

The editorial writer must think of the audience being addressed. Little purpose is served if the editorial is simply targeted at people who already agree with the editorial writer's point of view. The true power of the press is to convince and persuade those who disagree with you—to change their minds. Of course, that often provokes heated public debate—and even angry letters sent back to the newspaper by those who aren't convinced. That's OK. Publishers know that controversy usually sells papers, and angry letters to the editor are a cheap way of filling up all of that space in between advertisements.

Assuming your goal is to change a few minds, those who teach persuasion say the best defense of a premise must have a balance of emotional, logical and ethical appeal. Leaning heavily on any one won't be very persuasive. Here are some hints:

Emotional editorials without any logical appeal might stir feelings but will rarely convince nonbelievers.

Logical editorials without ethical or emotional appeal are usually too dry to be interesting. Don't bore the reader with pure logic. Show some emotion.

Ethical editorials without a balance of logical and emotional appeal come off as preachy, especially to those who do not hold the same moral standards as the writer.

Remember that you are writing for people who do not think like you do. Leave the cheerleading for the pep rally, and use this opportunity to unleash your skills as a reporter and a writer.

Style

Reporters learn a great deal about how the world works while covering important events; they yearn to take sides while writing their stories but cannot. Though it is not appropriate for a reporter to be writing a hard-news story and an editorial about that event in the same issue of a newspaper, a few years of experience as a journalist can only improve editorial pieces. The hard-news reporting skills will be valuable in constructing logical appeal to back your premise. Great opinion writing without facts to back it up is rarely convincing.

The storytelling skills gained as a news writer can help in constructing the emotional and ethical arguments needed to back your premise. These skills all relate to earlier lessons learned in this course about journalism style and the art of brevity.

Thomas Hylton, a Pulitzer Prize winner for a 20,000-circulation newspaper in Pottstown, Pennsylvania, has this to say about writing editorials:

"It's harder to write short than long. It's easy to write short and shallow. The next thing is to write long and meaningful. The hardest thing is to write short and meaningful."

Richard Aregood agrees. "Say it as briefly as possible," he says. "You don't have to tell everybody everything you know. I think that's the most important thing young reporters should think about. You've got to learn a lot of stuff to cover the story. Probably 80 percent of it doesn't matter. Take every possible word out— every possible word that doesn't advance the story or editorial."

Editorials to Avoid

That's enough for now about how to write editorials that work.

Here are common kinds of beginner's editorials you should avoid.

THE WHINER Who wants to read a monotonous inventory of complaints? An editorial like this is less creative than a shopping list. Simply detailing a list of problems makes a very poor editorial; offering a solution, and defending it, is generally considered better writing.

THE '60s FOLK SINGER Why are there taxes? Why are they taxing me? Why aren't they taxing the rich? Why are they spending the tax dollars so quickly? Who invented taxes, anyway? Why is this editorial so taxing?

At least Bob Dylan suggested that "the answer, my friend, is blowing in the wind."

A barrage of questions, even rhetorical questions, does little to support your argument or convince your reader. The most likely reaction, instead, is for the reader to ask, "Why am I reading this?"

THE I, ME, US, WE There's nothing more self-serving than an editorial or column with a picket fence of first-person pronoun I. There "I" was backstage with Aerosmith. "I" asked the lead singer if "I" could help myself to the free cold cuts and beer. "I" thought the band was really gnarly, rad and cool.

"It's OK to write about personal things," says Dave Barry. "I do it. I think a lot of people do it. But as soon as you get the feeling when you're reading a column that the basic point that the person's making is 'Boy, am I more fascinating than anyone else in the whole world,' then you lose it. That's a mistake a lot of would-be columnists make. They're just self-involved. And they think that anything that happens to them is fascinating to everyone else. It isn't. You have to make it interesting."

HUMOR WRITING

Columnist Michael Tomasky, who writes fairly serious opinion columns about New York City politics for the *Village Voice*, still understands the power of a good laugh in any kind of persuasion. "No matter how dry the subject or how boring you think it might seem to readers, always use quotes that are funny. Always try to coach them out of people," he says.

Pulling humorous quotes from news makers' interviews requires a bit of luck as well as skill. Amusing the reader with your own words takes a lot of hard work.

"I am an obsessive rewriter," says Dave Barry. "If they ever had one of those programs that shows all the different versions of a document, mine would be in the thousands for almost every column I write. It's supposed to look like it just came out—and you were probably drinking when you did it—in five minutes. But for me it's hour after hour after hour of staring at the screen and just changing, changing, changing."

Andy Rooney, Dave Barry, Scott Ostler and Joel Achenbach—all journalists interviewed for the telecourse—are considered among the most skilled and successful humorists in journalism. They all agree that trying too hard to be funny can kill the fun of comic writing.

According to Rooney, "E. B. White once said, 'Analyzing humor is like trying to understand the theory of flight by dissecting a sparrow.'

"I think that it would be wrong for me to start out with nothing in mind but being funny," says Rooney.

The better approach, he says, is to practice good journalism and let the humor grow out of the irony inherent in real life.

"We do quite a bit of reporting here," Rooney says. "If you really get something that you know is true, and you can back it up, you can hang a piece that amuses people on just a few little facts. You can take apart the ingredients on a package of corn flakes or anything else—a drug product, or something—and if you get something in there that is absurd and wrong, and dishonest in the sense that so much advertising is dishonest, then you can hang a whole piece on that . . . and it strikes people funny."

Scott Ostler, humor columnist for the *San Francisco Chronicle*, has a similar approach. Ostler's beat is the world of professional sports—a business as rife with pathos as it is with irony and sarcasm.

"I found that you can make serious comments by using humor, and not only get your point across but get people to read it," Ostler says. "If you start out saying, 'I'm going to write something very serious today about steroids,' people are gone. If you start out with saying something kind of humorous or off the wall then you grab people. So it's weird. I don't try to write funny stuff. It just comes out that way.

"I don't know what makes people laugh," Ostler continues. "I guess the unexpected—the Chevy Chase thing, where he's walking out in a dignified suit and he trips and falls. I guess, over the years, I've developed some sort of laugh filter that allows me to figure out a twist or a play on words that might make people laugh. But, if you watched me writing a column, you would probably think I was writing a phone book. I'm very serious. I don't type a line and say, 'Ho ho ho, that's really funny.' For me, it's kind of a grim process."

Of those interviewed for the telecourse, Dave Barry felt the most comfortable talking about what works in humor and what doesn't. Being successfully funny, he says, has a lot to do with understanding why people laugh.

"Humor is really closely related to fear and despair," Barry says. "I believe the reason people have a sense of humor is if they didn't, then they would look around; they would realize, with their perfectly rational brains, that we live in an extremely dangerous, scary world, run by all kinds of forces over which we have no control, and we're all going to get older and sicker and die. It's a scary thing. And if we can't react to that in some way that allows us to release the fear and the anxiety, we're in deep trouble. So we laugh."

Those who don't laugh, Barry says, are "the humor impaired. I know they're out there. I get letters from them.

"I give up on trying to answer the question why are certain things funny and why they aren't," he says. "You need to have a real strong sense of pacing. Too many attempts at humor fail because it takes forever to get to what's supposed to be funny. The writing just wanders around before it gets there. Or, once it gets there, it says it over and over and over. It doesn't get out of there quickly. It's a lot like stand-up comedy, in a sense. You don't let the reader see it coming, you hit the reader with it, and then you get out of there and go to something else the reader doesn't see coming."

"I try to be funny; I typically strain," says Joel Achenbach, whose work also reads like the punch lines came effortlessly. "Sweat beads up on my forehead. I try so hard to be funny, and it doesn't come easy for me. I'll spend half an hour on a joke. And other times, they just pop right out; it's hard to know. I'll really pound the keyboard, trying to make a line work. And sometimes you end up with a joke that runs on and on and on and on. Like 'I am so grateful that you are taking my wife.' No, it doesn't work. 'Take my wife, please.' You have to make it punchy."

CRITICAL REVIEW

The critic has earned one of the most unusual positions at any newspaper. While the rest of the staff is ethically bound to be as objective as possible, the critic's role demands complete subjectivity.

Roger Ebert says, "I had a little quotation—over my typewriter, when I had a typewriter—from a book called *The Immediate Experience* by Robert Warshaw. He said, about film criticism, 'A man goes to the movies and the critic must be honest enough to admit that he is that man.'

"Of course, you could say man or woman—he was a little bit sexist," Ebert adds, with a laugh. "But the point is, you went to the movies. The group didn't go to the movies; a demographic segment didn't go to the movies; kids didn't go to the movies; adults didn't go to the movies.

"You went to the movies. What happened to you? If it happened, you have to admit it. If you laughed, say you laughed. If you cried, say you cried. If you were bored, say how bored you were."

Both Ebert and his cohort Gene Siskel advise students not to write a critical review as if it were a mere set of facts about a performance. Instead, they say, make a value judgment. And back it up. Don't just say it was good or bad.

Say it was heartfelt, melancholy, amusing, charming or thought-provoking. Or say it was dreadful, hackneyed, tedious or tasteless. State a specific criticism or endorsement, and defend your position.

Gene Siskel advises students to start the review with the most unusual or stimulating thing—negative or positive—about the movie or play or musical event they are reviewing. If the event was completely bland, start the review saying that nothing stood out about the production at all. Or, have some fun, and tell the reader something more entertaining, like, "Three hours will pass, and it will seem like you never got off your couch to leave home."

"I say the dominant thing I want to tell you and then support the hell out of that opinion," Siskel says. "The readers don't want to know the whole story. They want to know the most interesting things you can tell them about the story. Then document it. When you say it's 'bad acting,' don't just say that. Support it. And acting is a very difficult thing to write about. Because it's so mysterious to those of us who aren't actors. Get specific."

Say the actress mumbled her lines. Or say the actor was so convincing, you forgot it was just a movie. Say the guitarist sounded like a worn-out chainsaw. Or say the fiddle player caused the tough truckers to cry in their lite beers. You don't have to be an expert on acting or music—describe specific feelings or reactions caused by the event.

But, as much as you must write the review from your own point of view, be careful how much of yourself you actually put in the column. It's a delicate balance.

"I see a lot of book columns where the writer tries to explain to you why he basically should have written the book," says Siskel. "Think about it. You may be not as successful as the guy who has written the book, and you have all these revenge qualities in your heart. Forget it. The readers aren't interested in that. They want to know about the book. They don't want to know about your failed, miserable life. Get out there and talk about the book. Recognize why people are reading the column. They're really not interested in you. They're interested in the movies; they're interested in the music; they're interested in the book. Don't ever forget it. You come second. Your opinion comes first, but you personally come second."

The Carole Rich textbook *Writing and Reporting News: A Coaching Method* does not include a unit on editorial or opinion writing. In fact, most textbooks for beginning news writing classes do not. And, most textbooks for editing classes also do not concentrate on the writing of editorials. Instead, they focus on page design, copy editing, headline writing and other related issues.

Where does a journalist learn about opinion writing? Perhaps the best answer is, on the opinion/editorial page of the newspaper. Also, you can learn much from reading columns and reviews. Read the works of the writers featured in the telecourse. Books and articles by Dave Barry, Andy Rooney, Roger Ebert, Gene Siskel and Joel Achenbach are readily available. Columns by Richard Aregood are available in collections of Pulitzer Prize winners. And syndicated opinion pieces written by many of the featured writers in the telecourse (including Scott Ostler, Larry King, John Katsilometes, Peter Berkow, Rooney, Siskel, Ebert, Barry and others) might be available in your hometown newspaper.

FINAL THOUGHTS: GET ME REWRITE

So, what do the Pulitzer Prize winners and celebrity columnists featured in this unit of the telecourse have in common? Are they all natural born writers?

Gene Siskel doesn't think so.

"I think everyone would realize that the so-called 'natural writer'—the one who makes you feel 'I'm so inadequate—I'll never be as good as him or her'—is not so natural. Let's see their rough drafts," Siskel says. "That will make you feel more comfortable. And also, it shows the working out of a problem. I'd rather study one paragraph and all of the various drafts of that one paragraph than a whole full review."

"No matter how disciplined a writer you are, you are going to waste words," Richard Aregood says. "Good newspaper writing is sometimes poetry and sometimes inspired hackwork. If you're self-editing the inspired hackwork, sometimes you get poetry."

Did you know that Dave Barry won the Pulitzer Prize, in spite of (and perhaps, because of) his sarcastic attitude toward the value of journalism awards?

"I think that it's an indication of how bad the drug problem is in this country, that I won the Pulitzer Prize," Barry quips.

"I think I know what happened. After I won it, I went to New York for two years to be on the jury that picks the finalists that go to the committee to pick the winners. It's in winter, and it's in New York City. It's not really the best time to be in New York. You sit in a kind of stuffy room, on hard chairs, and go through an enormous amount of Pulitzer Prize nominees. Anybody can be nominated to win a Pulitzer Prize—anybody who pays the money is nominated. So there are thousands of entries. By the end of this week there are two things in the world you really hate. One is New York City, and the other is Pulitzer Prize entries. All these gaseous, bilious stories flowing over. My editor, when he nominated me—maybe it was just luck and maybe it's just he's real smart—sent in fewer than the maximum number of columns. He only sent seven. He could send 10.

"Two of those columns—one of them was a vicious attack on New York City, and the other was a vicious attack on the Pulitzer Prizes, which actually proposed that I should win one and then I would split the money with the judges. I think that's why I won it. Revenge. Angry people in a room in New York City."

"I do that with coffee," says Scott Ostler. "If I'm sitting at the keyboard, and I'm kind of dozing off, then nothing works. If I can get really fired up and sort of sweating, and the hair messed up, then I usually write better. So I'll drink excessive amounts of coffee. Later on, my stomach is killing me and there's all of these horrible coffee aftereffects, but I've written an OK column. I'll go back and I'll play with it for another half an hour, an hour, two hours, and just kind of polish it up. As I'm doing it, I find that—especially when I'm drinking a lot of coffee and getting really wired—more things start falling into place."

"I don't even remember how I used to write without a computer because I have to change everything so often," adds Dave Barry. "I write every sentence dozens of times—that's literally true. I just change, change, change, change every little word, keep changing, then as soon as I finished a paragraph, go back, read it all over again, and probably change again."

Fahizah Alim, Sacramento Bee*: "I express my emotions in my column."*

Roger Ebert, Chicago Sun-Times*: "There has to be some reporting in every review."*

Four esteemed columnists, including three Pulitzer Prize winners, have offered their opinion pieces for student review in this unit of the telecourse. You've met them in the telecourse; now you can read their work. Following is a piece by Richard Aregood—a classic example of a mainstream political editorial from the op/ed page of a daily newspaper.

BUSH PARDONED SIX—AND HIMSELF

By Richard Aregood
Philadelphia Daily News

Great. Now we've got the criminals forgiving themselves. Even Richard Nixon, the Prince of Darkness himself, had the good taste to find some poor boob to blow out the charges against him.

Too chancy for a sleaze like George Bush. Or maybe he knew that Bill Clinton wasn't likely to indulge himself in self-destructive stupidity like honest but dim Gerry Ford was.

It was as if Nicky Scarfo, aglow with the holiday spirit and aware that hardly anybody pays attention to the news on Christmas Eve, had the power to drop charges against a bunch of his hit men before they could rat him out.

That statement contains about the nicest thing you can now say about George Bush. At least he didn't have the witnesses against him terminated with extreme prejudice. That's Washington for *whacked*.

Forget about all the crap the Reaganisti are spreading around about Iran-contra. Bush said the case against former Secretary of Defense Caspar Weinberger, arrogant liar Elliot Abrams and the others amounted to the "criminalization of policy differences."

The fact is the policy was a criminal policy, administered in secret by criminals. This is a lot more than an ideological difference of opinion over a regulation.

These guys—Ronald Reagan, George Bush and those who are freshly pardoned—decided that the law and the Constitution were inconvenient to them. They decided that the balance of power in our government should be eliminated in favor of an all-powerful strongman who can do anything he wants. They decided that our president should not be hampered by messy democracy, that he should have absolute power, like Saddam Hussein or George III. As always, Bush gives the lie to his own words about the grand principle behind his pardons. He didn't stand up before the election and state his position boldly. He waited until any backlash wouldn't matter to his own future and sneakily made his move.

He and this un-American band of conspirators have dragged this matter out for years—lying, destroying documents, concealing or withholding others, delaying, obfuscating and attacking the prosecutor, an old-fashioned, Constitution-believing distinguished Republican lawyer who believes no man is above the law. Then they complain that the investigation is taking too long and costing too much.

These men are not patriots, no matter how many flags they wrap themselves in. You cannot be a patriot while believing this great nation should ignore its own greatness and its own laws and behave like some homicidal junta.

For two decades, we have mostly been ruled by men for whom the American Way is nothing more than a totem to be whipped out to flash for us irrelevant citizens. They are scoundrels, not heroes.

Bush and Reagan even outdid Nixon in the seriousness of the offenses and the baldness of the cover-up. Nixon, after all, was only trying to subvert parts of the government. Reagan and Bush wanted to tear up the Constitution, then make it impossible to enforce the criminal law.

With no pressure on witnesses against them, and the still-potent magic of Reagan's "I'm just a kindly old smiling moron who didn't know what was going on," there won't be a clear picture of what happened until most of us are dead, if then. The bad guys won.

And now they plead that for the sake of national unity, we forget their crimes. Like Nixon.

The sycophants at the *Wall Street Journal* urge exactly that, that we not hound these men. They deserve hounding for what they did and also for what they cheapened.

VIETNAM WAR STILL CLAIMING VICTIMS

By Fahizah Alim
Sacramento Bee

David is a black Vietnam vet. That's his identity. Beginning early next year, the phrases "Vietnam War" and "Vietnam vet" will resurface in the minds of many Americans as we begin focusing on the 20th anniversary of the ending of that divisive war and its spiritual, mental and physical impact on our country.

The scenes of armed young men and even younger widows will remind us how terrible war is.

But for some, like David, the Vietnam War has never ended.

For too many of our homeless, unemployed, drug-addicted, mentally ill and imprisoned young men, their life conditions are a constant reminder that the Vietnam War was their springboard to nowhere.

We have all heard repeatedly about the disproportionate number of African American men that commit crimes, go to jail, drop out of school, lose their jobs, kill each other and so forth and so on.

Here's another place where black men were disproportionately represented. In Vietnam. On the front line. In the obituaries and among the walking wounded.

David was one day past his 18th birthday when he got his draft notice. David is now 45 and lives in Sacramento. That's not his real name—he didn't want to be identified because he fears the government that sent him to war.

Eleven months after receiving his high school diploma, David was on a boat in a murky Vietnam river with an M-14 rifle on his side.

"Eighteen was pretty young to be sending a kid to Vietnam," says David, "but I was all red, white and blue when I went to Vietnam. I put my hand over my heart for the flag.

"I don't mind going to kick butt, but it was a humbug war and we went over there to do a political number for the rich and got back here and couldn't get nothing. Not even a funky job."

David doesn't like talking about war. "Napalmed bodies, halved bodies, dead friends. We who came back with 10 fingers and 10 toes thought we were all right," he says with a bitter laugh. "But I scared my mama so bad she regrettably had to ask me to leave her house. It would be two in the morning, and I would be crouched down under the window sill eating a package of cigarettes.

"I was real bitter when I first came back, but I've mellowed out now."

Oh, yes. I remember when David, the brother of a good friend, would come to visit here on holidays and he wouldn't sit down.

Whatever the conversation was, he would find a way to turn it around to what he called the "hypocrisy of the government."

"I came back and took the civil service test for the police and fire departments at home and scored a 96," he says. "But they weren't hiring blacks, especially Vietnam blacks. I found out that instead of giving us freedom the war had closed even more doors to us.

"I knew a guy who would go to the Veterans Administration building on Wilshire Boulevard once a week and throw a red brick through a windowpane, shouting 'I'm a Vietnam vet and I want a job.' They'd pick him up, commit him and give him some Thorazine to keep him quiet for a while. But when he got out, he'd do the same thing again."

When America revisits the Vietnam War next year, many will feel pain for a devastating war that few understood.

But how many of those will feel pain for those disproportionate number of African American men that the Vietnam War has yet displaced?

David, who's unemployed now, will continue to fill out job applications. He will write after his name that he is a black Vietnam vet.

It's a war that gave him his identity. It's a war that he can't forget.

PITHY INTO THE WIND

By Dave Barry
Miami Herald

The burgeoning Iran-Contra scandal is truly an issue about which we, as a nation, need to concern ourselves, because (Secret Note to Readers: Not really! The hell with the Iran-Contra affair! Let it burgeon! I'm just trying to win a journalism prize here. Don't tell anybody! I'll explain later. Shhh.)

When we look at the Iran-Contra scandal, and for that matter the mounting national health-care crisis, we can see that these are, in total, two issues, each requiring a number of paragraphs in which we will comment, in hopes that (. . . we can win a journalism prize. Ideally a Pulitzer. That's the object, in journalism. At certain times each year, we journalists do almost nothing except apply for the Pulitzers and several dozen other major prizes. During these times you could walk right into most newsrooms and commit a multiple ax murder naked, and it wouldn't get reported in the paper, because the reporters and editors would all be too busy filling out prize applications. "Hey!" they'd yell at you. "Watch it! You're getting blood on my application!")

We can possibly, through carefully analyzing these important issues—the Iran-Contra scandal, the mounting national health-care crisis, and (while we are at it), the federal budget deficit—through analyzing these issues and mulling them over and fretting about them and chewing on them until we have reduced them to soft, spit-covered gobs of information that you, the readers can (. . . pretty much ignore. It's OK! Don't be ashamed! We here in journalism are fully aware that most of you skip right over stories that look like they might involve major issues which you can identify because they always have incomprehensible headlines like "House Parley Panel Links NATO Tax Hike to Hondurans in Syrian Arms Deal." Sometimes we'll do a whole series with more total words than the Brothers Karamazov and headlines like: "The World Mulch Crisis: A Time to Act." You readers don't bother to wade through these stories, and you feel vaguely guilty about this.

Which is stupid. You're not *supposed* to read them. We *journalists* don't read them. We use modern computers to generate them solely for the purpose of entering them for journalism prizes. We're thinking about putting the following helpful advisory over them: "Caution! Journalism Prize Entry! Do Not Read!")

Again, through a better understanding of these very important issues—the Iran-Contra scandal, the health-care crisis (which as you may be aware is both national AND mounting), the federal budget deficit, and yes, let's come right out and say it, the Strategic Defense Initiative—you readers can gain a better understanding of them, and thus we might come to an enhanced awareness of what they may or may not mean in terms of (. . . whether or not I can win a Pulitzer Prize. That's the one I'm gunning for. You get $1,000 cash, plus all the job offers the mailperson can carry. Unfortunately, the only category I'd be eligible for is called "Distinguished Social Commentary," which is a real problem, because of the kinds of issues I generally write about. "This isn't Distinguished Social Commentary!" the Pulitzer judges would say. "This is about goat boogers!" So today I'm trying to class up my act a little by writing about prize-winning issues. OK? Sorry.)

How we, as a nation can, through a deeper realization of the significance of these four vital issues—health care in Iran, the strategic federal deficit, mounting the Contras, and one other one which slips my mind at the moment, although I think it's the one that's burgeoning—how we can, as a nation, through Distinguished Social Commentary such as this, gain the kind of perspective and foresight required to understand (. . . a guy like noted conservative columnist George Will. You see him, on all those TV shows where he is always commenting on world events in that snotty smartass way of his, with his lips pursed together like he just accidentally licked the plumbing in a bus-station restroom, and you quite naturally say to yourself, as millions have before you: "Why doesn't somebody just take this little *dweeb* and stick his bow tie up his nose? Huh?" And the answer is: Because a long time ago, for reasons nobody remembers anymore, George Will won a *Pulitzer Prize*. And now he gets to be famous and rich and respected *for ever and ever*. That's all I want! Is that so much to ask?!) what we, and I am talking about we as a nation, need to have in order to deeply

understand all the issues listed somewhere earlier in this column.

And although I am only one person, one lone Distinguished Social Commentator crying in the wilderness, without so much as a bow tie, I am nevertheless committed to doing whatever I can to deepen and widen and broaden and lengthen the national understanding of these issues in any way that I can, and that includes sharing the $1,000 with the judges.

REVIEW: ALL THE PRESIDENT'S MEN

By Roger Ebert
Chicago Sun-Times

All the President's Men is truer to the craft of journalism than to the art of storytelling, and that's its problem. The movie is as accurate about the processes used by investigative reporters as we have any right to expect, and yet process finally overwhelms narrative—we're adrift in a sea of names, dates, telephone numbers, coincidences, lucky breaks, false leads, dogged footwork, denials, invasions and sometimes even the truth. Just such thousands of details led up to Watergate and the Nixon resignation, yes, but the movie's more about the details than about their results. That's not to say the movie isn't good at accomplishing what it sets out to do. It provides the most observant study of working journalists we're ever likely to see in a feature film. (Bob Woodward and Carl Bernstein may at last, merciful God, replace Hildy Johnson and Walter Burns as career models.) And it succeeds brilliantly in suggesting the mixture of exhilaration, paranoia, self-doubt and courage that permeated the *Washington Post* as its two young reporters went after a presidency.

Newspaper movies always used to play up the excitement and ignore the boredom and the waiting. This one is all about the boredom and the waiting and the tireless digging. It depends on what we already know about Watergate to provide a level of excitement. And yet, given the fact that William Goldman's screenplay is almost all

dialogue, almost exclusively a series of scenes of people talking (or not talking) to each other, director Alan J. Pakula has done a remarkable job of keeping the pace taut. Who'd have thought you could build tension with scenes where Bernstein walks over to Woodward's desk and listens in on the extension phone? But you can. And the movie's so well paced, acted and edited that it develops the illusion of momentum even in the scenes where Woodward and Bernstein are getting doors slammed in their faces.

When Robert Redford announced that he'd bought the rights to *All the President's Men*, the joke in the newsroom was about reporters becoming movie stars. What in fact has happened is that the stars, Redford as Woodward and Dustin Hoffman as Bernstein, became reporters: They sink into their characters and become wholly credible. There's not a false or "Hollywood" note in the whole movie, and that's commendable—but how much authenticity will viewers settle for? To what secret and sneaky degree do they really want Redford and Hoffman to come on like stars?

There must have been a temptation to flesh out the Woodward and Bernstein characters, to change the pace with subplots about their private lives, but the film sticks resolutely to its subject. This is the story of a story: Of two reporters starting with an apparently minor break-in and following it, almost incredulously at times, as it finally leads all the way to the White House. At times the momentum of Watergate seems to propel Woodward and Bernstein, instead of the other way around. It must have occasionally been like that at the time, and it's to the movie's credit that it doesn't force its characters into the center of every scene.

All the President's Men doesn't dwell on the private lives of its characters, but it does have a nice touch with their professional lives, and especially with their relationships with editors. The Watergate story started as a local story, not a national one, and it was a continuing thorn in the side of the *Post*'s prestigious national staff as Woodward and Bernstein kept it as their own. We meet the *Post* metro editor, Harry Rosenfeld (Jack Warden), defending and badgering "Woodstein" as the team came to be known. Martin Balsam plays Howard Simons, the managing editor, and Jason Robards is Benjamin Bradlee, the executive editor. All three are well cast; they may never have been in a newspaper office before, but they've learned the correct tone, they carry on a news conference as if they've held one before, and they even exhibit typical shadings of office fashion—the closer in time you are to having once covered a daily beat, the more you're permitted to loosen your tie and have baggy pants.

The movie has dozens of smaller character roles, for all the people who talked to Woodstein, or who refused to, and there's one cameo from real life: Frank Wills, the Watergate guard who found the fateful tape

on the lock, plays himself. Some of the other roles tend to blend into one faceless Source, but Robert Walden makes a memorable Donald Sgretti, playing the "dirty tricks" expert with bravado shading into despair. And two of the key informants are portrayed in interestingly different ways. Jane Alexander is a bookkeeper who gives the team some of their best leads and is plain, honest and scared; Hal Holbrook, as the mysterious "Deep Throat," the source inside the administration, is disturbingly detached, almost as if he's observing the events with a hollow laugh.

All of these elements in *All the President's Men* are to be praised, and yet they don't quite add up to a satisfying movie experience. Once we've seen one cycle of investigative reporting, once Woodward and Bernstein have cracked the first wall separating the break-in from the White House, we understand the movie's method. We don't need to see the reporting cycle repeated several more times just because the story has grown longer and the sources more important. For all of its technical skill, the movie essentially shows us the same journalistic process several times as it leads closer and closer to an end we already know. The film is long and would be dull if it weren't for the wizardry of Pakula, his actors and technicians. What saves it isn't the power of narrative but the success of technique. Still, considering the compromises that could have been made, considering the phony "newspaper movie" this could have been, maybe that's almost enough.

ALTERNATIVE VIEWS

There's some dispute in journalism about whether writing in the first person works. All opinions expressed about this subject are, of course, quite subjective. The author of this student study guide feels that readers could get bored hearing the word *I* too often— even in a review—as in "There I was backstage with the band, because I had a press pass, and I thought the band was pretty cool, and they even let me have a free beer."

Critic Gene Siskel expresses a parallel point of view.

"Recognize why people are reading the column," Siskel says. "They're really not interested in you. They're interested in the movies; they're interested in the music; they're interested in the book. Don't ever forget it. You come second. Your opinion comes first, but you personally come second."

As usual, Siskel and his partner in criticism differ. Only, this time, it's not about a movie—it's about writing style.

"If you write a nice perfect, little textbook third-person review," Ebert says, "It's going to be boring. If you write as yourself, with your own voice and your own tone, . . . well, any criticism, . . . implicitly or not, is in the first person.

"In criticism, there's no such thing as science," Ebert says. "Or objectivity. It's all opinion. It's all subjective. I developed a first-person style while in school. I was learning to write a nice inverted pyramid and a respectable lead—going through the motions of learning how to write in an ordinary (unbiased) journalistic way. But at the same time, the people who were my heroes, the people who I was reading, were first-person writers.

Andy Rooney, critic for the television news show "60 Minutes," has a similar attitude toward using the words *I* and *me*.

"I do write in the first person a lot," Rooney says. "I think it's a mistake not to. I think it's false not to."

Rooney offers this actual example: "A news correspondent asked a question of the president, and the president was pretty sore. Later, in putting the piece together [the correspondent] said, 'A reporter asked the president a question.' He [the correspondent] did not use the first person. Journalists classically do not use the first person. I very often find it false.

"When I use the first person, I am usually not thinking 'I'; I am thinking 'you.' I think people associate themselves with me when I use the word *I*. I do not use *one*; one does not use *one*, if one is a grown-up writer in America these days. So to that extent, I am nervous about it sometimes. I very often take some *I*'s out, *I, I*. It is quite possible to overdo it, but it's false never to use *I*."

GLOSSARY

COLUMN	A column, in most newspapers and magazines, is where a journalist is encouraged to express his or her own point of view. Many columnists are local celebrities, and the publications feature their photos at the head of the piece. Most columns are personal opinion reflections about current topics in news, politics, sports, or daily life. Often, columnists specialize in writing that evokes emotion, especially humor.
CRITICAL REVIEW	A critical review is an opinion piece in which a writer is expected to cast judgment on a performance—usually music, theater, movies, art, dance, literature and other forms of entertainment.
EDITORIAL	An opinion piece (usually political in nature) that is meant to represent the views of the editor or publisher or, in some cases, the entire publication.

OP/ED PAGE   The section of a mainstream newspaper in which opinions of the publisher and editor (as well as the reading public, in the letters to the editor section) are displayed.

Pick a topic to write about as an exercise to learn opinion and editorial style. Make sure the topic is somewhat controversial—it will serve little purpose if most readers agree with you. Take a strong stand on one side of the issue, and support it with good reporting as well as good opinion writing. Fill out the following checklist first, and submit it to your teacher or editor. Then, follow through with a completed piece. If you don't publish your editorial in the school newspaper, submit this opinion piece as a letter for publication in the "Letters to the Editor" section of your local newspaper.

Editorial Writer's Checklist

My premise is:

My purpose for writing this opinion piece is:

Some different kinds of persuasion I can use to convince those who don't agree with me:

Ethical arguments:

Emotional arguments:

Logical arguments:

Facts gathered in the reporting process that will help back up my arguments:

Typical objections that those who don't agree with me are most likely to voice, and my methods of refuting them:

QUIZ

Choose the best answer.

1 According to Gene Siskel and Roger Ebert, good critical review writing

 a. is stronger if it avoids a formalized, third-person English essay style approach.
 b. allows the writer to develop a "voice."
 c. should let the reader know how you personally reacted to the event you are reviewing.
 d. all of the above
 e. none of the above

2 According to Roger Ebert,

 a. it is important not to offend someone by saying something that will offend a racial or ethnic group.
 b. a critic should never give away the ending or plot to a movie or a play.
 c. political correctness is the fascism of the nineties.
 d. all of the above
 e. none of the above

3 Gene Siskel says he usually starts his movie reviews for the *Chicago Tribune*

 a. writing much like a beat reporter who was covering a fire—only his hard news is the reaction to the picture.
 b. with a vivid description of the most important scenes in the movie.
 c. by disagreeing with Roger Ebert's opinion of the movie.
 d. with his thumbs-up or thumbs-down judgment of the movie.
 e. with a list of the most important actors, directors and script writers involved with the project.

4 According to humor columnist Dave Barry,

 a. the punch lines need to be written before the rest of the column.
 b. even a humor columnist is more effective if he or she learns the skills of hard-news reporting first.
 c. the adjective is the most important part of humor writing.
 d. aspiring reporters shouldn't even consider a career before finishing journalism school.
 e. one unforgiving copy editor can kill more good jokes than 10 humor columnists can create.

5 Conservative editorial columnist Dorothy Rabinowitz and liberal editorial writer Richard Aregood and teacher Carole Rich all agree that

 a political editorial writing has little in common with hard-news writing.
 b. good editorial writers give both sides of an argument a fair, balanced and objective treatment before reaching a conclusion.
 c. a writer has to care a lot about a subject, and express a strong opinion, to write effective editorials.
 d. all of the above
 e. none of the above

6 According to Andy Rooney, the humor of his short "60 Minutes" pieces

 a. depends on crafty punch lines.
 b. is built around a bit of hard-news reporting.
 c. is built on passionate argument techniques.
 d. depends more on images, as opposite to a newspaper column that depends on words.
 e. has little in common with newspaper humor columns.

7 Fahizah Alim's opinion column for the *Sacramento Bee*, which was highlighted in the telecourse program for this unit,

  a. reflects her strong personal emotions connected to her ethnic background.
  b. reflects a news element (reporting within an opinion piece) about the high number of minority Vietnam veterans who are homeless.
  c. uses one veteran as a vehicle to report a situation and express an opinion.
  d. all of the above
  e. none of the above

8 Richard Aregood, Pulitzer Prize–winning editorial writer, suggests students can write more effective opinion pieces if

  a. they say as much as possible with as few words as possible.
  b. they use as many adjectives as possible to add color and emotion to the opinion piece.
  c. they avoid personal bias.
  d. they learn to write in the third person only.
  e. they learn to address the reader, using the second person.

9 Sports columnists, movie reviewers, political editorial writers and opinion column writers all have the following in common:

  a. They are given the freedom, in their space, to express personal opinions.
  b. They usually include some sort of hard-news reporting within the context of their writing.
  c. They are encouraged to stimulate, provoke, entertain, outrage or inspire the readers.
  d. all of the above
  e. none of the above

10 At mainstream daily newspapers, reporters and editorial writers have the following in common:

  a. They are both encouraged to express their personal point of view.
  b. They are both encouraged to be completely objective.
  c. They are both expected to conform to *Associated Press Stylebook* language guidelines.
  d. They are both expected to use humor whenever possible.
  e. They both receive the same salaries.

SELF-TEST

1 Richard Aregood considers himself an "extremely liberal" political editorial writer, yet he says he finds much in common with good conservative editorial writers. What attributes do they have in common?

2 Paraphrase the attitude expressed by both Roger Ebert and Gene Siskel toward the concept of political correctness, as it applies to opinion writing.

3 What qualities of good writing do political editorial writers, entertainment critics, humorists and columnists all have in common?

4 What are the differences between hard-news writing and editorial writing? What are the similarities?

5 Find a passage, written by a columnist, that made you laugh. (Try the Dave Barry pieces in this textbook. If they don't amuse you, check out your local newspaper. If it doesn't have a humor columnist, seek out syndicated writing by Joel Achenbach, Scott Ostler, Andy Rooney or any other humor columnist.) Write the passage down in the space provided, and attempt to explain what makes people laugh.

COVERING DISASTERS

Nothing can completely prepare you for the state of mind you'll be in when covering a catastrophe—not even prior experience. Many of the journalists interviewed for the telecourse had covered airliner crashes, chemical spills, earthquakes, fire storms, tornadoes, hurricanes, blizzards and wars. None admitted to being unperturbed by tragedy. A reporter is a human being, and the emotions experienced witnessing the grief of others can be overpowering.

Still, the printing presses don't wait; the evening news must air at the normally scheduled time. Viewers and readers will demand quick, accurate and thorough reporting. News agencies that fail the public during a crisis often suffer financially, shortly after.

Reporters find it easier to function under such pressure if they know their craft instinctively.

Many of the techniques taught in this beginning course on news writing will become essential when covering your first natural or human-made disaster. Those skills will be reviewed in this unit of the telecourse. And, by observing how the reporters in the video portion of this unit cover the Crystal Peak fire with calm professionalism, you'll be presented with some excellent role models to emulate when you're called on to cover a similar event.

OBJECTIVES

By observing reporters who are covering a natural disaster, you will review the skills taught in the first 12 weeks of the telecourse and gain insight on how to behave if you are thrust into a similar situation.

BEFORE YOU WATCH

This program demonstrates how journalists, under unusual pressure, must apply the principles taught in the first 12 lessons of the telecourse while writing stories—on deadline—that can save lives and help readers deal with natural or human-made disasters.

•**Pay close attention to the ways journalists and teachers use the following terms in this program:**

News judgment	Interviews
Summary lead	Public relations
Style	Feature news
Story development	Ethics

WHILE YOU WATCH

1. Ask yourself how you would function in a newsroom, if it was your job to cover a similar disaster.

2. Note which of the lessons learned in this telecourse would be most helpful when writing a disaster story on a deadline.

3. Observe the differences in approach between the *Sacramento Bee* reporter and the reporters from KOLO television.

4. Consider the differences between public relations as we normally think of it and the role of the public information officer during the reporting of this fire.

AFTER YOU WATCH

•**Address the following questions in your journal. Or, if there's time, discuss them in class:**

1. What kind of disasters have affected your local community within the past few years? Was the local media coverage of the disaster effective? Why?

2. Does the media intrude when victims of disasters are asked for quotes? What is the value of showing a victim's pain and other emotions?

3. Can good news coverage of a disaster make it easier for a community to cope with the effects? How?

4. What are the different roles of radio, television and newspaper news teams during disaster coverage?

THE
LESSON

"IT WON'T
HAPPEN TO ME"

The unit on covering disasters has two missions. First, this section is designed to communicate at least some of the feeling and responsibility felt when journalists are reporting on natural or human-made disasters. It is hard for a beginning journalism student to imagine being thrust into such an intense reporting environment. These events have an almost otherworldly feel; it is easy to assume that "such exciting (or horrible) events like that will never happen to me." However, disasters occur frequently, usually when you least expect it.

Even the production team that created this telecourse ran across disaster stories—frequently. During the four years the team was producing the Annenberg/CPB television shows, we ran across what seemed like an unusually high number of disasters near our home base of northern California—starting with an earthquake that interrupted the World Series between the Oakland Athletics and the San Francisco Giants. In what seemed like six-month intervals, the production crew was able to observe reporters in both large and small markets as they covered

•a snow storm that nearly crushed the town of Paradise, California;

•a train derailment that ended up in a chemical spill that wiped out trees and fish along the upper Sacramento River;

•several airplane crashes, both at air shows and near passenger terminals;

•several more earthquakes of varying sizes;

•less noisy and immediate disaster trends, including the near extinction of salmon native to California's rivers;

•a bomb scare that required the evacuation of a nearby community; and

•fire storms that wiped out metropolitan neighborhoods near Oakland and rural communities in the Sierra Nevadas as well as tens of thousands of acres of trees and wildlife in California's forests.

Many of those events have been incorporated into the telecourse.

The second mission of this unit and program is to review what you've learned from the telecourse, up to this point. Reporters who are covering disasters must be prepared to use all of the tools we have discussed in this introductory journalism class—while meeting inflexible publication deadlines that don't bend for the circumstances caused by catastrophic events.

By using the forest fire near Reno, Nevada, as a vehicle, we can show how the writers, broadcasters and public information officers from television station KOLO, the *Sacramento Bee* and the California Department of Forestry worked in harmony to bring vital information to the endangered communities—applying the principles that we have been discussing for the past 12 instructional units. We also get an advance look at the 14th and 15th weeks of the series, as some of the ethical and legal considerations of reporting on the fire are considered.

REPORTING ON DISASTERS

NEWS VALUE

The first instructional unit of this course illustrated a common theme voiced in newsrooms across the country: The media need to strike a balance between reporting what the public needs to know and what the public wants to know. Some journalists call this understanding news value.

Often, the information the public needs to know is less interesting, and, unless packaged with flash, it won't necessarily increase a newspaper's circulation or boost a television or radio station's ratings.

On the other hand, catering only to information the public wants to know often results in the kind of news coverage that makes editors, news directors and reporters associated with mainstream news organizations uncomfortable.

"We say the reader has a right to know," says Carole Rich, "but the reader has a want to know a lot of prurient things, which is why the *National Enquirer* sells more papers than the local newspaper or the *New York Times*. But does the reader really have a need to know? In what way are you empowering that reader by printing what you're printing?"

In the case of a natural disaster, the information that the public needs to know intersects naturally with the information the public wants to know. Reporters have little trouble satisfying readers and viewers if they deliver the breaking news accurately and in a timely fashion.

LEADS

The basic, on-the-spot reporting of a disaster best illustrates these journalists applying the lessons of a beginning reporting class under pressure. As a rule, the latest breaking news makes the best lead. The summary lead (discussed in Unit Two) becomes more than a formula in such a situation. It develops into the most basic tool necessary for a reporter to file a story on time, summarizing the Who, What, When, Where, Why and How under unusual pressure. Even as the disaster unfolds, the deadlines of broadcast and print news remain inflexible. And the desire to scoop the competition with accurate reporting and compelling storytelling certainly doesn't disappear just because the community is suffering a disaster. Mastering the summary lead helps the reporter with all of these challenges.

Editors and news directors are often warned by an ALERT icon that blinks through their computer screens. This signal is designed to prompt attention for very important wire service stories, such as disasters. Usually, the summary lead is the first—and only—element of the story that will initially go out on the wire. If you are writing a story that will be picked up by news organizations in other communities, the lead may be the only news about the disaster you are reporting on that they will get in time to publish. In this kind of situation, it is all the more important to learn creativity within the formula of reporting the basic Who, What, When, Where, Why and How summary.

Once the breaking news of the disaster has been reported, writers need to work a little harder to grab readers. If the unusual nature of the event no longer automatically attracts attention to an important disaster sidebar story, a good lead can captivate.

"There's going to be a lead to your story," says Karen Reuter, morning news anchor of KOLO television in Reno.

"There's some hook that makes you want to do the story, whether it is the fact that last night the fire was tame, and today they're going to be able to get a handle on it better than they have in the previous three days, or that last night was wild, was totally out of control and today it's going to be chaos. If you've got a focus of your story, you're going be able to go from there. But there's always a lead."

STYLEBOOK

In all the confusion of covering a disaster, it is important not to forget about correct language use. Reporters rarely have the chance to lug an *Associated Press Stylebook* along while covering such an event, and their editors back at the office often have to clean up the sloppy copy. Experienced reporters, with a previous knowledge of style rules, clearly have an advantage over inexperienced reporters. The *AP Stylebook* demands precise language use for disaster stories; these rules can make the difference between clear or muddled reporting.

The television program gives several examples of style rules related to covering a fire. The *AP Stylebook* also has specific guidelines for weather-related disasters.

Norm Goldstein, editor of the *AP Stylebook*, says the book, which many in the newsroom call the reporters' bible, "tries to be a ready reference for writers so that they don't have to go scurrying around to a dictionary every time. We try and have a list, for example, of the worst hurricanes of the century in there, for quick reference . . . [to] look it up and put things in perspective without scurrying for data retrieval systems or encyclopedias."

The references under "Weather Terms" also give very precise definitions for important terms such as *blizzard, severe blizzard, thunderstorm, severe thunderstorm, tornado* and *funnel cloud*. The differences are subtle, but important. The indiscriminate use of words such as these, without a thorough and specific understanding of their definitions, can lead to vague, sloppy reporting.

The reference under "Earthquakes" is a good example of how the *AP Stylebook* can be invaluable during the stressful conditions of reporting on a disaster. The *Stylebook* gives a listing of notable quakes from the recent past so that a reporter can compare the scope of the damage. Spellings of troublesome words such as *temblor* and *epicenter* are listed, and a precise explanation of the *Richter Scale* is also included.

STORY DEVELOPMENT

The inverted pyramid (explained in Unit Four) becomes the other fundamental tool when covering breaking news like the Crystal Peak fire, which is the center-piece of Unit Thirteen. The inverted pyramid is the natural development style for breaking hard-news events. Even television journalists—who in Unit Eight explained how the inverted pyramid is avoided when constructing news pack-ages—tend to use a pyramid-like structure when ad-libbing a story live, on camera, from the scene of the disaster. It makes sense. Without a script or a TelePrompTer, the natural tendency is to tell the audience what just happened, with the most recent and most important breaking news reported in the first few sentences.

The other important information is related soon after, with the reporter tossing in anecdotes and nonessential details as he or she runs out of steam—toward the end of the live stand-up.

The print reporter, filing a news story about the same event—usually from a portable computer through a modem—will automatically also package the information using the inverted pyramid style, assuming the newspaper will have limited space for the piece and the editor will have to cut from the bottom. If the story goes over a wire service, newspapers around the country will have a varying amount of reader interest or space for a remote disaster and will automatically cut from the bottom, sometimes using only the first paragraph or two.

As the breaking news settles down, reporters are allowed to pursue more cre-ative story development styles while writing feature stories that spin off from the main event.

QUOTES AND SOURCES

Covering a disaster presents unusual challenges when a reporter is looking for quotes—whether the interviews are with victims or with rescue workers. Many involved are grieving, exhausted or busy—and reluctant to talk to the media. Others are cooperative and realize that their comments can help readers and view-ers cope with the disaster.

"For me it's the most uncomfortable kind of story," says Karen Reuter, "because there's a certain element of competition, where you want to be the one to talk to the family who was burned out, and you want to get the poignant and gut-wrenching kind of information . . . get at the heart of what this feels like to lose your home. But you're invading their privacy in an unbelievable way. And when someone tells you, 'Get out of here. You have no business being here' or 'How could you be so heartless?' it hurts. Because you don't want to be heart-less—you want to do a good story. But doing a good story sometimes means invading someone's privacy."

Sensitivity to victims of a disaster is governed by law as well as guided by a personal sense of ethics.

According to Terry Hendry, also of KOLO, "If they ask you to leave, legally you have to leave. And you'd want to, anyway. You don't want to be seen as an intruder . . . you're going to stay in this community long after the story is over with. If you make people mad there, they'll stay mad with you forever. And of course we live and die by how many people watch us."

Still, the reporters know that getting strong quotes not only helps report the story, it also often serves the community.

"I pretty much go with my gut level to know when it's absolutely inappropriate," says Reuter.

"I never take an obnoxious approach because I think that will always turn people off. I try to take a sensitive approach, and if I really feel like this is not going to work, I leave. I tell them why it's important for them to talk to us. I say, 'People want to know. There are people in this community riveted to this fire. You've lost your home; people want to know what has happened to you and how this fire has devastated you. It's information that people really want to find out.'"

The reporters covering the Crystal Peak fire found access to some astonishing sources. In one instance, family members cooperated even while collecting valuables and abandoning their home. Another man, who refused to evacuate, agreed to talk to reporters even while working alongside the firefighters who were attempting to save his home. In both instances, the information reported by the media helped explain the human drama of the story—making it more than a dry report filled with numbers of acres and homes lost to the fire. The resulting stories were also viewed by many neighbors who were themselves making decisions about whether to evacuate or stay to fight the fire near their own homes.

Nancy Vogel, reporter from the *Sacramento Bee*, also gathered some astonishing quotes.

"Actually, under a disaster like a wild fire, people are unbelievably accessible," Vogel says. "Even when their belongings are packed in their car and they're trying to get out of there. They always seem to take at least a minute or two to tell you who they are, and how this feels and where they're headed. A couple times out of three, people will say, 'I just can't talk about it.' I understand that and walk away. The firefighters are sometimes tough because they're shy. But, without a camera, when I'm armed with just a notebook and a pen, they're much more open to me."

In addition to the victims, the rescue workers on a disaster are clearly important sources for quotes. During the Crystal Peak fire, many of the firefighters took the time to give the reporters a quote or two. The reporters themselves had to be diplomatic and take care not to add to the confusion of the event. Because of their sensitivity, the reporters were rewarded with insight and information that those affected directly by the fire wanted to share with newspaper readers and television viewers.

"On a fire this big, there's going to be plenty of people to talk to," says Reuter. "There's no reason to make somebody angry because you're getting in their face and they're really tired. Or maybe they're in the middle of going to a planning meeting. You can't stop them, you can't interrupt them, because it's rude. You use basic common sense. If there's someone who you absolutely have to talk to, the only person that you need to interview, if you've got to talk to that person, you've got to work with them. You've got to work around their schedule. I'd say, 'I'd really like to interview you—what's you're schedule like this morning? It looks like you're going into a meeting. Is there a time I can talk to you after that meeting? Do you know how long that will last?' And people are in general very cordial, and they'll work with you. If you are polite and pleasant first, they'll reciprocate."

WRITING VERSUS REPORTING

A running theme through Unit Six was that, in their zeal to write well and tell a good story, writers can sometimes forget their original goals of good reporting.

A similar phenomenon can be seen when journalists are too eager to scoop the competition, telling a good story while getting some of the facts wrong. In the case of the Crystal Peak fire, one broadcast news organization reported rumors that the main artery between Reno and California (Interstate Highway 80) had been closed by the fire. Though the rumor was corrected shortly, such inaccurate information could cause panic among the viewers and should be rigorously avoided.

Disaster stories offer many opportunities for good writing. The scenes lend themselves to eloquent description; the people involved often give the writers plenty of quotes to bring out the emotional impact. But journalists must take extra care not to be too caught up in the words. Accurate reporting in all journalism is essential; inaccurate reporting of evacuation routes, emergency procedures, injury updates and other details about a disaster can be a matter of life and death. Often, in the haste to scoop the competition, bad mistakes can be made—mistakes that are inexcusable on several levels.

According to Terry Hendry, "The tendency is to be there first. . . . It is an absolute mistake. When you hear something like a highway is closed, it's always best to double-check those things. I've found, and I think this is 100 percent in my case, when you don't check twice, you always get burned. The viewer is always questioning your credibility at that point, from then on."

BEAT REPORTING

Unit Seven of this series took a look at beat reporting. Though it would be easy to assume the beat reporters who specialize in public safety stories would be the most likely to cover a disaster, reporters from almost any beat can be asked to pitch in during the chaos that ensues. During the infamous World Series earthquake in San Francisco, the sports beat reporters who were broadcasting the interrupted game had to become hard-news reporters in an instant. Thousands were trying to evacuate the stadium and find ways home, even though the city's main artery through the Bay Bridge had been damaged. Their only link to essential survival information and breaking news was through the sports journalists and other live announcers reporting news through their car radios.

Nancy Vogel, who was covering the Crystal Peak fire for the *Sacramento Bee*, was usually an education beat reporter. But, after covering a disaster for the *Bee*, she said, "I got addicted, on my very first fire.

"I'd never seen anything that beautiful. We were actually, at one point, running to the truck to try to get away from it, and there were deer and fox running up the road with us. There's this incredibly deep silence right before it starts to pick up, and then the trees just start exploding around you and I got hooked after that. And I also got to know how well folks come together from different agencies to fight these things. I don't think people really appreciate how quickly they move on them most of the time. I'm not saying it's always flawless. The fire is its own animal, and so is the fire-fighting effort."

BROADCAST WRITING

Unit Eight compares the similarities and differences between broadcast journalism and print journalism. Those comparisons are illustrated again as we see both television and newspaper reporters covering the same fire.

Television's immediacy can be an advantage during a disaster, and news directors can have the power to supersede commercial programming with live reports from the scene. This kind of journalism can certainly help communicate information needed to cope with the aftermath of a catastrophic event.

"In the live shots where you're standing there and you're talking about what happened," says Terry Hendry, "expect to be scared. Most people see the cool, calm journalist on television, and they seem to have their hair all in place and everything is in order. . . . It's not that way. Equipment's breaking in the field, information is usually strewn about. Nine times out of 10 your producer will send you out there with only seconds to spare before you're on the air and you have little information to go with. The only thing you can do is turn to yourself and rely on yourself and tell the truth.

"You'd say a few things: 'There's a fire here, people are being evacuated.' And then you would go to video." Hopefully, the rest of the team has the pictures that will tell the story.

Skilled photography can tell more of the story than the words written or narrated over the images. Perhaps the most powerful moment of reporting from the Crystal Peak fire was captured by KOLO camera operator Brian Pogue, with the simple ambient sound and video of trees exploding into flames like giant Fourth of July sparklers lighting up the night sky.

"A news team is a reporter and a photographer, and they are that: a team," Karen Reuter says. They have got to work together.

"You don't want to have the reporter running around getting interviews, the photographer running around getting pictures, and no communication to pull it together."

However, television programmers must be careful to address a common criticism—that they are merely capitalizing on the misfortunes of others to capture shocking images and higher ratings. Solid reporting of essential information can usually counter these claims.

"We are criticized a lot because people say that television is shallow, it's superficial," says Hendry. "You know when you're covering a story and you're doing it well when you feel the emotions, and then you take those emotions and you're able to translate them and show people just exactly what's going on and what people are feeling out there that are involved in the disaster."

Good reporting of a disaster—without capitalizing on or exaggerating the event—includes accurate communication of both the facts and emotions. Good journalists such as Hendry find the balance.

"You can't ad-lib and fake something like that," she says. And that's another thing that people tell you over and over in the television biz. Don't fake it. If you don't know it, don't say it; if you don't feel it, don't try to show it. Be yourself. Be yourself and try and be as accurate as you can.

"You can't help but get involved. There's so many different emotions tugging on you. The only thing that you don't want to do is lose clarity of mind. Hysteria is not a good thing. Panic is your worst enemy. We always kid each other by saying that, but it really is. Panic is a bad thing, and you want to avoid that. But the other emotions, sadness—seeing a natural disaster, nature at work—it is awe inspiring, and it makes you just take a deep breath and look at it and think, 'My gosh, this is incredible.' You want to bring that story home, so that not only people can watch but if you're lucky, maybe they'll be moved by it."

Newspapers can't report live from the scene and are limited to frozen (though still powerful) images of the wake of the disaster. Nancy Vogel says, "A newspaper, we're one day late always on where the evacuation center is or who to call. And we have to keep that in mind. But, we can be more useful, I think, than television, in perhaps running down the list of what to pack. How to be prepared. What you should have ahead of time. What your escape route should be, that sort of thing."

While the television station can report that nearly a thousand firefighters are on the scene, the newspaper can detail the specific divisions that have arrived—an important detail if the reader is concerned about the safety of a loved one who fights fires.

While the television station can report that 6,000 acres and three small communities have been affected by the blaze, the newspaper can supply a detailed map.

And it was the thorough reporting of a newspaper staff that uncovered the possible origins of the Crystal Peak fire, which was reported vaguely by television as "caused by some type of machinery."

Ironically, that machinery had been operated by a subcontractor hired by the Forest Service—the very agency responsible for preventing and combating forest fires.

PUBLIC RELATIONS

When a reporter covers a disaster, public relations representatives from the government or local relief agencies can be invaluable sources of information.

Fire Information Officer Peggi Lawrence made her first appearance in this telecourse during Unit Nine, on public relations writing. In this program, we see how her job is very different than those in public relations whose primary mission is to sell or create an image for a product, person or company.

In the video, we see Karen Reuter seek out Lawrence at the fire command center immediately, before even starting on her story.

"Peggi got me oriented right away," Reuter says. "I talked to her first thing, and she said, 'This is where the fire is. These were our trouble spots last night, and this is our concentration today.' So that when I go to talk to some of the operations chiefs and the safety officer, I don't sound like I don't know anything about this fire. It's important for you not necessarily to be an expert but to know the basics, so that you can ask intelligent questions, ask questions that are going to be pertinent to your story and make sense to the people you're talking to."

During the fire, Lawrence functions as a vital link between those battling the blaze and the journalists covering the event. Through the mass media, Lawrence is able to communicate to local residents survival information such as

•when and if residents should evacuate,
•who has been hurt by the fire,
•how residents can assist firefighters in their work,
•what progress has been made in containing the fire, and
•where the fire is burning and where it is likely to spread.

Ultimately, Lawrence and other public relations representatives for the Forest Service had to explain the "why" of the story—a touchy subject when it was discovered that a subcontractor working directly for the Forest Service worker might have initially sparked the blaze. Even in such a potentially embarrassing situation, Lawrence explains, a public relations person's best approach is honesty. You'll notice the subject is addressed in Lawrence's example press release, reproduced on page 275.

FEATURE STORIES AND SIDEBARS

Once the breaking-news headline stories are covered, readers will be receptive to almost every sidebar and follow-up story about human interest angles and personality profiles of the victims and rescue workers. Background and trend stories about the disaster's causes—as well as possible solutions to avoid future incidents—give numerous opportunities for writers to explore both in-depth reporting and creative writing approaches. The lessons covered in Unit Eleven, which introduced feature news writing styles, are reinforced as the reporters discuss and show how they sought out and offered as many angles on the fire story as possible.

"On a fire like this that's lasted for several days, it's hard to be fresh," says Karen Reuter. "A lot of the stories are stale, because you've done the battle of the flames for the last three days. And that's when your ability to be creative and to think of interesting sidebars really comes out."

The Carole Rich textbook *Writing and Reporting News: A Coaching Method* features a chapter titled "Disasters and Tragedy" (pp. 479–512 in the second edition) that covers many of the same topics as this unit of the telecourse does. An important checklist of information to collect on a disaster story is included, as well as information about the importance of follow-up stories and insight on how to deal with interviewing grief-stricken survivors or victims of disasters.

The best sidebars, according to Reuter, are "personal stories. Maybe one firefighter's personal decision—why they're here. Maybe there's an incident commander who was personally burned in a fire and has made the choice to come back and continue to fight fires as . . . some kind of personal resolve. There's a story."

Terry Hendry has a similar approach to features. "What you want to do is take these people that are involved and focus in on one small section," she says. "If they're being evacuated, how is that going? If there are people out on the field and they're collapsing from exhaustion, how is that going? How is the smoke affecting people who have asthma? What you do is you try and take a little slice of how people are affected, and you try and bring that back to the folks who are watching."

ETHICAL DILEMMAS

The most obvious area of sensitivity, which teeters on the border of both media ethics issues and media law issues, would be in the area of invasion of privacy. We've already heard from several reporters about their approaches to gathering quotes.

Another ethical and legal challenge comes when the law enforcement authorities create artificial boundaries over which journalists are asked not to cross in order to take photographs, notes or video images. While such lines are usually drawn with "public safety" in mind, we'll find out in Unit Fifteen that the government has a history of hiding newsworthy information in the name of protecting the public from itself—and that journalists have been fighting these practices for hundreds of years.

Is it unethical or illegal for journalists to cross into "restricted" zones created by the local police and the firefighters? Is it even legally possible for these officials

Nancy Vogel, Sacramento Bee*: "I got addicted, on my very first fire. . . . There's this incredibly deep silence, then the trees just start exploding around you. I got hooked after that."*

Charles Kuralt, CBS News*: "Covering the scene of a plane crash, I forced myself to go into the terminal and talk to friends and relatives who were waiting for that plane to land. I was surprised to find that some of them really did want to talk. It relieved the tension."*

to restrict access by the press? Several of the journalists who covered the Crystal Peak fire freely admitted that they had gathered spectacular still and video images by pushing into areas that officials specifically asked them not to enter. These journalists took great care not to interfere with the fire-fighting efforts, but they took an equal amount of care not to get caught in their zeal to scoop the competition.

Objectivity, balance, truth and fairness also play a role in the covering of a disaster. While it is easy to emphasize the horrors of a forest fire, reporter Nancy Vogel of the *Sacramento Bee* characterized it as "beautiful." In a way, a forest fire is a normal occurrence in nature—caused even more often by lightning than by careless campers. So often, in fact, that shortly after the Crystal Peak fire, the *Sacramento Bee* did a series of stories about how people's interference with natural fires has caused a dangerous situation in which normally small fires become out-of-control fire storms feeding on dried fuel that has been building up for decades.

Would a news organization be remiss in emphasizing the tragic nature of a forest fire near this suburban subdivision if it was not reported that lightning-caused timber fires had been Mother Nature's method of pruning and revitalizing the ecosystem for millions of years before humans tried to civilize the neighborhood?

As with much news writing, the better stories reach beyond the hackneyed look at the surface level. It's the good reporter's ethical responsibility to look beyond the obvious—to think, and research, and reflect, until good reporting and good writing merge to create good journalism.

FIRE RACES TOWARD TINY SIERRA TOWN: FIVE BUILDINGS BURNED IN BLAZE NEAR I-80

By Nancy Vogel
Sacramento Bee

A raging, out of control wildfire shot flames more than 100 feet into the air Thursday after exploding in sick, dry forest northeast of Truckee. It burned at least 3,000 acres, destroyed at least five buildings and threatened the small Nevada town of Verdi.

While hundreds of firefighters assaulted the inferno from hillsides and aircraft, struggling to save million-dollar homes, curiosity-seekers gathered in droves beside roads to gawk at the reddened sky and shoot souvenir photographs.

"It looks like they're watching the Fourth of July," said Jimbo Cronon, general manager of the Gold Ranch Casino in Verdi. "The first thing I sold out at my store is film."

The fire, dubbed Crystal Peak, was noticed about 2 p.m. as a billow of smoke near Stampede Reservoir, about 10 miles northeast of Truckee. Flames spread to the Sunrise Basin subdivision, forcing evacuation, and by 11 p.m. were within a few hundred yards of Verdi, a town of roughly 1,400 people along Interstate 80.

Fire officials predicted that the superhot, white-capped blaze, which created its own wind, would be a "major rager" and launched a massive effort to stop it.

"It's going forever," said Josh Bradley, a state firefighter from Nevada City, as he headed to a fire line on the west side of Crystal Peak. "This thing just took off up over the ridge, and it looks like a pretty serious fire."

Tahoe National Forest spokesman Steve Larrabee said Verdi was in a precarious situation. "Usually on the east side, the wind has a tendency to blow down-canyon, toward Verdi," he said. "So that's our concern tonight."

Cronon watched as wind-whipped flames raging like "100-foot twisters" threatened to overtake Verdi late Thursday night.

"It looks like flame throwers in old movies," he said. "The fire looks like a small tornado the way it's going up and down."

Huge tongues of flame were lapping to within three-quarters of a mile of Interstate 80 by 10:30 p.m. Thursday. Fire officials first called for voluntary evacuations in Verdi and later ordered some residents to leave.

"It's very scary," said Lisa Bonauro, who lives with her family on Hansen Street in Verdi. "We're very nervous."

Like many Verdi residents, however, Bonauro was reluctant to leave her home.

"We're staying up all night," she said.

The wildfire sparked to life in Tahoe National Forest, and gusty winds whipped it northeastward into the Toiyabe National Forest in Nevada over a ridge carpeted with drought- and beetle-killed trees. The fire had consumed more than 3,000 acres by 10:30 p.m. and destroyed five structures—at least three of them homes—despite the frantic work of more than 700 firefighters, 40 fire engines, 12 bulldozers, eight air tankers, three helicopters and 16 crews of firefighters.

Twice as many firefighters are expected to be rushed to the steep burning mountainsides today, said Larrabee.

Homes in the threatened area ranged up to $1.5 million in price, according to Robert Herbert of the Nevada National Guard.

A fire lookout station that the Forest Service announced in May it could not staff full time for lack of money sat within sight of the volcano-like blaze, which devoured towering pines and nearly blackened the sky with smoke.

Phil Horning, a spokesman for the state Department of Forestry and Fire Protection, said the fire started in a steep area where at least half the trees are dead or dying. The area's timber had been sold, and logging was scheduled.

A U.S. Forest Service equipment operator first noticed the fire, Horning said.

While scores of people with video cameras lined smoky Interstate 80 between Boomtown and Verdi to capture the fire's red glow, the Red Cross prepared an evacuation center at B.D. Billinghurst Middle School in Reno. Food and shelter were ready for 200 people, spokeswoman Christine Price said.

Chief Alan Van Guilder of the Reno Fire Department said firefighters would soon begin lighting backfires to try to starve the blaze.

Crystal Fire
Information

The Crystal Fire, on the Tahoe and Toiyabe National Forests, has increased to more than 6,000 acres. This was due to late-Friday afternoon erratic winds causing several spot fires on the north and south flanks.

During the spot fire activity, several homes near the Gold Ranch area were threatened and some people evacuated. One outbuilding was destroyed, and several others damaged.

Fire suppression efforts for today will focus on the "hot spots" on the north and south flanks and building additional fireline in those areas. The fire crews on the ground will have air support with 8 helicopters and 5 air tankers to make water and retardant drops on the fire. There are also 83 engines and 17 dozers in use.

The structure protection group (50 engines plus crews) will be stationed strategically in residential areas for fire protection and community assistance.

The fire is 20% contained.

There are now 1,400 persons assigned to the fire. They represent 20 Federal, State, County and Municipal agencies, Volunteer Fire departments and other organizations, and the Nevada National Guard.

Persons who are not residents in the fire areas are asked to remain away from the fire areas and keep the roads available for local residents and emergency vehicles. Many of the roads are narrow and are currently restricted to one-way fire traffic as a safety precaution.

Interstate 80 remains open. Visibility may be slightly decreased due to smokey conditions.

FIRE INFORMATION CENTER
August 6, 1994   Phones: 345-1754; 345-1756; 345-1758
10:00 AM

CDF press release.

ALTERNATIVE VIEWS

Carole Rich, author of *Writing and Reporting News: A Coaching Method*, has covered her share of disasters. She had these observations on the difference between the traditional approach to reporting and a modern student's first instincts.

"So much of my life as a reporter and editor seemed to be covering disasters of one form or another, I thought it was very important [to include a chapter in the textbook]. But one of the funniest things that has happened shows a generational change. . . . There are things nobody tells you about on how to cover disasters. Like, what do you take before you leave the newsroom? What should you think about before you leave the newsroom? And my students say, 'Look at a map for alternate routes' and I'm real proud of them.

"And then I say, 'OK, what do you need so that you can communicate with the newsroom before you leave—things you should think about?' And they say, 'Pack your Powerbook.'

"One said, 'Take your cellular phone.' And another one said some other piece of equipment, and I stood in front of the classroom and roared. I said, 'All I wanted you to do was take a pocket full of quarters so you can call back to the newsroom.'

"The generation gap really hit me. They have all these electronic gizmos like a fax that they're going to carry around in their pockets. But I think nobody prepares you well to cover a disaster. In a sense, it's no different than any other story. Good reporting is good reporting, whether you're going out on a police accident or an earthquake. But there's a mass of material that you should probably think about. And I guess that's why I include a specific chapter on it.

"You can't take a checklist to a disaster. I think an easier way of visualizing reporting . . . [is to imagine] you're waiting for some loved ones to come in on a plane at your local airport. And you hear on the radio that a plane has crashed. What do you want to know? I think role-playing helps you a lot more in being a good reporter. If you were in this position, what would you want to know? People are desperately waiting for news. If you were one of those people desperately waiting for news, what's absolutely crucial to you? Forget the checklist. Just be human."

GLOSSARY

The disaster-related terms in the following glossary are defined in the *Associated Press Stylebook*. Precise use of language is important for accurate reporting in such situations. Most of these terms are found listed under "Weather Terms" in the *Stylebook* and are cited here courtesy of the Associated Press.

BLIZZARD
Wind speeds of 35 mph or more and considerable falling and/or blowing of snow with visibility near zero.

CYCLONE
A storm with strong winds rotating about a moving center of low atmospheric pressure. The word sometimes is used in the United States to mean *tornado* and in the Indian Ocean area to mean *hurricane*.

DUST STORM
Visibility of one-half mile or less due to dust, wind speeds of 30 mph or more.

EPICENTER
Refers to the point on the earth's surface above the underground center, or focus, of an earthquake.

FLASH FLOOD
A sudden, violent flood. It typically occurs after a heavy rain or the melting of a heavy snow.

FUNNEL CLOUD
A violent, rotating column of air that does not touch the ground; usually a pendant from a cumulonimbus cloud.

GALE
Sustained winds within the range of 39–54 mph (34–47 knots).

HEAVY SNOW
It generally means a (1) fall accumulating to 4 inches or more in depth in 12 hours or (2) fall accumulating to 6 inches or more in depth in 24 hours.

ICE STORM
Describes the freezing of drizzle or rain on objects as it strikes them. *Freezing drizzle* and *freezing rain* are synonyms for ice storm.

SANDSTORM
Visibility of one-half mile or less due to sand blown by winds of 30 mph or more.

SEVERE BLIZZARD
Wind speeds of 45 mph or more, great density of falling and/or blowing snow with visibility frequently near zero and a temperature of 10 degrees or lower.

SEVERE THUNDERSTORM
Describes either of the following: (1) winds—thunderstorm-related surface winds sustained or gusts 50 knots or greater; (2) hail—surface hail three-quarters of an inch in diameter or larger. The word *hail* in a watch implies hail at the surface and aloft unless qualifying terms such as *hail aloft* are used.

TEMBLOR
A synonym for *earthquake*. Do not spell the word as *trembler* or *tremblor*.

TORNADO

A violent rotating column of air forming a pendant, usually from a cumulonimbus cloud, and touching the ground. It usually starts as a funnel cloud and is accompanied by a loud roaring noise. On a local scale, it is the most destructive of all atmospheric phenomena.

TROPICAL STORM

A warm-core tropical cyclone in which the maximum sustained surface wind ranges from 39 to 73 mph (34–63 knots) inclusive.

TYPHOON

A warm-core tropical cyclone in which the minimum sustained surface wind is 74 mph or more. Hurricanes are east of the international date line. Typhoons are west of the line. Both are known as cyclones in the Indian Ocean. When a hurricane or typhoon loses strength (wind speed), usually after landfall, it is reduced to tropical storm status.

WIND CHILL INDEX

Also known as the *wind chill factor*. No hyphen. The wind chill index is a calculation that describes the combined effect of the wind and cold temperatures on exposed skin. The wind chill index would be minus 22, for example, if the temperature was 15 degrees and the wind was blowing at 25 mph—in other words, the combined effect would be the same as a temperature of 22 below zero with no wind. The higher the wind at a given temperature, the lower the wind chill reading, although wind speeds above 40 mph have little additional cooling effect.

SUGGESTED WRITING EXERCISES

Ethical and legal challenges involving disaster coverage come when the law enforcement authorities create artificial boundaries over which journalists are asked not to cross—even if they need to gather quotes, take photographs or gather video images. While such lines are usually drawn with "public safety" in mind, we'll find out in Unit Fifteen that the government has a history of hiding newsworthy information in the name of protecting the public from itself—and that journalists have been fighting these practices for hundreds of years.

1 Is it unethical or illegal for journalists to cross into "restricted" zones created by the local police and the firefighters?

2 Is it a good idea for government officials to restrict access by the press?

3 Several of the journalists who covered the Crystal Peak fire freely admitted that they had gathered spectacular still and video images by pushing into areas that officials specifically asked them not to enter. These journalists took great care not to interfere with the fire-fighting efforts, but they took an equal amount of care not to get caught in their zeal to scoop the competition. How would you have approached the same situation, if you were reporting on the same fire?

4 Objectivity, balance, truth and fairness also play a role in the covering of a disaster. Would a news organization be remiss in emphasizing the tragic nature of a forest fire near this suburban subdivision if it was not reported that lightning-caused timber fires had been Mother Nature's method of pruning and revitalizing the ecosystem for millions of years before humans had tried to civilize the neighborhood? Why?

QUIZ

Choose the best answer.

1 When broadcast journalists report live from the scene of a disaster, they

    a. construct the stories in an identical manner to most other broadcast stories.

    b. often use the inverted pyramid form of development, which is rarely used in broadcast news.

    c. try to find a feature angle for the live stand-up.

    d. all of the above

    e. none of the above

2 In a disaster situation, reporters

    a. never trust information given to them from public information officers.

    b. often depend on public information officers for essential data.

    c. can trust anything given to them by a PIO, since it is an emergency situation.

    d. all of the above

    e. none of the above

3 The summary lead is

    a. a good beginning for a press release written about a disaster.

    b. a standard approach for a hard-news story written for a newspaper about a disaster, especially when the writer is on a tight deadline.

    c. rarely used in broadcast journalism but is an acceptable beginning for a story about a disaster—especially if the reporter is broadcasting live from the scene.

    d. all of the above

    e. none of the above

4 When leaving to cover a disaster, a reporter might be well advised to bring along

    a. a good map of the area.

    b. pocket change for pay phones.

    c. a portable computer with a modem.

    d. all of the above

    e. none of the above

5 Reporters who are gathering quotes from disaster victims

    a. sometimes encounter hostility.

    b. often encounter people who find talking about their grief to be therapeutic.

    c. must be aware of trespassing and invasion of privacy issues.

    d. all of the above

    e. none of the above

6 Feature news stories about disasters are

    a. rare and usually considered inappropriate, because the readers want the hard news.
    b. especially appropriate in second- and third-day coverage, as follow-up and behind-the-scenes stories about the human interest angles of the disaster.
    c. almost always favored by newspapers, since the broadcast news reporters usually scoop them on the hard news.
    d. all of the above
    e. none of the above

7 Karen Reuter's story about the fire, featured in the telecourse program,

    a. tried to avoid the cliché "show them the flames" approach.
    b. used nat-sound to create atmosphere.
    c. featured sound bites from several different news makers to supplement the reporter's point of view.
    d. all of the above
    e. none of the above

8 The difference between newspaper coverage and broadcast coverage of the Crystal Peak fire was

    a. newspapers always scooped the broadcast news agencies.
    b. television delivered live coverage while newspapers gave a more in-depth look at issues such as evacuation routes, causes of the blaze, areas that were threatened and costs of fighting the fire.
    c. newspapers depended on public information officers, while broadcast agencies did not.
    d. all of the above
    e. none of the above

9 The impression given by the public information officer was that

    a. the press works well in cooperation with the government to help the public cope with a disaster.
    b. the press often gets in the way of disaster-relief efforts.
    c. the public relations department often has an antagonistic relationship with the press.
    d. all of the above
    e. none of the above

10 Reporters who had covered earthquakes, airline crashes and other disasters

    a. found that their experiences were completely different when they covered the Crystal Peak fire.
    b. found that disaster victims rarely wanted to talk to the press.
    c. experienced many of the same emotions and challenges that come with covering a disaster.
    d. all of the above
    e. none of the above

SELF-TEST

1 List at least four things that are different about the way print and broadcast news teams cover disasters.

2 List at least four things that are the same about the way print and broadcast news teams cover disasters.

3 List at least four functions that hard-news stories have in disaster coverage.

4 List at least four functions that feature news stories have in disaster coverage.

5 How do public relations professionals and journalists interact during a disaster?

JOURNALISM
ETHICS

Superman had a day job.

When he wasn't saving the world from total destruction, he passed the time as a newspaper reporter. Even then, his motto was "Truth, justice and the American way."

Your personal code of ethics won't be the same as Clark Kent's—each journalist must fashion his or her own set of rules. Ultimately, each journalist must decide what is the most honorable way to act in a given situation.

Each news organization has its own written code of ethics, but few of the journalists interviewed for this telecourse could recall the specifics of their own company policies.

Instead, the reporters, editors and broadcasters expressed a strong sense of personal commitment to serve the public in the most noble way possible.

The reasons given were many. Most wanted to just feel honest about the job they were doing. Others were quite preoccupied with the public view of the news business and felt that strong ethical practices would lead to **credibility**.

Of course, like any other business, some individuals have a higher standard of ethics than others. That truism is evident even in the brief half-hour video presentation.

As students, you will be able to judge for yourselves what is fair, equitable, virtuous and moral behavior in the newsroom. The process of creating a personal code of ethics should start with this introduction to journalism. In an ideal academic setting, the process might continue with an entire course in ethics. But the continual reevaluation of personal ethics is a quest that should never end. Hopefully, all the student journalists inspired by this course will continue to reevaluate and strengthen their personal codes of ethics throughout an entire career.

OBJECTIVES

This unit and program surveys the ethical challenges and attitudes of some of America's most noteworthy journalists. You will be encouraged to start creating your own code of ethics based on the video presentation and the exercises contained in the student study guide.

Codes of ethics in newsrooms across the country address many of the same topics. And, though the nature of news beats varies widely, the ethical challenges from reporter to reporter bear many similarities.

•**Pay close attention to the ways the featured journalists in both the video presentation and the textbook use these terms:**

Conflict of interest	Anonymous source
Gratuities/freebies	Accuracy
Deception	Advocacy
Fairness	Admissions
Objectivity	Relationships/friendships
Balance	Plagiarism
Credibility	Privacy
Off-the-record source	Sensitivity

1. Think about the different approaches to ethics as practiced by mainstream journalists, advocacy journalists and tabloid journalists.

2. Look for the different ethical challenges Monica Davey, reporter for the *St. Petersburg Times*, encounters as she works on a story about the city council trying to close down businesses that feature erotic dancers, X-rated videos and magazines and other "adult" entertainment.

3. Listen for reporters' tone when they describe the relationship between credibility and profit.

4. Watch for differences in ethical challenges for different newsroom beats.

5. Notice how broadcast reporters and newspaper reporters have subtly different concerns about journalism ethics.

•**Address the following questions in your journal. Or, if there's time, discuss them in class.**

1. Explain the difference between a "red light" and a "green light" approach to ethics, as explained by Bob Steele of the Poynter Institute. What would be the dif-

ference between a red light approach to **deception** and a green light approach to posing, if a reporter was working on the same story about the "adult entertainment" businesses in St. Petersburg?

2. In his defense of the practice of paying for interviews, Brian Williams from the *National Enquirer* says that at least it is clear what the motive of the news maker is. In this defense, Williams questions the motivation of people who talk to the mainstream press. Do you buy the argument?

3. How would an ABC newsmagazine or *National Enquirer* cover the story about the St. Petersburg City Council's battle against the X-rated businesses differently than the local newspaper?

THE
LESSON

Bob Woodward is arguably the most renowned journalist of the 20th century. His reputation was launched while he was half of the Woodward and Bernstein reporting team that uncovered the Watergate scandal and ultimately led to the resignation of President Richard Nixon in August 1974. Since that time, Woodward has written many best-selling books that also have relied on investigative journalism techniques. (Recommended reading: *Wired*, *The Brethren*, and *The Agenda*.) Woodward has also continued to work for the *Washington Post* as a respected editor and investigative reporter.

In his opening statement of the telecourse program on ethics, Woodward suggests that students should "pretend that there's somebody from the *Columbia Journalism Review* or the local journalism review listening and watching you operate." Woodward then advises students to ask themselves the question "Does it seem like somebody I know would be bothered by my behavior?"

He doesn't mean to imply that a journalist should back off from a story that irritates people. Woodward himself has "bothered" numerous news makers, politicians, scholars and journalists with his reporting style. While Woodward was in the process of dethroning Richard Nixon, his ethics were being questioned by many critics.

For writing stories linking Nixon with sabotage of the Democratic Party headquarters, Woodward and the *Washington Post* were criticized by Republican Senator Bob Dole for being presidential candidate George McGovern's "partner-in-mudslinging." Nixon's campaign director Clark MacGregor accused Woodward of using "innuendo, third-person hearsay, unsubstantiated charges, anonymous sources and huge scare headlines."

In his book *All the President's Men*, written with Carl Bernstein, Woodward himself admits making mistakes (and some ethical lapses in judgment) during the uncovering of the Watergate scandal.

The flip side of this criticism is that newspapers have an ethical responsibility to publish important news stories, even in the face of severe public criticism. During the time period that the *Washington Post* continued to run front-page stories about Nixon and Watergate—in spite of ridicule and condemnation by other news organizations—the television networks and the majority of daily newspapers in the country virtually ignored the incident. Nixon ran for re-election with very little scrutiny. On the eve of the election, pollsters showed only 52 percent of the American voters had even heard the word *Watergate*. Nixon won in a landslide.

Clearly, what one reporter justifies as ethical behavior can easily bother others. A historical study of Watergate and Woodward's contribution to journalism reinforces many of the concepts illustrated in this unit of the telecourse, including this primary theme: Each reporter, ultimately, is responsible for constructing his or her own code of ethics.

ANONYMOUS SOURCES: OFF-THE-RECORD COMMENTS

The most celebrated bit of journalism of this century—Woodward and Bernstein's investigative reporting on Nixon—relied heavily on **anonymous sources** and **off-the-record** comments. Years later, journalists are still split on the correct ethical approach to using these techniques to gather information for the news.

Many editors and reporters are still troubled by all variations of off-the-record comments, anonymous sources, confidential sources, background sources or deep background sources.

"I think there's a rare story that needs an anonymous source," says Shirley Biagi, of California State University, Sacramento. "I think the reader wonders about the believability. If you want to be credible with your readers, . . . try to take the story to the point where you can use someone's actual name. If you can't, take the anonymous information and verify it elsewhere. Find other information that can be used on the record and try to use it on the record."

Woodward, on the other hand, steadfastly defends using anonymous sources and off-the-record comments.

"I am incredulous that some editor would say, 'Never use an anonymous source,'" he says. "I think that is so naive about journalism and about the world. Who publicly declares their most important secrets regularly? Just doesn't happen."

And, Woodward points out, in certain circumstances, a government official is just as likely to lie as an anonymous source.

"If I quote the president of the United States accurately, and it turns out he's lying, it's not my fault," Woodward says. "It's the president's fault." Still, he says, the impression of the public would be "the president lied; Woodward, the reporter, just got snookered.

"We've got this idea that you take yourself off the hook by putting it on the record," he says. "I disagree. I think the standard should be 'Is it really true?' In journalism, there's a feeling of 'Oh, we can wash our hands of that, because the official lied.' I think it's our job to check."

This brings us, again, to the main theme of this unit in the telecourse. With regard to anonymous sources and off-the-record comments, as well as most other journalism ethics decisions, every reporter must devise his or her own personal set of values. No one person can tell you everything that is correct or incorrect in journalism ethics. After hearing Woodward, Biagi and others discuss the pros and cons of using anonymous sources, it is up to you—the student reporter—to design your own personal philosophy about the practices.

As an entry-level journalist, many of your values will be affected by your mentors and peers in the newsroom. This telecourse will start you on the way through that process with a fairly noteworthy cast of characters.

One of those characters is Monica Davey, a reporter for the *St. Petersburg Times*. As the camera follows Davey working on the story about the city's efforts to shut down "adult entertainment" spots, notice how Davey approaches each ethical decision.

For instance, during her telephone interviews, Davey is told (off the record) by one bar owner that the dancers in a competing establishment practice prostitution. Davey's approach is similar to Biagi's advice. She doesn't include the anonymous comment in her story but considers the information as part of the bigger picture when investigating the whole piece.

FAIRNESS

If a single thread can be unraveled from the comments about ethics in the televised portion of this unit, it is that good journalists are preoccupied with being fair. From the *National Enquirer* to the *New York Times*, from ABC News to the *Village Voice*, reporters, editors and broadcasters all voiced concerns about being fair to the people who are covered by the news.

Carole Rich sums up the concerns by asking, "Who will be hurt by your story?"

The ultimate balance to that question is answering, "What is the newsworthiness of the story? Does the public's right to know outweigh the pain or embarrassment caused to the news maker?"

The real challenge to answering all three questions is understanding that journalists must not be timid. Unfortunately, some members of the populace commit hideous acts or do embarrassing things. It is often a reporter's job to observe unsavory aspects of society and write about them. In the process, the public sees the world as it is. The ugly (and even not so ugly) truth often hurts.

Fairness, however, is not the same as **objectivity** and **balance**. Michael Tomasky, of the *Village Voice*, suggests that **advocacy** journalists embrace the concept of fairness while rejecting the need for balancing a story. According to Tomasky, his job is to state a point of view in his writing, take a side and support the case with as much good reporting as possible.

Harry Smith, morning anchor for CBS News, offers a more mainstream point of view. According to Smith, reporters should avoid bias and always strive for one thing: Truth.

You'll see Monica Davey grapple with issues such as fairness, objectivity and bias in the television program, as she attempts to screen out her personal feelings about pornography and sex for sale in the story about the St. Petersburg night-clubs.

RED LIGHT/ GREEN LIGHT

Bob Steele, director of the ethics program at the Poynter Institute for Media Studies, introduces a concept in which he advocates a "green light" metaphor for an approach to journalism ethics. It is important, Steele says, to not get so carried away with a fear of hurting somebody's feelings that a personal code of ethics or morality gets in the way of good reporting.

"The biggest ethics weakness in journalism is not sensationalism," Steele says, "but rather that journalism is too timid. . . . It doesn't aggressively go after the right stories in the right way.

"A democracy functions well with more information. . . . The public's right to know is the starting point. In some situations, rare though they might be, the person's right to **privacy** will outweigh that public right to know."

GREEN LIGHT APPROACH—AN EXAMPLE

Steele suggests that the struggle to fairly report a problem such as suicide will illustrate his point. Suicide is a topic that is badly underreported, in Steele's opinion. Especially at colleges, where potential news stories about suicide come up frequently.

"I once worked in a television station," he says. "When I first got there . . . there were two [suicides], in a school, and I thought it was fairly significant. Somebody said, 'Don't waste your time thinking about running this story—we haven't done a suicide story in 20 years.' I said, 'Why not?' He said, 'Well, 20 years ago I did a story, and . . . the owner of the TV station stormed into the newsroom and said, 'That's the last blankety-blank time we'll ever run a suicide story.' He'd gotten a lot of angry response from his friends in the community.'"

Steele suggests that a solution to that kind of negative thinking would be to avoid writing stories about the specifics of certain suicides. Instead, a reporter could write about the issue itself.

"I think that at a college press where that is clearly an issue, it's important to weigh the situation and figure out ways you can report a suicide story which still recognize the potential of great harm to some vulnerable people—the family, the victims and others," Steele says.

"Still, you have the responsibility of getting some important information out about that particular event to prevent rumor and innuendo from causing problems, to make sure it's as accurate as possible. And, most importantly, to give a large contextual element to a story which has great social significance. That's a challenge. But that's that green light notion.

"A red light approach," Steele says, "would be to say, 'You don't do stories like that, because they hurt people.' The green light notion is figure out ways to do it which minimize harm and reveal perspective. And truth."

CONFLICT OF INTEREST

One topic of great concern to all of the journalists interviewed for the news-writing telecourse was **conflict of interest**.

"We have to hold ourselves to the same standards that we hold to the people that we cover," says Elizabeth Arnold, of National Public Radio. Arnold covers politicians who, she says, are attacked if they exhibit behavior even "remotely connected" with a conflict of interest. In her view, journalists should have even higher standards.

One aspect of journalism ethics is how to deal with friendships. Sports reporters become friends with coaches, and then find they must write about a recruiting scandal. Public safety reporters become friends with police officers, and then have to cover a story in which the officer is accused of wrongdoing.

"You always have that problem," says Kurt Loder of MTV News and *Rolling Stone*. "It's not a good thing to be friends with people you're covering. It's tempting, but they're not going to consider you their friend anyway. They just know that you're somebody who can do something for them. So you shouldn't really flatter yourself that they want to be your buddy. They don't. Generally, they want you for some reason or other, and you just have to fend that off all the time. You can't really cover people critically that you're friends with."

Student reporters should be especially cautious of any stories involving friends or organizations that they might be associated with. A good approach would be to ask an editor to re-assign the story to another writer.

CREDIBILITY

Two motifs emerged when journalists interviewed for the news-writing telecourse talked about credibility.

First, reporters simply want to feel good about what they do, and they want to be believed by the public.

The second school of thought is a bit more cynical, even if it is completely practical. If the public doesn't believe a news organization, nobody buys the truth it's trying to sell—literally.

"The bottom line," says Michael Brown, of the *Chicago Defender*, is to "write the newspaper so somebody will buy it. Newspapers aren't a public service. Newspapers are in business to make money. It has nothing to do with ethics. It has to do with what's going to make money for this newspaper."

Brown was not the only journalist interviewed for the news-writing telecourse to express this view. But, he also adds, it's not the company code of ethics that is important.

"What it comes down to here is . . . does it go against your personal principles?"

It's an attitude that has much in common with most other mainstream journalists.

"The mainstream press," says Bob Steele, of the Poynter Institute, has a "primary responsibility . . . to serve the public in the way no other profession does. Not medicine, not law, not architecture. Nobody else has that responsibility except journalists—of seeking the truth and reporting as fully as possible."

THE TABLOID PRESS

The tabloid press, Steele says, has a completely different mission. "That's to go out and make money in any way possible. Their vehicle happens to be on paper, with clearly salacious or sellable stories that take great liberty with the truth and are highly sensationalistic. I think in a democracy, that should be allowed. I don't have any problem with that. They should honor the notions of not causing undue harm to people, in an ethical sense, or in violating laws in a legal sense. And they should be held accountable in the same way.

"They are on the product shelf. In a supermarket, there's some things that we may not buy, and we might laugh at them. I guess the same exists with the tabloid press; they have a right to be. Our response in mainstream journalism should not be to push them away but rather to do what we do all the better."

The most obvious difference between the tabloid approach to journalism and the mainstream approach is in the willingness to pay for interviews.

Brian Williams, general editor of the *National Enquirer*, defends his publication's approach in the telecourse program on ethics.

"If I'm paying you, I know what your motivation is," he says. "We're just real clear about it. We pay you. Here's a check, report it to the government, pay taxes on it. OK, now let's see if the information's true. The point of it is, is the information true? Just because I paid you for it doesn't mean I'm going to print it . . . or believe it. And that's the key point: Is it true?"

Journalists from mainstream news organizations are just as clear about their position on the subject. Paying for interviews reduces credibility, and the practice is forbidden.

Williams suggests that the line between mainstream and tabloid journalism is not as distinct as it once was.

"It's always interesting where the lines were drawn in that regard," he says. "I think a good case in point was when the *Star*, another tabloid, broke the Gennifer Flowers story." (Flowers had claimed a longtime affair with then–presidential candidate Bill Clinton.)

According to Williams, during the Clinton era (which overlapped the infamous O. J. Simpson murder trial), a pattern that had been emerging for years became firmly established. The tabloid press would break a gossip or scandal story, and the mainstream press would do stories about how the tabloid press was covering the scandal. In the process, the mainstream press gained an excuse to cover the same scandals—from a mainstream point of view.

POSING

Some journalists have gained impressive information by pretending not to be journalists. The *Chicago Sun-Times* won a Distinguished Service Award from the Society of Professional Journalists in 1978 by exposing shakedowns from government inspectors. The information on the crooked inspectors was gathered when the *Sun-Times* purchased its own bar, the Mirage, and staffed it with journalists pretending to be employees. The resulting stories were spectacular. Although the series was nominated for a Pulitzer Prize, the prize committee rejected it, citing misgivings about the undercover style of reporting.

Though impressive stories can be gained through such subterfuge, the journalism community is split on whether such practices should be rewarded or chastised.

Several times during the telecourse program on ethics, you'll hear city editor Kim Kleman and reporter Monica Davey acknowledge the *St. Petersburg Times* policy against **posing**. It would have been much easier for Davey to gain information about the adult entertainment clubs she was investigating if she had pretended to be a patron instead of a journalist. But many mainstream journalists feel uneasy about these types of practices.

"Should journalists go undercover?" asks Bob Woodward. "Should they pretend they are something they are not? I say no. I say that it's a kind of false witness. It is pretending, and pretending doesn't work very well in journalism.

"I just wouldn't do it," says Woodward. "I'd be embarrassed. When I talk to somebody, I want them to know who I am and what I'm doing."

A related issue is the use of hidden cameras by television news organizations. "At [the newsmagazine show] 'Prime Time Live,' we began to make it one of our main tools for investigating wrongdoing," says Sam Donaldson, of ABC News. "For investigating crooks and people who, if you ask them a question, would tell you a lie. And the camera would in fact show you a reality."

Donaldson says that ABC and other networks are evolving an ethical code that will address the appropriate and inappropriate use of hidden cameras.

"I'm not proud of everything we've done during this evolution," he says. "I think we've come to a point now where we've got it down . . . when to use the hidden cameras and when not to use them. Clearly, a hidden camera is not to be used for something frivolous and trivial. It ought not to be used when there are other means available. A hidden camera, while by the very nature of the device, is a subterfuge."

FREEBIES

In the telecourse segment on ethics, reporter Monica Davey and editor Kim Kleman joke about the awkwardness of turning in expense reports to the newspaper's accounting department for admission fees to adult entertainment clubs. But the paper's policy is clear. Readers tend to mistrust the objectivity of reporters who receive gifts, **gratuities**, free admissions and the like.

Often, owners of restaurants, nightclubs, record companies and other entertainment industries try to subtly (and not so subtly) gain favor from a critic by bestowing gifts. Professional sports franchises, politicians and retailers also attempt to influence news organizations with samples, free records, backstage passes and so forth. Many smaller publications allow their poorly paid employees to accept such perks; a good critic would never let a free ticket or tape influence the outcome of a review. The bigger newspapers and television stations have strict policies against accepting anything.

Sometimes news makers sincerely want to make personal gestures by offering insignificant tokens of thanks; rejecting their generosity creates more confusion or awkwardness than credibility. In such circumstances, many newspapers allow reporters to accept small gifts but require that they be donated to charity.

THOROUGHNESS

At the core of any discussion of ethics is a commitment to good journalism. Sometimes, the dedication to ethics involves a more mundane attention to details and thoroughness than it does loftier, controversial concepts such as conflict of interest, posing or use of anonymous sources.

ACCURACY

It is Monica Davey's—and every other reporter's—ethical responsibility to triple-check every detail published in a story.

The promise of accuracy is often overlooked when ethics are discussed, partially because the other controversial issues are more interesting. Checking facts, to some reporters, seems too much like getting a bothersome chore out of the way, instead of striving for high-quality journalism.

In this unit's television program, Davey avoids a potential error of labeling certain businesses as "adult entertainment" on a map suggested by the editor—even though the city of St. Petersburg listed the same businesses in its investigation. Since the city had not officially formalized its own legal definition of the term "adult entertainment," Davey felt uncomfortable using it as a broad umbrella that would cover everything from stores that sold pornographic magazines to nightclubs that featured glorified go-go girls. The resulting story used either "sex-oriented entertainment" or "adult businesses" but not "adult entertainment."

The attention to detail in language saved the *St. Petersburg Times* from receiving angry phone calls from business owners, not to mention potential lawsuits.

ASKING TOUGH QUESTIONS

One aspect of this commitment to thoroughness is the willingness to ask questions that will make the news source uncomfortable. Often, it is the ethical responsibility of the reporter to be aggressive and a bit pushy.

As Monica Davey points out in the telecourse, if the reporter doesn't ask the same tough questions that readers are asking in their own minds as they read the story, the newspaper will get tossed in the trash.

If the tough questions reflect a lack of bias, news makers on both sides of a controversy will be put on the spot.

During the television program, you'll see Davey ask city officials why they are so set on closing the adult businesses. Among other questions, she asks, "Don't the concepts of free speech and liberty to pursue happiness, as guaranteed in the Constitution, cover a citizen's right to pursue erotic entertainment? What are the city's real motives for shutting down these businesses?"

Davey's questions to those who run the establishments are equally tough.

One owner was asked why she would not want her own daughter to be a dancer in the club she owned. And Davey asks point-blank if the dancers participate in prostitution.

Those are some of the questions people are going to be asking when they read the story.

It's Davey's ethical responsibility to ask those questions, and others, without flinching if they make the news makers uncomfortable.

ETHICAL CHALLENGES FOR DIFFERENT TYPES OF JOURNALISTS

The program on ethics ends with several reporters giving brief glimpses of the ethical challenges on their particular beats. We'll supplement those brief glimpses with a survey of some sound bites that didn't make the final cut on the television program.

A WHITE HOUSE REPORTER

White House Correspondent Helen Thomas says journalists should ask tough questions, especially of military flacks, or even presidents, who try to cover up the horrors of war with hackneyed platitudes such as, "It's a beautiful day for bombing." Thomas speaks from experience. She served with the UPI White House press corps throughout the Vietnam War and the Watergate scandal, watching much of the press lob softball questions at Richard Nixon and his entourage.

"You know what your profession is," Thomas says. "You don't let your personal feelings get involved. When the chips are down, in the case of Watergate, you had to go with the story. You had to ask the president the question if you had the opportunity. The burning question of the day. Even though you knew it would hurt.

"The press conference is the only forum in our society where a president can be questioned," Thomas says. "It's not in the Constitution, but that's absolutely necessary in a democracy . . . to question a president, or anyone in power. Otherwise, they wouldn't have to explain anything. A president could rule by edict. He could be a dictator, if he wasn't questioned. People in power have to be accountable. To us. 'Us,' meaning the American people. And we default when [journalists] don't ask the questions that the people want to know. We have a big responsibility, a real burden to ask. Reporters . . . are the representatives of the people."

Thomas also says the same ethical duty to ask tough questions is important for journalists covering every level of government—from the president's office right down to the local city council or student government at your school.

A RUSSIAN JOURNALIST

Andrew Loschilin works for ITAR-TASS, the Russian news agency. His ethical challenges are starkly different than those of American journalists. Journalists who worked in the former communist state (called the Soviet Union before it became the democratic Russia) were little more than government propaganda writers. The young journalists of the new Russia are intimately involved in the revolt against communism—their success is essential for the emerging democracy.

"People covering the events within the former Soviet Union face ethical choices daily," Loschilin says, "because of the people who want to bribe them or to incriminate something against their political foes . . . or because of the widespread crime in Russia. The job as a journalist in Russia is not only difficult but dangerous—physically dangerous—for people who work there.

"Of course, I know personally some people who've been journalists who were attacked on the streets, who were robbed, who were beaten . . . or publicly humiliated because of the things they wrote in their newspapers. There are hot spots in Russia, or in the territory of the former Soviet Union, where journalists are killed."

A MINORITY JOURNALIST

Terry Armour, sports columnist for the *Chicago Tribune*, is up-front about his view of working as an African American in a business dominated by Caucasians. The ethical challenges, he says, involve pressures from two directions.

"The hardest thing—not just for African Americans, but for any kind of minority—when you are dealing with subjects about your race is to stay on the fence and not have any opinion one way or another," Armour says.

"That doesn't mean you can't actively go out and seek stories that might back up your feelings about some subject. But, there are two standards there. From the black community, it's 'Hey, you're one of us. You're going to help our community. You aren't going to say anything bad about us.' But, when you do, it's, 'Aw, man, I thought you were one of us.'

"I have to say, 'You can't look at me like that—you have to look at me as a writer from the *Chicago Tribune*—not as black or white.'"

From some people, Armour says, there is resentment from those who feel minorities are only hired to fill quotas. "I would hope they would eventually judge me by my writing," he says.

Claudio Sanchez, of National Public Radio, says that having minorities in the newsroom serves a much larger purpose than trying to be fair about hiring practices. A diversity of employees, he says, leads to better reporting.

"There is a whole area of cultural ethics that is far more prominent these days in journalism," Sanchez says. "Newsrooms in this country have realized that in order for us to really be fair and thorough in covering communities, . . . that we're up against 90–150 dialects in any given community—in places like Los Angeles, New York, and Miami.

"As accurate as we are when we're covering the English-dominant communities, we cannot ask anything less of a reporter to be able to be accurate and to look out for those things—and not to paint with a broad brush minority communities that have their own story to tell. The journalistic ethics of covering those stories are mysterious in many ways, because we've not been schooled in those things."

A simple solution, Sanchez suggests, is to have reporters who can accurately understand the cultures through deep familiarity with community languages, social structures, attitudes and beliefs. Reporters who have lived in ethnic communities are not treated like outsiders and can oftentimes bring the newspapers, radio stations and television stations a more genuine understanding of complex story angles.

A CRITIC

Roger Ebert, Pulitzer Prize–winning critic, believes critics, students—in fact, all journalists—should beware of trying to be "politically correct" in the attempt to behave ethically.

"Political correctness is the fascism of the nineties," Ebert says.

"It's kind of this rigid feeling that you have to keep your ideas and your ways of looking at things within very narrow boundaries or you'll offend someone. Certainly one of the purposes of journalism is to challenge just that kind of thinking. And certainly one of the purposes of criticism is to break boundaries; it's also one of the purposes of art.

"When you're politically correct, you're training yourself at a very young age to lie. It's so tragic that today, on the campus, there's really such tunnel vision when it comes to political correctness that people are afraid to use terms or to have feelings that haven't been approved."

A BUSINESS REPORTER

Susan Antilla, business reporter for the *New York Times*, expresses caution about potential conflict of interest from investments, as well she should. R. Foster Winans, writer of a regularly featured *Wall Street Journal* column about stock market trends, was sentenced in 1985 by a federal district court to 18 years in prison, after being found guilty on charges of securities fraud for misappropriating privileged information—otherwise known as insider trading. Not only was Winans's behavior unethical, it was illegal.

AN OBITUARY WRITER

Jim Nicholson, known nationwide for preserving the obituary as an art form, has some unusual challenges in his beat. How do you approach the obituary of a dead person who lived a regrettable life?

"Most of the ethical standards that apply to news or features apply to obituaries," Nicholson says. "But all you have to do to be in my column is to be dead."

The Carole Rich textbook *Writing and Reporting News: A Coaching Method* includes a complementary chapter on "Media Ethics" (pp. 321–337 in the second edition). Of particular interest are the excerpts from codes of ethics of the following organizations: Society of Professional Journalists, Public Relations Society of America and the *Philadelphia Inquirer*.

Rich also includes the Poynter Institute Model, which is explained by Bob Steele, one of the guests in the telecourse program.

Even if the deceased has been convicted of a crime, Nicholson tries to write a positive story. But his policy is not to ignore the crime. "I can't sweep that under the rug," he says. "I call the family and say, 'Guess what? Uncle Ralph did three years for armed robbery.' They say, 'You can't say that.' Well, then we can't do an obituary. Certainly people are going to read the obituaries and say, 'How come they didn't talk about [the felony]? It was in all the papers.'"

At Nicholson's newspaper, the policy is to let the family decide whether to run a truthful obituary or none at all. The same policy applies to suicides.

"A suicide must be called a suicide," he says. "Same as any violent death; we can't just say, 'So-and-so died' if they OD'd on a lot of heroin or if they stopped a bullet. So, again, I give the family a choice. I say we can do a fine story—this person's life isn't defined by those last few seconds. Some choose 'Yes, let's do an obituary; include the fact that he or she killed themselves.' Others say, 'No, I can't do that.' That tells more about the living than the dead, really."

A BROADCAST JOURNALIST

Linda Ellerbee tells students in the telecourse program: Don't fake the news! She makes a reference to "GM and NBC" that might be obscure for those who haven't studied journalism ethics. The reference is about a famous case in which a television network faked the cause of explosion in the demonstration of an allegedly dangerous gas tank design in a popular-selling truck. In the news broadcast, the truck appeared to explode upon simple impact—with shocking and very impressive flames. The producers of the show later admitted helping the explosion along, for the camera's sake. Whether the reference is familiar or not, Ellerbee's point is universal. Journalists shouldn't make the news—they should report it. This is an

Did you know the word *ethic* comes up in another related aspect of journalism? Commitment to getting the complete story—and utter dedication to accuracy—is an essential ingredient to any personal code of ethics. It is also intimately connected to a reporter's work ethic.

"Nobody's ever gonna tell you to stay until seven o'clock so you can make a phone call and find somebody at home," says two-time Pulitzer Prize winner Tom Knudson. "Sometimes, you just have to do that. Sometimes it pays off; sometimes it doesn't. When I see people who will go to work at nine o'clock, and then go home after seven and a half hours and refuse to work more than they're legally obligated to do, at the *Bee*, it just seems like hocus-pocus to me."

"It's not just passion to work long hours," says Bob Woodward. "I think it's practical. If I work 10 hours on a story, I now know basically what the story is—and more importantly, I know what I don't know.

"If I spend two more hours on this story, I probably can double the quality of information I have. So the last hour you spend on anything is so much more valuable than the first. And if you're interested in high-quality stories, and they've assigned you to spend two days on a story, you spend part of one of your own nights. I think you can make the story two times as complete, sometimes 10 times as complete, and sometimes 100 times better."

---

easier proverb to create than to follow, especially in a situation such as a disaster, when a reporter could lend a hand to victims instead of dispassionately covering the scene.

In television, following this basic rule of journalism is even more difficult than in the print business. As Ellerbee points out, flames sell. A fire—or other spectacular disaster—looks good on the tube. If a reporter is late on the scene, it is tempting to nudge reality along for the sake of a better picture. For example, one television reporter admitted (off camera) to the producers of this telecourse that he once arrived on a murder scene after the corpse had been placed in an ambulance. The reporter convinced the ambulance driver to put the body bag—with corpse—back on the pavement for one quick camera shot.

Most news directors would have shot the reporter, if he had admitted the lapse in ethics. But he did receive a better image for that evening's news.

Brian Williams, National Enquirer: *"Paying for information . . . we'll do that and see no problem with it. I for the life of me cannot see that as big an issue as it is."*

Sam Donaldson, ABC News: "Credibility is important. . . . The audience has a right to say, 'Well, if you lied to him, how come you're not lying to me?'"

A related issue in television news ethics is the staging of news with actors and actresses.

"Re-enacting the news is greatly frowned on now," says Rick Kaplan, executive producer of "ABC World News Tonight," though he admits that the networks experimented with the practice in the 1980s.

"When they've hired actors to portray [news making] figures, that's always caused a great stir in our business and frankly brought most programs so much criticism, it wasn't worth the trouble."

A HUMOR COLUMNIST

"I have no ethics," says humor columnist Dave Barry. "We're mostly scum. I lie all the time in print. So what possible ethical challenge can I have?"

But, seriously, folks, when pressed, even Barry admits to certain on-the-job ethical challenges.

"If you have a column that gets wide circulation, people are always going to want to be favorably mentioned in it," he says. "They're fools. . . . I never favorably mention anybody. People mail me things all the time. We have to constantly be sending stuff back. I'll write about a product, making fun of it. Then 1,500 companies will mail me their products, hoping that I'll make fun of them too. And then you're always asking yourself, 'What do I do with this thing?' Sometimes you send it back, but if it's like cookies, what do you do?"

CLOSED? OR ARE THEY?

By Monica Davey
St. Petersburg Times

One elbow propped on the long counter, Stacy Harp looks around his dimly lit business and shrugs. He doesn't know what he'll do Jan. 29, the day the city wants his 5-year-old business to close.

But Harp, a burly, bearded man, isn't worried. It probably will be business as usual at the Centerfold Club, one in a row of exotic dance clubs along Central Avenue.

"Just let them cite us," Harp said. "They're violating our rights."

The Centerfold Club, where women in skimpy clothes dance seductively on table tops in the afternoon, is one of 11 establishments that sell sex-oriented entertainment in St. Petersburg. A city law, which will take effect Jan. 29, could outlaw all the sex-oriented businesses, including topless dance clubs, X-rated video rental and viewing booths, and stores that sell sex magazines, erotic toys, lotions and gadgets.

No one's sure whether all 11 businesses qualify as "adult" joints under the city's anatomically detailed rule, but one thing is certain: The law allows no "adult use establishments" in the places where they are now. So, come the end of this month, St. Petersburg likely will have no legal nude bars or lewd bookstores.

"That's the intent of it," Mayor David Fischer said last week. "The intent of it is to close them down."

One Very Strict Law
St. Petersburg's is one of the toughest such laws in the country. Even the city's attorney, who may have to defend the ordinance in court, acknowledges that.

It was prompted several years ago by gripes from frustrated neighborhood groups, Fischer said. Unlike the layout of some larger cities, St. Petersburg's major roads and commercial strips often sit right next to residential neighborhoods, Fischer said. And putting exotic dancing spots near family playgrounds, not surprisingly, created a struggle, he said.

What makes St. Petersburg's law so strict isn't its 700-foot-restriction, which forces the businesses to stay at least that far from residential neighborhoods, schools, day-care centers, churches or parks, said Assistant City Attorney Mark Winn. Plenty of cities and counties, including Pinellas, Hillsborough, Tampa, Clearwater, Largo and Tarpon Springs, have similar setback requirements for sex-oriented entertainment.

St. Petersburg's stands out from the rest, though, because of what the restriction really means in this city: There are just 15 sites, including The Pier, the Gateway Mall and some locations at Tyrone Square Mall, where the businesses can meet the 700-foot restriction, Winn said.

"I would say that the number of sites is one of the smallest, the fewest, in the country," said Winn. Legal precedents have allowed local governments elsewhere to restrict sex-oriented entertainment, but have required them to give the businesses reasonable sites to relocate to.

When the city council adopted the ordinance a year ago, it gave the clubs and shops a one-year grace period to comply with the new rule—by putting more clothing on the dancers, changing the focus of their businesses, moving elsewhere, or closing down. The grace period will end Jan. 28. A day later, city workers can go after them.

Code enforcement officials and police have yet to figure out exactly what they'll do that day. Police likely will issue ordinance citations against violating clubs and shops, said Steve Wolochowicz, a city planner. Procedures for what will happen after that are still in the works, city officials said.

Ours Is a Nice Place
Ellen Blackstock doesn't want to see anyone go out of business. Nevertheless, the manager at the Pleasure Dome says, some of the other dance clubs frankly aren't as nice as hers.

"There are some really sleazy clubs," said Blackstock, 50, whose son-in-law owns the exotic dance club at 55 32nd St. N. "Ours is as respectable a place as possible for this kind of place.

"Men are going to have adult entertainment no matter what," she said. "They always have. So you need to keep it behind closed doors, and you need to keep strict values."

St. Petersburg's adult businesses aren't exactly banding together to fight the law that threatens their existence. In fact, it is quite the opposite.

Several store owners contacted in recent weeks criticized the other clubs, saying that they were unsanitary or disreputable, or that they drew a crooked crowd, including drug dealers and prostitutes.

The fact is, the establishments are all different. They range from dark, carpeted rooms, with little more in the way of decoration than old easy chairs, to flashy bar rooms decked with Christmas lights and thumping rock music.

Some of the stores are barely recognizable from the street, with muted-beige walls and discreet signs. Others scream "GIRLS" in neon, and their painted silhouette stencils promise curvy women.

Those differences may explain why the businesses chose not to pull together when it came to fighting the city's new law.

"They're all dumps," said Bob Green, vice president and general manager of the Office Lounge, a dance club inside the Executive Motor Lounge at 3080 34th St. N. "We're the only legitimate nightclub in the city."

The Office Lounge, at 20 years old, is the city's oldest club. Its 40 dancers draw clients from 21 to 90 years old, and even attract couples to the seven-day-a-week business, Green said. "We're very successful," he said. "It's just a nice, clean club."

The Office Lounge isn't sure whether it will be breaking the city's law come the end of the month, Green said. It's not alone in its uncertainty.

In tedious detail, the ordinance defines all kinds of terms: Sexual activity, adult uses, adult materials, adult booths, adult bookstores, adult photographic studios, adult physical establishments, adult arcades, adult theaters and so on.

City officials list the 11 establishments as those that may fall into the city ordinance. No city staffers have visited the businesses to make a final ruling, though, and some business owners say they probably don't qualify. Several exotic dance facilities, for example, said their employees wear "pasties" to cover parts of their breasts, and would not fall under the guidelines of the rule. Winn, the city's lawyer, disagrees.

The Office Lounge will do whatever it takes—more clothing, for example—to come into compliance, it says. On Friday, city officials received a letter from the Lounge, asking for city guidance on the matter. "We want to work with the city," the letter said.

Others interviewed seemed less interested in changing.

Most said they plan nothing different Jan. 29. They'll wait and see what the city does to them.

Three have applied for and been denied variances to the law during the year. One of those, the Blue Garter, has appealed its case to a judge. Another, the Paradise Club, already has been shut down after being declared a public nuisance under another ordinance.

More recently, five other businesses requested exceptions to the city rule. The city council will hear those cases Thursday.

The council likely will refuse them, most business owners think.

"They'll turn them all down," said Harp, of the Centerfold Club, which accepts major credit cards and where a sign at the door pledges no prostitutes. The club's variance request already was denied. Harp said the issue will come down to someone going to court.

The Sixty-Sixer Adult Video Center, at 3800 66th St. N., has sued the city for an amendment to the city law. But that suit, still waiting to be heard, doesn't tackle the ordinance itself, said Luke Lirot, the store's lawyer in the case.

"There's no question that somebody's going to go after it," said Lirot. "It's depriving people of their civil rights." If no variances are granted Thursday, Lirot predicts, representatives of some of the businesses will file a suit.

Derek Coombs has seen what topless bars do to a neighborhood, he says.

Coombs, a minister at Northside Baptist Church, says it's not so much an issue of what goes on in the dark clubs, it's what the clubs dredge up with them. "I think we can demonstrate . . . that wherever they have located, they have attracted trouble," said Coombs, who supported creating the ordinance along with hundreds of other residents last year.

Like Coombs, supporters of the measure say sex-oriented entertainment businesses tend to bring criminals to an area, to lower property values and to create unsafe conditions. Those so-called "adverse secondary effects" have been documented at similar businesses nationwide, he said.

"I believe that somewhere along the way, you have to take a stand for what is right," said Coombs. "Through the years, people have too often said, 'Whatever goes.' This is about what we as citizens believe is right or wrong."

The businesses have options, Coombs said. That the management at The Pier, St. Petersburg's premier tourist attraction, turned down a recent request to rent space to an adult business is irrelevant, Coombs said. "From my standpoint, the alternatives have been provided," he said. "Because somebody won't rent to them, well, that's unfortunate."

Mayor Fischer agrees.

"We're trying to give them alternatives," Fischer said. "But we don't consider them an asset to the neighborhood. As a matter of fact, an adult use is a deterrent to the success of other small businesses near it."

Not everyone is so sure.

Most of Ola Glover's customers don't even notice the bookstore that sits smack against the side of her business. Inside the 4th Street Books and Video, at 1427 Fourth St. S., customers check out rows of magazines, rubber toys and sex-enhancing oils.

"I don't have any problem with it," said Glover, whose motto is: "You buy it, I fry it."

"They keep the parking lot clean and well-lit," she said. Some of the bookstore's customers, Glover said, drive fancy cars and wear three-piece suits. "People come here, get out of their cars, go in there, come out and leave. There's no loitering."

There is no moral question on her block, she said.

"I'm a grown person," said Glover, 55. "If something is offensive, you don't go."

David Perfetto sees that concept's flip side: People who want something will find a place to get it, regardless of laws.

Perfetto, 24, is a customer at the Blue Garter, at 2744 Central Ave. He is browsing through fleshy magazines that cover one wall, across from another wall of plastic inflatable dolls. Individual booths offer several noontime customers quick movies, while a longer movie is playing in a nearby room that seats 20.

Asked whether his girlfriend knows where he is this afternoon, Perfetto laughs and says he's unsure. She never asked, he says.

The Blue Garter serves a purpose, Perfetto said.

"This is what's saving these people," he said. "Places like this are keeping people away from prostitutes and AIDS. This way, they're doing it by themselves in safe places."

ALTERNATIVE VIEWS

Brian Williams, of the *National Enquirer*, expresses views on ethics that sound much the same as those expressed by journalists from the mainstream publications.

Here are a few samples. You be the judge. How different is tabloid journalism from the typical daily newspaper today?

On anonymous sources:

"Most [mainstream] political coverage that I read is from unnamed administration officials," says Williams. "I think that's the way it's done politically. I think the importance is not how you label that source but how accurate that information is. Obviously, the ideal situation is somebody on the record. That's the ideal. But if the information can only be gotten by protecting someone's anonymity, then our compact is with the reader to get that reader the information. And we'll do that."

On objectivity:

"I think that it's almost a scientific method in terms of reporting," Williams says. "You start out with a premise, and you try to prove that premise. And in the process of doing that, if you're doing it honestly, then that premise may change.

"I can't be objective. I don't know anyone that can. I can be truthful. I can be honest. And I think that's the criteria I want to hold myself to. When I start a story I start from believing something. Otherwise I can't put any energy in it. It's naive. It's like sending someone out to find out what the weather is. That's not what I want to do."

GLOSSARY

ADVOCACY
A style of journalism in which a reporter is expected to take sides in controversial issues and develop a point of view. Advocacy journalists assume their role is to interject a personal bias into a story—the opposite of mainstream journalism, in which reporters are expected to be as objective as possible and opinions are supposedly left for columns or editorials.

ANONYMOUS SOURCE
If a reporter quotes a source and purposely does not name the source, that source is called an anonymous source. Usually, the reporter is trying to protect the source by not including the name with the attribution.

BALANCE
When reporters strive to balance a story, they work to give each side of an issue an equal say. A story that quoted those who supported one side more than it quoted the other might be unintentionally unbalanced. The same unbalanced effect might be achieved by including an equal number of comments from both sides, but playing all the quotes from one side near the top of a story and shoving all the quotes from the other side for the end of the story.

CONFLICT OF INTEREST
A conflict of interest is created in journalism when a writer allows personal interests (friendships, family, business connections, etc.) to influence the outcome of a story.

CREDIBILITY
The credibility of a writer or a publication is equivalent to the believability of that writer or publication.

DECEPTION/POSING
A journalist who pretends not to be a journalist while collecting information for a news story is posing and practicing deception.

GRATUITIES/FREEBIES
When a reporter accepts gifts, free entry or any other benefit that would otherwise cost money, the common label is "accepting freebies" or gratuities.

OBJECTIVITY   Objectivity in journalism is trying not to make a judgment, or take sides, when covering a controversial issue. Writers who cover hard news for mainstream newspapers are encouraged to remain objective and filter out as much personal bias as possible when reporting a story.

OFF THE RECORD   When a source tells a reporter something that he or she does not wish to be repeated, that comment is said to be "off the record." In most situations, people who are being interviewed know that everything they say may end up in the news story. That information is on the record.

PLAGIARISM   Plagiarism is using the work of another person (in journalism, the written words of another writer or publication) and calling that work your own.

PRIVACY   Privacy is difficult to define when practicing journalism. Many news makers would prefer not to have their wrongdoings made public. The law does not usually recognize their right to keep that information private. However, in certain situations (when journalists gain the information through intrusion, or when the information published is a private fact not considered newsworthy), the courts (and most ethical journalists) recognize the individual's right to privacy. This issue will be explored in depth in Unit Fifteen.

SUGGESTED WRITING EXERCISES

1 What is your feeling about reporters pretending not to be reporters to get a good story? Can you think of any situation in which the practice might be justified?

2 Michael Brown, of the *Chicago Defender*, discusses the difference between a reporter's personal code and a company code of ethics. Why is this an important distinction?

3 George Thurlow, of the *Chico News & Review*, suggests that reporters often have to decide between hurting a friend or reporting the truth. Is this dilemma unavoidable? How would you personally react if presented with this choice?

4 Michael Brown says the "bottom line" of any ethical code is profit. Peter Berkow, the host of the telecourse, implies that the concern with credibility by many news organizations is directly linked with the practicalities of staying in business. Are these overly cynical attitudes? Isn't the desire to be credible also linked with a journalist's personal desire to do good and behave morally?

5 Mainstream publications work hard to maintain believability quotients with their readers. Is it possible that tabloid publications profit from exactly the opposite image? Where do advocacy publications fit in this discussion?

6 Explain the difference in attitudes toward fairness and balance, as expressed by both Sam Donaldson of ABC and Michael Tomasky of the *Village Voice*. What is your personal understanding of the following journalism ethics concepts listed below?

Objectivity

Fairness

Balance

QUIZ

Choose the best answer.

1 Monica Davey, the reporter from the *St. Petersburg Times* who was working on the story about the city council closing the adult businesses in town, had to deal with which of the following ethical issues?

  a. whether a reporter should pay an entrance fee to enter a business that she is reporting on.
  b. whether a journalist can keep his or her personal feelings out of the reporting of a story.
  c. whether a journalist should ask tough questions at the risk of seeming rude or invading the privacy of a news source.
  d. all of the above
  e. none of the above

2 According to Monica Davey, accepting anonymous tips about prostitution at an adult business

  a. would be a good way to get anonymous quotes for her stories about why the city of St. Petersburg was trying to close down X-rated businesses.
  b. would never be a good way to get information for her stories about why the city of St. Petersburg was trying to close down X-rated businesses.
  c. might be a good way to get a tip for a story that would require more research and confirmed facts but would be inappropriate as an anonymous quote.
  d. all of the above
  e. none of the above

3 One way to write a story about the adult businesses in St. Petersburg would have been to have reporters pose as normal customers. The attitude expressed by City Editor Kim Kleman and reporter Monica Davey toward this approach to journalism is that

  a. it is a good approach to get information that would never be revealed to an identified reporter.
  b. concealing the identity of a reporter is appropriate only in stories that are designed to uncover a scandal.
  c. the *St. Petersburg Times* never recommends that a reporter conceal his or her identity while working on a story.
  d. all of the above
  e. none of the above

4 According to Michael Tomasky, of the *Village Voice*, in his style of advocacy journalism

  a. objectivity is important, but accuracy is not.
  b. fairness is more important than balance in advocacy journalism.
  c. both balance and fairness are unimportant in advocacy journalism.
  d. all of the above
  e. none of the above

5 Jeff Chapman, a sports reporter from the *Oakland Tribune*, says writers on his beat

  a. have few ethical challenges.
  b. must be careful about gratuities, gifts and other perks offered by sports franchises.
  c. should be careful not to let their personal opinions color the balance or objectivity of their writing.
  d. all of the above
  e. none of the above

6 According to Anita Creamer, columnist for the *Sacramento Bee*,

a. columnists should be careful not to let their personal opinions color the balance or objectivity of their writing.

b. columnists should protect their sources, especially if the source has never been interviewed by a newspaper.

c. columnists do not have to worry about conflict of interest, because their job is to express opinions.

d. all of the above

e. none of the above

7 Helen Thomas, UPI White House reporter, says that reporters

a. must be very careful about national security issues.

b. must show respect to the president at all times.

c. who cover presidents or military experts must ask tough questions about issues such as conduct in war.

d. all of the above

e. none of the above

8 One theme agreed on by almost all of the journalists interviewed for this series—from mainstream newspapers to advocacy papers to tabloids—is that journalists

a. should never, ever accept a gift.

b. should never vote, in order to stay unbiased.

c. should strive to be fair.

d. all of the above

e. none of the above

9 Bob Steele, of the Poynter Institute for Media Studies, uses a red light/green light metaphor to represent

a. a positive approach to doing aggressive and fair journalism, as opposed to timid journalism.

b. a symbol for denying temptation to accept perks and being receptive toward reader reaction.

c. red light for anonymous sources, green light for good public relations.

d. all of the above

e. none of the above

10 *National Enquirer* and other tabloids

a. have no difference in ethical policy from mainstream newspapers.

b. are willing to pay for interviews, while mainstream newspapers avoid such practices.

c. are identical to advocacy publications in their approach to media ethics.

d. all of the above

e. none of the above

SELF·TEST

In the space provided, identify and discuss the ethical challenges that faced reporter Monica Davey in the televised portion of this unit, as she reported the story about St. Petersburg's attempt to close adult businesses. Explain how you would react in a similar situation.

1 *Balance, fairness and objectivity*—How does she separate her personal feelings about X-rated adult entertainment businesses from writing about this issue? Could you keep your personal feelings out of the writing and reporting of the story?

2 *Anonymous tips*—How did Davey handle the anonymous tips about prostitution at certain clubs? How would you handle the situation, if you knew there was a high probability that the claims were true?

3 *Paying to get in: Cover charges*—What were the issues in this story? Could the reporter get better quotes if she paid for interviews?

4 *Posing*—Davey had the opportunity to pretend she was just a regular customer. Are there circumstances when posing might make sense, or deliver a better story, when covering the same issue?

5 *Accuracy*—Why are accuracy and thoroughness part of an ethical code? What does this have to do with being ethical or having a sense of morals? How did Davey's commitment to accuracy and detail lead to a better story in this specific instance?

6 *Tough questions*—Why is the willingness to ask tough questions part of an ethical code? Is there anything wrong with simply being polite? What tough questions does Davey ask in her work on the story? What additional questions would you ask?

7 *Freedom of speech and the First Amendment*—How do these issues relate to this story about pornography? Why is it part of the reporter's ethical code to consider this aspect of the story?

8 *Red light/green light*—How would Bob Steele's metaphor for ethical decisions apply to the reporting of this story?

9 *Shortcuts*—Monica Davey worked for a solid week on this story. How would taking shortcuts in the work lead to a lapse of ethics?

10 *Other publications*—How would the *National Enquirer* or the *Village Voice* approach this story differently than the *St. Petersburg Times*?

MEDIA LAW

At this point, you have survived 14 weeks of this introductory news-writing class. Soon, you'll be writing stories for the school newspaper or working as an intern for the daily newspaper.

It is a daunting responsibility. Unlike many other school activities you could participate in—or other entry-level jobs you could accept—the results of your work will affect other people directly. Even though you print the truth and don't intend to hurt anybody, the people you write about could be embarrassed and offended by what you say. An innocent error could lead to somebody getting fired or a loss of customers at a business.

Even the most innocent stories could lead to controversy. What the writer construes as a compliment is often considered an insult by the source.

Of course, it could be your legitimate intent and duty as a journalist to expose a fraud or finger a crook. In any case, if the news maker didn't like what you said or how you got the information, litigation could result.

The First Amendment, in a sense, guarantees the freedom of the press. Publishers are free to print whatever they want. Prior restraint, where the government would actually step in and turn off a printing press, is extremely rare in our society. (Child pornography is one subject that is not tolerated—as of now. And, the government is even undecided against prior restraint with the publishing of stories that might threaten national security, such as reporting the recipe for creating your own atomic bomb.)

In spite of the lack of prior restraint, once something has been published, the subject of the story has recourse through the legal system to sue the writer and publisher if false information has been published that causes harm. In fact, the courts have recently decided that a news maker may sue even if the information published was true—if the journalist obtained the information through an invasion of privacy.

Any introductory journalism course should give an overview of the laws that govern media, including the laws that guarantee free access to the information needed to report the news. But this unit should be viewed only as an introduction to media law. Students who are preparing to write regularly for the school newspaper or who will be soon seeking an entry-level news-writing position should be required to take an entire course in media law.

This unit should give you a head start on any such course. Think of it as a very condensed half-hour with three classy attorneys who could easily be charging you more that $100 per hour each, and absorb as much of the information as you can.

OBJECTIVES

This unit will tell you how to avoid potential violations of libel and invasion of privacy laws, as you prepare to publish your first news stories. It will outline defenses against threats of such litigation, if a lawsuit can't be avoided. The lesson will also introduce laws that guarantee reporters access to information.

BEFORE YOU WATCH

This program introduces students to the legal issues that face journalists. A student journalist must understand the principles covered here before publishing news stories.

•**Pay close attention to the ways journalists and teachers use the following terms in this program:**

Libel	Public's right to know
Slander	Public figure
Invasion of privacy	Public official
Absolute defense	Shield law
Conditional defense	Open meeting laws
Defamation	Sunshine laws
Truth	FOIA

WHILE YOU WATCH

1. Pay close attention to the attorneys' pointers; normally, you might have to pay more than $100 an hour to hear the same advice.

2. Think of ways student journalists could unintentionally involve themselves in publishing-related lawsuits. Imagine how you would avoid those pitfalls.

3. Consider the relationship between the advice you are listening to and the First Amendment to the Constitution.

4. Notice the contrast between invasion of privacy and libel issues.

5. Review the laws designed to protect a journalist's rights to freely report the news.

6. Observe how many issues addressed in this unit Bruce Lang and Mike Donnelly must consider when they discuss the approach to Donnelly's story about the man who survived after his wife, doctor, and hospital had already prepared documents to allow him to die.

AFTER YOU WATCH

•**Address the following questions in your journal. Or, if there's time, discuss them in class:**

1. Do the laws discussed in this unit favor the public's right to know over an individual's right to privacy?

2. Do these laws favor a journalist's rights to report the news accurately and freely—without intervention from the government—over the rights of the general public?

3. Should a reporter go to jail to protect an anonymous source?

4. What is the best way for a student newspaper editor to respond if an irate caller is on the phone threatening a libel suit?

5. What rights do you have in your state if the student government wants to withhold access to documents or bar school newspaper reporters from selected student government meetings?

6. How could a powerful person try to intimidate a reporter such as Mike Donnelly from reporting a controversial story? Does the public have a right to know about a story like the one Donnelly reported in this unit of the telecourse? Why?

THE LESSON

If you walk away from this unit on media law with only two thoughts in your mind, they should be the following: First, journalists in the United States are protected. A study of libel laws should not result in a timid approach to reporting. If anything, a student of news writing should be comforted that our society values and protects aggressive journalism. Second, journalists have an intimate relationship with the truth.

The word *truth* is viewed from several different angles in the study of media law. Protection from a libel suit is not guaranteed just because a journalist knows something is true.

The best absolute defense in a libel lawsuit is *provable truth.*

Any subject of a news story who feels a news story has been defamatory (harmful and embarrassing) can threaten a libel lawsuit. And, if the plaintiff can find an attorney who will take the case, the plaintiff can almost always sue. However, to win, the news maker must prove (in most cases) that disputed information is false. In other words, according to the attorneys consulted for this unit, the burden is usually on the plaintiff to prove falsity.

Still, most editors advise reporters that provable truth is the best defense.

The plaintiff must also prove that he or she was identified in a published story and that the journalist being sued was responsible to some degree of fault (negligence or actual malice) for including information that was false and actually defamatory—not just unpleasant.

The vast majority of people who threaten libel suits never go beyond making an angry phone call. Once they understand what the legal definition of libel is, they usually realize intimidation doesn't go far with professional journalists.

And most of those who take a suit all the way to court lose, because most good journalists are smart enough not to print facts they can't prove as true—or because the plaintiff cannot prove they are false.

Many conditional (or qualified) defenses can convince a judge or jury to rule in a news writer's favor if a libel suit has been filed, even if the absolute defense of provable truth cannot be used.

CONDITIONAL DEFENSES

FAULT STANDARDS

To win a libel suit, a plaintiff must prove a **fault standard**. In other words, the plaintiff has to prove that the journalist was at fault.

There are two different types of fault standards for two different types of news makers. This is because society, and the courts, recognize that journalists should have the right to freely scrutinize and criticize the behavior of public officials and public figures—without constant fear of a libel suit.

ACTUAL MALICE

The fault standard that must be proven by public figures or public officials to win a libel suit in most states is called *malice*. It is also referred to as **actual malice** or *constitutional malice*.

(According to Jane Kirtley, an attorney with the Reporters' Committee for Freedom of the Press, some states—Indiana is one—use actual malice as the standard for all plaintiffs, not just public figures or public officials.)

Journalism students often wrongly assume that proving malice means these plaintiffs must show a reporter was "out to get them." Actually, malice as a legal term means that a reporter printed a false statement with *knowledge of falsity* or *reckless disregard for the truth*.

Mark Goodman, an attorney with the Student Press Law Center, explains that the different standard applies toward public figures and public officials because it makes it more difficult for them to be successful in libel claims.

"There's an interest in having full discussion of those people's lives and activities," Goodman says.

Nevertheless, Goodman warns, "You shouldn't be thinking, 'Is this person a public official or a public figure or a private person? Have I exercised malice here?' It's an indication that you're not doing a very good job of reporting, because your concern should be accuracy and if you're accurate, you're never going to have to worry about a successful libel claim."

NEGLIGENCE

The fault standard that must be proven by a private individual (in most states) to win a lawsuit is much less difficult to establish in a trial. It is known, in legal terms, as **negligence** or *simple negligence.*

A writer who does not work within the normal journalistic rigors to make sure all information published is accurate or true could be considered negligent. If, on the other hand, false information was printed that was unknowingly false, and the reporter had made an understandable mistake, the plaintiff might not win a libel suit. In simpler terms: A sloppy, lazy journalist is negligent; a journalist who acts reasonably is not.

For example, if a journalist had mistakenly reported that an individual had been arrested for a crime, and the incorrect name had been supplied by a normally credible source (police department, court clerk, etc.), the reporter could hardly be considered negligent (especially if the reporter had double-checked the name or had received confirmation from more than one source).

Our society (and our court system) recognizes the importance of printing the truth, but it also understands that reporters should be able to function in their jobs unencumbered by a fear that they might get sued for routine, forgivable mistakes.

According to attorney and author John Zelezny, in libel cases against the media, in which the suing party has to show negligence, the plaintiff would have to show that you didn't act like a reasonable reporter.

"For example," Zelezny says, "you didn't contact the person who the story was about. You didn't check with another source, even though the story was pretty outlandish or suspect in some way . . . or even, as a matter of routine in certain kinds of reports, where you would tend to check with another source, you didn't do that. You rushed the story through. You didn't look at warning signals along the way. Those could be the signs of simple negligence."

PRIVILEGE

Another important concept beginning students must learn is that of privilege. Again, this is a conditional defense against libel that applies only to certain members of society.

There are two types of privilege. Public officials are protected from libel (or slander) suits from each other by a concept called **absolute privilege**. Because of absolute privilege, one public official can't sue another public official about something said or written while working as a public servant. For example, one senator cannot successfully sue another senator for something libelous said on the senate floor. That statement is protected by absolute privilege. (The same libelous statement uttered at an Elk's Club luncheon speech or printed in a campaign flyer would not be protected by absolute privilege, because neither libelous statement was made while the senator was working for the public.)

Journalists in some cases may be protected by a conditional defense called a **qualified privilege**. The journalist has a qualified privilege to report what a public official says while the politician is protected by an absolute privilege, even if the statement by the public official was libelous.

In other words, the law traditionally allows politicians to lie without getting sued (as long as they're at work). You, as a reporter, have a limited right (qualified privilege) to print those lies. (This privilege also covers, in most states, fair and accurate reports of official proceedings and documents.)

Mark Goodman warns that this is a risky defense, emphasizing that a journalist must not deceive viewers or readers by putting that information in a misleading context. "The privilege can be overcome if the person suing you for libel can show that you didn't accurately or fairly report what happened in [a government] meeting.

"If you report something, for example, that is in a police record or that happens in a city council meeting, that will be something where you are protected in a libel context . . . as long as your report is fair and accurate. But be careful to check—not all meetings are covered."

OTHER DEFENSES

Opinion is protected by the First Amendment, although the distinction between opinion and fact is sometimes blurred. Opinion is usually defined as statements that are neither provably true nor provably false.

Some reporters work a beat where critique of performance (especially in areas such as sports or entertainment) requires a routine amount of opinion—much of it derogatory. These writers are protected by the doctrine of *fair comment and criticism*.

"To say the person is good versus bad is not something that, empirically, evidence can prove or disprove," Mark Goodman explains. "It is true that those kind of statements can have an impact . . . a devastating impact on the livelihood of the person who they're about. The courts, nonetheless, recognize that's not something that's capable of being libelous. If I say that an author is the worst author to have ever written a book . . . and because I'm so influential that book doesn't sell, that author would have no cause of action against me because the statements that I'm making are simply my own opinions."

This brings up one aspect of libel that has yet to be addressed fully in this unit: **Defamation**.

News makers are defamed if information printed is harmful to their reputation. This becomes a particularly thorny issue if the defamatory article impairs the news maker's ability to earn an income or if it causes extreme embarrassment.

Nevertheless, it is the duty of a good critic to sometimes print material about performers that some (especially the performer) might consider defamatory.

In other beats, much of the information printed is routinely defamatory. Clearly, if a news maker is accused of a heinous crime, the article reporting that fact could be considered defamatory by the above definition.

Still, if an article that harms an individual's reputation is based on pure opinion or on facts that are provably true, the plaintiff is unlikely to win a lawsuit against a journalist—unless the information printed constitutes an invasion of privacy.

PRIVACY

This brings us back to one of the original premises of this unit on media law: Journalists have an intimate relationship with the truth.

Examine the following statement again: If an article that harms an individual's reputation is based on pure opinion or on facts that are provably true, the plaintiff is unlikely to win a lawsuit against a journalist.

Notice the word *unlikely*. Notice the wording *"unlikely to win a lawsuit."* These are the kinds of trick phrases journalism teachers frequently use on exams about media law. They are also the kinds of tricky distinctions that can trip up a rookie reporter on the most mundane of stories.

We have learned that the only absolute defense against a libel suit is that the disputed information is provably true.

But a relatively new and unusual area of the law *assumes that the disputed information is true*. The plaintiff's gripe is that the newspaper had no right to print it. This area of the law is called *invasion of privacy*.

There are four torts, or categories of violations, within invasion of privacy law:

Appropriation
Public disclosure of private facts
Intrusion
False light

APPROPRIATION OR MISAPPROPRIATION

Perhaps it would be easier for a reporter to stomach if the first aspect of invasion of privacy examined is one that involves the advertising department.

Imagine that some mindless account representative has decided to design an advertisement for a brand of pork and beans and has used your photo with the caption "Our best reporters eat Granny's Pork & Beans."

This would be an invasion of your privacy, known in the legal world as *appropriation*, **misappropriation** or *commercialization*, depending on the state. The use of a person's name or likeness in the selling of a product without an individual's permission is particularly intolerable, according to the law, when that person's character or reputation has some marketability. For example, before invasion of privacy laws were passed, a number of companies used Babe Ruth's face and name on their packaging without the home-run king's permission. These days, many athletes make more money from endorsement deals than they do from their players' salaries.

In 1994, for example, Michael Jordan, the basketball legend, earned about $30 million. The next-highest-paid athlete made $15 million. But, in '94, Jordan was earning only about $1,000 per month—as a minor league baseball player. The rest was earned from selling products with his name and image.

News departments must be aware of appropriation laws when using old stories (during sweeps week for a broadcast news organization or a circulation drive for a publication) as promotion, instead of for the news. Special care must be taken with images that might make it look like a news maker was endorsing a publication or a broadcast news company.

The other three recognizable areas of invasion of privacy concern journalists more directly.

PUBLIC DISCLOSURE OF PRIVATE FACTS

Public **disclosure** of private facts is a category of invasion of privacy law that allows a plaintiff to claim damages from reported facts in a news story, even if those facts are provably true. This area of the law assumes that certain facts, while true, are not newsworthy. For the plaintiff to claim damages, the judge or jury must decide that the news maker's right to privacy outweighs the public's right to know.

According to Mark Goodman, "If you can show the newsworthiness of what you're publishing overcomes the privacy interest the individual has in it, then they're not going to be successful in a privacy suit against you."

For instance, a woman might usually have a legitimate disclosure complaint if a newspaper published a story saying she had had an abortion—if she can establish the abortion was not newsworthy.

But, Goodman explains, "If that woman happened to be a very prominent member of a right-to-life organization, revealing the fact that she [once] had an abortion might be exactly the kind of thing that is newsworthy enough to overcome the privacy interest that she would have in it."

Jane Kirtley's definition of disclosure of private facts is similar:

"The publication of truthful information about someone that is nevertheless highly offensive and, when published, does not give rise to a newsworthiness defense that would justify the publication."

Like Goodman, Kirtley says the definition of the concept is still very vague in the courts. To help students understand better, she offers this clarification and example: "It's important to draw a distinction between whether the subject is newsworthy and whether the individual you're writing about is newsworthy in his or her own right. There was a case some years ago involving a young man who had fathered a child out of wedlock. He was a minor, and the newspaper interviewed him without his parents' permission but with his permission. He was identified as an unwed father, and the family subsequently sued for private facts, invasion of privacy. And the court said that there was no question that teen-age pregnancy, birth out of wedlock, was a very important subject, very newsworthy. But that the identity of this particular young man was not."

INTRUSION

Another type of invasion of privacy is known as **intrusion**. This area of the law specifically addresses the news-gathering stage. This tort again assumes that the information published is true. It may even be information that is newsworthy, about a newsworthy person—and, therefore, not disclosure of private facts. However, if the information has been obtained through methods not deemed appropriate by the courts (or by statutes in some states), the plaintiff still has the right to sue.

The most common examples of this kind of violation involve some sort of trespass to gain information.

Jane Kirtley describes this tort: "Physical intrusion into someone else's private space. Obviously that includes physical trespass, walking into somebody's house or apartment without their permission. But it also encompasses the use of hidden microphones, tape recording devices, tapping into a telephone, hidden cameras of any kind. All of those can be subject to punishment either under a civil lawsuit or, in some states, under criminal prosecution."

It can be a tough claim to defend, Kirtley says. "One of the things I always emphasize is . . . the fact that you're a journalist is not, in and of itself, a ticket of admission to anyplace you want to go."

In some situations, such as natural disasters, the courts have ruled that journalists have the right to enter residential areas that would usually be defined as private as a part of routine journalistic fact finding. Otherwise, a good guideline would be to respect the normally accepted boundaries of residential privacy.

A photographer invades privacy by entering, without invitation, a person's home and taking pictures. But, sometimes, legal trespass is not even required for the plaintiff to have a successful invasion of privacy lawsuit.

According to John Zelezny, "A classic case out of California involved a situation where two reporters were doing a story about an individual who was practicing medicine without a license out of his home. And the reporters managed to gain entry into the home by going to the front door and simply saying, 'We need some medical help and one of your friends sent us.' And so they gained access.

"So far no legal problem. Kind of sneaky, but no legal problem. But when they got into the house and went back into the den, they then started taping with hidden microphones and photographing with hidden cameras. And the individual sued and won."

Notice, again, this invasion involves the collection of information. Truth is assumed.

FALSE LIGHT

The final area of invasion of privacy law is called **false light**. The courts have almost as much trouble defining this area of the law as journalism students do.

"False light is probably the least commonly recognized kind of invasion of privacy," Mark Goodman explains. "It's very similar to a libel claim, and for that reason many courts say we don't recognize it as separate from a libel claim. False light is when someone has been presented in a fashion that is misleading and that results in extreme embarrassment and humiliation."

Unlike the other kinds of invasion of privacy, the contested statement in a false light case must be false.

"But the difference between a false light invasion of privacy and a libel claim is that unlike a libel claim—where damage to reputation has to be shown—in a false light claim typically all that's necessary is that the person show that they've been extremely humiliated or embarrassed," says Goodman.

John Zelezny adds this example for clarification:

"The specific description of the tort of false light will vary a little bit from state to state, and in some states it's not even recognized as a separate tort from libel. But most states recognize it as a separate type. And where they do, the distinction might be best illustrated by an older case, a 1950s case, in which a youngster had been just barely missed by a motorist.

"The youngster was a pedestrian at the time. It was a very close call. She was brushed down to the street and bystanders rushed to help her up. And a news photographer captured a dramatic photo of this event. It ran in the newspaper, I believe it was the next day, about this very close call. And that's fine, that's no problem. But a couple of years later, this photo is then pulled out of the file, to illustrate a magazine story, titled 'They Ask to Be Killed' about careless pedestrians and how pedestrians are just asking for it.

"They needed a graphic; they went back to the file and found this picture. Fact of it was . . . in this case the pedestrian, this girl, was not careless. It had been the motorist's fault. So she's now portrayed in public, in association with this story, as a careless pedestrian. A careless person who nearly cost her own life. When in fact that was not true. So there's your falsehood. Now, is it libelous? No. Where's the lowered reputation?

"That's not the kind of thing that reduces a reputation with your peers or others in the community. And yet inside she might really hurt by this portrayal in public as something very contrary to what she was. If it's offensive enough, it may rise to the level of a false light claim. And she won."

■NVASION OF PRIVACY: FINAL COMMENTS

Most invasion of privacy disputes can be avoided by common sense and a strong code of ethics. Unfortunately, when enough reporters offend society with invasive, sloppy and unethical journalism, the state governments often feel empowered to chip away at the First Amendment to pass additional laws that abridge the freedom of the press.

This process can be seen at work with the specific example of printing the names of rape victims.

For many years, journalists have voluntarily and routinely avoided exposing the victims of rape. However, there have been numerous instances when editors have felt a justification for printing names of rape victims or "alleged" rape victims. A rash of recent celebrity-rape cases has caused publications ranging from the *New York Times* to the *National Enquirer* to have to break from their normal policies.

The key to this example is that the editors, not those who run the government, make the decisions about what to publish and what not to publish. Some editors have, however, made decisions to publish names of rape victims that most other editors (and many readers) felt should have remained private.

The knee-jerk reaction of several state legislatures was to criminalize the publishing of truthful information—in other words, prohibiting publications from making their own decisions.

Bob Steele, of the Poynter Institute, has these observations on the phenomenon:

"I think it is important that we as a profession [in journalism] recognize responsibility of being fair or accurate and all the other elements of ethics—so that others on the outside aren't shackling us with some sort of laws that prevent the dissemination of important information. Some states still have laws on the books dealing with the ability of the press to get the names of rape victims. And in many states, including here in Florida, that law has been challenged and the press has been found in favor of being able to get that information. Still, in Florida, very few organizations would use the name of a rape victim, even though the courts have now said that it is legal for the press to receive and publish that information."

This example of the relationship among the journalism profession, society and the government over one specific issue (naming rape victims) illustrates a pattern that is often repeated. Reporters control their own behaviors by self-imposed codes of ethics. But, if the behavior of those in the news-writing profession offends or irritates the society at large, the government (as a representative of the people) steps in with an excuse to try disciplinary action.

John Zelezny cites another example of this pattern:

"This whole area of privacy clearly involves ethical decisions apart from the legal ones. They overlap, but even if you settle the legal question, you may still have a terrific ethical question to resolve. The business of hidden cameras, little tiny microphones and so on, is an issue that we're going to see become pervasive in the future. These things are easy to obtain. You can go to a neighborhood electronics shop and get things that you couldn't get a decade ago that make these intrusions easier. Legally speaking, it will not be a violation. Unless you intrude into an area where somebody reasonably could expect solitude. And that's why in TV news today, you will often see hidden microphones and cameras used. But that doesn't mean automatically it's a legal violation. If they're used in the marketplace or the street corner, or something like that, people don't have a reasonable expectation of privacy. The place where it's a real danger is private residences. Motel rooms. Maybe private hospital rooms. That sort of thing."

The misuse of hidden electronic devices has already inspired several branches of government to pass laws limiting their use in news gathering. For instance, it would be a good idea for you to check what the laws in your state are with regard to using an audiotape recorder during an interview, without the news maker's consent or knowledge.

A covert recording of a conversation is extremely easy to accomplish, and many student journalists innocently violate these laws while taping telephone interviews without permission.

"In Britain—oddly enough, a country that one thinks of as putting a premium on privacy—they don't have privacy laws," says Jane Kirtley.

"For several years they've been tinkering with the concept. And one of the most powerful arguments the press has been making that keeps scuttling it, is that privacy laws are frequently used by those in positions of power to keep the public from finding out things that they're doing. Things they don't want the public to know.

The Carole Rich textbook *Writing and Reporting News: A Coaching Method* has a chapter called "Accuracy and Libel" that covers many of the same issues that this unit discusses (pp. 303–318 in the second edition). The emphasis on accuracy in reporting as the best defense against libel cannot be overemphasized. Invasion of privacy issues are addressed in the ethics chapter of Rich's book (pp. 321–337 in the second edition).

Since most teachers assign the *Associated Press Stylebook* for this course, now would be the time to notice the title is actually the *Associated Press Stylebook and Libel Manual*. The section on libel and invasion of privacy issues is an excellent reading assignment to complement this unit of the telecourse.

It should be emphasized that this unit of the telecourse is only an introduction to the issues of media law. Students who are interested in a career in journalism should take entire courses in media law, with an emphasis on the history as well as the recent changes in the field. Self-starters would be well advised to read a textbook by one of the guests in this unit of the telecourse, attorney John Zelezny: *Communications Law: Liberties, Restraints and the Modern Media.*

Students should also be encouraged to correspond with both the Student Press Law Center and the Reporters' Committee for the Freedom of the Press. Both organizations publish magazines that address current legal developments affecting the way journalists do their jobs. Reading literature from these organizations will help keep your school newspaper up-to-date with the latest changes in the law.

- **Student Press Law Center: (703) 807-1904**

- **Reporters' Committee for Freedom of the Press: (703) 807-2100**

"The irony—and I think one of the things that makes invasion of privacy law of doubtful constitutionality—is the fact that it does create a construct under which publishing absolutely true information can give rise to liability. The private facts tort is all based on the fact that the information you're publishing about someone is absolutely true. If it were false, they'd be suing for libel. This is one of those examples where truth is not a defense at all. A defense for private facts is newsworthiness. Not truth."

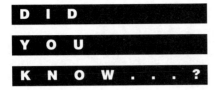

Newspapers can get sued for letters to the editor. Republishing of libel is still libel. A disclaimer stating the information in the published letters does not represent the newspaper is of little help. Editors must screen the letters to separate opinion from false statements of fact.

Advertisements are not exempt from libel claims. Printing false information, even if the advertiser provides camera-ready copy, is still republication of libel.

Sometimes the simple wrong choice of words can lead to a lawsuit. The following categories of words or expressions could be considered defamatory and, if false, could lead to a libel suit:

Words implying an individual was charged or convicted of a crime

Words implying an individual is a racist or bigot

Words implying an individual has lied

Words implying an individual has a loathsome disease

However, words that are opinion words are protected by the First Amendment. The problem, Mark Goodman points out, is that writers who use these words often cannot restrain themselves—and they often cross over from mere opinion to accusations involving facts.

Here are examples of some words that are routinely used in good reporting. Double-check their accuracy in every instance.

abuse	gay	prostitute
AIDS	guilty	rape
bankrupt	illegal	sexual harassment
criminal	junkie	thief
drunk	liar	unmarried mother
ex-convict	mentally ill	
felon	overdose	

John Zelezny, teacher and author: "Privacy is a tough area, because it's different in each state . . . and it's an area where law and ethics are hard to separate."

Jane Kirtley, attorney: "One of the things that I see in young journalists is what I consider to be a dangerous respect for authority. That when recordkeepers say, 'No, you can't have this record,' that becomes the end of this discussion."

PUBLIC FIGURES

It has been noted that **public officials** and **public figures** are not treated exactly the same in invasion of privacy or libel laws. (The glossary for this unit has brief definitions of both terms.) However, Jane Kirtley warns students that there are different kinds of public figures.

"You can be an all-purpose public figure," she says. "One who has become so prominent, who is in the spotlight in such a pervasive way, that virtually anything you do or say is a matter of public interest and concern." However, only a few news makers are considered this prominent.

"You can be a limited-purpose public figure, meaning that either because of circumstances or because of the fact that you have become prominent in a particular field—let's say you're a heart surgeon, anything having to do with your heart surgery and your skills—if you were killing patients, that would clearly be a matter of public interest and concern. But your private life, unless it has some effect on your ability to carry out your job, probably wouldn't be.

"There are certain times when an individual will thrust himself into the public eye. It could be standing up at a public meeting and making a speech or comment. It could be like Oliver Sipple, the guy who deflected an attempted assassination of President Ford, who was just a guy in the crowd until he reached forward and grabbed the gun. That suddenly made him a public figure, the court said, when he subsequently sued because his homosexuality was revealed in a news story. It's

Mark Goodman, attorney: "It really is vital that student journalists understand that the First Amendment gives them a lot of leeway. The reason for that is the basic belief that we have in a democratic society that free expression and press freedom are good things."

obvious that there are times when by your very actions, you can become a public figure. But, if a journalist has gone out and dug up somebody who up until that point has been completely anonymous, that in and of itself will not make him a public figure and won't make the public figure defense available."

SHIELD LAWS

Reporters' rights are protected as well as news makers' rights. Some of the laws that govern these rights are called **shield laws**. According to Jane Kirtley, as of 1995, 29 states and the District of Columbia have such laws to give journalists special privileges that the ordinary citizen does not have.

Most of the laws protect the journalist from being compelled either to testify or to reveal written information in a court proceeding or an administrative inquiry.

According to Kirtley, shield laws exist "because of the important recognition that journalists are not investigators for the government, nor do they act as the agents of any special interest. In my view, it's tremendously important that journalists not be co-oped into being used as cheap or free investigators for people who are simply too lazy to do their own work. It can hurt your objectivity both in actual fact as well as in appearance, it is a tremendous time waster, it uses up personnel that ought to be reporting, and I think that more and more, we're seeing states recognize that it's important for journalists to have these special privileges.

"I have seen that in some states, the First Amendment is not enough protection. In fact, in some states, if you don't have a statute, a journalist will be compelled to testify or will go to jail if he or she fails to do so. On the other hand, I've been privileged to do work in a number of developing democracies in Eastern and Central Europe. They are trying very hard to come up with laws that would grant the press many of the freedoms that we take for granted in this country. Without exception, their press laws are lengthy, they are detailed, and they are replete with, yes, rights, but also responsibilities that journalists must carry out before they may exercise those rights.

"And it seems to me that there's a lesson to be learned from that for us, too. Which is that what the government gives us in terms of special rights and privileges, it can either exact behavior in return, or it can take them away if we don't perform in the way that they want. And I think that if we're going to be truly independent, the best protection really does rest with the First Amendment to the Constitution."

Document access and open meeting laws, which are mentioned in the television program, are addressed more fully in Unit Six, "Writing Versus Reporting."

The following is the raw script for Mike Donnelly's story.

Nat sound, music: "If You Came Back from Heaven."

SOT open, SOT Wanda: "I had this gut feeling he was coming back.". . . 3:37 (Or miracle type bite)

VO [Voiceover]: It was Monday, March 14th, when 56-year-old Jim Mewes suffered a massive stroke. What happened in the next few months is an extraordinary tale of love, faith and the will to survive. It's also a story about modern medical technology . . . and its effects on how we live . . . and how we die.

DISSOLVE TO: STAND-UP Celebration of Christmas, Wanda Mewes . . . Jim's wife is sending out this newsletter to friends.

She writes . . . "As the celebration of the birth of Christ approaches, Jim and I want to express our gratefulness to those of you who helped us through the darkest days of our lives." She talks about Jim's coma and writes "the doctors again maintained that Jim would never survive and implored me to do the unthinkable. They informed me that Jim's chances of ever waking up were one in a billion, and if he did . . . he would be blind, paralyzed and retarded forever. Again, knowing Jim is a one in a billion man . . . I refused.

SOT NAT SOUND, VAN DOOR/LIFT: Ten months ago, when Jim Mewes had his stroke, he was taken first to Oroville Hospital, and then transferred to Enloe Hospital in Chico. Records show he was suffering from a massive intracerebral hemorrhage and was paralyzed on his left side. One document says the following: "I again

had long discussions with the wife who was again adamant about total, supportive measures. This despite the fact that the patient was felt to be a very poor candidate for a good quality of life." It was signed by Dr. Jeffrey Lobosky, the neurosurgeon in charge.

On March 22nd, Jim went into a coma.

SOT (When he went into his coma, there was nothing there . . . no sign of life.) 3:22 Bad shot, must be under video.

VO: Every doctor and medical professional we talked to said 99 percent of the patients in Jim's condition would most likely die. The patients that might survive would be expected to have an extremely poor quality of life. Four days after Jim went into a coma, nurses notes say Dr. Lobosky suggested to the family that if there was no improvement, "the family should consider allowing the patient to die." (Graphic showing comment with date of 3/26)

STAND-UP (HOLDING UP HOSPITAL RECORDS): Hospital records tell an incredible story of a woman with unbelievable faith. Wanda Mewes was so determined to keep her husband alive, she became a hospital staff's worst nightmare. She was called disruptive, unrealistic and demanding. Time after time, the records portray her as woman who would not accept the probable death of the man she's loved for more than 20 years.

SOT: "I was a monster . . . ." (Third obit. tape)

VO: Jim remained in his coma. Eventually, his sons believed he would not wish to live this way and gave consent to allow him to die. And then, even Wanda began to break down. She finally started to consider the possibility Jim's life might be over and gave permission for DNR . . . "Do not resuscitate." She contacted a funeral home and even wrote up an obituary for Jim.

SOT (WANDA READING OBIT) VO: But then, something strange happened. On April 3rd . . . Easter Sunday, she says Jim moved his jaw. She immediately rescinded the "Do not resuscitate" orders.

SOT VO: On April 12th, after 23 days in a coma, Jim began to awake.

SOT: Wanda STAND-UP: But even after he came out of his coma, there was still a question of Jim's quality of life. Dr. Lobosky believed strongly enough in his opinion Jim should be allowed to die. . . . He presented his case before the bio-ethics committee. The committee is meant to facilitate communication and make ethical recommendation when faced with a moral dilemma. Its discussions are kept confidential. . . . But Channel 12 has been told the committee confirmed Wanda Mewes's right to make the ultimate decision regarding her husband's fate. But the committee also acknowledged Dr. Lobosky's dilemma of having a patient who by all rational standards was dying. Being faced with the likelihood of continuing agonizing treatment and tying up valuable resources in vain, the committee reportedly agreed with Dr. Lobosky's opinion that he could not, in good conscience, continue futile care.

(DISSOLVE TO JIM, HOLDING PICTURE OF LEE MARVIN)

NAT SOUND SOT: "Well, Jim, you are supposed to be dead." Jim says, "I'm alive" etc.

VO: Today, eight months after the bio-ethics discussed the case, and about nine and a half months after he had his stroke, Jim is home and has the spark of life.

SOT JIM: Although he remains paralyzed and must be fed through a tube to his stomach, his condition is said to be improving. But now he has fear. Fear that the people who are supposed to save his life . . . will take it.

SOT: Jim says he won't go back to Enloe Hospital, saying, "I'm afraid they will put me to sleep."

VO: It's one thing to be a Monday morning quarterback, quite another to be a Monday morning neurosurgeon. Hospital records indicate there were times when Jim himself communicated a wish to die. With medical technology becoming so advanced it's possible to artificially prolong life for months, sometimes years.

This has created one of the great conflicts of our times. When do we draw the lines between care and torture . . . hope and reality?

Dr. Patrick Tedford is the chair of the bio-ethics committee.

SOT: from Tedford VO: Dr. Lobosky has refused to comment because the Mewes family is filing a lawsuit. The Mewes are alleging Jim's coma was caused by negligence, not his stroke. Enloe Hospital officials have also refused to talk about the case. Dr. Gerard Valcaringi, the pulminologist who is credited by the Mewes with saving Jim's life during respiratory failure, calls Jim's story a miracle. He says Jim was not to have survived, that he defied medical statistics. Although he refused to go on camera, saying he doesn't want to step on any toes, he acknowledges the case shows the medical community should take a closer look at how it defines "a miracle."

SOT MUSIC: On July 23rd, Jim and Wanda Mewes renewed wedding vows.

MUSIC—ON-SET COMMENTS from Donnelly: Everyone I talked to in the medical community says Dr. Lobosky is an excellent neurosurgeon and made the logical and expected recommendations. At least two doctors told me that if they tried to save every patient in Jim's condition, only 1 percent would survive. And even then, the quality of life would be expected to be very poor. The question is, should doctors take such extraordinary measures at such a tremendous expense to save that 1 percent? Especially when many people who fall under that 1 percent would not want to live under those conditions.

ALTERNATIVE VIEWS

CHEATING

The discussion of media law in this telecourse has centered primarily around issues such as libel, invasion of privacy, shield laws and sunshine laws. But one journalist and educator interviewed for the project felt there is one other aspect of media law that is too frequently overlooked in beginning news-writing courses.

"Somewhere in this course you're going to have to say, 'Do not make things up and do not steal other people's writing,'" says Mitchell Stephens, of New York University. "That unfortunately needs to be said a couple of times in any basic journalism course.

"I had a student write me a note, last semester here at NYU, saying that a few times, in courses he'd taken during the past year, he'd heard students talking about having made up aspects of stories. And that drives me crazy. It drives me crazy for two reasons—not just because I'm prudish and I can't stand any sort of deviation from the straight and narrow; it drives me crazy because it's unfair to everybody else who's working. And to be a journalist is to work to get things right and to try to find out what really happened. This is not fiction writing. This is trying to get it right. And when people cheat, it's just unfair. It's wrong. If you choose to become a journalist, you're volunteering to become people's eyes on what's going on in society around them. Your first responsibility in assuming that is to tell things straight. To tell it true.

"Students really have to be reminded that you can't make things up and you can't steal other people's work. As a student journalist, you're going to be out covering a story and maybe somebody from the newspaper is out there too and it's really tempting to borrow something from that newspaper version or take something from somewhere else. You can't do that. Not be a journalist. That's cheating."

TABLOID JOURNALISM AND THE LAW

"We'll print it, if we think that's what the reader wants to know," says Brian Williams, of *National Enquirer.* "We'll take that risk [of getting sued]. Will we callously or carelessly print something? No. Will we do anything that's necessary that's legal to find something out? Yes. Absolutely, without question.

"I think we're careful at the *Enquirer* as far as lawsuits go. A lot of what we write about are public figures. So invasion of privacy is a very narrow area there. I think the rest of the press is catching up to where we've been. They want to do our kinds of stories. I think there was an op/ed piece in the *Times* a couple years ago, and it talked about the fact that the *Enquirer* is actually one of those operations that's always pushing the First Amendment. I think in a sense we do. I think we do a service to the rest of the press because we're out there and we're willing to; we have the resources to be able to defend ourselves if we're attacked.

"We don't get sued very often at all. Suits get announced—there's a public relations dance that goes on. We print something, somebody doesn't like it, announces that they're going to sue us for $100 million. They hold a press conference, pass out a press release and that's the end of it. Nothing ever happens. If you look at the number of suits we have pending, say, compared to "60 Minutes" or the *New York Times* or *Time* magazine, [our lawsuits] probably are much less. It's surprising."

GLOSSARY

This glossary was assembled with the aid of Mark Goodman, Jane Kirtley and John Zelezny. Some of the definitions were excerpted from *Communications Law: Liberties, Restraints and the Modern Media* (Belmont, CA: Wadsworth, 1993).

ACTUAL MALICE
A fault standard that must be proven by a public official (and in some cases, by a public figure) in order to win a libel suit. It is also known as **constitutional malice**. The legal definition of the term has nothing to do with ill will. It means that when defamatory statements were published, the reporter knew they were false or published the statements with reckless disregard for the truth.

DEFAMATION
A key ingredient in the definition of libel, defamation is usually understood as an attack on the reputation of another person. It is also sometimes defined as something published or said that causes harm, embarrassment or loss of income. Legally, defamation means damaging a reputation, not just attacking.

DISCLOSURE (OF PRIVATE FACTS)
The most commonly thought-of invasion of privacy tort, disclosure can be defined as unwarranted publicity about a person's private life. Private facts are harder to define—facts that are intimate and highly offensive to a reasonable person. No liability exists under this tort for giving further publicity to information that was generally available to the public or information that was public record. The plaintiff must also prove that the disclosure clearly overstepped prevailing notions of decency. The best defense against this claim of invasion of privacy is that the information was newsworthy and that the public's right to know outweighs the individual's right to privacy.

FALSE LIGHT
One of four branches of invasion of privacy recognized by the law. It is a tort similar to defamation or libel—the representation of an individual in a false and highly offensive manner before the public. The subtle difference between libel and false light (which is recognized only in some states) is that the person suing for false light might claim only embarrassment or anguish, as opposed to injury to reputation.

FAULT STANDARD
When reporters are sued for libel, the plaintiff must prove some degree of fault on the defendant's part. Negligence and malice are fault standards that apply to different segments of the population.

INTRUSION	A branch of invasion of privacy laws, intrusion can be defined as the intentional invasion of a person's physical seclusion or private affairs in a manner that would be highly offensive to a reasonable person.
LIBEL	Publishing of false information that identifies and defames an individual. A successful libel suit must establish the following: (1) The contested information was false; (2) the contested information was published; (3) the contested information injured or damaged reputation; (4) the plaintiff was identified; (5) a fault standard is shown of (a) malice, in the case of a public official or public figure (in most states) or (b) negligence, in the case of a private individual.
MISAPPROPRIATION	One of the four identifiable areas of invasion of privacy. This aspect of invasion of privacy applies to the unauthorized use of an individual's name or likeness for commercial purposes, especially in advertising. (Also called *appropriation* or *commercialization* in some states.)
NEGLIGENCE	A fault standard in some states that allows private individuals, as plaintiffs, to recover in a libel suit upon evidence of mere negligence in the performing of a reporting job. In other words, the writer failed to take precautions that a reasonable journalist would take under similar circumstances to ensure that libelous information would not be included in a news story.
OPEN MEETING LAWS	The public (and therefore the press) is guaranteed access to attend and observe most government proceedings in most states. Though journalists must sometimes demand access to these meetings, knowledge of your state laws regarding the matter can create access to information that some politicians or bureaucrats would rather keep from the public. (See Public records.)
PLAINTIFF	In the case of a libel lawsuit or invasion of privacy lawsuit, the plaintiff is the person who sues, claiming damages by the defendant (or communicator.)
PUBLIC FIGURE	The public figure classification applies to plaintiffs who have assumed special prominence in the resolution of public issues or the character of public events. Entertainers and individuals who voluntarily involve themselves in news events are public figures. In many cases, the classification of public figure or private individual is decided in a hearing before a judge. The laws involving fault standards (malice and negligence) and invasion of privacy vary, depending on whether the plaintiff is a private individual or a public figure.
PUBLIC OFFICIAL	A public official is an individual who is a public servant. Public officials include elected representatives and others (not elected) who work for national or local government agencies. (Some states require that the official have some degree of authority. Not everyone on a government payroll is a public official.) The laws involving fault standards (malice and negligence), privilege and invasion of privacy vary, depending on whether the plaintiff is a private individual or a public official.

PUBLIC RECORDS The Supreme Court (and most states) have recognized the right of access for the public (and therefore, the press) to most government documents. The federal version of this principle is the Freedom of Information Act (FOIA). In the case of invasion of privacy lawsuits, information contained in public records cannot be protected by a plaintiff. In the case of libel suits, producing a document that is public record can often prove the truth of the disputed, defamatory statement.

QUALIFIED PRIVILEGE A conditional defense against a libel claim. A reporter has the qualified privilege to publish what a public official has the **absolute privilege** to say. Absolute privilege is the protection given by law against a libel claim over something said or written by a public official while that official is performing as a public servant.

SHIELD LAWS Shield laws are designed to protect a reporter's rights. Though they vary from state to state, shield laws usually offer some degree of protection for the reporter to resist court subpoena and to keep private unpublished notes and photographs as well as confidential sources, anonymous sources and background sources. Seizure and newsroom searchers are usually dealt with by separate laws, such as the Privacy Protection Act.

SLANDER Slander is similar to libel, only it is spoken instead of published. (In most states, broadcast information is considered under libel laws.)

TORT A *torte* is a multilayered cake, usually with a rich frosting. A *tort* is a legal term that means a wrongful act for which a civil suit can be filed.

SUGGESTED WRITING EXERCISES

1 Carefully read the text of Mike Donnelly's news story. What is the significance of the following terms, if Donnelly was to be sued for libel or invasion of privacy?

Truth

Defamation (injury to reputation)

Public figure

Constitutional malice

Negligence

Disclosure of private facts

Intrusion

2 In your opinion, from the conversation you were able to witness in the tele-course program, what measures did news director Bruce Lang and Mike Donnelly take to make sure the television station was protected from a libel or invasion of privacy lawsuit resulting from this story? Did they also take care to make sure the story was fair and balanced? Why?

3 In the case of this story, is the law constructed in such a way that the reporter is intimidated from good reporting for fear of a suit? How could legal intimidation become a factor that inhibits good journalism?

QUIZ

Choose the best answer.

1 Which of the following is not relevant in establishing libel?

 a. That the information published defamed or injured the plaintiff's reputation
 b. That the information published was false
 c. That the information published invaded the plaintiff's privacy
 d. That the information was actually published
 e. That the information published identified the plaintiff

2 Which of the following is not true about actual malice?

 a. Lack of actual malice is a conditional defense against a libel claim.
 b. The plaintiffs have to prove the journalist had feelings of malice, hatred or scorn or was "out to get them."
 c. Actual malice is reckless disregard of the truth.
 d. Actual malice is also sometimes called constitutional malice.
 e. Actual malice is a defense in a libel claim from a public official or, sometimes, a public figure, but does not always apply in a defense in a libel claim from a private individual.

3 Shield laws are laws that

 a. in every state protect journalists' rights.
 b. allow journalists to make some forgivable mistakes in a libel suit.
 c. allow journalists access to documents or meetings that the rest of the public does not have access to.
 d. in some states protect journalists from court subpoenas involving unpublished notes, unpublished photos and confidential sources.
 e. in some states protect journalists from getting speeding or parking tickets while performing basic reporters' duties.

4 Sunshine laws are laws that

 a. allow journalists access to documents or meetings that the rest of the public does not have access to.
 b. are exactly the same in every state.
 c. guarantee journalists access to all documents and meetings.

d. allow access for all citizens to some government documents and meetings that had been closed to the public in the past.

e. guarantee that journalists who work with computers in gloomy offices get at least two 15-minute breaks "in the sunshine" a day—as a health precaution against problems resulting from indoor work.

5 Invasion of privacy laws

a. are exactly the same in every state.
b. protect all citizens equally from unfair press scrutiny.
c. have been around longer than libel laws.
d. unlike libel, usually assume the disputed information is true.
e. are different for tabloid publications than they are for mainstream newspapers.

6 Qualified privilege

a. allows journalists to print some of what government officials have absolute privilege to say.
b. allows journalists access to rock concerts, movie theaters and other places of entertainment, without having to pay, as long as the reporter is writing a review.
c. is an absolute defense in a libel case.
d. protects newspapers against libel claims, if the quoted information is accurate.
e. is the privilege senior reporters hold over rookie reporters.

7 Truth is not an absolute defense in a lawsuit in which

a. the plaintiff is suing for disclosure of private facts.
b. the journalist cannot prove disputed information in a libel suit.
c. the plaintiff is suing for intrusion.
d. all of the above
e. none of the above

8 Intrusion

a. involves printing of false information.
b. is a tort of invasion of privacy that involves the fact-gathering stage.
c. is a tort of invasion of privacy in which the plaintiff must prove malice to be successful.
d. all of the above
e. none of the above

9 A complaint of misappropriation by a plaintiff

a. usually applies to the advertising department but can apply to the news department in special circumstances.
b. involves using the name of an individual in commercial enterprises without the individual's permission.
c. is one of the torts of invasion of privacy law.
d. all of the above
e. none of the above

10 The following is an absolute defense in a libel suit:

a. fair comment and criticism
b. provable truth
c. qualified privilege
d. all of the above
e. none of the above

SELF-TEST

1 List five things that must be established to win a libel suit.

2 Which invasion of privacy tort is associated with the information-gathering stage of news writing? Define this tort.

3 Explain how libel-law fault standards differ for reporting about various types of news makers.

4 What is the difference between absolute privilege and qualified privilege, in the context of libel law?

5 The best defense for one invasion of privacy tort is to claim the public's right to know is more important than an individual's right to privacy. Which tort is this? Why is this a good defense?

6 Provable truth is a very important defense in a libel suit. Is it good defense for invasion of privacy suits? Why?

7 Define actual malice (also known as constitutional malice).

8 What is the purpose of shield laws?

9 What are sunshine laws? Give at least one example.

10 Assume your student newspaper is sued for libel because of a very opinion-ated letter to the editor published on the op/ed page. What are the determining factors for whether the litigation will be successful?